# LIST OF PERSONS,

RESIDENTS OF THE

# STATE OF WISCONSIN,

REPORTED AS DESERTERS

FROM THE

# MILITARY AND NAVAL SERVICE

OF THE

# UNITED STATES.

MADISON, WIS.:
ATWOOD & RUBLEE, STATE PRINTERS, JOURNAL OFFICE.
1867.

# LIST OF PERSONS,

RESIDENTS OF THE

# STATE OF WISCONSIN,

REPORTED AS DESERTERS

FROM THE

# MILITARY OR NAVAL SERVICE

OF THE

# UNITED STATES.

MADISON, WIS.:
ATWOOD & RUBLEE, STATE PRINTERS, JOURNAL OFFICE.
1867.

# STATE OF WISCONSIN,

## OFFICE OF THE SECRETARY OF STATE,

MADISON, July, 1867.

By the provisions of Chapter 57 of the General Laws of 1867, which may be found on the following pages, it was made the duty of the Secretary of State to procure from the War Department a list of deserters from the military and naval service and from the draft. The accompanying list has accordingly been procured, and corrected as far as possible from the records in the office of the Adjutant General of this State. The names of all reported as deserters from the several regiments of this State have been compared with the muster-out rolls, and many originally reported as deserters have been omitted from this list.

The first of these lists contains the names of those who were reported at the War Department as deserters, and also so appear on the muster-out rolls of their respective companies. The second list contains the names of those who, when drafted, failed to report. All such are declared deserters by both National and State laws. That many are erroneously reported, is doubtless true. Many so reported were absent in Hospitals or on detached service, but their whereabouts being unknown to their company commanders, they were dropped, under orders, as deserters. Many who were drafted, were already in the army, but as they did not report to the Provost Marshal, they were marked as deserters. But probably a large majority of those reported were either actual deserters or absent without leave and were justly so reported.

In order that no injustice may be done, attention is called to the instructions accompanying the Election Laws, of which each Inspector will have a copy. And it is earnestly suggested to any and all who find their names on these lists erroneously, that they furnish to this office, at once, evidence of the facts in the case, so that the proper corrections may be made.

Copies of these lists must be posted up at the polls on election day, and under the law, are *prima facie* evidence of desertion. Boards of Registry have no right to register the name of any person found on these lists, without satisfactory evidence that the charge of desertion was false. Neither can the vote of any such person be received without the production of similar evidence. Trusting that all officers will unite in sustaining and enforcing the law, and that injustice may be done no one individual, these lists are submitted and certified.

THOS. S. ALLEN,
*Secretary of State.*

## CHAPTER 67—General.

[*Published April* 2, 1867.]

AN ACT to authorize the secretary of state to procure and furnish to clerks of county boards of supervisors authenticated lists of deserters from the military and naval service of the United States, and to provide for their distribution.

*The people of the state of Wisconsin, represented in senate and assembly, do enact as follows:*

Section 1. The secretary of state is hereby authorized and required forthwith to procure from the secretary of war of the United States, an authenticated list of all persons who, being residents of the state of Wisconsin, at any time deserted from the military or naval service of the United States, or from any draft into such service duly ordered, and who are now enrolled in the office of said secretary of war as such deserters; which said list shall be alphabetically arranged, according to the respective surnames of such deserters, and shall state as near as may be the time of each such desertion, and the place of residence of each such deserter at the time he deserted from said service, and which said list shall be kept and preserved in the office of the secretary of state, and shall be open to public inspection.

Section 2. The secretary of state is hereby further authorized and required to furnish and transmit to all clerks of county boards of supervisors, in the same manner and at the same time in each year, that blank returns of elections are now transmitted, a sufficient number of copies of said list, duly certified by him, as will supply the board of registry for each town, ward or village with one copy thereof, and the inspectors of election in each election precinct in any county with three copies of said list.

Section 3. It shall be the duty of each and every clerk of the county board of supervisors in this state to whom copies of said list are so transmitted, to deliver or cause to be delivered to the board of registry in each town, ward and incorporated village in his county, on or before the day of their last meeting preceding any general election, one copy of said list, and to the inspectors of election at each election precinct in his county, at any general election, three copies of said list, which shall be posted up by said inspectors in conspicuous places at the polls of such election, for public inspection.

Section 4. A copy of said list, duly certified by the secretary of state, shall be *prima facie* evidence in all courts and places, of desertion from the military or naval service of the United States, by the person therein named as a deserter from such service.

Section 5. Any clerk of the county board of supervisors and any inspector of election who shall refuse or neglect to perform any of the duties which by this act he is required to perform, shall be deemed guilty of a misdemeanor, and shall be liable to a fine of fifty dollars and costs of prosecution for each and every offense.

Section 6. This act shall take effect and be in force from and after its passage.

Approved March 29, 1867.

# DESERTERS FROM REGIMENTS.

NOTE—ABBREVIATIONS—"C," Cavalry; "H A," Heavy Artillery; "L A," Light Artillery; "I," Infantry.

A

| *Reg't.* | | *Name.* | *Residence.* | *Date.* |
|---|---|---|---|---|
| 1 | I | Auger, Henry | | |
| 2 | I | Agnew, Henry | Salem | Jan. 20, 1863 |
| 2 | I | Anderson, John H. | Racine | |
| 2 | I | Allen, Luman E. | | Nov. 20, 1861 |
| 2 | I | Andrew, Nickerson | Columbus | May 5, 1864 |
| 3 | I | Anderson, Andrew | Moscow | May 8, 1865 |
| 3 | I | Altyhein, Chas. | | July 5, 1865 |
| 5 | I | Ackerman, John | | Aug. 2, 1861 |
| 5 | I | Anderson, Lewis | Janesville | Aug. 31, 1863 |
| 5 | I | Allen, Joseph R. | | Sept. 19, 1863 |
| 5 | I | Atkinson, James | Fond du Lac | Sept. 30, 1863 |
| 5 | I | Anderson, Peter | Grand Rapids | June 19, 1862 |
| 5 | I | Arlt, William | Brookfield | |
| 6 | I | Allen, Wm. G. | | Nov. 6, 1861 |
| 6 | I | Amos, Albert | | Sept. 14, 1862 |
| 6 | I | Allen, Andrew | | Jan. 17, 1863 |
| 6 | I | Anderson, Lewis | | Aug. 31, 1863 |
| 6 | I | Austin, Arva O | | Sept. 12, 1862 |
| 8 | I | Allen, Wm. H. | New York | |
| 8 | I | Aleroft, George | | Jan. 16, 1862 |
| 9 | I | Augustin, Buschlin | | July 27, 1862 |
| 10 | I | Allen, Samuel | Clifton | July 10, 1862 |
| 10 | I | Austin, Jonathan | Oxford | Sept. 7, 1862 |
| 11 | I | Alpress, William | | Feb. 24, 1863 |
| 11 | I | Anderson, Johnson | | Dec. 14, 1862 |
| 11 | I | Adney, Perry | Wisconsin | |
| 13 | I | Austin, Jas. A. | Janesville | June 19, 1865 |
| 13 | I | Allensworth, Jacob | | |
| 13 | I | Anderson, Wm. H. | | Oct. 1, 1864 |
| 14 | I | Austin, Alonzo J. | Wisconsin | July 20, 1865 |
| 14 | I | Austin, Alonzo J. | Plover | July 17, 1865 |
| 15 | I | Anderson, Henry | Batte de Norte | |
| 15 | I | Alby, Byron | Berlin | |
| 17 | I | Ashman, John | | May 24, 1864 |
| 51 | I | Alche, Geo | Milwaukee | Mar. 28, 1865 |
| 51 | I | Ander, Jno | Fond du Fac | April 1, 1865 |
| 51 | I | Andrew, Thomas | Princeton | |
| 50 | I | Armstrong, Bernard | Westport | May 26, 1865 |
| 50 | I | Anderson, James | Crawford Co. | Sept. 8, 1865 |
| 50 | I | Applefellow, Hermon | Neenah | Aug. 24, 1865 |
| 50 | I | Altmere, Nicholas | Green Bay | Aug. 26, 1865 |

| *Regt.* | | *Name.* | *Residence.* | *Date.* |
|---|---|---|---|---|
| 48 | I | Armstrong, Wm. S | Milwaukee | Mar. 17, 1865 |
| 48 | I | Andrew, Thomas | Milwaukee | Mar. 5, 1865 |
| 48 | I | Arthur, Chas | Milwaukee | Mar. 5, 1865 |
| 48 | I | Andrew, Thomas | Milwaukee | Mar. .., 1865 |
| 44 | I | Anderson, John | | Jan. 7, 1865 |
| 44 | I | Alvord, Edward | Milwaukee | Feb. 12, 1865 |
| 44 | I | Anderson, Chas | Fond du Lac | Aug. 22, 1865 |
| 42 | I | Agen, Chas | Beloit | Sept 20, 1864 |
| 38 | I | Ailey, Jno | Janesville | Sept 18, 1864 |
| 37 | I | Allen, Thos. J | Delavan | May 1, 1864 |
| 37 | I | Allen, Lloyd W | | May 23, 1865 |
| 35 | I | Adams, John | Milwaukee | Feb. 27, 1866 |
| 34 | I | Adamsen, Martin | Bristol | Mar. 5, 1863 |
| 34 | I | Anderson, Paul | Adams | Jan. 30, 1863 |
| 34 | I | Albrecht, Chas | Abbott | Jan. 21, 1863 |
| 34 | I | Andie, A. John | Lincoln | Jan. 31, 1863 |
| 34 | I | Adrian, Francis | Sturgeon Bay | Jan. 31, 1863 |
| 34 | I | Ausloos, Baptist J | Green Bay | Jan. 31, 1863 |
| 34 | I | Auflink, Hiram | Wauwatosa | Jan. 31, 1863 |
| 32 | I | Austin, Jos. P | Oshkosh | Oct. 29, 1862 |
| 32 | I | Allen, Noah | Oxford | Nov. 12, 1862 |
| 32 | I | Allen, Geo. A | Calamus | Oct. 12, 1863 |
| 31 | I | Ames, Louis | Milwaukee | Mar. 2, 1863 |
| 31 | I | Adair, Alexander | Monroe | June 23, 1863 |
| 30 | I | Adams, Chas. F | Ridgeway | May 22, 1863 |
| 30 | I | Anderson, Jno. W | | Mar. 24, 1864 |
| 30 | I | Abbott, James | | Mar. 14, 1864 |
| 29 | I | Alexander, Arthur | Watertown | Jan. 10, 1863 |
| 29 | I | Alexander, James | Hartford | July 9, 1863 |
| 27 | I | Ahrnsbrach | Herman | Mar. 30, 1863 |
| 27 | I | Abrahamson, Jans F | Fort Washington | Mar. 23, 1863 |
| 24 | I | Allen, Chas. W | Milwaukee | |
| 24 | I | Allen, Alexander | Milwaukee | April .., 1863 |
| 21 | I | Adalgo, Antonio F | Waupun | Feb. 9, 1865 |
| 20 | I | Anderson, Jno | Racine | April 1, 1863 |
| 20 | I | Ackerson, David E | Boscobel | Oct. 31, 1864 |
| 18 | I | Atwood, Austin L | Plover | |
| 18 | I | Allen, Geo. G | | |
| 1 | C | Alby, Edwin T | Cape Giradeau, Mo | Nov. 10, 1862 |
| 1 | C | Adams, Andrew | | Mar. 15, 1862 |
| 1 | C | Adney, Jno. T | Soldiers' Grove | Oct. 1, 1862 |
| 1 | C | Adams, Geo | | Dec. .., 1864 |
| 2 | C | Andrews, Thos. B | | Jan. 28, 1863 |
| 2 | C | Alexander, Morris | | Dec. 4, 1862 |
| 2 | C | Allen, James | Dodgeville | |
| 3 | C | Allen, Theodore S | Janesville | Oct. .., 1862 |
| 4 | C | Alft, Michael | | Oct. 20, 1684 |
| 4 | C | Allen, O | Whitewater | Jan. 29, 1863 |
| 4 | C | Alexander, James | Manitowoc | Feb. 14, 1862 |
| 4 | C | Allstone, Isaac | Baton Rouge, La | Apr. 26, 1866 |
| 1 | H A | Antoine, Benjamin | Fond du Lac | |
| 1 | H A | Amos, Robt | Neenah | Oct. 21, 1863 |
| 1 | H A | Austin, Jno | | Oct. 8, 1863 |
| 1 | H A | Avery, Edwin | Milwaukee | Sept 11, 1863 |

## B

| | | | | |
|---|---|---|---|---|
| 1 | I | Burlinggame, Edward | | |
| 1 | I | Baker Henry | | |

| Reg't. | | Name | Residence. | Date. |
|---|---|---|---|---|
| 1 | I | Babcock, Clinton | | |
| 1 | I | Brown, Alfred | | |
| 1 | I | Burns, Wm | | |
| 1 | I | Brodbent, Thos. C. | | |
| 2 | I | Beroy, Harmon H | Randolph | Dec. 1, 1861 |
| 2 | I | Brown, Wm. J | | Aug. .., 1861 |
| 2 | I | Brackett, Jefferson W | | Dec. 12, 1862 |
| 2 | I | Barnes, Robt | | Jan. 21, 1863 |
| 2 | I | Brookens, Thos. S | | .., 1862 |
| 2 | I | Blake, Henry | Madison | July 21, 1861 |
| 3 | I | Booth, Geo. L | | |
| 3 | I | Beoupray Leon | Boscobel | .., 1864 |
| 3 | I | Brown, John | Milwaukee | |
| 3 | I | Brown, Thos. | | |
| 3 | I | Baker, Wm. H | Madison | Nov. 7, 1864 |
| 3 | I | Berdeman, Fredk | | |
| 3 | I | Buck, Joseph | Milwaukee | |
| 3 | I | Berigan, John | Milwaukee | |
| 5 | I | Bentley, George | | May 11, 1862 |
| 5 | I | Benedict, Geo. L | Forrest | May 2, 1862 |
| 5 | I | Barnum, Marens H | Warsaw | Jan. 18, 1863 |
| 5 | I | Brown, James W | Janesville | Aug 13, 1863 |
| 5 | I | Blake, David A | Stevens Point | Oct. 3, 1864 |
| 5 | I | Benness Andrew J | Waukesha, | Oct. 20, 1862 |
| 5 | I | Bonell, George E | Eau Claire | |
| 5 | I | Bendey Charles | | .., 1862 |
| 6 | I | Bonney, Winfield S | | Sep. 25, 1862 |
| 6 | I | Baldwin, Danl. W | | Sep. 14, 1862 |
| 6 | I | Beatti, John | Janesville | Aug. 31, 1863 |
| 6 | I | Bly Geo. W | | Oct. 27, 1861 |
| 6 | I | Bury, G. J | Michigan | July 8, 1861 |
| 6 | I | Burs, H. S | Vienna | July 6, 1861 |
| 6 | I | Best, George | Westport | July 6, 1861 |
| 6 | I | Beardsley, John E | | |
| 7 | I | Beebe, David | | Sep. 27, 1862 |
| 7 | I | Blakinton, Noble | | Dec. 11, 1862 |
| 7 | I | Black, James | Lancaster | May 4, 1863 |
| 7 | I | Bogel, Fred | Milwaukee | Dec. 20, 1864 |
| 7 | I | Bogle, Frank | | Feb. 6, 1865 |
| 8 | I | Barnes Ferdinand | Bridgeport | |
| 8 | I | Bassett, Martin | Farmington | |
| 8 | I | Burnett, Joseph | Plymouth | |
| 8 | I | Briedlon, Bacon | Janesville | |
| 8 | I | Bellesfield, Samuel | | July 24, 1864 |
| 8 | I | Beuley, Henry C | | Feb. .., 1863 |
| 9 | I | Bauer, John | Burlington | Sep. 27, 1864 |
| 9 | I | Brenninger, William | Green Bay | Sep. 10, 1865 |
| 10 | I | Burke, Geo. W | Menasha | Aug. 7, 1862 |
| 10 | I | Bush, Alson | Wyocena | Sep. 7, 1864 |
| 10 | I | Best, John P | Big Spring | Aug. 4, 1862 |
| 10 | I | Bowers, Thomas D | | |
| 10 | I | Best, John N | Big Spring | Dec. 25, 1862 |
| 10 | I | Ballou, Alvin B | Harrison | |
| 11 | I | Berg, John | | |
| 11 | I | Blighton, George | | Nov. 25, 1862 |
| 11 | I | Bowman, E. J | | Nov. 20, 1862 |
| 11 | I | Bishop, Vernon V | | Mar. 17, 1863 |
| 11 | I | Barnes, Harvey | West Point | Oct. 11, 1863 |
| 11 | I | Bishop, V. V | Millville | Mar. 16, 1863 |

| Reg't. | | Name. | Residence. | Date. |
|---|---|---|---|---|
| 11 | I | Bingham, Newell H | Richland | Nov. 19, 1861 |
| 11 | I | Baret, John | Roche-a-cris | July 27, 1863 |
| 11 | I | Brown, James | | Oct. 4, 1861 |
| 11 | I | Blake, John | | Oct. 19, 1863 |
| 12 | I | Benjamin, Wm | Bangor, Maine | May 27, 1862 |
| 13 | I | Box, Edmond | Waverly, Tenn | June 17, 1865 |
| 13 | I | Barnes, Joseph | Stoughton | June 14, 1865 |
| 13 | I | Branon, Thomas W | Janesville | July 10, 1865 |
| 13 | I | Barnard, Martin V | | |
| 13 | I | Barnard, Elliott D | | |
| 13 | I | Baine, Edgar J | | |
| 13 | I | Baker, Frank | Janesville | Jan. 15, 1863 |
| 14 | I | Blakesler, Chauncy | | Aug. 18, 1862 |
| 14 | I | Burke, Ed. J | Milwaukee | Feb. 10, 1865 |
| 14 | I | Bury, John | Milwaukee | Feb. 10, 1865 |
| 14 | I | Bradley, John W | Milwaukee | Jan. 29, 1865 |
| 14 | I | Brent, Wm. T | Milwaukee | Jan. 29, 1865 |
| 14 | I | Blasier, John J | | July 30, 1862 |
| 14 | I | Brown, Henry | | Aug. 19, 1862 |
| 14 | I | Betts, Isaac | | Aug. 19, 1862 |
| 14 | I | Baker John H | | Aug. 18, 1862 |
| 14 | I | Brooks, Wm. H | | Jan. 21, 1863 |
| 14 | I | Bills, Walter M | Omro | |
| 14 | I | Boon William | Lake Milwaukee | Nov. 10, 1862 |
| 15 | I | Brown, Nils | Chicago | |
| 15 | I | Bleye, John | Chicago | |
| 15 | I | Berg, Anders | Colman, Iowa | |
| 16 | I | Beitheir, John | | April 1, 1864 |
| 16 | I | Burrett, Roland | Mauston | Aug. 18, 1865 |
| 17 | I | Bates, Alonzo | | |
| 17 | I | Burnes, Philip | | |
| 17 | I | Broit, F. A. E | | Mar. 19, 1862 |
| 17 | I | Barnes, J. W | | Mar. 19, 1862 |
| 17 | I | Blondell, Wm | | July 25, 1862 |
| 17 | I | Berry, Isaac | | July 31, 1862 |
| 17 | I | Burnbridger, John | | Mar. 20, 1862 |
| 17 | I | Brown, John | | April 19, 1862 |
| 17 | I | Binsion, Samuel O | | June 25, 1862 |
| 17 | I | Bird, John | | |
| 17 | I | Blood, Egbert J | | Mar. 20, 1862 |
| 17 | I | Brown, John | Fond du Lac | April 19, 1864 |
| 17 | I | Black, Wm. H | Clayton | May 4, 1864 |
| 17 | I | Bates, Alonzo | New Buffalo | April 6, 1862 |
| 17 | I | Bosee, Jonathan | | April 14, 1862 |
| 17 | I | Bearg William | | |
| 17 | I | Baisler, Charles H | | April 25, 1862 |
| 17 | I | Bombazer, John | Appleton | Feb. 28, 1863 |
| 17 | I | Briggman Otto | Milwaukee | July 2, 1865 |
| 52 | I | Baxter, Geo. R | | March 2, 1865 |
| 52 | I | Baxter, Jno. H | | March 2, 1865 |
| 52 | I | Burke, Michael | | March 3, 1865 |
| 52 | I | Burnes, Jno | Madison | |
| 52 | I | Brashier, Geo | | |
| 52 | I | Bennett, Ira | | |
| 52 | I | Brown, Thos | Madison | May 7, 1865 |
| 51 | I | Burns, Jno | Milwaukee | April 9, 1865 |
| 51 | I | Bennett, Martin | Milwaukee | Mar. 28, 1865 |
| 51 | I | Brownell, David | Milwaukee | June 2, 1865 |
| 51 | I | Bush, Alfred | Milwaukee | April .., 1865 |

| Reg't. | | Name. | Residence. | Date. |
|---|---|---|---|---|
| 51 | I | Brinker, John | La Crosse | July .., 1865 |
| 50 | I | Boyle, Wm | Westport | Mar. 26, 1865 |
| 50 | I | Brown, Wm | Hampden | Mar. 1, 1865 |
| 50 | I | Bonner, Wm | New Diggings | Aug. 29, 1865 |
| 50 | I | Bamin, Jno | Green Bay | Aug. 27, 1865 |
| 50 | I | Bamin, Frank | Green Bay | Aug. 28, 1865 |
| 50 | I | Bachelor, Jno. M | Prescott | Aug. 29, 1865 |
| 50 | I | Berg, Jno. W | Moscow | Aug. 27, 1865 |
| 50 | I | Bum, Jacob R | Menomonee | Aug. 30, 1865 |
| 50 | I | Britton, Jno | | Mar. 27, 1865 |
| 50 | I | Bibbe, Anton | Green Bay | Aug. 26, 1865 |
| 50 | I | Benton, Geo | Dumfries | |
| 49 | I | Burns, Dennis | Madison | Mar. 12, 1865 |
| 48 | I | Berg, Henry | Eagle Mills | Sept. 7, 1865 |
| 48 | I | Broze, Wm | Waumanda | Sept. 7, 1865 |
| 48 | I | Bonman, Geo | Belvidere | Sept. 7, 1865 |
| 48 | I | Broker, Chas | Belvidere | Sept. 7, 1865 |
| 48 | I | Bohrie, Gottlieb | Taunton | Sept. 7, 1865 |
| 48 | I | Briggs, W. Carter | Portage | Sept. 6, 1865 |
| 47 | I | Beck, Jno | | Feb. 22, 1865 |
| 46 | I | Burns, Andrew | Milwaukee | Mar. 6, 1865 |
| 45 | I | Broshore, Wm | Madison | Dec. .., 1864 |
| 44 | I | Brannon, Jas | | Jan. 7, 1865 |
| 44 | I | Banks, Jno | | Jan. 7, 1865 |
| 44 | I | Bowley, Thos | Milwaukee | Feb. 12, 1865 |
| 44 | I | Blakely, Wm | Milwaukee | Feb. 12, 1865 |
| 44 | I | Butler, Jno | Milwaukee | Feb. 21, 1865 |
| 44 | I | Bailey, Thos | Fond du Lac | Aug. 22, 1865 |
| 43 | I | Brown, Wm. C | | |
| 43 | I | Burns, Dan'l | Milwaukee | Oct. 14, 1864 |
| 43 | I | Bussell, Jno | Milwaukee | Oct. 2, 1864 |
| 43 | I | Browel, Otis | Milwaukee | Sept. 7, 1864 |
| 42 | I | Baker, Jno. H | Madison | Aug. 30, 1864 |
| 42 | I | Burk, Wm | Madison | Aug. 30, 1864 |
| 42 | I | Butts, Jas. H | Columbus | Sept. 9, 1864 |
| 42 | I | Blair, Jno | Madison | Sept. 17, 1864 |
| 42 | I | Bates, Jno | Oshkosh | Sept. 17, 1864 |
| 41 | I | Baker, Henry | Madison | June 9, .... |
| 38 | I | Branners, Henry | Milwaukee | April 28, 1864 |
| 38 | I | Brink, Lemuel | Milwaukee | June 15, 1864 |
| 38 | I | Brown, Jno | Milwaukee | July 28, 1864 |
| 38 | I | Boss, Jno. W | Janesville | Sept. 18, 1864 |
| 38 | I | Brady, Chas | | Sept. 27, 1864 |
| 38 | I | Brudent, H. R | Fond du Lac | Dec. 9, 1864 |
| 38 | I | Bresenthal, Fred'k | Princeton | Nov. 19, 1864 |
| 38 | I | Bowers, Alfred | Madison | Dec. .., 1864 |
| 37 | I | Ball, Julian | | April 26, 1864 |
| 37 | I | Bentley, Seneca | Plainfield | June 14, 1864 |
| 37 | I | Bagg, James | | May 3, 1864 |
| 36 | I | Brown, Harvey | Gilmanton | Oct. 31, 1864 |
| 36 | I | Beggs, David | Madison | May 3, 1864 |
| 36 | I | Brinie, Jno | Madison | April 26, 1864 |
| 36 | I | Bery, Jhial S | Sparta | April 19, 1864 |
| 35 | I | Burke, Martin | Milwaukee | Feb. 23, 1864 |
| 35 | I | Brown, Thos. H | Fond du Lac | Mar. 9, 1864 |
| 35 | I | Blakesly, Forrest L | Mineral Point | May 18, 1864 |
| 35 | I | Buckley, Wm. H | Burk | Dec. 19, 1864 |
| 35 | I | Breed, Jason | Byron | Jan. 2, 1865 |
| 35 | I | Bullis, Oliver R | Avon | Nov. 11, 1865 |

| Reg't. | | Name. | Residence. | Date. |
|---|---|---|---|---|
| 35 | I | Brink, Geo | Madison | Feb. 27, 1866 |
| 35 | I | Bacon, Henry S | Madison | Feb. 27, 1866 |
| 35 | I | Brock, James | Janesville | Jan. 8, 1864 |
| 34 | I | Bleanser, Fred | Cedarburg | Jan. 14, 1863 |
| 34 | I | Behrens, Fred | Cedarburg | Jan. 29, 1863 |
| 34 | I | Bartlett, Geo | Mequon | Jan. 31, 1863 |
| 34 | I | Barth, Peter | Mequon | Jan. 30, 1863 |
| 34 | I | Brasch, Frank | Grafton | Jan. 29, 1863 |
| 34 | I | Becker, Peter | Grafton | Jan. 30, 1863 |
| 34 | I | Burmoch. Michael | Grafton | Jan. 15, 1863 |
| 34 | I | Burke, John | Grafton | Dec. 16, 1862 |
| 34 | I | Burns, Thos | Grafton | Dec. 12, 1862 |
| 34 | I | Brown, Benj. N | Madison | Dec. 18, 1862 |
| 34 | I | Brokhofy, Jno | Milwaukee | Feb. 2, 1863 |
| 34 | I | Binkers, Leopold | Sumner | Jan. 30, 1863 |
| 34 | I | Bishop, Nelson | Ridgeway | Feb. 1, 1863 |
| 34 | I | Bishop, Horace | Ridgeway | Jan. 30, 1863 |
| 34 | I | Bartla, John | Mt. Point | Jan. 31, 1863 |
| 34 | I | Bues, Ernst | Bells Harbor | Jan. 31, 1863 |
| 34 | I | Befay, Emil | Sturgeon Bay | Jan. 15, 1863 |
| 34 | I | Baugret, Anton | Brussell | Jan. 31, 1863 |
| 34 | I | Backen, Owen | Boltonville | Jan. .., 1863 |
| 34 | I | Baden, Christian | Staatsville | Mar. 16, 1863 |
| 34 | I | Boesch, Charles | Grandville | Dec. 31, 1863 |
| 34 | I | Bull, Mathias | Menomonee | Jan. 31, 1868 |
| 34 | I | Belden, John | Princeton | Jan. 29, 1863 |
| 34 | I | Barnard, John | Manchester | Jan. 31, 1863 |
| 34 | I | Bamberg, William | Hamburg | Jan. 31, 1863 |
| 34 | I | Bhelke, August | Shields | Jan. 31, 1863 |
| 34 | I | Barnes, Jno | Milwaukee | Dec. 15, 1862 |
| 34 | I | Brill, Geo | Fish Creek | Feb. 1, 1863 |
| 33 | I | Barnes, Jas. H | Missouri | Dec. 22, 1862 |
| 33 | I | Balser, Henry | St. Louis | Dec. 22, 1862 |
| 33 | I | Bruce, Erastus W | Osagel, Co. Mo. | May 1, 1863 |
| 33 | I | Baker, Wm | St. Louis | Oct. 19, 1862 |
| 33 | I | Blunt, John | Breckenridge, Mo. | Feb 23, 1863 |
| 33 | I | Blackwell, W. S | Breckenridge, Mo. | Oct. 18, 1862 |
| 33 | I | Brimmer, Ezra | Boscobel | Oct. 15, 1862 |
| 33 | I | Button, Thos. G | Kenosha | July 28, 1865 |
| 32 | I | Behnkin, Louis | Metomen | Jan. 27, 1863 |
| 32 | I | Barnett, Robert | Rushford | Dec. 29, 1862 |
| 32 | I | Batterson, L | Eden | Ap'l 19, 1864 |
| 32 | I | Beauchamp, Anthony | Berlin | June 15, 1864 |
| 32 | I | Barrett, Henry | Center | June 15, 1864 |
| 31 | I | Briggs, Eugene | Pr. du Chien. | June 17, 1863 |
| 31 | I | Buckingham, Rich'd | Dodgeville | Mar. 4, 1863 |
| 31 | I | Baker, John F | Crawford Co | Mar. 7, 1863 |
| 31 | I | Brown, Gideon P | Green Co | Feb. 26, 1863 |
| 31 | I | Bush, Geo | Kenosha Co | Feb. 24, 1863 |
| 31 | I | Burwell, Otis | Milwaukee | Feb. 11, 1863 |
| 31 | I | Britt, Emanuel | | Mar. 2, 1863 |
| 31 | I | Burt, Geo | Albany | Sept. 6, 1863 |
| 31 | I | Band, Geo. W | Dodgeville | Dec. 4, 1863 |
| 31 | I | Bevins, Eli | Madison | Mar. 27, 1864 |
| 30 | I | Benson, Eugene | Galesville | Oct. 28, 1863 |
| 30 | I | Baker, Geo | | Apr. 16, 1864 |
| 30 | I | Bauman, Geo | Madison | Dec. 25, 1862 |
| 30 | I | Brown, Geo | | Mar. 1, 1864 |
| 29 | I | Baker, Ira R | | Jan. 23, 1863 |

| Reg't. | | Name | Residence. | Date. |
|---|---|---|---|---|
| 29 | I | Butler, Fred'k | Oak Grove | Oct. 31, 1862 |
| 29 | I | Bortsch, Chas | Horicon | Apr. 10, 1863 |
| 29 | I | Burns, Jno | Oak Grove | May 26, 1865 |
| 28 | I | Bump, Wm. H | Waukesha | Feb. 25, 1863 |
| 28 | I | Bramer, James | Palmyra | Nov. 10, 1862 |
| 28 | I | Burger, August | Waukesha | Mar. 1, 1862 |
| 28 | I | Boyle, Thomas | Milwaukee | |
| 28 | I | Bulman, Nathaniel | Waukesha | Jan. 29, 1865 |
| 27 | I | Bristol, Wm | Wolf River | Mar. 30, 1863 |
| 27 | I | Burt, Wm. A | Lima | Mar. 29, 1863 |
| 27 | I | Berger, Jacob | Milwaukee | Oct. 8, 1862 |
| 27 | I | Barber, Thos | Milwaukee | Jan. 2, 1863 |
| 27 | I | Brown, Edward | Milwaukee | Jan. 2, 1863 |
| 27 | I | Brust, Nicholas | Milwaukee | Feb. 1, 1863 |
| 27 | I | Busch, Thos | Milwaukee | Jan. 2, 1863 |
| 27 | I | Bingham, Geo. C | Milwaukee | Mar. 10, 1863 |
| 27 | I | Brand, August | | |
| 27 | I | Brown, James | | |
| 27 | I | Bente, Wm | Herman | Jan. 15, 1863 |
| 26 | I | Barbenire, Gusseppe | Milwaukee | June .., 1863 |
| 25 | I | Burdick, Alfred | Ithaca | Oct. 10, 1862 |
| 25 | I | Burlingame, Phillip | Tomah | May 14, 1863 |
| 24 | I | Brown, Wm | Milwaukee | |
| 24 | I | Burgess, Ezra | Wauwatosa | |
| 24 | I | Baker, Alonzo W | Milwaukee | |
| 24 | I | Barron, Russell J | Milwaukee | |
| 24 | I | Barry, Patrick | Milwaukee | |
| 24 | I | Brown, John | Milwaukee | |
| 24 | I | Brewer, Horatio S | Milwaukee | June 23, 1863 |
| 24 | I | Brundage, Alfred M | Milwaukee | Feb. 1, 1863 |
| 24 | I | Bauer, Herman | Milwaukee | May 1, 1863 |
| 24 | I | Bradt, Peter | | |
| 22 | I | Boodle, David | Lynn | Dec. 13, 1862 |
| 22 | I | Briggs, Jas. C | Delavan | Feb. 20, 1863 |
| 22 | I | Baker, Frank | Delavan | Feb. 27, 1863 |
| 22 | I | Barrett, Wm | Mt. Pleasant | Sep. 10, 1862 |
| 22 | I | Barnum, Samuel | Plymouth | Sep. 5, 1862 |
| 22 | I | Burst, Wm | Plymouth | May 15, 1863 |
| 21 | I | Budd, Jno. H | | Oct. 8, 1862 |
| 21 | I | Bennett, Henry D | Menasha | May 1, 1863 |
| 21 | I | Bennett, Harvey D | New London | Dec. 31, 1862 |
| 21 | I | Bartlett, Frank H | Janesville | Jan. 20, 1865 |
| 20 | I | Bombard, Peter | Lone Rock | |
| 20 | I | Bracht, Henry | Sheboygan | |
| 19 | I | Benedict, Cyrus | Oshkosh | Feb. 12, 1862 |
| 19 | I | Barker, Isaac W | Racine | Oct. 3, 1864 |
| 19 | I | Bruggen, Wm | Jefferson | July 11, 1865 |
| 19 | I | Brashneener, Jno | Bradley, Mich | June 6, 1862 |
| 19 | I | Bloods, Gall | Milwaukee | |
| 18 | I | Bixby, Harmon | Springville | |
| 18 | I | Bancroft, Edwin | Plover | |
| 18 | I | Beadle, Joel S | Plover | |
| 18 | I | Blair, Wm. G | Plover | |
| 18 | I | Bacon, Thos. G | Plover | |
| 18 | I | Brewster, Jerome | Berlin | |
| 18 | I | Brown, Hiram H | Columbus | |
| 18 | I | Brown, Joseph M | Portage | |
| 18 | I | Berry, James | Berlin | |
| 18 | I | Baker, H. L | Retreat | |

| Reg't. | | Name. | Residence. | Date. |
|---|---|---|---|---|
| 1 | C | Bessett, John | Beef Hill | Mar. 8, 1862 |
| 1 | C | Brown John | Fond du Lac Co., | Jan. 26, 1862 |
| 1 | C | Briggs Oscar | Berlin | |
| 1 | C | Bender Geo. J | Token Creek | Dec. 29, 1862 |
| 1 | C | Baker, James | Detroit, Mich | July 10, 1862 |
| 1 | C | Brown, Jno | | |
| 1 | C | Buckley, Timothy | Madison | May 3, 1864 |
| 1 | C | Brown, Wm | | Dec. 1, 1864 |
| 1 | C | Burdick, Thos. J | | Dec. 3, 1864 |
| 1 | C | Baldace, Joseph | Janesville | Jan. 15, 1865 |
| 1 | C | Buckhultz, August | | Dec. 31, 1863 |
| 1 | C | Brown, Judah | Lind | Nov. 9, 1864 |
| 2 | C | Bowers, Chas. L | Hudson | Sept. 1, 1864 |
| 2 | C | Barrett, Ogden | Milton | Nov. 18, 1864 |
| 2 | C | Bramer, Walter | Big Piney | June 28, 1865 |
| 2 | C | Brown, John | La Crosse | July 13, 1865 |
| 2 | C | Boulonger, Edward | Green Bay | Oct. 18, 1865 |
| 2 | C | Burgen, Chas | | Dec. 7, 1862 |
| 2 | C | Burk, James | Milwaukee | Mar. 24, 1862 |
| 2 | C | Breed, S. H | Darien | |
| 2 | C | Bishop Albert E | La Crosse | May 17, 1863 |
| 2 | C | Blair, Louis | | Oct. 15, 1862 |
| 3 | C | Baker, Thomas | Berlin | June 14, 1864 |
| 3 | C | Bub, George | Watertown | July 6, 1864 |
| 3 | C | Bowie, William | | Oct. 20, 1864 |
| 3 | C | Burges, Fred'k E | Van Buren, Ark | Aug. 27, 1864 |
| 3 | C | Blake Albert J | Sparta | April 21, 1865 |
| 3 | C | Bowie William | | Oct. 20, 1864 |
| 1 | H A | Bates, Jno. R | Columbia Co | Sept. 16, 1864 |
| 1 | H A | Baker Chaney | Alexandria, Va | Feb. 11, 1865 |
| 1 | H A | Bliss, Edward L | Fitchburg | Mar. 21, 1865 |
| 1 | H A | Barnes, Amandus | Milwaukee | May 10, 1861 |
| 1 | H A | Bronson, Amos | Milwaukee | Mar. 5, 1864 |
| 1 | H A | Barson, Wm | Milwaukee | Sept. 11, 1863 |
| 1 | H A | Burns, John | Racine | Oct. 18, 1864 |
| 2 | L A | Burnett, Andrew | Millville | Nov. 1, 1861 |
| 5 | L A | Barling, Rufus R | Monroe | Sept. 26, 1862 |
| 6 | L A | Barbarin, Edmond W | Pr. du Sac | Jan. 27, 1862 |
| 6 | L A | Bell Jno. (col'd) | | Feb. 17, 1863 |
| 7 | L A | Banks, Francis | Spring Green | July 1, 1864 |
| 8 | L A | Bradley, Warner | Omro | Mar. 14, 1862 |
| 8 | L A | Bligth, Chas. G | Monroe | May 27, 1862 |
| 8 | L A | Boyd, Joseph W | Watertown | June 2, 1862 |
| 9 | L A | Barber, Jervis | Burlington | Aug. 31, 1865 |

## C

| Reg't. | | Name. | Residence. | Date. |
|---|---|---|---|---|
| 1 | I | Cody Michael | | |
| 2 | I | Coffin Abner | Dane Co | Dec. 30, 1862 |
| 2 | I | Cuddeback, Solomon | Randolph | |
| 2 | I | Casey, Francis | Ridgeway | Dec. 18, 1862 |
| 3 | I | Chapman, Willis A. | Platteville | Apr. 23, 1862 |
| 3 | I | Crane, James | Milwaukee | |
| 3 | I | Church, M. A | | July 1, 1863 |
| 5 | I | Cox, William | | |
| 5 | I | Carr, J. B | | May 24, 1863 |
| 5 | I | Carr, J. B | Janesville | |
| 5 | I | Clapps, C. C | Virginia | July 19, 1864 |
| 5 | I | Carpenter, Danford D | Prairie du Chien | May 3, 1863 |

| Reg't. | | Name. | Rssidence. | Date. |
|---|---|---|---|---|
| 5 | I | Culver, Artemus | Waukesha | Oct. 20, 1862 |
| 6 | I | Cosely, Henry | Madison | |
| 6 | I | Clay, C. H | Prairie du Chien | May 20, 1864 |
| 6 | I | Conklin, Jas. G | | Nov. 3, 1861 |
| 6 | I | Crevosse, John | | Nov. 6, 1861 |
| 6 | I | Comstock Leander | | Sep. 14, 1862 |
| 6 | I | Cormor, James | | Sep. 14, 1862 |
| 6 | I | Cayzar, John T | | Sep. 14, 1862 |
| 6 | I | Cardy, Henry, J | | Aug. .., 1863 |
| 6 | I | Closson George | Michigan | July 8, 1861 |
| 7 | I | Carman, Frank G | | Jan. 20, 1863 |
| 7 | I | Chapel, William | | |
| 7 | I | Carl, William J | | |
| 7 | I | Chapman, David | | |
| 7 | I | Clark, James | | June 14, 1865 |
| 8 | I | Clark, Jos D | Waupaca | |
| 8 | I | Crandall, R. W | Plymouth | |
| 8 | I | Chilson, Jos. O | Mauston | |
| 8 | I | Cooly, Arthur O | | Oct. 20, 1864 |
| 8 | I | Cassady, Edward | | Feb. 10, 1865 |
| 8 | I | Carr, James C | Janesville | July 14, 1865 |
| 8 | I | Christianson, Peter | | Sep. 15, 1865 |
| 9 | I | Cook, George | Madison | Feb. 21, 1865 |
| 10 | I | Cone Norris D | | |
| 10 | I | Cronkhile Chas. T | Chester | Oct. 31, 1862 |
| 11 | I | Collins Dennis | | Mar. 19, 1863 |
| 11 | I | Conant, James B | | Mar. 10, 1863 |
| 11 | I | Conkle J. J | | Mar. 15, 1863 |
| 11 | I | Conkle, Daniel | | Mar. 15, 1863 |
| 11 | I | Chapman, F. B | | Feb. 20, 1863 |
| 11 | I | Chamberlain, Thos | | Mar. 1, 1862 |
| 11 | I | Carr, Robt | | Apr. 26, 1863 |
| 11 | I | Collins Dennis | Milwaukee | Mar. 18, 1863 |
| 11 | I | Corvant, James | Johnson's Creek | Mar. 10, 1863 |
| 11 | I | Conkel, Daniel | Richland | Mar. 14, 1863 |
| 11 | I | Conkel John J | Richland | Mar. 15, 1863 |
| 12 | I | Campion, Edward | Cooperstown | Nov. 20, 1861 |
| 12 | I | Coly, Joseph L | Grand Rapids | Nov. 17, 1861 |
| 13 | I | Chemshom, Spooner | Janesville | June 14, 1865 |
| 13 | I | Croft, Wm | Janesville | June 16, 1865 |
| 13 | I | Cron, Christian | Sharon | |
| 13 | I | Cole, Henry S | | |
| 13 | I | Calnen, Thomas | | |
| 13 | I | Croft, William | | |
| 13 | I | Coshall, Wm | | |
| 13 | I | Chamberlain, Carlos, E | | May 10, 1864 |
| 13 | I | Cooper, Elijah E | | May 10, 1864 |
| 14 | I | Curbey, Augustus W | | Aug. 18, 1862 |
| 14 | I | Cready, John | | May 22, 1863 |
| 14 | I | Cooley, Oscar | Depere | Aug. 2, 1864 |
| 14 | I | Chester, Henry | Milwaukee | Feb. 15, 1865 |
| 14 | I | Christian, Daniel | | Jan. 11, 1862 |
| 14 | I | Comer, Wm E | | Jan. 20, 1862 |
| 14 | I | Clark, Edward | | Aug. 18, 1862 |
| 14 | I | Crish, Thos B | | July 7, 1862 |
| 14 | I | Crish, Elijah J | | July 7, 1862 |
| 15 | I | Chroshong, Wm | Waterford | |
| 16 | I | Caswell, Jas | | April 2, 1864 |
| 16 | I | Cole, Ambrose B | Hillsboro | Aug. 18, 1862 |

| Reg't. | | Name | Residence. | Date. |
|---|---|---|---|---|
| 16 | I | Clark, John | Fox Lake | |
| 16 | I | Claflin, Lorenzo | Seven Mile Creek | April 6, 1862 |
| 17 | I | Caughlin, David | | Mar. 20, 1862 |
| 17 | I | Cline, Michael | | Feb. 9, 1862 |
| 17 | I | Coales, Israel | | Feb. 18, 1862 |
| 17 | I | Connelly, John | | Apr. 18, 1862 |
| 17 | I | Casleman, Thos | | Mar. 20, 1862 |
| 17 | I | Christopherson, Thos | | Mar. 20, 1862 |
| 17 | I | Childs, Seldon | | Aug. 6, 1862 |
| 17 | I | Campbell, John D | | Mar. 22, 1862 |
| 17 | I | Cobis, Silas | | Mar. 20, 1862 |
| 17 | I | Caipson, John C | | Jan. 20, 1862 |
| 17 | I | Cooney, Michael | | Jan. 20, 1862 |
| 17 | I | Connell, Michael | | Jan. 20, 1862 |
| 17 | I | Crawford, Levi | | Mar. 26, 1862 |
| 17 | I | Clark, Michael | | Aug. 9, 1862 |
| 17 | I | Cawley, Farrell | | July 9, 1862 |
| 17 | I | Chambers, John | | Mar. 19, 1862 |
| 17 | I | Clany, John C | | Dec. 26, 1864 |
| 17 | I | Costellon, Peter | Beaver Dam | April 27, 1864 |
| 17 | I | Clark, John G | Chicago | April 27, 1864 |
| 17 | I | Campbell, Spencer | | Jan. 1, 1865 |
| 17 | I | Coats, Israel | | Feb. 18, 1863 |
| 52 | I | Carr, Thos | | April 9, 1865 |
| 52 | I | Coleman, Edward | | Feb. 26, 1865 |
| 52 | I | Canes, Isaiah | | Mar. 3, 1865 |
| 52 | I | Callaghan, Jno | | |
| 52 | I | Condon, Jno | | |
| 52 | I | Callahan, Jno | Madison | April 22, 1865 |
| 51 | I | Carr, Henry N | Milwaukee | Mar. 4, 1865 |
| 51 | I | Caswell, James | Milwaukee | Mar. 4, 1865 |
| 51 | I | Cook, Chas | Milwaukee | April 9, 1865 |
| 51 | I | Casey, George | Milwaukee | April 9. 1865 |
| 51 | I | Condor, Richard | Milwaukee | April 15, 1865 |
| 51 | I | Crowell, Geo | Milwaukee | Mar. 8, 1865 |
| 51 | I | Corwin, Jas. W | Milwaukee | Mar. 28, 1865 |
| 50 | I | Cooley, Chas | Vernon Co | Aug. 25, 1865 |
| 50 | I | Croft, Wm | New Diggings | Aug. 29, 1865 |
| 50 | I | Comstock, Chas | Horicon | July 5, 1865 |
| 50 | I | Clarke, Jno | Morrison | Aug. 27 1865 |
| 50 | I | Cole, Albert | | Sept. 4, 1865 |
| 48 | I | Cheesebro, Nicholas | Chilton | Sept. 6, 1865 |
| 48 | I | Cook, Jno | Milwaukee | Feb. 19, 1865 |
| 48 | I | Carty, James | Milwaukee | Feb. 28, 1865 |
| 48 | I | Caravans, Fredrick | Milwaukee | Feb. 24, 1864 |
| 48 | I | Casser, Sebastian | Milwaukee | Mar. .., 1865 |
| 48 | I | Cassady, Frank | Milwaukee | Mar. .., 1865 |
| 47 | I | Colton, James | | Feb. 22, 1865 |
| 46 | I | Cameron, Jno | — | Mar. 1, 1865 |
| 46 | I | Cain, Patrick | Milwaukee | Mar. 6, 1865 |
| 44 | I | Cram, Ransom | Muscoda | Aug. 9, 1865 |
| 43 | I | Collins, Jno | | |
| 43 | I | Cooper, Geo. H | | |
| 43 | I | Coon, Jno | | |
| 43 | I | Clare Jno | Milwaukee | Sept. 24, 1864 |
| 43 | I | Crutch, Wm | Mineral Point | Sept. 23, 1864 |
| 39 | I | Callahan, James | | Jan. 10, 1864 |
| 38 | I | Canada, Michael | Marinette | June 15, 1864 |
| 38 | I | Campen, Jno | Madison | June 15, 1864 |

| *Reg't.* | | *Name.* | *Residence.* | *Date.* |
|---|---|---|---|---|
| 38 | I | Carey, Richard | Palmyra | June 29, 1864 |
| 38 | I | Castello, Thos | Madison | Sept. 12, 1864 |
| 38 | I | Carr, Michael | Milwaukee | Sept. 16, 1864 |
| 38 | I | Chase, Henry | Madison | Sept. 23, 1864 |
| 38 | I | Conderman, Geo. A | | Sept. 22, 1864 |
| 37 | I | Cole, Geo | Madison | May .., 1864 |
| 36 | I | Christensen, Peter | Milwaukee | May 9, 1864 |
| 36 | I | Calkins, Albert | Sparta | Aug. 31, 1864 |
| 35 | I | Clark, John | Milwaukee | April 18, 1864 |
| 35 | I | Cleaver Thos | Milwaukee | Sept. 16, 1865 |
| 35 | I | Chamberlain, Frank | Prairie du Chien | Feb. 27, 1866 |
| 35 | I | Cox, Harry | Milwaukee | Feb. 27, 1866 |
| 35 | I | Casban, John | Madison | Feb. 27, 1866 |
| 35 | I | Cullong Lewis | Milwaukee | Aug. 1, 1864 |
| 34 | I | Carroll, Richard | Mequon | Dec. 10, 1863 |
| 34 | I | Crown, Conrad | Fredonia | Dec. 10, 1863 |
| 34 | I | Childs, Wm | Milwaukee | Jan. 5, 1863 |
| 34 | I | Collingwood Jno | Dodgeville | Jan. 13, 1863 |
| 34 | I | Christiansen, Peter | Highland | Jan. 21, 1863 |
| 34 | I | Conrad, Ferdinand | | Jan. 25, 1863 |
| 34 | I | Costerman, Peter | Holland | Jan. 31, 1863 |
| 34 | I | Coco, Ferdinand | Green Bay | Jan. .., 1863 |
| 34 | I | Curry, James | Farmington | Dec. 25. 1862 |
| 34 | I | Conard, John | Lincoln | Jan. 5, 1863 |
| 34 | I | Callahan, Jeremiah | Mequon | Dec. 19, 1862 |
| 34 | I | Clampe, John, jr | Crystal Lake | Jan. 31, 1863 |
| 34 | I | Carroll, John | Menomonee | Jan. 30, 1863 |
| 34 | I | Choulnig, Frederick | Milwaukee | Dec. .., 1862 |
| 33 | I | Clogston, Wm | Tepton, Mo | Jan. 4, 1863 |
| 33 | I | Cowell, Andrew | Bennett's Mills | Nov. 26, 1862 |
| 33 | I | Calvin, Jas. H | St. Louis | Oct. 19, 1862 |
| 33 | I | Crane, Wm. L. sr | Tuscumbia | Feb. 10, 1863 |
| 33 | I | Crane, Wm. L. jr | Tuscumbia | Feb. 10, 1863 |
| 33 | I | Cooper, John | St. Louis, Mo | Dec. 23, 1862 |
| 33 | I | Campbell, Rob't A | Boscobel | Oct. 15, 1862 |
| 33 | I | Coffee, James | Janesville | May 10, 1863 |
| 33 | I | Clark, Abner | Boscobel | Oct. 25, 1862 |
| 33 | I | Clarmont, Lewis | St. Louis, Mo | Feb. 24, 1863 |
| 33 | I | Crangle, Henry | Racine | Nov. 23, 1864 |
| 32 | I | Campbell, Jno | Springvale | Oct. 7, 1862 |
| 32 | I | Conklin, Lorenzo | | Feb. 22, 1864 |
| 32 | I | Culbertson, Dan'l B | Berlin | May 22, 1864 |
| 32 | I | Cady, Andrew J | Green Bay | July 1, 1864 |
| 31 | I | Cashman, Thomas | Prairie du Chien | Sept. 16, 1863 |
| 31 | I | Cowan, Henry | | July 16, 1864 |
| 31 | I | Crawford, Thos. B | Nashville, Tenn | July 17, 1864 |
| 30 | I | Cook, Robert | Galesville | Feb. 15, 1863 |
| 30 | I | Clark, Jno | | Feb. 4, 1864 |
| 30 | I | Cunningham, Thos | Chippewa | Jan. 31, 1865 |
| 30 | I | Cunningham, Jno | Madison | Oct. 20, 1864 |
| 30 | I | Cowley, Thos | | Oct. 20, 1864 |
| 30 | I | Coon, Darius E | Fulton Creek | April 1, 1864 |
| 29 | I | Chapman, Milo | Horicon | Feb. 10, 1863 |
| 29 | I | Chandler, Jno. C | Horicon | Feb. 10, 1863 |
| 29 | I | Cole, Lucius | Randolph | Jan. 23, 1863 |
| 29 | I | Carter A. M | Hartford | Jan. 22, 1863 |
| 29 | I | Corlis Edward | Burnett | Jan. 23, 1863 |
| 28 | I | Crowels, Samuel | Lisbon | Oct. 20, 1863 |
| 28 | I | Clock, Wm | Waukesha | Feb. 27, 1862 |

| Reg't. | | Name. | Residence. | Date. |
|---|---|---|---|---|
| 28 | I | Clawson, Garrett | Walworth | July 1, 1863 |
| 28 | I | Cardwell, Richard | Milwaukee | |
| 28 | I | Cook, Benj. S | Brookfield | Oct. 16, 1862 |
| 28 | I | Campbell, Hiram | Oconomowoc | Oct. 14, 1862 |
| 28 | I | Chaffe, Jno. W | Summitt | July .., 1863 |
| 28 | I | Connolly, Jno | Milton | July 21, 1863 |
| 27 | I | Cummings, J. B | | Mar. 18, 1863 |
| 27 | I | Carroll, James | Clyde | Sep. 30, 1863 |
| 27 | I | Curtiss, Jno | | |
| 27 | I | Cole, Geo | Carlton | Aug. 18, 1862 |
| 26 | I | Crashart, Lewis | | Mar. 20, 1863 |
| 26 | I | Czarnecki, Valendi | Fond du Lac | July 1, 1863 |
| 26 | I | Cohill, John | Janesville | Apr. 24, 1865 |
| 26 | I | Chamicke, Valenti | | July 1, 1863 |
| 26 | I | Cuhn, Martin | Two Rivers | |
| 24 | I | Carney, John C | Milwaukee | |
| 24 | I | Curley, Wm | Milwaukee | |
| 22 | I | Carey, Peter S | Hudson | Jan. 15, 1862 |
| 22 | I | Cathoon, Jas. M | Janesville | Mar. 12, 1863 |
| 22 | I | Cole, Amos H | Monroe | Nov. .., 1862 |
| 22 | I | Carver, Evi B | Plymouth | Sep. 5, 1862 |
| 21 | I | Campbell, Ithamer | Janesville | Oct. 8, 1862 |
| 20 | I | Carroll, Michael A | Madison | June 4, 1863 |
| 20 | I | Clarke, Wm | Ripon | Aug. 8, 1863 |
| 20 | I | Cole, Jno | Ripon | Oct. 1, 1862 |
| 20 | I | Cole, Geo. C | Racine | Aug. 25, 1862 |
| 20 | I | Coon, Henry | Richland Center | Aug. 11, 1862 |
| 19 | I | Clary, Wm | Waukesha | June 2, 1862 |
| 19 | I | Cutz, Michael | Milwaukee | Feb. 10, 1862 |
| 19 | I | Connell, John | Milwaukee | Oct. 3, 1864 |
| 18 | I | Cory, Rowell F | Readstown | |
| 18 | I | Corrigan, Matthew | Hampden | |
| 18 | I | Cummins, H | Springville | |
| 1 | C | Connor, Richard | Milwaukee | July 7, 1862 |
| 1 | C | Commen, John | | June .., 1863 |
| 1 | C | Carson, Jno. A | Kenosha | Dec. 7, 1863 |
| 1 | C | Conant, Jno. A | Geneva | Dec. 1, 1862 |
| 1 | C | Caswell, Geo. A | Kilbourn City | Apr. .., 1862 |
| 1 | C | Clanson, Geo. H | Markesan | |
| 1 | C | Carney, Michael | Kenosha | |
| 1 | C | Clark, Jno. B | | Dec. 14, 1864 |
| 1 | C | Chatfield, Theodon | Milwaukee | Nov. 30, 1864 |
| 2 | C | Coons, Geo. H | La Crosse | July 31, 1863 |
| 2 | C | Carpenter, Elliott | | Aug. 28, 1862 |
| 2 | C | Carter, Jas. L | Richland Co | Oct. 10, 1865 |
| 2 | C | Cobb, Albert C | Janesville | Oct. 15, 1865 |
| 2 | C | Carman, James | Janesville | Oct. 14, 1865 |
| 2 | C | Covey, Geo. W | Mauston | July 10, 1865 |
| 2 | C | Craig, Steward | Wingville | July 25, 1865 |
| 2 | C | Cohart, Jno | | |
| 3 | C | Campbell, Robert | Watertown | July 6, 1864 |
| 3 | C | Cannon, Gouvernon | Van Buren, Ark | Oct. 14, 1864 |
| 3 | C | Carter, Albeon J | Appleton | Oct. 14, 1864 |
| 3 | C | Chapman, Wm. B | Bloomfield | June 21, 1865 |
| 3 | C | Conway, Geo. (col'd) | Janesville | Aug. 27, 1865 |
| 3 | C | Colomino, Chas. A | Janesville | June 14, 1865 |
| 3 | C | Cooper, Samuel | Platteville | June 6, 1864 |
| 3 | C | Craigie, Thos. H | Milwaukee | Dec. 31, 1862 |
| 3 | C | Carmon, John W | Van Buren, Ark | Mar. 10, 1864 |

| Reg't. | | Name. | Residence. | Date. |
|---|---|---|---|---|
| 3 | C | Chappell, Walworth | Kingston | , 1862 |
| 3 | C | Clarey, James C | Waukesha | Feb. 14, 1862 |
| 3 | C | Conrad, Phillip | Utica | Feb. 6, 1862 |
| 3 | C | Cook, Herbert | Merton | Oct. 20, 1862 |
| 3 | C | Carson, Chas W | La Crosse | Jan. 6, 1864 |
| 3 | C | Carr, Abraham C | Sparta | July 3, 1863 |
| 3 | C | Connor, Wm H | Oshkosh | Feb. 7, 1863 |
| 4 | C | Church, G. W | Jefferson | July 5, 1865 |
| 4 | C | Comstock, John E | Hudson | Jan. 29, 1865 |
| 4 | C | Clark, Wm | Madison | |
| 4 | C | Cobbin, Wm. | Chippewa Falls | |
| 4 | C | Curran, James | | |
| 4 | C | Carroll, Patrick | | |
| 1 | H A | Comstock, Chas | New Bedford | |
| 1 | H A | Chapman, Edwin | Lodi | May 20, 1863 |
| 1 | H A | Coy, Kendall M | Omro | Oct. 18, 1863 |
| 1 | H A | Cunningham, Andrew | Madison | Aug. 9, 1865 |
| 1 | H A | Clark, James | Milwaukee | Sep. 10, 1863 |
| 1 | L A | Craft, Geo | | Sep. 15, 1863. |
| 4 | L A | Clifford, Jno N | Portsmouth | May 27, 1863 |
| 4 | L A | Carroll, Edward | Portsmouth | July 21, 1865 |
| 6 | L A | Christman, Andrew | St. Louis, Mo | Aug. 3, 1863 |
| 7 | L A | Coon, Chas | Milwaukee | Dec. 29, 1863 |

## D

| Reg't. | | Name. | Residence. | Date. |
|---|---|---|---|---|
| 1 | I | Donner, George | | |
| 1 | I | Dikeman, Henry | | |
| 1 | I | David, Henry V | | Dec. .., 1862 |
| 1 | I | De Groff, Richard L | Waupun | May 9, 1864 |
| 2 | I | Dailey, Arthur J | Beaver Dam | Nov. 1, 1862 |
| 2 | I | Dilly, Geo. W | Mineral Point | 1862 |
| 2 | I | Donovan, John | Rocktown | |
| 2 | I | Dean, Elisha A | Fall River | |
| 2 | I | Dasy, Wm. R | Potosi | July 21, 1861 |
| 3 | I | Dugent, John | | |
| 3 | I | Dowery, Hiram | Wisconsin | Apr. 23, 1865 |
| 5 | I | Darling, Otis | | May 3, 1862 |
| 5 | I | Doyle, Edward | Fond du Lac | Sep. 30, 1864 |
| 5 | I | Dongan, James | Hudson | May 31, 1863 |
| 5 | I | Davis, Edward | Muskeego | Mar. 1, 1864 |
| 5 | I | Davenport, James H | Beaver Dam | May 5, 1864 |
| 5 | I | Dellehasy, Wm | | July 28, 1861 |
| 5 | I | Deney, John J | | July 20, 1861 |
| 5 | I | Davis, Wm. H | | July 27, 1865 |
| 7 | I | Dunavan, Edw'd. | | Sep. 6, 1865 |
| 7 | I | Durhans, John S | Milwaukee | Feb. 11, 1865 |
| 7 | I | David, Peter | Cedar Creek | Apr. 25. 1865 |
| 8 | I | Disbrow, Philip | Dayton | |
| 8 | I | Devoo, Isaac | Eau Claire | |
| 8 | I | Dennison, James | Viroqua | |
| 8 | I | Donnelly, Pat | La Crosse | July 23, 1864 |
| 8 | I | Dom, Dewey | | Nov. 23, 1864 |
| 8 | I | Dunham, Charles | | Sep. 5, 1863 |
| 9 | I | Dennis, Theodore | | Feb. 11, 1863 |
| 9 | I | Drews, Gottleib | Milwaukee | |
| 10 | I | Dillon, James | New York | Oct. 30, 1862 |
| 10 | I | Dow, Lorenzo H | | |
| 11 | I | Donna, John | | Mar. 15, 1863 |
| 11 | I | Dowdna, John M | Richland | Mar. 15, 1863 |

| Reg't. | | Name. | Residence. | Date. |
|---|---|---|---|---|
| 11 | I | Dally, Daniel | Oregon | Nov. 3, 1861 |
| 12 | I | Draper, Jason | Juneau Co. | May 4, 1862 |
| 12 | I | De Lane, Wm. W | Oconto | Oct. 19, 1862 |
| 12 | I | Doyle, Thomas D | Walworth | Jan. 20, 1862 |
| 12 | I | Dean, James W | Wisconsin | May 1. 1864 |
| 13 | I | Doyle, Patrick | | Jan. 14, 1865 |
| 13 | I | Dake, Jas. K | Green Bay | July 15, 1865 |
| 13 | I | Dunn, Michael | Janesville | |
| 13 | I | Dodge, Peter | | June 12, 1865 |
| 14 | I | Davis, John | La Crosse | July 1. 1865 |
| 14 | I | Doxtator, Jacob | Oneida | Nov. 30, 1864 |
| 14 | I | Doxtator, Cornelius | | Nov. 30, 1864 |
| 14 | I | Delk, David M | | July 7, 1862 |
| 14 | I | Dunham, Levi | | Jan. 18, 1862 |
| 14 | I | Davis, David | | Jan. 21, 1863 |
| 14 | I | Delk, W. K | | July 7, 1862 |
| 14 | I | Darrell, Henry | | |
| 15 | I | Dingman, Robt. S | Waterford | May 2, 1862 |
| 16 | I | Denick, Thomas | Princeton | Aug. 18, 1862 |
| 16 | I | Daily, Edward | Eau Claire | Apr. 30, 1864 |
| 16 | I | Downing, Elias | Plymouth | Aug. 18, 1862 |
| 16 | I | Devine, John P | Deerfield | Feb. 20, 1862 |
| 16 | I | Dudley, Oscar L | Wisconsin | July 17, 1862 |
| 17 | I | Discon, Anthony | | Mar. 20, 1862 |
| 17 | I | Duggan, John | | Mar. 20, 1862 |
| 17 | I | Dewyer, Cornelius | | Mar. 20, 1862 |
| 17 | I | Diamond, Jas | | Mar. 14, 1862 |
| 17 | I | Dailey, James | | Mar. 15, 1862 |
| 17 | I | Donshan, Philip | | Mar. 23, 1862 |
| 17 | I | Dixon, Bercly A | Vicksburg, Miss | May 1, 1865 |
| 17 | I | Deryer, Wm | Vicksburg, Miss | May 7, 1865 |
| 17 | I | Dayton, John W | Beaver Dam | Aug. 27, 1864 |
| 17 | I | Dennis, Frank | | Mar. 20, 1862 |
| 17 | I | Daily, James | Milwaukee | Mar. 13, 1864 |
| 17 | I | Dayton, Geo. W | Beaver Dam | Apr. 26, 1864 |
| 17 | I | Dushane, Thomas | | June 29, 1864 |
| 17 | I | Detry, Augustine | Green Bay | May 29, 1864 |
| 17 | I | Denyat, Cornelius | New Berlin | Apr. 6, 1862 |
| 17 | I | Deorne, Martin | Eagle | Apr. 7, 1862 |
| 17 | I | Danks, Augustiene | New London | Apr. 6, 1862 |
| 52 | I | Daniels, Michael | | |
| 51 | I | Davis, Geo. H | Milwaukee | Mar. 28, 1865 |
| 50 | I | Dowling, Wm | Fulton | Mar. 27, 1865 |
| 50 | I | Drinks, Barnard | Appleton | Aug. 30, 1864 |
| 50 | I | Dowd, Geo. W | | Aug. |
| 50 | I | Dawson, Jno | New Diggings | Aug. 27, 1865 |
| 50 | I | Dean, Lucius M | Seneca | Aug. 28, 1865 |
| 50 | I | Dodge, Hiram P | Arena | Sep. 9, 1865 |
| 48 | I | Donley, Michael | Prairie du Chien | Sep. 6, 1865 |
| 48 | I | Duefram, Barnard | Boscobel | Sep. 19, 1865 |
| 47 | I | Dunn, Wm | | Feb. 22, 1865 |
| 47 | I | Dailey, Henry | | Feb. 22, 1865 |
| 46 | I | Dusenbury, Hiram | Wautoma | Mar. 5, 1865 |
| 44 | I | Duffy, Jno | | Jan. 7, 1865 |
| 44 | I | Dunlary, Cornelius | | Jan. 7, 1865 |
| 44 | I | Donovan, Dan'l | | Jan. 7, 1865 |
| 44 | I | Donally, James | | Jan. 8, 1865 |
| 44 | I | Donally, Frank | | Jan. 8, 1865 |
| 44 | I | Dunn, Jno | Milwaukee | Feb. 12, 1865 |

| *Reg't.* | | *Name.* | *Residence.* | *Date.* |
|---|---|---|---|---|
| 44 | I | Duryea, Jno | Milwaukee | Feb. 16, 1865 |
| 44 | I | Dolan, Chas | Milwaukee | Feb. 16, 1865 |
| 44 | I | Dyer, Chas A | Peshtigo | June 12, 1865 |
| 43 | I | Delany, Patrick | Milwaukee | Oct. 13, 1864 |
| 43 | I | Dayley, Thos | Stoughton | Sep. 7, 1864 |
| 43 | I | Demerest, Andrew J | Milwaukee | Sep. 25, 1864 |
| 38 | I | Dean, Henry | Milwaukee | Aug. 22, 1864 |
| 38 | I | Duffey, Patrick | Milwaukee | Aug. 17, 1864 |
| 38 | I | Duncan, John R | Milwaukee | Aug. 28, 1864 |
| 38 | I | Daniels, Leonard | Berlin | Jan. 29, 1865 |
| 37 | I | Dyke, Wm. H | | May 3, 1864 |
| 36 | I | Dyke, George | Monroe | May 9, 1864 |
| 36 | I | Donaldson, Seymour | Eau Claire | May 7, 1864 |
| 36 | I | Doyle, Wm | Madison | Aug. 31, 1864 |
| 35 | I | Dapper, Martin | Cedar Creek | Nov. 27, 1863 |
| 35 | I | Duggan, John | Milwaukee | Feb. 10, 1864 |
| 34 | I | Daiken, Wm | Milwaukee | Jan. 30, 1863 |
| 34 | I | Donebar, James | Chicago | Jan. 10, 1863 |
| 34 | I | Delsant, Henry | Sturgeon Bay | Feb. 4, 1863 |
| 34 | I | Dellahue, Michael | Red River | Jan. .., 1863 |
| 34 | I | Debeck, Lepold | Green Bay | Feb. 2, 1863 |
| 34 | I | Dellaronelle, Hector | Green Bay | Jan. 30, 1863 |
| 34 | I | Dailey, Thomas | Meeker | Jan. 1, 1863 |
| 34 | I | Degritz, Carl | Fillmore | Jan. 1, 1863 |
| 34 | I | Dabus, Joseph | Menomonee | Jan. 31, 1863 |
| 34 | I | Dage, August | Crystal Lake | Jan. 29, 1863 |
| 34 | I | Deineit, Wm | Cedarburg | Jan. 28, 1863 |
| 34 | I | Durwald, Christian | Hartford | Jan. 31, 1863 |
| 33 | I | Dayer, Daniel | St. Louis, Mo | Dec. 22, 1862 |
| 33 | I | Dobson, Carroll | Tuscumbia, Mo | Feb. 22, 1863 |
| 33 | I | Doyle, Walter | | Mar. 17, 1863 |
| 32 | I | Delany, John | | Oct. 14, 1862 |
| 32 | I | Dean, James | Westfield | Dec. 4, 1862 |
| 31 | I | Detling, John | Green county | Mar. 6, 1863 |
| 31 | I | Davis, Edward | Dodgeville | Mar. 4, 1863 |
| 31 | I | Dale, Alfred | Dodgeville | Mar. 4, 1863 |
| 31 | I | Dunn, Phillip | Milwaukee | Jan. 3, 1863 |
| 31 | I | Durkee, Henry | Madison | Mar. 2, 1863 |
| 31 | I | Douglass, Samuel | Mineral Point | Jan. 23, 1863 |
| 30 | I | Delamater, Samuel | Janesville | Dec. 6, 1863 |
| 30 | I | Delamater, Henry C | Janesville | Dec. 6, 1863 |
| 30 | I | Dunn, Wm. C | Madison | Dec. 10, 1863 |
| 30 | I | Dockailler, Jacob | Taunton, Mass | Jan. 7, 1864 |
| 30 | I | Duffee, Charles | Milwaukee | April 9, 1864 |
| 30 | I | Denno, Laber | | Mar. 24, 1864 |
| 30 | I | Donahue, Patrick | | Jan. 1, 1864 |
| 30 | I | Dolan, James | Sun Prairie | April 1, 1864 |
| 29 | I | Danley, Silas | Horicon | Mar. 14, 1863 |
| 29 | I | Dunham Hezekiah | | Feb. 9, 1863 |
| 29 | I | Davis, L. M | Westport | Jan. 23, 1863 |
| 28 | I | Dailey, John | Milwaukee | |
| 28 | I | Dailey, James | Ottawa | Sept. 18, 1863 |
| 27 | I | Davis, Thos | Milwaukee | Jan. 2, 1863 |
| 27 | I | Devine, Corney | Milwaukee | Jan. 2, 1863 |
| 27 | I | Doud, Jno | Milwaukee | Mar. 31, 1863 |
| 27 | I | Debano, Jno | | Mar. 7, 1863 |
| 26 | I | Daub, Jno | Milwaukee | Sept. .., 1862 |
| 25 | I | Dayton, Justus A | Durand | Apr. 11, 1863 |
| 24 | I | Duffy, Jas | Milwaukee | |

| Reg't. | | Name. | Residence. | Date. |
|---|---|---|---|---|
| 24 | I | Dewey, Guy | Milwaukee | Oct. 29, 1864 |
| 24 | I | Daggett, Wm. E | Milwaukee | Dec. 31, 1862 |
| 22 | I | Dwyer, James | Milwaukee | Jan. 10, 1863 |
| 22 | I | Davis, Morris O | Racine | May 20, 1863 |
| 21 | I | Deiter, George W | | Oct. 8, 1863 |
| 21 | I | Dwaporte, David | Fond du Lac | June .., 1863 |
| 21 | I | Davis, Robert | Nekimi | Dec. 31, 1862 |
| 21 | I | Demouth, Geo | Milwaukee | June 15, 1864 |
| 20 | I | Delaney, Thos | Elkhorn | |
| 20 | I | Dugan, James | Milwaukee | Mar. 31, 1864 |
| 19 | I | Doney, Alfred R | La Crosse | May 29, 1862 |
| 19 | I | Doty, W. H | Oshkosh | Feb. 12, 1862 |
| 19 | I | Decolm, Richard | Oshkosh | Feb. 12, 1862 |
| 19 | I | Drew, James | Milwaukee | June 16, 1862 |
| 18 | I | Doud, George W | Berlin | |
| 18 | I | Drake, Samuel | Plover | |
| 18 | I | Day, Martin V. B | Reedstown | |
| 18 | I | Davis, Thomas J | Newton | June 21, 1865 |
| 1 | C | Doblen, John F | | Feb. 1, 1864 |
| 1 | C | Davis, Ferdinand G | Madison | Dec. 26, 1864 |
| 2 | C | Dodge, Sherman | Stockbridge | Aug. 30, 1863 |
| 2 | C | Downing, Harry | Utica | Oct. 30, 1863 |
| 2 | C | Downing, Robert | Yorkville | Mar. 5, 1862 |
| 2 | C | Dequire, Felix | | Feb. .., 1862 |
| 2 | C | Doran, James | Memphis, Tenn | Aug. 11, 1862 |
| 2 | C | Davis, John | Patch Grove | Aug. 19, 1863 |
| 2 | C | Delniche, Andre | Mishicott | |
| 2 | C | Dufram, Isidore | Fond du Lac | June 23, 1865 |
| 3 | C | Durfee, Charles H | Madison | June 14, 1864 |
| 3 | C | Dred, Andrew | | June 7, 1865 |
| 3 | C | Denison, Royal L | Baraboo | June 10, 1862 |
| 3 | C | Dunbar, Oscar A | Eau Claire | Jan. .., 1862 |
| 3 | C | Dunn, Robert | Waukesha | Jan. 29, 1862 |
| 3 | C | Dunlap, James F | Sparta | Sept. 19, 1862 |
| 3 | C | Davitz, Ernst | Watertown | July .., 1863 |
| 4 | C | Dellseil, Jno | Milwaukee | Apr. 23, 1866 |
| 4 | C | Delston, J | | Apr. 25, 1866 |
| 4 | C | Debert, Jno | Milwaukee | Apr. 23, 1866 |
| 4 | C | Daley, Barney | Baton Rouge, La | Aug. 30, 1863 |
| 4 | C | Doyle, Alexander | New River | June 10, 1864 |
| 4 | C | Douglass, James | Jackson county | Apr. .., 1864 |
| 4 | C | Dabzell, James | Baton Rouge, La | Sept. 27, 1865 |
| 1 | H A | Dunn, Joseph | Milwaukee | |
| 1 | H A | Dolan, Henry J | Milwaukee | |
| 1 | H A | Downing, Charles E | Fond du Lac | |
| 1 | H A | Dussing, Christian | Milwaukee | Apr. 1, 1865 |
| 1 | L A | Denurse, Michael | Lockport, Ill | Nov. 26, 1862 |
| 4 | L A | Davis, Charles D | Milwaukee | Oct. .., 1864 |
| 4 | L A | Denning, Caron | Beloit | Oct. 12, 1861 |
| 12 | L A | Dietz, Christian | | Mar. 2, 1865 |

## E.

| Reg't. | | Name. | Residence. | Date. |
|---|---|---|---|---|
| 2 | I | Erhart, Joseph | Beloit | Apr. 30, 1863 |
| 5 | I | Estis, Edwin | | July 30, 1861 |
| 6 | I | Ernisse, Isaac | Holland | June 25, 1865 |
| 7 | I | Elliott, Jacob | | Dec. 13, 1862 |
| 7 | I | Exbanks Joseph | | Oct. 30, 1862 |
| 7 | I | Earl, Wm. J | Platteville | Aug. 19, 1861 |
| 7 | I | Edgar, John | Milwaukee | Dec. 17, 1864 |

| *Reg't.* | | *Name.* | *Residence.* | *Date.* |
|---|---|---|---|---|
| 8 | I | Earl, John | | Apr. 30, 1863 |
| 9 | I | Eckert, Michael | | Feb. 11, 1863 |
| 11 | I | Evans, William | | Jan. 14, 1863 |
| 11 | I | Evans, James | | Jan. 1, 1863 |
| 13 | I | Edwards, Wm | | June 29, 1865 |
| 13 | I | Eames, Wm. P. | | |
| 14 | I | Eveland, Andres | | Aug. 18, 1862 |
| 14 | I | Elliott, David | | June 28, 1862 |
| 15 | I | Everson, Erick | Spring Grove, Minn. | |
| 15 | I | Errickson, K. | | |
| 17 | I | Evans, Edward | Jackson, Miss. | Nov. 14, 1864 |
| 52 | I | Egan, Jno | | |
| 51 | I | Edwards, Jno | Milwaukee | Mar. 4, 1865 |
| 51 | I | Edwards, Wm | Milwaukee | July 1, 1865 |
| 51 | I | Evans, James | Milwaukee | Apr. .., 1865 |
| 51 | I | Edmunds, Charles R. | Lowell | July 16, 1865 |
| 50 | I | Elliott, George W. | Blooming Grove | Mar. 1, 1865 |
| 50 | I | Everson, Fred'k | | Aug. 29, 1865 |
| 48 | I | Esses, Jacob | Milwaukee | Mar. 1, 1865 |
| 46 | I | Ellentson, Herman | Milwaukee | Apr. 18, 1864 |
| 34 | I | Erickson, Andreas | Carrolton | Jan. 29, 1863 |
| 34 | I | Ebel, Chas | Milwaukee | Jan. 30, 1863 |
| 34 | I | Eisold, John | Sheboygan | Jan. 2, 1863 |
| 34 | I | Eckis, Nicholas | West Bend | Jan. 30, 1863 |
| 34 | I | Erickson, Andrew | Kewaska | Jan. 5, 1863 |
| 34 | I | Ewer, Thomas | Hartford | Feb. 1, 1863 |
| 33 | I | Estes, John L. | Missouri | Feb. 6, 1863 |
| 31 | I | Edson, Chas | Milwaukee | Jan. 1, 1863 |
| 27 | I | Ellis, James | Milwaukee | Dec. 30, 1862 |
| 25 | I | Erickson, Orloff | La Crosse | Sept. 20, 1862 |
| 24 | I | Edwards, Wm. H. | Milwaukee | |
| 24 | I | England, George A. | Milwaukee | |
| 24 | I | Ellmaker, Chas. | Milwaukee | Dec. 31, 1862 |
| 22 | I | Enockson, Ole | Clinton | May 14, 1864 |
| 22 | I | Edwards, John K. | Richmond | Nov. 10, 1864 |
| 19 | I | Enigh, Wm. E. | Kenosha | June 8, 1862 |
| 18 | I | Edmonster, Ruben | Plover | |
| 18 | I | Evans, George W. | Plover | |
| 18 | I | Eaton, Jno | Dayton | June 25, 1865 |
| 1 | C | Evans, Vernon | Ripon | Nov. 1, 1861 |
| 1 | C | Eldridge, Ephraim | Oshkosh | |
| 1 | C | Ellis, Fred'k G. | Beaver Dam | July 1, 1863 |
| 1 | C | Easlewin, George | Monroe | Dec. 3, 1864 |
| 1 | C | Ellis, Wm | Beaver Dam | July 1, 1863 |
| 2 | C | Engel, Theodore | | Dec. 7, 1862 |
| 2 | C | Etlope, Richard | | Feb. 11, 1863 |
| 2 | C | Erich, Rudolph | Milwaukee | |
| 3 | C | Eddy, Cassius | Janesville | Aug. 26, 1865 |
| 3 | C | Eckhart, George | Camp Benton | Oct. 7, 1862 |
| 3 | C | Edwards, John | Ft. Leavenworth | Aug. 4, 1862 |
| 4 | C | Epham, Dockerty | | |
| 4 | C | Ely, John H. | Fond du Lac | Dec. 31, 1865 |
| 1 | H A | Elliott, John H. | Milwaukee | Sept. 11, 1863 |
| 4 | L A | Ellsworth, John L | | Dec. 14, 1861 |
| 4 | L A | Ennis, Daniel | | Aug. 15, 1862 |
| 4 | L A | Elliott, Elias B | | Oct. 1, 1862 |

## F

| Reg't | | Name | Residence. | Date. |
|---|---|---|---|---|
| 1 | I | Feeley, Thomas | | |
| 1 | I | Fuller, Julius | | |
| 1 | I | Fritzgerolds, Jeremiah | | |
| 1 | I | Farrer, Geo | | |
| 1 | I | Farnsworth, Allen | Fond du Lac | May 19, 1864 |
| 1 | I | Fry, George | Sheboygan | May 12, 1864 |
| 2 | I | Franklin, Wm | Dane Co | Dec. 12, 1862 |
| 2 | I | Flemming, Geo. W | La Crosse Co | Dec. 30, 1862 |
| 2 | I | Fenton, John H | Madison | May 30, 1863 |
| 2 | I | Foust, Henry | Sauk City | |
| 2 | I | Frey, Sebastian | Dane Co | |
| 2 | I | Foot, William H | Janesville | |
| 3 | I | Fitzgerad, Thomas | Milwaukee | June 17, 1865 |
| 5 | I | Frye, Christian S | | May 17, 1862 |
| 5 | I | Fay, Stewart J | Berlin | Oct. 11, 1863 |
| 5 | I | Fault, Jos. T | Theresa | Aug. 5, 1863 |
| 5 | I | Foster, Alex | Virginia | July 27, 1864 |
| 6 | I | Forsyth, George | | Apr. 5, 1862 |
| 6 | I | Fuller, Wm. A | | Sep. 14, 1862 |
| 7 | I | Foster, Sylvester | | Sep. 12, 1862 |
| 7 | I | Franklin, N. C | | Apr. 19, 1862 |
| 8 | I | Fuller, Dana S | Buffalo | |
| 8 | I | Fennel, Abel S | Green Prairie | |
| 8 | I | Fields, Harrison D | Oshkosh | Apr. 1, 1864 |
| 9 | I | Fi nie, Frederick | | |
| 9 | I | Fleak, Wm | St. Louis | Aug. 8, 1864 |
| 10 | I | Fellows, Oliver | | |
| 11 | I | Freeman, Hiram | Rockbridge | May 10, 1863 |
| 11 | I | Franklin, William | | Oct. 19, 1863 |
| 13 | I | Foster, Edwin | Leroy | July 20, 1865 |
| 13 | I | Ford, James | | |
| 13 | I | Frisby, David C | | |
| 13 | I | Filkins, Geo | | |
| 14 | I | Flanders, John | | |
| 16 | I | Fisher, Dave | | June 7, 1864 |
| 16 | I | Field, Jos ah W | Wisconsin | Apr. 6, 1862 |
| 17 | I | Fitzpatrick, Patrick | | Mar. 20, 1862 |
| 17 | I | Fitzgibben, Stephen | | June 30, 1862 |
| 17 | I | Flinn, Chas | | Dec. 28, 1864 |
| 17 | I | Fife, Andrew J | Vicksburg, Miss | May 1, 1865 |
| 17 | I | Fife, Farris A | Vicksburg, Miss | May 1, 1865 |
| 17 | I | Farrell, Thomas | Madison | |
| 52 | I | Foote, Henry | | |
| 52 | I | Foote, Chas | | |
| 51 | I | Ferier, Anthony | Milwaukee | Mar. 15, 1865 |
| 51 | I | Frank, Gerhard | Milwaukee | Mar. 8, 1865 |
| 51 | I | Finnegan, Thomas | Milwaukee | Mar. 28, 1865 |
| 51 | I | Franklin, Archer | Janesville | Aug. 26, 1865 |
| 50 | I | Fortner, Geo | Delavan | Aug. 29, 1865 |
| 50 | I | Faulkner, Ed | Dale | Aug. 24, 1865 |
| 50 | I | Fry, Leonard | Ashland | Sep. 9, 1865 |
| 50 | I | Fowles, Wm. E | Fort Howard | |
| 48 | I | Fields, Lemuel | Chilton | Sep. 6, 1865 |
| 48 | I | Ford, Jno | Milwaukee | Feb. 28, 1865 |
| 48 | I | Fowley Jno | Milwaukee | Feb. 24, 1865 |
| 47 | I | Fie, Thomas | | Feb. 22, 1865 |
| 47 | I | Fitzpatriek, Dan'l | | Feb. 22, 1865 |

| Reg't. | | Name. | Residence. | Date. |
|---|---|---|---|---|
| 47 | I | Fleming, David | | Feb. 9, 1865 |
| 43 | I | Feenney, Jno | Janesville | Oct. 5, 1864 |
| 42 | I | Fiddler, Merrill | Fond du Lac | Sep. 17, 1864 |
| 38 | I | Frasier, Wm | Sheboygan | Aug. 25, 1864 |
| 38 | I | Frasier, Franklin | Sheboygan | Aug. 25, 1864 |
| 38 | I | Fitzgibbon, James | Fond du Lac | Sep. 2, 1864 |
| 37 | I | Fe elson, Jonas | | May 3, 1864 |
| 35 | I | Fishback, Nicholas | Fond du Lac | Aug. 1, 1864 |
| 35 | I | Farrow, Alex | | Feb. 27, 1866 |
| 35 | I | Feisler, Eugene | Madison | Feb. 9, 1866 |
| 34 | I | Fulz, Michael | Belgium | Jan. 18, 1863 |
| 34 | I | Faber, Jno | Belgium | Jan. 26, 1863 |
| 34 | I | Foster, Jno | Milwaukee | Jan. 12, 1862 |
| 34 | I | Fisher, Capitan | Milwaukee | Jan. 29, 1863 |
| 34 | I | Farley, Jno | Racine | Dec. 29, 1862 |
| 34 | I | Frohlich, Jno | Paris | Jan. 31, 1863 |
| 34 | I | Fox, John | Chicago | Jan. 9, 1863 |
| 34 | I | Fogal, John | Farmington | Jan. 31, 1863 |
| 34 | I | Fuss, Fred'k | Theresa | Jan. 26, 1863 |
| 34 | I | Feiereisen, John | Madison | Jan. 16, 1863 |
| 34 | I | Fellerer, Joseph | Sheboygan | Jan. 31, 1863 |
| 34 | I | Fennendal Honnore | Red River | Jan. 31, 1863 |
| 34 | I | Forsyth, Jerome | Preble | Feb. 1, 1863 |
| 34 | I | Forsyth, Henry | Preble | Jan. 4, 1863 |
| 34 | I | Fulton, Geo | Schiller | Feb. 1, 1863 |
| 33 | I | Faherty, Mark | St. Louis, Mo | Sep. 28, 1862 |
| 33 | I | Feltz, Emaul | Perry Co., Mo | Oct. 22. 1862 |
| 33 | I | Fink, Michael A | Trenton, Mo | Feb. 24, 1863 |
| 33 | I | Fortuno, J. Willis | St. Louis, Mo | Sep. 22, 1862 |
| 32 | I | Fairfield, Jefferson | Oshkosh | Oct. 7, 1862 |
| 31 | I | Flood, Peter | Albany | Sep. 26, 1864 |
| 31 | I | Faulds, Jno | Glencoe | Jan. 23, 1863 |
| 30 | I | Farleigh, Francis | Boscobel | Sep. 26, 1863 |
| 30 | I | Foster, Jacob | | Dec. 25, 1862 |
| 29 | I | Forsyth, Wm | Watertown | Jan. 9, 1863 |
| 28 | I | Festus, Clark H | Summitt | Dec. 20, 1862 |
| 26 | I | Fuelling, Adam | Waukesha | May 9, 1863 |
| 25 | I | Fitts, Jas. F | Platteville | Sep. 1, 1862 |
| 24 | I | Farroll, Thos | Milwaukee | Apr. .., 1863 |
| 24 | I | Finnegan, Thos. D | Milwaukee | May 10, 1865 |
| 22 | I | Fuller, Wm | Union Grove | Jan. 24, 1863 |
| 22 | I | Fitch, Jno | Delavan | Sep. 10, 1862 |
| 21 | I | Fowler, Thos. H | Menasha | May 25, 1863 |
| 21 | I | Fitzgerald, Jeremiah | Kenosha | Oct. 12, 1864 |
| 20 | I | Foss, Jno | Ripon | |
| 20 | I | Fitzparrick, O. P | Ripon | Aug. 8, 1863 |
| 19 | I | Fort, Martin, | Milwaukee | Feb. 12, 1862 |
| 19 | I | Filmore Jos. H | Madison | July 3, 1863 |
| 18 | I | French, Chas | Franklin | |
| 18 | I | Fennell, Jas | | |
| 18 | I | Facy, Alonzo H | Oshkosh | |
| 18 | I | Fitzpatrick, Jas | Berlin | |
| 18 | I | Fust August | Amherst | |
| 1 | C | Flenk, August | Clyman | June 2, 1863 |
| 1 | C | Fee, Arthur, | Ripon | Dec. 20, 1863 |
| 2 | C | Fairfield, Wm | | June 4, 1862 |
| 2 | C | Founcer, Louis | Green Bay | June 26, 1863 |
| 2 | C | Fuller, Henry | Beloit | Oct. 15, 1865 |
| 2 | C | Farrell, James | La Crosse | July .., 1864 |

| Reg't. | | Name. | Residence. | Date. |
|---|---|---|---|---|
| 2 | C | Franke, Hugo | Milwaukee | |
| 3 | C | Fry, Isaac | Janesville | June 14, 1864 |
| 3 | C | Fitch, Henry A | Madison | Oct. .., 1864 |
| 3 | C | Fisher, George | Waukesha | Feb. 6, 1862 |
| 4 | C | Fogle, Geo. W | Sauk Co | |
| 4 | C | Fairfield G. N | Appleton | Feb. 12, 1862 |
| 4 | C | Fayhay, Jas. B | Madison | Apr. 8, 1863 |
| 4 | C | Fulkerson, Geo. W | Oconto | Mar. 28, 1864 |
| 1 | H A | Fehrenbach, Rich'd | Milwaukee | May 19, 1864 |
| 1 | H A | Fessenden, Albert | Milwaukee | Aug. 10, 1865 |
| 1 | H A | Fulton, Thos. W | | Aug. 10, 1865 |
| 2 | L A | Frank, Henry | Milwaukee | July 12, 1862 |
| 3 | L A | Fitzpatrick, Pat | Berlin | Jan. 2, 1862 |
| 7 | L A | Folsom, Chas. M | Milwaukee | Dec. 29, 1863 |
| 9 | L A | Fullerton, Henry | Jackson | May 28, 1862 |
| 10 | L A | Frood, Jno | Osceola | Oct. 7, 1867 |

## G

| Reg't. | | Name. | Residence. | Date. |
|---|---|---|---|---|
| 1 | I | Graham, Thomas R | | Nov. .., 1862 |
| 1 | I | Gates, Francis | | Dec. 20, 1862 |
| 2 | I | Gallatin, Baltis | Madison | Nov. 28, 1862 |
| 2 | I | George, F. Marshall | La Crosse | June 17, 1864 |
| 5 | I | Grimes, John W | | June 30, 1862 |
| 6 | I | Geisber, John | | Sep. 14, 1862 |
| 6 | I | Gibbs, Chas. J | | Sep. 14, 1862 |
| 6 | I | Garthwaite, Jacob H | | Sep. 14, 1862 |
| 6 | I | Graves, Milo | | July 2, 1865 |
| 7 | I | Gaunt, Henry | | Aug. 9, 1862 |
| 7 | I | Gilmore, John P | Chippewa Falls | June .., 1864 |
| 8 | I | Grosbeck, Louis | Kickapoo | |
| 8 | I | Grinnell, Henry | Ripon | |
| 8 | I | Grasser, Ferdinand | Eau Claire | |
| 8 | I | Gowers, William W | Janesville | .., 1863 |
| 11 | I | Grimes, Jerome | | Feb. 23, 1863 |
| 11 | I | Gregory Alonzo G | | Nov. 20, 1861 |
| 12 | I | Goothe John F | Fort Howard | Oct. 27, 1862 |
| 12 | I | Gribner, Henry | Fond du Lac | Sep. 23, 1862 |
| 12 | I | Gear, Elmore | Wyoming | Nov. 19, 1862 |
| 12 | I | Gaynon, Lewis | | May 1, 1864 |
| 14 | I | Guyette, Antoni | Mosinee | May 11, 1863 |
| 14 | I | Gummer, H. B | | Dec. 23, 1861 |
| 15 | I | Gilbert, Gulbrand | | |
| 16 | I | George, David H | Germantown | Aug. 18, 1862 |
| 17 | I | Grogeu, John | | Apr. 15, 1862 |
| 17 | I | Guest, Louis | | Mar. 19, 1862 |
| 17 | I | Gould, Alonzo C | Beaver Dam | May 20, 1864 |
| 17 | I | Gillispie, Silas | Madison | Apr. 18, 1864 |
| 52 | I | Gietezon, Anton | Port Washington | Apr. 28, 1865 |
| 51 | I | Glen, Wm | Milwaukee | Apr. .., 1865 |
| 50 | I | Gromby Patrick | Beaver Dam | Aug. 30, 1865 |
| 50 | I | Gill, Wm | Vernon Co | Mar. 17, 1865 |
| 50 | I | Gorslini, Alex | Vernon Co | Aug. 25, 1865 |
| 50 | I | Gillman, J. W | Vernon Co | Aug. 26, 1865 |
| 50 | I | Guntley, Jno. G | Fond du Lac | Aug. 27, 1865 |
| 50 | I | Guilleman, Adolph | Lisbon | Aug. 26, 1865 |
| 50 | I | Gee, Geo. A | Belmont | Aug. 29, 1865 |
| 50 | I | Giersch, Hendrick | Jefferson | July 10, 1865 |
| 48 | I | Gillett, Wm | | Sep. 8, 1865 |

| *Reg't.* | | *Name* | *Residence.* | *Date.* |
|---|---|---|---|---|
| 48 | I | Grugan, James | Milwaukee | Feb. 28, 1865 |
| 48 | | Griffin, David | Milwaukee | Feb. 24, 1865 |
| 48 | I | Goulden, Geo | Milwaukee | Feb. 24, 1865 |
| 48 | I | Gum, Franklin | Omro | Apr. 1, 1865 |
| 48 | I | Grey, Henry | Milwaukee | Mar. 1, 1865 |
| 47 | I | Gilliams, Edward | | Feb. 22, 1865 |
| 46 | I | Grady, James | Milwaukee | Mar. 6, 1865 |
| 44 | I | Gibbs, Artemus | Boscobel | Mar. 9, 1865 |
| 44 | I | Gulliford, Wellington | Boscobel | Feb. 18, 1865 |
| 43 | I | Gober, Cable | Milwaukee | Oct. 3, 1864 |
| 43 | I | Gloster, Richard | Milwaukee | Sep. 7, 1864 |
| 42 | I | Gualke, Fred'k | Pewaukee | Dec. 10, 1865 |
| 42 | I | Golf, Jno | Madison | Oct. 15, 1865 |
| 34 | I | George, Jno | Belgium | Jan. 31, 1863 |
| 34 | I | Gardner Dan'l | Chicago | Jan. 5, 1863 |
| 34 | I | Gilvin, Thos | Chicago | Jan. 11, 1863 |
| 34 | I | Gelbank, Mark | Iron Point | Jan. 31, 1863 |
| 34 | I | Geller, John | Pepin | Jan. 31, 1863 |
| 34 | I | Grentz, Wm | Shields | Dec. 17, 1862 |
| 34 | I | Geberling, Nicolaus | Lomira | Jan. 22, 1863 |
| 34 | I | Guday, Thos | Iron Point | Jan. 31, 1863 |
| 34 | I | Genneseo, Julian | Sturgeon Bay | |
| 34 | I | Grassel, John | Milwaukee | Jan. 1, 1863 |
| 34 | I | Geralds, Orrin | Madison | Jan. 20, 1863 |
| 34 | I | Golvin, Thomas | Casco | Jan. 26, 1863 |
| 34 | I | Giese, August | Kewaska | Feb. 1, 1863 |
| 34 | I | Glass, Geo | | Feb. 22, 1863 |
| 34 | I | Gilmore John | Trenton | Feb. 1, 1863 |
| 34 | I | Goeden, Peter | Menomonee | Jan. 31, 1863 |
| 33 | I | Gilleland, Wm. D | Jefferson City, Mo | Sep. 24, 1862 |
| 33 | I | Gruben, Cloves H | Syracuse, Mo | Oct. 18, 1862 |
| 33 | I | Guenstrad, Irvin | Tuscumbia, Mo | Feb. 22, 1863 |
| 33 | I | Golden, John | Tuscumbia, Mo | May 19, 1863 |
| 33 | I | Goetsch, Henry | St. Louis, Mo | Mar. 29, 1863 |
| 32 | I | Grimmer, Harrison B | Shawano | Oct. 28, 1862 |
| 30 | I | Gibbons, Patsey | Hudson | Sep. 25, 1862 |
| 30 | I | Gile, Halmuth | Madison | Jan. 16, 1863 |
| 30 | I | Gill Robert | | Feb. 10, 1864 |
| 30 | I | Griswold, Samuel | | Mar. 16, 1864 |
| 30 | I | Gould, W. K | Westford | Jan. 23, 1864 |
| 30 | I | Giannicelli, Ludwig | Cross Plains | Oct. 27, 1862 |
| 30 | I | Groth, John F | Walworth | Dec. 20, 1862 |
| 28 | I | Golden, Daniel | Menomonee | July 21, 1863 |
| 27 | I | Govro, Henry C | | Mar. 18, 1863 |
| 27 | I | Gutter, Franz | | Jan. 2, 1863 |
| 27 | I | Gerbach, Jno | Saukville | Jan. 2, 1863 |
| 27 | I | Gibbs, Edward | | |
| 26 | I | Gasper, Wm | | June 6, 1863 |
| 26 | I | Gasser, Jacob | Prairie du Sac | July 1, 1863 |
| 25 | I | Gray, Enoch | Richland | July 30, 1863 |
| 25 | I | Gahn, Michael | Point Bluff | Feb. 17, 1863 |
| 24 | I | Griffith, Jno | Milwaukee | |
| 24 | I | Glyn, Edw'd | Milwaukee | |
| 24 | I | Gaynor, Thomas | Milwaukee | Dec. 31, 1862 |
| 24 | I | Gilbert, Benjamin | Milwaukee | Feb. 1, 1863 |
| 24 | I | Gallagher, Phillip | Milwaukee | |
| 24 | I | Gorberty Jno | Milwaukee | Apr. 2, 1864 |
| 22 | I | Groushong, Wm | Delavan | Nov. 20, 1862 |

| Reg't | | Name | Residence | Date |
|---|---|---|---|---|
| 22 | I | Green, Jeremiah | Waterford | Feb. 28, 1863 |
| 22 | I | Godden, Thos | Janesville | Sep. 5, 1863 |
| 22 | I | Garrmiger, Addison | Plymouth | Jan. 24, 1863 |
| 20 | I | Grant, Albert | Elkhorn | |
| 20 | I | Gage, Geo | Raymond | June 3, 1863 |
| 20 | I | Griffin, Jno | Shullsburg | June 1, 1865 |
| 19 | I | Gunderson, Andrew | La Crosse | May 29, 1862 |
| 19 | I | Gray, Almon R | Coloma | Nov. 1, 1862 |
| 19 | I | Gaffney, James | Waterford | Apr. 15, 1862 |
| 19 | I | Ga B | Mliwaukee | Feb. 10, 1862 |
| 19 | I | Gjermanson, Ole G | La Crosse | |
| 19 | I | Gleason, Ebenezer | Milwaukee | |
| 18 | I | George, Joseph L | | |
| 18 | I | Guist, O. B | Viroqua | |
| 18 | I | Grace, Wm. H | Portage | |
| 18 | I | G een, Chas C | Columbus | |
| 18 | I | Getter, Ferdinand | Milwaukee | Mar. 14, 1862 |
| 1 | C | Gilbert Sylvester | Burnett | |
| 2 | C | Goslin, Claron J | | Apr. 3, 1863 |
| 2 | C | Grant, Ben F | | Jan. 31, 1863 |
| 2 | C | Gordon, Alden W | Mauston | July 10, 1865 |
| 2 | C | Gates, Merrill R | | Aug. 26, 1864 |
| 3 | C | Goff, John | Van Buren, Ark | June 18, 1864 |
| 3 | C | Gardner, Chas. H | Fairplay | July 20, 1862 |
| 3 | C | Gun, Silas T | Platteville | Sep. 12, 1862 |
| 3 | C | Garvey, Michael | Janesville | Mar. 26, 1862 |
| 3 | C | Gardner, Alfred C | Oshkosh | June 27, 1862 |
| 3 | C | Gill, Myron | Oshkosh | July 30, 1863 |
| 3 | C | Gottfixdt, Adolph | Watertown | Sep. 12, 1862 |
| 3 | C | Gilbert, Curtis E | Walworth | Oct. .., 1862 |
| 4 | C | Gannon, James | Madison | |
| 4 | C | Gleason, James | Madison | |
| 4 | C | George Joseph L | Kenosha | Feb. 18, 1862 |
| 4 | C | Gale, Sam'l | | Nov. 22, 1863 |
| 4 | C | Greenleaf, Isaac J | Green Co | Mar. .., 1864 |
| 4 | C | Geer, Henry H | Madison | Sep. 27, 1865 |
| 4 | C | Gilson, Wm | Tomah | July 6. 1865 |
| 1 | H A | Gilber, Dona | East Troy | |
| 1 | H A | Grave, Joseph | Milwaukee | July 26, 1861 |
| 1 | H A | Gordon, Thos | Milwaukee | Aug. 10, 1865 |
| 1 | H A | Gros, Jno | Milwaukee | Sep. 1, 1863 |
| 1 | L A | Goslan, Anthony | La Crosse | Sep. 26, 1862 |
| 2 | L A | Garvin, Danl W | Millville | Feb. 8, 1862 |
| 4 | L A | Grun, Patrick | | Jan. 25, 1862 |
| 4 | L A | Gunning, James | | June 10, 1862 |
| 4 | L A | Gilbert, Patrick | La Crosse | Aug. 16, 1864 |
| 7 | L A | Goodnough, Dwight | Racine | Mar. .., 1863 |
| 8 | L A | Gilholly, James | Wausau | May 29, 1862 |
| 12 | L A | Greenway, James B | Janesville | Mar. 12, 1864 |

## H

| Reg't | | Name | Residence | Date |
|---|---|---|---|---|
| 1 | I | Hill, George | | |
| 1 | I | Hallas, Chas | | |
| 1 | I | Huntsley, Chas | | |
| 1 | I | Hall, John | | |
| 1 | I | Holderness, Wm | | Dec. 24, 1862 |
| 2 | I | Hanes, Freeman R | Otsego | Sep. 23, 1861 |
| 2 | I | Hammont, Sam'l H | Kingston | Apr. 1, 1862 |

| Reg't | | Name | Residence. | Date |
|---|---|---|---|---|
| 2 | I | Harler, Carl | Sauk Co | Sep. 15, 1862 |
| 3 | I | Hagerman, William | | Dec. 4, 1861 |
| 3 | I | Hart, Edmond | | Dec. 11, 1862 |
| 3 | I | Harris, Amos E. | | |
| 3 | I | Hanish, Anthon | Wisconsin | May 3, 1865 |
| 3 | I | Hanskee, Oren | Wisconsin | May 3, 1865 |
| 3 | I | Hovenstadt, J B. | | May 2, 1864 |
| 5 | I | Hart, David P. | | May 3, 1862 |
| 5 | I | Hunter, Levi | Lancaster | May 4, 1863 |
| 5 | I | Hunter, John | Lancaster | May 1, 1863 |
| 5 | I | Hartman, John | Menomonee | Aug. 31, 1863 |
| 5 | I | Hill, James | Stevens Point | Oct. 3, 1864 |
| 5 | I | Hannon, John | | Aug. 31, 1863 |
| 6 | I | Harvey, Samuel P. | Prairie du Chein | Aug. 31, 1863 |
| 6 | I | Holmes, Volney | New Lisbon | May 7, 1864 |
| 6 | I | Harbough, Geo W. | | Sep. 14, 1862 |
| 6 | I | Hartman, John | Menomonee | Aug. 31, 1863 |
| 6 | I | Hennan, Ganter | | Mar. 30, 1862 |
| 7 | I | Hinton, Cyrus R. | Otsego | Dec. 28, 1862 |
| 7 | I | Houghton, Henry J | | Nov. 10, 1862 |
| 7 | I | Henlon, E. R. | | Nov. 30, 1862 |
| 7 | I | Hogan, James | Milwaukee | Dec. 17, 1864 |
| 7 | I | Hart, Charles | St. Croix Falls | Nov. 30, 1864 |
| 8 | I | Hedge, Riley | Eau Claire Co | |
| 8 | I | Harrington, Hinman | Halington | |
| 8 | I | Hadfield, Jos. J | Racine | |
| 8 | I | Hammond, John | Wisconsin | |
| 8 | I | Hollis, Francis | Fitchburg | |
| 8 | I | Haywood, Levi T | Fond du Lac | |
| 8 | I | Henry, Jacob W | | Dec. 15, 1864 |
| 8 | I | Heavrin, James H | | June .., 1862 |
| 8 | I | Humes, Edward W | | July 30, 1865 |
| 9 | I | Hauk, Fred | Prairie du Chein | Aug. 8, 1864 |
| 9 | I | Hesse, Adolph | Kenosha | Feb. 1, 1865 |
| 10 | I | Harrington, Woodbury | Sugar Creek | Nov. 1, 1862 |
| 10 | I | Hathaway, Elmer | Kilbourn City | Sep. 7, 1862 |
| 10 | I | Howe, Orin R | Hartford | Feb. 28, 1864 |
| 10 | I | Hulet, Benjamin | Jackson Co | June 16, 1863 |
| 11 | I | Hilterbrand, M | | |
| 11 | I | Houghton, Milo | Prairie du Sac | Oct. 1, 1863 |
| 11 | I | Herman Patrick | | Nov. 20, 1861 |
| 12 | I | Herriman, Peter H | St. Croix | Nov. 23, 1861 |
| 12 | I | Haunony, Wm | Vermont | Jan. 5, 1862 |
| 12 | I | Hale, Lewis | Fort Howard | Oct. 5, 1862 |
| 12 | I | Howard, Chas | Wisconsin | Mar. 18, 1864 |
| 13 | I | Hadley, Geo A | La Crosse | June 14, 1865 |
| 13 | I | Helmes, Sylvanus A | Edgerton | Sep. 30, 1865 |
| 13 | I | Hancock, Elijah | | |
| 13 | I | Hotelling, Joseph | | |
| 13 | I | Hutchins, Ward S | | |
| 13 | I | Hughes, Benjamin | Fort Deposit | Sep. 15, 1864 |
| 13 | I | Hart, Corn R | | June 30, 1865 |
| 14 | I | Hammond, Harvey P | | Aug. 18, 1862 |
| 14 | I | Hodges, Richard | | Aug. 19, 1862 |
| 14 | I | Harrington Jos | | Dec. 21, 1861 |
| 14 | I | Hall, John | Polk | Dec. 8, 1865 |
| 14 | I | Hill, Joseph | Kossuth | July 22, 1864 |
| 15 | I | Helgeson O | Elgin | |
| 15 | I | Hanson, Mathew | Monroe Co | |

| Reg't. | | Name | Residence | Date. |
|---|---|---|---|---|
| 15 | I | Halvorson, H. O | Kilbourn City | |
| 15 | I | Hanson, John | | |
| 15 | I | Holm, Jakob B | Raymond | |
| 15 | I | Holland, Thos | Port Washington | |
| 16 | I | Harvey, Robt E | | Feb. 27, 1864 |
| 16 | I | Horton, Geo H | Madison | July 28, 1864 |
| 16 | I | Heath, Jefferson | Atlanta | Nov. 12, 1864 |
| 16 | I | Holdridge, Wm G | Watertown | Apr. 6, 1862 |
| 16 | I | Hall, Charles V | Hazel Green | July 2, 1865 |
| 17 | I | Hatchins D. W | | Jan. 17, 1862 |
| 17 | I | Harrington, Pat | | Mar. 20, 1862 |
| 17 | I | Hogan, John C | | Jan. 20, 1863 |
| 17 | I | Harrison, Wm | | Feb. 27, 1862 |
| 17 | I | Holdridge, Henry | | Apr. 18, 1862 |
| 17 | I | Hoy, Francis C | | Mar. 20, 1862 |
| 17 | I | Haunt, Michael | | Apr. 18, 1862 |
| 17 | I | Hasmer, Thos | | Apr. .., 1862 |
| 17 | I | Hattersly, Samuel | | Mar. 19, 1862 |
| 17 | I | Hope, Wm | Fond du Lac | May 1, 1865 |
| 17 | I | Heegan, Frank | Chicago | Apr. 18, 1864 |
| 17 | I | Hamilton, James | Kildare | Apr. 9, 1862 |
| 17 | I | Holden, Ira | Primrose | Apr. 9, 1862 |
| 17 | I | Horrigan, Mathew | Milwaukee | May 19, 1863 |
| 52 | I | Hughes, Edw'd A | | Apr. 26, 1865 |
| 52 | I | Hogan, Henry | | |
| 51 | I | Heggans, Jno | Milwaukee | Mar. 4, 1861 |
| 51 | I | Hawes, Nathaniel | Milwaukee | |
| 51 | I | Hassersey, John | Milwaukee | |
| 51 | I | Herron, Sam'l | Milwaukee | Mar. 28, 1865 |
| 51 | I | Hoffman, Thodore | Milwaukee | Mar. 29, 1865 |
| 51 | I | Hughes, Francis | La Crosse | Apr. 12, 1865 |
| 51 | I | Hessler, Christian | Sheboygan | |
| 50 | I | Hartley, Wm | Hampden | Mar. 3, 1865 |
| 50 | I | Harrington, Lyman | Madison | Apr. 25, 1865 |
| 50 | I | Horn, Jeremiah | Wiota | Aug. 29, 1865 |
| 50 | I | Hannock, Wm | Fond du Lac | Aug. 28, 1865 |
| 50 | I | Heuthorn, Washington | Yankeetown | Aug. 27, 1865 |
| 50 | I | Hendricks, Jno | Green Bay | Aug. 26, 1865 |
| 50 | I | Harrison, Heth | | Sep. 1, 1865 |
| 50 | I | Harker, Jno C | New Diggings | Sep. 1, 1865 |
| 50 | I | Hawley, Oscar S | Prescott | Sep. 9, 1865 |
| 50 | I | Hewitt, Henry | Waushara Co | Sep. 9, 1865 |
| 49 | I | Hooker, Clark P | La Crosse | Sep. .., 1865 |
| 48 | I | Harris, Chas | Sheboygan Falls | Sep. 10, 1865 |
| 48 | I | Hotchis, Horace | | Sep. 7, 1865 |
| 48 | I | Herold, Wm | Belvidere | Sep. 6, 1865 |
| 48 | I | Haag, Geo | Taunton | Sep. 7, 1865 |
| 48 | I | Howard, Wm | Milwaukee | Mar. 26, 1865 |
| 48 | I | Heath, Jeremiah | Burlington | Sep. 19, 1865 |
| 48 | I | Howard, Chas | Fox Lake | Sep. 6, 1865 |
| 48 | I | Hays, James | Milwaukee | Mar. 1, 1865 |
| 48 | I | Higgins, Thos. G | Augusta | Apr. 8, 1865 |
| 47 | I | Harris, Chas | | Mar. 2, 1865 |
| 45 | I | Harris, Wm | Madison | Feb. 12, 1865 |
| 44 | I | Heart, James | Milwaukee | Feb. 12, 1865 |
| 44 | I | Hudson, David B | Milwaukee | Feb. 21, 1865 |
| 44 | I | Hudson, Chas. E | Milwaukee | Feb. 21, 1865 |
| 44 | I | Hamilton, Robert | Boscobel | Feb. 12, 1865 |

| Reg't. | | Name. | Residence. | Date. |
|---|---|---|---|---|
| 44 | I | Hayes, Enoch | Peshtigo | June 12, 1865 |
| 43 | I | Hill, Lucien P. | Shopiere | Jan. 24, 1865 |
| 43 | I | Hickey, John | Janesville | |
| 43 | I | Heserodt, Lee | Milwaukee | Oct. 7, 1864 |
| 38 | I | Hurley, Wm | Fond du Lac | Apr. 28, 1864 |
| 38 | I | Harp, Wm | Milwaukee | June 15, 1864 |
| 38 | I | Haring, Thos | Milwaukee | July 28, 1864 |
| 38 | I | Holton, Jno | Deerfield | July 12, 1864 |
| 38 | I | Hacket, Wm | Milwaukee | Aug. 28, 1864 |
| 38 | I | Hamilton, James | | Sep. 22, 1864 |
| 38 | I | Holden, Jno. Jr | | Feb. 28, 1865 |
| 37 | I | Henry, James | Milwaukee | May 3, 1864 |
| 37 | I | Hammond, Abner | Hustisford | June 26, 1864 |
| 37 | I | Holbrook, Geo. F | Eau Claire | July 13, 1864 |
| 37 | I | Hughbanks, Dana | Pr. du Chien | May 2, 1864 |
| 36 | I | Hansen, Hans | Milwaukee | May 3, 1864 |
| 36 | I | Haskins, Horatio | Sheboygan | Apr. 8, 1864 |
| 36 | I | Hall, Wm | Madison | Apr. 6, 1864 |
| 36 | I | Haskell, Martin | Madison | May 7, 1864 |
| 36 | I | Horton, Geo | Milwaukee | Apr. 18, 1864 |
| 35 | I | Hobbs, Thos | Madison | Feb. 26, 1864 |
| 35 | I | Henker, Chas | Williamstown | July 4, 1864 |
| 35 | I | Harland, Edward | Monroe | Feb. 11, 1865 |
| 35 | I | Hitsman, Adam | Fond du Lac | Aug. 14, 1865 |
| 35 | I | Haak, Fred. Wm | Milwaukee | Feb. 27, 1866 |
| 35 | I | Hubbell, Edwin | Janesville | Jan. 8, 1864 |
| 34 | I | Hooper, Phillip | Mequon | Jan. 3, 1863 |
| 34 | I | Howard, Geo. | Mequon | Jan. 23, 1863 |
| 34 | I | Helmke, John | Cedarburg | Feb. 1, 1863 |
| 34 | I | Hettinger, Michael | Cedarburg | Dec. 26, 1862 |
| 34 | I | Heitzel, Leonard | Dodge Co. | Jan. 31, 1863 |
| 34 | I | Houlgrave, Thos | Milwaukee | Jan. 31, 1863 |
| 34 | I | Hausen, Ole | Watertown | Jan. 31, 1863 |
| 34 | I | Harris, Alexander | Lisbon | Dec. 18, 1862 |
| 34 | I | Heath, John | | Jan. 22, 1863 |
| 34 | I | Halblein, John | | Jan. 30, 1863 |
| 34 | I | Horlage, Alexander | Sturgeon Bay | Jan. 31, 1863 |
| 34 | I | Hoslet, John Baptist | Red River | Jan. 29, 1863 |
| 34 | I | Hilner, Frederick | Fillmore | Jan. 31, 1863 |
| 34 | I | Hegg, John | Boltonville | Jan. 26, 1863 |
| 34 | I | Hageman, Frederick | Franklin | Jan. 16, 1863 |
| 34 | I | Hankey, John | Neshkoro | Jan. 31, 1863 |
| 34 | I | Heller, Geo | Milwaukee | Dec. 15, 1862 |
| 34 | I | Hill, Ole | Fish Creek | Feb. 1, 1863 |
| 34 | I | Hubsch, John | Mequon | Jan. 29, 1863 |
| 33 | I | Hammond, David | Syracuse, Mo | Nov. 5, 1862 |
| 33 | I | Heatculd, Earnest J | St. Louis | Dec. 22, 1862 |
| 33 | I | Hill, Wm | St. Louis | Nov. 25, 1862 |
| 33 | I | Hatcher, Wm | Breckenridge, Mo | Nov. 22, 1862 |
| 33 | I | Holden, Patrick | St. Louis | Sep. 24, 1862 |
| 33 | I | Haly, Patrick | St. Louis | Dec. 23, 1862 |
| 33 | I | Heher, Patrick | Janesville | Oct. 25, 1862 |
| 33 | I | Hunnekins, Jno | Racine | Nov. 27, 1862 |
| 33 | I | Hopkins, John W | St. Louis | Feb. 24, 1863 |
| 33 | I | Herbert, Michael | St. Louis | Dec. 23, 1862 |
| 33 | I | Hill, Lucien P | Shopiere | Jan. 24, 1865 |
| 32 | I | Haley, Wm | Oshkosh | Oct. 28, 1862 |
| 32 | I | Hakes, Azro S | Montello | Jan. 31, 1863 |
| 32 | I | Hancy, Jas | Montello | Dec. 31, 1862 |

| Reg't. | | Name | Residence. | Date. |
|---|---|---|---|---|
| 32 | I | Hanks, Orin H | Harrisville | Jan. 31, 1863 |
| 32 | I | Hoffner, Wm | | |
| 32 | I | Higgins, Geo. W | Stockton | Mar. 25, 1864 |
| 31 | I | Hayes, James | Gratiot | Feb. 21, 1863 |
| 31 | I | Halton, Cornelius | Milwaukee | Feb. 4, 1863 |
| 31 | I | Huggannin, Leonard | | Mar. 2, 1863 |
| 31 | I | Hewitt, Edwin D | Milwaukee | July 3, 1863 |
| 30 | I | Henris, Wm | | Apr. 16, 1864 |
| 30 | I | Hudson, John S | Milwaukee | Apr. 21, 1864 |
| 29 | I | Harney, Thos | Oak Grove | Jan. 23, 1863 |
| 28 | I | Hanley, Patrick | Lisbon | Dec. 19, 1862 |
| 28 | I | Heider, Jno | Brookfield | June 2, 1864 |
| 28 | I | Hasler, Jno | Brookfield | Dec. 20, 1862 |
| 28 | I | Hadfield, Jno. J | Pewaukee | Jan. 26, 1863 |
| 28 | I | Hurbert, Jacob | Milwaukee | |
| 28 | I | Hamilton, Wm | Milwaukee | |
| 28 | I | Hays, Alonzo | Milwaukee | |
| 27 | I | Hays, Richard | Lima | Mar. 29, 1863 |
| 27 | I | Holhedge, John W | Milwaukee | Jan. 15, 1863 |
| 27 | I | Heller, Geo | Milwaukee | Jan. 2, 1863 |
| 27 | I | Holland, Geo. W | Milwaukee | Apr. 1, 1863 |
| 27 | I | Helfric, Frederick | Milwaukee | Mar. 10, 1863 |
| 27 | I | Hinckley, Robert | Milwaukee | Mar. 10, 1863 |
| 27 | I | Helfrich, J | | |
| 27 | I | Hollingshead, Jos | | |
| 27 | I | Heyden, Chas | | |
| 26 | I | Hinrichs, John | | Nov. 2, 1863 |
| 26 | I | Hartner, Anton | Sauk City | July 3, 1863 |
| 26 | I | Boehne, J. W. F | Milwaukee | June 5, 1863 |
| 26 | I | Helgar, Henry | Milwaukee | Dec. 5, 1863 |
| 26 | I | Heme, Antone | Rhine | Oct. 10, 1862 |
| 26 | I | Hauser, Jacob | Troy | Oct. 6, 1862 |
| 25 | I | Hubbard, Harvey B | Sparta | Sep. 10, 1862 |
| 25 | I | Hanwood, Geo. D | Durand | Sep. .., 1863 |
| 24 | I | Howard, Alonzo | Milwaukee | |
| 24 | I | Hill, Geo | Milwaukee | |
| 24 | I | Heth, Wm. H | Milwaukee | |
| 24 | I | Hopkins, W. H | Milwaukee | Mar. 13, 1864 |
| 24 | I | Hamilton, Henry O | Milwaukee | |
| 24 | I | Hickley, Nicholas | Milwaukee | Dec. 31, 1862 |
| 22 | I | Horton, Samuel | Janesville | Jan. 28, 1863 |
| 22 | I | Hall, Thos | Racine | Jan. 27, 1863 |
| 22 | I | Hitchcock, Wm | Racine | |
| 21 | I | Hill, J. N | | Dec. 10, 1862 |
| 21 | I | Hill, Jediah | | Dec. 10, 1862 |
| 21 | I | Herbert, Peter | Fond du Lac | June 18, 1863 |
| 21 | I | Harris, Jno. C | Waupaca | June 4, 1863 |
| 21 | I | Holland, Lot | Byron | Mar. 4, 1863 |
| 21 | I | Hamhey, Michael | Fond du Lac | Feb. 13, 1864 |
| 21 | I | Horton, Richard | Fond du Lac | Oct. 28, 1862 |
| 21 | I | Hyde, W. F | | May 7, 1864 |
| 20 | I | Holland, C. O | Elkhorn | |
| 20 | I | Hall, Jno. B | Ripon | Aug. 30, 1864 |
| 19 | I | Hurley, Timothy | Reedsburg | Mar. 21, 1862 |
| 19 | I | Holverson, Gunder | La Crosse | June 2, 1862 |
| 19 | I | Hill, Seth C | La Crosse | May 31, 1862 |
| 19 | I | Homer, Joel | Racine | June 2, 1862 |
| 19 | I | Harriman, Abner | Bear Creek | June 3, 1862 |
| 19 | I | Haye, Lawrence | Milwaukee | Feb. 25, 1862 |

| Reg't. | | Name. | Residence. | Date. |
|---|---|---|---|---|
| 19 | I | Hazelton, James A | Sparta | June 1, 1862 |
| 18 | I | Hornby, Jos | Franklin | |
| 18 | I | Halliday, Cornelius H | Plover | |
| 18 | I | Hughes, Wm. J | Columbus | |
| 18 | I | Hooker, Andrew | Kilbourn City | |
| 18 | I | Harrington, A. B | Portland | Aug. 18, 1862 |
| 1 | C | Hart, David | Ft. Atkinson | Mar. 10, 1862 |
| 1 | C | Hobbs, Walter | Milwaukee | July 7, 1862 |
| 1 | C | Hanchet, Alanson | Paris | Oct. 24, 1862 |
| 1 | C | Howard, Moses | | Dec. 9, 1864 |
| 2 | C | Hetzel, Peter | Milwaukee | July 2, 1863 |
| 2 | C | Hamilton, Duane | | Mar. 8, 1862 |
| 2 | C | Hartwick, Johann | | Jan. 5, 1863 |
| 2 | C | Hutchins, Philander | | Mar. 24, 1862 |
| 2 | C | Hall, Wm. F | | Oct. .., 1862 |
| 2 | C | Hanler, D | Big Foot | Jan. 16, 1862 |
| 2 | C | Holman, Wm | Hudson | Feb. 2, 1863 |
| 2 | C | Honk, David | Eau Claire | Oct. 12, 1865 |
| 2 | C | Hill, Frederick | Madison | Oct. 25, 1865 |
| 2 | C | Haines, John B | Fond du Lac | Sep. 1, 1864 |
| 2 | C | Henson, Nis | La Crosse | Dec. 26, 1864 |
| 2 | C | Hope, Richard E | Eldorado | June 11, 1863 |
| 3 | C | Hickok, Philo | Watertown | July 6, 1864 |
| 3 | C | Hart, Dudley M | Watertown | Oct. 5, 1864 |
| 3 | C | Hughes, Wm. R | Madison | July 11, 1864 |
| 3 | C | Handy, Adam P | Janesville | June 22, 1865 |
| 3 | C | Hughes, Wm | Gennesee | Mar. 3, 1862 |
| 3 | C | Hastings, Alvin M | Fall River | Mar. 25, 1862 |
| 3 | C | Hendricks, Henry J | Van Buren, Ark | Mar. 10, 1864 |
| 3 | C | Helms, Wm. A | | Sep. 19, 1863 |
| 3 | C | Howard, Patrick | Elkhorn | May 8, 1862 |
| 3 | C | Huiman, Addison | Madison | May .., 1865 |
| 3 | C | Hall, Andrew J | Fairwater | June 11, 1862 |
| 3 | C | Hutchins, Philander | Waukesha | Jan. 29, 1862 |
| 3 | C | Hohn, Phillip | Utica | Feb. 6, 1862 |
| 3 | C | Howard, Chas. G | Genessee | Feb. 6, 1862 |
| 3 | C | Haitz, Chas | Leavenworth | Oct. 15, 1862 |
| 3 | C | Heger, Joseph | Watertown | Oct. 10, 1862 |
| 4 | C | Hopkins, Frank | Columbus | July 6, 1865 |
| 4 | C | Howard, J. C | New Orleans, La | Nov. 18, 1863 |
| 4 | C | Hitchcock, Rufus | | |
| 4 | C | Hueke, Chas | | |
| 4 | C | Higgings, Joseph E | Watertown | |
| 4 | C | Hunter, Peter | Whitewater | Jan. 29, 1863 |
| 4 | C | Higbie, Jno. F | Hebron | Sep. 2, 1861 |
| 4 | C | Heyer, Fred'k | Aztalan | July 9, 1861 |
| 4 | C | Harrington, Jno | Milwaukee | Mar. 30, 1864 |
| 4 | C | Holloway, Jno | Kenosha | Apr. 27, 1864 |
| 4 | C | Harris, Jno | | Oct. 5, 1864 |
| 4 | C | Hinnelbauer, Simon | Milwaukee | Feb. 6, 1866 |
| 1 | H A | Harvey, Henry A | Utica, N. Y | |
| 1 | H A | Hill, Rowland | Milwaukee | Feb. 8, 1864 |
| 1 | H A | Hill, Robt | Alexandria, Va | Apr. 1, 1865 |
| 1 | H A | Hayes, James | Milwaukee | Sep. 11, 1863 |
| 1 | H A | Harris, Henry | Milwaukee | Sep. 10, 1863 |
| 1 | H A | Heflin Thos | Alexandria, Va | Aug. 9, 1865 |
| 1 | H A | Hanson, Jacob | Chicago, Ill | Oct. 18, 1864 |
| 1 | L A | Hale, Jno | St. Louis, Mo | Feb. 28, 1863 |
| 1 | L A | Hutchins, Philander | Fond du Lac | Sep. 26, 1862 |

| *Reg't.* | *Name.* | *Residence.* | *Date.* |
|---|---|---|---|
| 1 L A | Holmes, Taylor | | July 19, 1864 |
| 1 L A | Harvey, Francis | | Dec. 15, 1864 |
| 3 L A | Hugg, R. H. N. | Green Lake | Oct. 12, 1862 |
| 4 L A | Hayes, Geo. W | Portsmouth | July 2, 1865 |
| 4 L A | Hugh, Riley | Portsmouth | July 2, 1865 |
| 7 L A | Higgins, Chas. A. J | Milwaukee | May .., 1863 |
| 7 L A | Hart, A. S | Milwaukee | Dec. 29, 1863 |
| 8 L A | Howe, Edwin R | Stevens Point | May 27, 1862 |
| 9 L A | Howard, Alonzo | Burlington | Apr. 25, 1862 |
| 10 L A | Hoyt, Sam'l W | Hillsboro | Mar. .., 1862 |
| 13 L A | Hunter, Jno | Milwaukee | Apr. 13, 1864 |
| 13 L A | Hanies, Jno. A | Milwaukee | Jan. 8, 1864 |

## I

| | | | |
|---|---|---|---|
| 4 C | Irwing, Girard | La Crosse, La Crosse Co | Mar. 20, 1866 |
| 50 I | Ingle, Sam'l | | Aug. 16, 1865 |
| 50 I | Ingraham, Oscar F | Darlington | Sep. 8, 1865 |
| 34 I | Ingraham, Henry | | Feb. 1, 1863 |
| 20 I | Ingals, Geo. A | Platteville | |
| 20 I | Ishmael, Rich'd | Beetown | June 5, 1863 |
| 3 I | Indian, Muschega | La Crosse | |
| 6 I | Immel, Nichlaus | | Feb. 27, 1863 |
| 9 I | Ignaty, Esser | | June 7, 1863 |

## J

| | | | |
|---|---|---|---|
| 1 I | Johnson, Henry | | |
| 2 I | Jones, John A. | Springfield | Dec. 13, 1862 |
| 2 I | Jacobson, John | Portage City | Apr. 1, 1862 |
| 3 I | Jackson, Richard | | Aug. .., 1862 |
| 3 I | Jones, John J | | May 29, 1862 |
| 5 I | Johnson, Lewis | Brothertown | May 2, 1863 |
| 6 I | Jay, Geo | | Sep. 14, 1862 |
| 6 I | Johnson, Joseph | | Sep. 14, 1862 |
| 6 I | Jessie, George | Appleton | July 3, 1861 |
| 7 I | Jones, J. W | Milwaukee | Dec. 17, 1864 |
| 8 I | Johnson, A. J | Sweetland | |
| 8 I | Jones, W. H. H | Exeter | |
| 8 I | Johnson, Wm. H | Hamburg, Miss | Feb. 5, 1865 |
| 9 I | Jung, Jacob | Milwaukee | Aug. 25, 1864 |
| 10 I | James, Harvey | Jackson Co | Nov. 5, 1861 |
| 11 I | Johnson, Wm. A | Baraboo | Oct. 17, 1863 |
| 11 I | Jordon, Ephraim J | New Orleans | Apr. 22, 1862 |
| 11 I | Juchmnick, Christian | Harrison | Aug. 27, 1865 |
| 12 I | James, George | Washington | Oct. .., 1862 |
| 12 I | Jones, John D | Mariette | May 1, 1864 |
| 13 I | Johnson, Nelson | Stevenson, Ala | June 15, 1865 |
| 13 I | Johnson, Wm | | |
| 14 I | Johnson, Peter | Oneida | Sep. 30, 1864 |
| 14 I | Jacobs, Aaron | | Jan. 11, 1862 |
| 14 I | Jordon, Luke | | Jan. 11, 1862 |
| 15 I | Jorgensen, L | Freeborn | |
| 15 I | Johnson, K. | | |
| 15 I | Johnson, Nils N | Leeds | |
| 16 I | Jellings, John | | Mar. 13, 1862 |
| 17 I | Jarvis, Rufus G | | Jan. 24, 1862 |
| 17 I | Johnson, Rasmus | Oconto | Jan. 20, 1863 |
| 52 I | Jackson, Jas | | |
| 51 I | Johnson, William | Milwaukee | |

| Reg't. | | Name. | Residence. | Date. |
|---|---|---|---|---|
| 51 | I | John, Gustave | Milwaukee | May 6, 1865 |
| 51 | I | Johnson, W. C | La Cross | |
| 50 | I | Johnson, Geo | Hampden | Feb. 28, 1865 |
| 50 | I | Johson, Jas W. | | Sep. 3, 1865 |
| 50 | I | Juleson, Ole | Ridgeway | Aug. 26, 1865 |
| 50 | I | Johnson, Andrew | | Aug. 28, 1865 |
| 48 | I | Jones, Chas | Fox Lake | Feb. 15, 1865 |
| 48 | I | Jackson, Chas. E | Milwaukee | Mar. 5, 1865 |
| 48 | I | Jackson, Jno. G | Fox Lake | Sep. 6, 1865 |
| 46 | I | Johnson, Wm | Milwaukee | Mar. 6, 1865 |
| 45 | I | Jorgensen, Ole | Liberty | Mar. 16, 1865 |
| 44 | I | Johnson, Sam'l | Chicago | Apr. 6, 1865 |
| 43 | I | Johnson, Wm. F | Milwaukee | Sep. 30, 1864 |
| 34 | I | Jansen, Lorenz | Cedarburg | Jan. 28, 1863 |
| 34 | I | Jonas, Chas | Cedarburg | Jan. 28, 1863 |
| 34 | I | Johnson, Jackson | Milwaukee | Jan. 5, 1863 |
| 34 | I | Jacobsen, Hans | Highland | Jan. 30, 1863 |
| 34 | I | Johnson, Christopher | Dodgeville | Jan. 31, 1863 |
| 34 | I | Jones, Robt | Sheb. Falls | Jan. 20, 1863 |
| 32 | I | Johnson, William | Oshkosh | Oct. 7, 1862 |
| 32 | I | Jones, David H | | Aug. 21, 1863 |
| 32 | I | Jones, Robt | Dodgeville | Mar. 4, 1863 |
| 32 | I | Jacobs, Wm. M | Albany | Mar. 6, 1863 |
| 30 | I | Jones, Geo. E | Lincoln | |
| 30 | I | Jeffert, Gustavus | | Feb. 10, 1864 |
| 30 | I | Johnson, Chas | Janesville | Dec. 25, 1863 |
| 28 | I | Jones, Wm | Waukesha | Feb. 24, 1863 |
| 28 | I | Johnston, John | Waukesha | Apr. 7, 1864 |
| 27 | I | J hnson, Henry | Milwaukee | Mar. 17, 1863 |
| 27 | I | Jamm, Emil | | Dec. 4, 1862 |
| 26 | I | Jacoby, Chas | Milwaukee | Aug. 31, 1863 |
| 24 | I | Johan, Mathias | Milwaukee | |
| 24 | I | James, Jno | Milwaukee | Jan. 8, 1863 |
| 22 | I | Jackson, Rich'd M | Plymouth | Jan. 24, 1863 |
| 22 | I | Jones, Rich'd R | Waukesha | May 20, 1863 |
| 21 | I | Jeffer, Julius M | Jefferon | June 11, 1863 |
| 21 | I | Johnson, John | Janesville | Mar. 22, 1864 |
| 21 | I | Johnson, Wm | | Oct. 12, 1864 |
| 20 | I | Johnson, J. R | Waukesha | |
| 20 | I | Johnson, Jno | Milwaukee | Mar. 31, 1864 |
| 18 | I | Jones, Jas | Milwaukee | |
| 18 | I | Jones, Aaron B | Berlin | |
| 18 | I | Johnson, Henry | Springville | Apr. 1, 1862 |
| 1 | C | Jones, Geo. C | Ripon | Nov. 21, 1863 |
| 1 | C | Jenney, Jacob | | Nov. 22, 1861 |
| 2 | C | Jones, Adam | Madison | Nov. 17, 1863 |
| 2 | C | Jones, David | | |
| 2 | C | Jones, Mitchell | Fox Lake | Oct. 12, 1862 |
| 3 | C | Jones, Henry | Genessee | Mar. .., 1862 |
| 3 | C | Judd, Levi | Mauston | June 10, 1862 |
| 3 | C | Johnson, Orson | Oconto | .., 1862 |
| 3 | C | Jeffers, Joseph | Fairwater | June 11, 1862 |
| 3 | C | Jones, William | Janesville | July 1, 1864 |
| 3 | C | Johnson, Ansel J | Oshkosh | Jan. 30, 1863 |
| 4 | C | Johnson C. M | Ripon | |
| 4 | C | Johnson, Andrew | | |
| 4 | C | Johnson, Spencer | Baton Rouge | |
| 4 | C | Johnson, George | Monroe | July 6, 1865 |
| 4 | C | Jenkins, Thos | | |

| Reg't. | Name. | Residence. | Date. |
|---|---|---|---|
| 1 H A | Johnson, Jno. M | Milwaukee | Aug. 23, 1864 |
| 8 L A | Jackson, Jepher W | Greenfield | Oct. 2, 1862 |
| 10 L A | Johnwell, John | Milwaukee | Oct. 7, 1862 |

## K

| Reg't. | | Name. | Residence. | Date. |
|---|---|---|---|---|
| 1 | I | Kent, Alonzo H | | |
| 1 | I | Kimson, Wm. M | Cascade | Dec. 20, 1866 |
| 1 | I | Knolitz, Fred | | |
| 2 | I | Kremison, Geo | Minnesota | Sep. .., 1861 |
| 2 | I | Kiel, S. M | Sauk City | Mar. .., 1862 |
| 3 | I | Kuplin, Michael | Watertown | |
| 3 | I | Kidder, John W | Fond du Lac | July 9, 1864 |
| 3 | I | Kenedy, John | Waupun | Dec. 4, 1861 |
| 5 | I | Kindness, Louis | | May 19, 1862 |
| 7 | I | Kee, Thomas | | Aug. 28, 1862 |
| 7 | I | Kellog, Henry C | | Sep. 13, 1861 |
| 8 | I | Keeley, Wm. H | | Oct. 20, 1864 |
| 9 | I | Klim John | La Crosse | May 4, 1864 |
| 11 | I | Kane, William D | | Jan. 1, 1862 |
| 12 | I | Kronberg, Elias | Sturgeon Bay | May 27, 1862 |
| 13 | I | Kamstrock, George | Milwaukee | June 20, 1862 |
| 14 | I | Kimball, Harvey | Barr | July 4, 1864 |
| 14 | I | Kimball, Harvey | La Crosse | July 11, 1865 |
| 14 | I | King, Nicholas | Onedia | Sep. 30, 1864 |
| 14 | I | Kindness, Thomas | | Jan. 11, 1862 |
| 14 | I | King, Martinus | | Jan. 19, 1862 |
| 14 | I | Kirchmer, Fred | | Jan. 20, 1862 |
| 14 | I | Keutner, Sherman R | | Jan. 21, 1863 |
| 15 | I | Kuesden, Christian | Spring Grove | |
| 15 | I | Kunson, Nils | Chicago, Ill | |
| 16 | I | Kruskie, Wm. J | Hustisford | June 3, 1862 |
| 16 | I | Kruskie, J. H | Hustisford | June 3, 1862 |
| 16 | I | Kruskie, Fred'k | Hustisford | June .., 1862 |
| 16 | I | Kogh, Edwin | Jackson Co | Mar. 13, 1862 |
| 17 | I | Kirwan, Ed | | Mar. 20, 1862 |
| 17 | I | Keenan, John | | Mar. 20, 1862 |
| 17 | I | Kelly, Michael | | Mar. 20, 1862 |
| 17 | I | Konse, Louis | Vicksburg, Miss | Oct. 8, 1864 |
| 17 | I | Killom, Owen | Cascade | Feb. 10, 1862 |
| 52 | I | Kinney, Thos | | |
| 51 | I | Kain, Thos | Milwaukee | Apr. 5, 1865 |
| 51 | I | Krouse, Carle | Milwaukee | Mar. 28, 1865 |
| 51 | I | Kelley, Frank | Milwaukee | Apr. .., 1865 |
| 51 | I | Krees, Franc | Cedarburg | |
| 51 | I | Knight, Chas | Milwaukee | July 5, 1865 |
| 50 | I | Kirkpatrick, Jno | Crawford Co | Sep. 3, 1865 |
| 50 | I | Kohen, Jacob | Fond du Lac | Aug. 27, 1865 |
| 50 | I | Kelly, Thos | Moscow | Aug. 26, 1865 |
| 50 | I | King, Gilbert | | Aug. 27, 1865 |
| 50 | I | King, Wm. M | | Aug. 27, 1865 |
| 50 | I | Kibbe, Anthony | Big Springs | Aug. 30, 1865 |
| 50 | I | Kelly, Jno | | Mar. 31, 1865 |
| 50 | I | Klaussen, Theodore | Green Bay | Aug. 27, 1865 |
| 50 | I | Kenroy, Peter | Fond du Lac | Aug. 26, 1865 |
| 50 | I | Kuhler, Norman | Delaware | Mar. 18, 1865 |
| 50 | I | Kilmeir, Wm | Beaver Dam | Aug. 25, 1865 |
| 48 | I | Kunze, W. F | Chilton | Sep. 6, 1865 |
| 44 | I | Kelly, Jno | Milwaukee | Oct. 27, |

| *Reg't.* | | *Name.* | *Residence.* | *Date.* |
|---|---|---|---|---|
| 43 | I | Kempf, James | Milwaukee | Sep. 25, 1864 |
| 38 | I | Keeler, Edw'd | Milwaukee | Aug. 17, 1864 |
| 38 | I | Kinney, Joseph | Milwaukee | Aug. 17, 1864 |
| 38 | I | Kilbourn, Michael | Milwaukee | Aug. 17, 1864 |
| 38 | I | Killean, Jno | | Sep. 15, 1864 |
| 37 | I | Kimball, Wm | Madison | Apr. .., 1864 |
| 37 | I | Klanck, Peter | Mequon | May 3, 1864 |
| 37 | I | Kelley, Thomas | Madison | Mar. 10, 1865 |
| 35 | I | Knox, Geo | Janesville | Feb. 26, 1864 |
| 35 | I | Kelley, Henry | Ironton | Apr. 14, 1864 |
| 35 | I | Krings, John | Theresa | Nov. 15, 1864 |
| 35 | I | Kruse, Fritz | Mayville | Dec. 19, 1864 |
| 35 | I | Kratsch, John | Milwaukee | Feb. 27, 1866 |
| 34 | I | Klansing, Frank | Mequon | |
| 34 | I | Klank, Mathias | Mequon | Jan. 28, 1863 |
| 34 | I | Kruer, Jno | Mequon | Jan. 28, 1863 |
| 34 | I | Kelly, Jas | Port Washington | Dec. 12, 1862 |
| 34 | I | Knutson, Niles | Franklin | Jan. 29, 1863 |
| 34 | I | Koble, Kaspar | Germantown | Jan. 31, 1863 |
| 34 | I | Kuchtan, Adam | Milwaukee | Jan. 27, 1863 |
| 34 | I | Kiris, H. H | Nelson | Jan. 31, 1863 |
| 34 | I | Kenton, Robert | Germantown | Dec. 26, 1862 |
| 34 | I | Knutson, Niles | Franklin | Jan. 16, 1863 |
| 34 | I | Koble, Casper | Franklin | Jan. 16, 1863 |
| 34 | I | Kohnke, August | Crystal Lake | Jan. 29, 1863 |
| 34 | I | Kreiger, Ludwig | Crystal Lake | Jan. 31, 1863 |
| 34 | I | Keiser, Chas | Mukwanago | Jan. 31, 1863 |
| 33 | I | Kirk, John W | St. Louis | Feb. 24, 1863 |
| 33 | I | Keyes, Wm. F | Beetown | Oct. 25, 1862 |
| 33 | I | Kerrunnals, Geo | Paris | Apr. 11, 1863 |
| 32 | I | Karles, Jno | Green Bay | Oct. 9, 1862 |
| 32 | I | Kileven, Patrick | Fond du Lac | Oct. 31, 1862 |
| 32 | I | Kendall, Wm | Cato | Feb. 8, 1864 |
| 32 | I | Kenniston, Chas | | Oct. 24, 1863 |
| 31 | I | Kemp, Chas | Monticello | Jan. 23, 1863 |
| 31 | I | Kemp, Wm | Monticello | Jan. 23, 1863 |
| 30 | I | Kingsley, John L | Chippewa Falls | Nov. 11, 1862 |
| 30 | I | Knight, John | | Mar. 6, 1864 |
| 29 | I | Kieth, E. D | Westford | Jan. 23, 1863 |
| 28 | I | Kellog, George | | June .., 1864 |
| 27 | I | Kent, John J | Sandy Bay | Mar. 30, 1863 |
| 27 | I | Klemme, Conrad | Sheboygan | Sept. 29, 1863 |
| 27 | I | Kull, Jacob | Sheboygan | Dec. 25, 1863 |
| 27 | I | Keuster, Joseph | Cooperstown | Jan. 15, 1863 |
| 27 | I | Kellog, James | | |
| 27 | I | Karstaedt, Wm | Herman | Aug. 13, 1863 |
| 26 | I | Krueger, August | | Dec. 15, 1862 |
| 26 | I | Klein, Jaçob | | |
| 26 | I | Klinke, Julius | Milwaukee | June 20, 1863 |
| 26 | I | Kaege, John | Milwaukee | Apr. 30, 1864 |
| 26 | I | Kamshulda, Clemens | Milwaukee | Oct. 4, 1864 |
| 25 | I | Kent, Herman H | La Crosse | Sept. 2, 1862 |
| 25 | I | Keys, Francis | Cassville | Sept. 27, 1862 |
| 24 | I | Kirk, Geo | Milwaukee | |
| 24 | I | Knight, Columbus G | Milwaukee | |
| 24 | I | Kelly, Eugene | Milwaukee | Aug. .., 1863 |
| 21 | I | Kendall, Levi G | | Oct. 8, 1862 |
| 21 | I | Kuter, Ezra | | Oct. 3, 1862 |
| 20 | I | Kimitzer, Chas | Watertown | June 4, 1863 |

| *Reg't.* | | *Name.* | *Residence.* | *Date.* |
|---|---|---|---|---|
| 19 | I | Kincannon, Edward | Fox Lake | Mar. 27, 1862 |
| 18 | I | Leah, Colin | Berlin | |
| 1 | C | Kelly, Thos | Token Creek | Apr. 4, 1862 |
| 1 | C | Kent, Jackson J | Janesville | Jan. 28, 1865 |
| 1 | C | Kirschua, Antum | | Jan. 12, 1864 |
| 1 | C | Kleusman, Bertin | Fond du Lac | July 7, 1865 |
| 1 | C | Kennedy, Jno | Beaver Dam | June .., 1862 |
| 2 | C | Knoll, Herman | | Sept. 23, 1862 |
| 2 | C | Kaster, Ferd | Warren Co., Mo | May 5, 1863 |
| 2 | C | Knofferl, Johann | Newberg | |
| 2 | C | Kramer, Henry | Milwaukee | |
| 2 | C | Killoran, Jno | Brown Co | June 23, 1865 |
| 2 | C | Kennedy, Michael | Janesville | Apr. 9, 1865 |
| 3 | C | King, Benjamin | | Sept. 10, 1864 |
| 3 | C | King, John | St. Louis, Mo | Aug. 10, 1862 |
| 3 | C | Kernest, Samuel | Oshkosh | June 11, 1862 |
| 3 | C | Karst, Frank | Watertown | Aug. .., 1862 |
| 4 | C | Keith, Franklin | Hart's Prairie | Mar. 18, 1863 |
| 4 | C | Keach, Albert | Green Bush | Aug. 1, 1862 |
| 4 | C | Kilbourn, R | Milwaukee | Feb. 14, 1862 |
| 1 | H A | Kirby, George C | Fulton | |
| 4 | L A | Kern, Demain | | Oct. 12, 1861 |

## L.

| | | | | |
|---|---|---|---|---|
| 1 | I | Lewis, Wm | | |
| 1 | I | Longstreet, B. K | | |
| 1 | I | Longstreet, Byron K | | Apr. 10, 1863 |
| 2 | I | Leach, James | La Crosse | Oct. 10, 1862 |
| 2 | I | Langhoff, Herman J | Janesville | Feb. 26, 1863 |
| 2 | I | Langhoff, Herman J | Janesville | Mar. 10, 1864 |
| 3 | I | Lammon, Joseph | Wisconsin | Apr. 2, 1865 |
| 3 | I | Londue, Nelson | | Dec. 4, 1861 |
| 5 | I | Laross, Chas | Superior | Oct. 1, 1864 |
| 5 | I | Labarge, Isaac | Menomonee | Apr. 29, 1863 |
| 5 | I | Leary, James | Milwaukee | Mar. 28, 1864 |
| 5 | I | Lamphere, Ezra D | Stevens Point | Oct. 3, 1864 |
| 6 | I | Lamore, Oleon | | Aug. 9, 1862 |
| 6 | I | Lansing, Wm. H | | |
| 6 | I | Loolin, Sidney B | | |
| 6 | I | Langsuer, Wm | Milwaukee | Oct. .., 1862 |
| 7 | I | La Prairie, Alerius | St. Croix Falls | Nov. 30, 1864 |
| 8 | I | Loomis, George A | Buffalo | |
| 8 | I | Love, Alfred | Viroqua | |
| 8 | I | Lee, Harry | Miss | |
| 8 | I | Liverman, Moses | La Crosse | |
| 8 | I | Loomis, Harrison | Gilmanson | July .., 1862 |
| 9 | I | Luck, John | | Aug. 4, 1862 |
| 9 | I | Leitner, John | St. Charles, Mo | |
| 10 | I | Lee, Rufus V | | |
| 11 | I | Leach, Levi J | | Jan. 16, 1863 |
| 12 | I | Langua, Eazer | Queen Bay | Aug. 1, 1864 |
| 13 | I | Livingston, Geo | Bradford | Jan. 19, 1865 |
| 13 | I | Lockridge, John A | Albany | Aug. 5, 1865 |
| 13 | I | Lain, David S | | |
| 13 | I | Lane, Austin E | | |
| 14 | I | Laundy, Andrew E | Lawrence | Dec. 17, 1864 |
| 14 | I | Lee, John W | | Aug. 31, 1862 |
| 14 | I | Lewis, Jack | | Jan. 11, 1862 |

| Reg't. | | Name. | Residence. | Date. |
|---|---|---|---|---|
| 14 | I | Loomis, Henry J. | | Jan. 18, 1863 |
| 14 | I | Liverson, John | Northward, Iowa | |
| 15 | I | Larson, Andreas | Leeland, Ill | |
| 16 | I | Lamphear, Ezra | Princetown | July 13, 1862 |
| 16 | I | Lamb, John | Wautoma | Aug. 18, 1862 |
| 16 | I | Lee, Henry C. | Princetown | Aug. 18, 1862 |
| 16 | I | Lawrence, John | Adams Co | Apr. 20, 1862 |
| 16 | I | Lane, James | Coloma | Jan. 18, 1863 |
| 16 | I | Lawrence, Henry J | Lemonweir | Aug. 18, 1862 |
| 17 | I | Leonard, George | | Aug. 16, 1862 |
| 17 | I | Leon, James | | Mar. 20, 1862 |
| 17 | I | Lynch, Dennis | | Mar. 20, 1862 |
| 17 | I | Larson, Hames | | Apr. 15, 1862 |
| 17 | I | Little, Atchson | | June 20, 1863 |
| 17 | I | Lambert, Alfred | Green Bay | Apr. 19, 1864 |
| 17 | I | Leuthier, Samuel | Beaver Dam | June 3, 1863 |
| 17 | I | Landers, Michael | Portage Co. | Apr. 18, 1864 |
| 17 | I | Lary, Timothy C | Darlington | Apr. 18, 1864 |
| 17 | I | Lyon, Laramie | Grand Rapids | June 3, 1864 |
| 17 | I | La Plante, Octave | Marquette | Jan. 20, 1863 |
| 52 | I | Long, Matthew | | |
| 51 | I | Lamberger, John | Milwaukee | Apr. 10, 1865 |
| 51 | I | Lynch, Jeremiah | Milwaukee | Mar. 18, 1865 |
| 51 | I | Love, Robert | Milwaukee | Mar. 28, 1865 |
| 51 | I | Lynch, John | Milwaukee | Apr. .., 1865 |
| 51 | I | Leonard, James | La Crosse | Apr. 6, 1865 |
| 51 | I | Leonard, Jones | La Crosse | |
| 50 | I | Lewis, Chas | Beloit | Mar. 7, 1865 |
| 50 | I | Lemminger, Fred'k | Morrison | Aug. 26, 1865 |
| 50 | I | Larschild, John | Green Bay | Aug. 26, 1865 |
| 50 | I | Leischer, Chas | Hudson | Oct. 31, 1865 |
| 48 | I | Lehner, Mathaus | Chilton | Sept. 10, 1865 |
| 48 | I | Loetz, Wm. | Belvidere | Sept. 7, 1865 |
| 48 | I | Lynk, Patrick | Milwaukee | Feb. 24, 1865 |
| 48 | I | Lorg, Daniel | Milwaukee | Feb. 24, 1865 |
| 48 | I | Larogue, Joseph | Prairie du Chien | Sept. 6, 1865 |
| 46 | I | Lawrence, Geo | Milwaukee | Mar. 6, 1865 |
| 43 | I | Lyman, Jno | Milwaukee | |
| 42 | I | Low, Jno | Oshkosh | Sept. 17, 1864 |
| 38 | I | Lindsay, Thos | Fond du Lac | Sept. 12, 1864 |
| 38 | I | Link, Battis | Palmyra | Sept. 21, 1864 |
| 38 | I | Lafferty, James | Milwaukee | Sept. 6, 1864 |
| 38 | I | Lawrence, Henry T | La Crosse | Sept. 22, 1864 |
| 38 | I | Leach, Alex | Oconto | May 8, 1864 |
| 37 | I | Lee, John | Dane | May 21, 1864 |
| 37 | I | Laflin, Lark E | La Crosse | Nov. 16, 1864 |
| 36 | I | Lorson, Martin | Eau Claire | May 7, 1864 |
| 35 | I | Lusch, John | Milwaukee | May 7, 1864 |
| 35 | I | Leddle, Wm. | Delavan | Dec. 31, 1865 |
| 35 | I | Lembke, Gottlieb | Milwaukee | Feb. 27, 1866 |
| 35 | I | Lenhardt, Conrad | Milwaukee | Feb. 27, 1866 |
| 34 | I | Lucke, Jno | | Dec. 12, 1862 |
| 34 | I | Lefevre, Chas | Franklin | Jan. 8, 1863 |
| 34 | I | Lowers, Martin | Granville | Jan. 5, 1863 |
| 34 | I | Laudflerd, Lucas | Beaver Dam | Jan. 31, 1863 |
| 34 | I | Looze, Antoine | Kewaunee | Jan. 31, 1863 |
| 34 | I | Lefevre, Alphons | Kewaunee | Jan. 31, 1863 |
| 34 | I | Lauer, John | Sheboygan | Jan. 31, 1863 |
| 34 | I | Lemince, Thiers | Green Bay | Jan. 31, 1863 |

| Reg't. | | Name. | Residence. | Date. |
|---|---|---|---|---|
| 34 | I | Leitch, Alex | Pepin | Jan. 31, 1863 |
| 34 | I | Leonais, Louis | Green Bay | Jan. 31, 1863 |
| 34 | I | Lemay, John Baptist | Green Bay | Jan. 30, 1863 |
| 34 | I | Lane, Patrick | Lowell | Jan. 31, 1863 |
| 34 | I | Langenberger, Herman | Milwaukee | Jan. 6, 1863 |
| 34 | I | Lamal, Andre | Red River | Jan. 5, 1863 |
| 34 | I | Luck, John | Port Washington | Dec. 13, 1862 |
| 33 | I | Le Grand, James | Pilot Knob, Mo | Nov. 5, 1862 |
| 33 | I | Loveall, Cyrus | Tuscumbia, Mo | Dec. 3, 1862 |
| 33 | I | Lyon, James | St. Louis | May 20, 1863 |
| 33 | I | Looby, Chas. | Lima | Oct. 25, 1862 |
| 33 | I | Longvalle, Augustus | St. Louis | Dec. 23, 1862 |
| 32 | I | Loomis, Elliott B. | | |
| 31 | I | Leonard, Albert | Albany | Feb. 24, 1863 |
| 31 | I | Lozier, George W. | Dayton | Feb. 28, 1863 |
| 30 | I | Leuther, John | Chippewa Falls | Mar. 29, 1863 |
| 30 | I | Lang, Daniel | | Dec. 25, 1862 |
| 29 | I | Larabee, Lamont | Portland | Jan. 23, 1863 |
| 29 | I | Larabee, Martin M | Portland | Jan. 23, 1863 |
| 28 | I | Larkin, Chas. A. | Waukesha | Jan. 25, 1863 |
| 28 | I | Love, Wadkins | Pine Bluff, Ark | May 31, 1865 |
| 27 | I | Lutz, Martin | Kewaunee | Mar. 30, 1863 |
| 27 | I | Linstromm, Wm. | Christiana | Jan. 2, 1863 |
| 27 | I | Leonhardt, Engle | Milwaukee | Dec. 30, 1862 |
| 27 | I | Long, Jefferson | Milwaukee | Jan. 2, 1863 |
| 27 | I | Laver, Geo | Lima | Mar. 7, 1863 |
| 25 | I | Long, Jonathan D. | Potosi | Dec. 10, 1863 |
| 24 | I | Leach, Chas | Milwaukee | |
| 24 | I | Lee, H. O | Milwaukee | Apr. .., 1863 |
| 24 | I | Lindham, Walter | Milwaukee | Apr. .., 1863 |
| 24 | I | Lawrence, Job C | Milwaukee | Apr. .., 1863 |
| 24 | I | Lowell, Chas. D | Milwaukee | Dec. 31, 1862 |
| 24 | I | Larmen, Eugen | | Dec. .., 1864 |
| 23 | I | Lee, James | Caledonia | Sep. 16, 1863 |
| 22 | I | Lee, Henry | Beloit | Oct. 29, 1862 |
| 21 | I | La Duc, Peter | | Jan. .., .... |
| 21 | I | Lynn, Thos | Wausaw | June 25, 1863 |
| 21 | I | Lawrence, Amos | Appleton | Sep. .., 1862 |
| 20 | I | Lucas, D. W. | Waukesha | |
| 20 | I | Lambert, Wm | Ripon | Aug. 8, 1863 |
| 19 | I | Larson, Elliff | Houston, Minn | May 29, 1862 |
| 19 | I | Lobdell, Augustus | Portage | Jan. 1, 1862 |
| 19 | I | Lampmenr, Peter | Racine | Mar. 28, 1862 |
| 18 | I | Levisse, Isaac | Plainfield | |
| 18 | I | Linden, Peter | Fond du Lac | June 28, 1865 |
| 18 | I | Lee, John | Burns | Aug. 18, 1862 |
| 18 | I | Loveless, Marson E. | Columbus | |
| 1 | C | Lampman, Isaac | Osbkosh | Oct. 24, 1862 |
| 1 | C | Lyons, Timothy | Ripon | Mar. 20, 1864 |
| 2 | C | Lee, Geo. W | Fond du Lac | |
| 2 | C | Lighetti, John H. | | Jan. 27, 1863 |
| 2 | C | La Chappelle, Jno | | Dec. 28, 1862 |
| 2 | C | Lowe, J. W. | Mauston | July 10, 1865 |
| 2 | C | Lang, Jacob | Milwaukee | July 22, 1865 |
| 3 | C | Lyth, John | Coloma | June 22, 1865 |
| 3 | C | Litnay, Joseph | Milton | Aug. 26, 1865 |
| 3 | C | Lord, Jerry W | Janesville | Aug. 27, 1865 |
| 3 | C | Lethard, Geo | Kingston | Feb. .., 1862 |
| 3 | C | Larabee, Hiram S | Eau Claire | Jan. .., 1862 |

| Reg't. | | Name. | Residence. | Date. |
|---|---|---|---|---|
| 3 | C | Leggett, Thos | Skirllville | Jan. 29, 1864 |
| 3 | C | Laula, Joseph | Janesville | Oct. 15, 1862. |
| 4 | C | Lutier, Wm | | |
| 4 | C | Ludvorg, Augustus | Milwaukee | Dec. 10, 1864 |
| 4 | C | La Grange, Andrew C | Ripon | Feb. 5, 1862 |
| 4 | C | Loper, Lyman | Ripon | July 27, 1861 |
| 4 | C | Laythe, Isaac C | Jefferson | Apr. 2, 1863 |
| 4 | C | Lisenbee, Chas. R | Sparta | Apr. .., 1864 |
| 4 | C | Lamont, S | Necedah | Oct. 31, 1864 |
| 1 | H A | Larsen, Andrew | Milwaukee | Mar. 17, 1865 |
| 1 | H A | Laven, Patrick | Milwaukee | Dec. 4, 1864 |
| 1 | H A | Larson, Andrew | Milwaukee | Mar. 7, 1865 |
| 8 | L A | Langwood, Andrew S | Menasha | Mar. 17, 1862 |
| 13 | L A | Lee, Eli | Baton Rouge, La | May 2, 1865 |
| 13 | L A | Lewright, Geo | Milwaukee | Jan. 27, 1864 |

## M

| Reg't. | | Name. | Residence. | Date. |
|---|---|---|---|---|
| 1 | I | Meehow, Peter | | |
| 1 | I | Molton, Harson | | |
| 1 | I | Martin, Peter | | Nov. 10, 1862 |
| 1 | I | Mitchell, Joseph | | Nov. 10, 1862 |
| 1 | I | Michaelson, Michael | | Jan. 29, 1864 |
| 2 | I | Miles, Geo. H | Waupaca | April 1, 1862 |
| 2 | I | Murphy, Thomas | | 1861 |
| 2 | I | Marty, Fredolin | New Glarus | Dec. 22, 1862 |
| 2 | I | Mevis, Chas. N | New York | |
| 3 | I | Myers, Chas | | |
| 3 | I | Martin, Wm | | Aug. 9, 1862 |
| 3 | I | Morris, Philip B | Monroe | June 9, 1863 |
| 3 | I | Mohony, Edward | Janesville | |
| 5 | I | Martin, Jacob | Stoughton | Apr. 1, 1865 |
| 5 | I | Meriur, Joseph | Menomonee | Apr. 29, 1863 |
| 5 | I | Masterson, W. D | Janesville | Aug. 31, 1863 |
| 5 | I | Mormon, John | Menomonee | Aug. 31, 1863 |
| 5 | I | Miller, Philip | Menomonee | Aug. 31, 1863 |
| 5 | I | Merrills, Jermiah | | Dec. 10, 1864 |
| 5 | I | Myers, Morris | | Sep. 20, 1864 |
| 6 | I | Messenger, Chester | Madison | |
| 6 | I | Mevis, Chas. A | Janesville | Jan. 6, 1865 |
| 6 | I | Mahony, Florence | | Apr. 4, 1862 |
| 6 | I | Murray, John | | Aug 7, 1862 |
| 6 | I | Moffatt, Arthur | | Sep. 14, 1862 |
| 6 | I | Masterson, Wm. D | | Aug. 31, 1863 |
| 6 | I | Mormon, John | | Aug. 31, 1863 |
| 6 | I | Miller, Philip | Menomonee | Aug. 31, 1863 |
| 6 | I | Morrison, Silas W | | |
| 6 | I | Martine, Ferdinand | | July 1, 1865 |
| 6 | I | Marshall, Geo. F | | |
| 6 | I | Miller, Martin | Waumandee | July 17, 1863 |
| 7 | I | Menandee, O. Santen | | Oct. 14, 1861 |
| 7 | I | Mackey, Edwin | | July 17, 1863 |
| 7 | I | Mathews, John | | |
| 8 | I | Makes, Geo. W | North Port | |
| 8 | I | Morris, Levi W | Little River | |
| 8 | I | Malony, Michael | Seneca | |
| 8 | I | Milton, Frank | Oshkosh | Apr. 1, 1864 |
| 8 | I | Morse, Ralph | Milwaukee | Sep. 5, 1865 |
| 9 | I | Meyer, Charles | | Feb. 21, 1863 |

| *Reg't.* | | *Name.* | *Residence.* | *Date* |
|---|---|---|---|---|
| 9 | I | Meyer, Frederick | | Feb. 21, 1863 |
| 9 | I | Mueller, Chas | Watertown | Sep. 12, 1863 |
| 10 | I | Mason, Geo | Clifton | July 10, 1862 |
| 10 | I | Money, Henry | | |
| 11 | I | Murphy, Dennis | | Mar 10, 1863 |
| 11 | I | Michael, Augustus | | Dec. 3, 1862 |
| 11 | I | Murphy, Dennis W | Kendall | Mar. 11, 1863 |
| 11 | I | Messtoe, Thos. C | | Nov. 20, 1862 |
| 12 | I | Matteson, Even | Dodgeville | Jan. 5, 1862 |
| 12 | I | Moshen, Festus D | Wisconsin | July 2, 1863 |
| 12 | I | Miller, Hartman | Milwaukee | Jan. 14, 1865 |
| 12 | I | Moore, Wm. D | La Crosse | June 14, 1865 |
| 12 | I | Monogan, Pat | Janesville | June 14, 1865 |
| 12 | I | Mayes, Samuel | Waverly, Tenn. | June 25, 1865 |
| 13 | I | Monroe, Jas | Maxonville | June 19, 1865 |
| 13 | I | Machamer, Martin | | |
| 13 | I | Morris, Thomas | | |
| 13 | I | Murray, Wm. H | | |
| 13 | I | Miller, Edgar L | | |
| 14 | I | Maitrejohn, Wm | Pittsburg Landing | May 19, 1863 |
| 14 | I | Motcholzky, Marion | | June 16, 1862 |
| 14 | I | Miller, Geo | Milwaukee | Dec. 15, 1864 |
| 15 | I | Mickelson, Andrew | | |
| 16 | I | Morgan, David | Richford | Apr. 6, 1862 |
| 16 | I | Moran, Jas | | Apr. 1, 1864 |
| 16 | I | Morehouse, Ben | Columbus, Ky | June 7, 1864 |
| 16 | I | Mott, Octavius A | Waushara | Apr. 6, 1862 |
| 17 | I | Montgomery, Edward | | Jan. 23, 1862 |
| 17 | I | Murphy, Pat | | Mar. 20, 1862 |
| 17 | I | Moran, Owen | | Mar. 2, 1862 |
| 17 | I | Merceir, Peter | | Jan. 19, 1863 |
| 17 | I | Marble, Seneca D | | |
| 17 | I | Mook, John | | Apr. 30, 1862 |
| 17 | I | Mullen, John | | Mar. 20, 1862 |
| 17 | I | Meagher, Pat | | Apr. 15, 1862 |
| 17 | I | Miller, Chas | | Aug. 3, 1862 |
| 17 | I | Markel, Joseph | | Dec. 26, 1864 |
| 17 | I | Myers, William | | Dec. 26, 1864 |
| 17 | I | Mincier, August | | Oct. 8, 1864 |
| 17 | I | More, Rhonson | | Mar 20, 1862 |
| 17 | I | Maher, Dennis | | Mar. 20, 1862 |
| 17 | I | Malerson, R. W | | June 20, 1862 |
| 17 | I | Minor, Augustus | Green Bay | Oct. 4, 1864 |
| 17 | I | Martin, Alex | | June 7, 1864 |
| 17 | I | Morrison, Thomas W | New Buffalo | Apr. 6, 1862 |
| 17 | I | Morrison, Alex | Madison | Mar. 21, 1862 |
| 17 | I | Murphy, Patrick | | Mar. 20, 1862 |
| 1 | I | McMannis, Patrick | | |
| 1 | I | McCarthy, Jas | | |
| 1 | I | McIntire, Hugh | | Sep. 28, 1862 |
| 1 | I | McDonald, Alex | | |
| 2 | I | McCoy, James | La Crosse | Aug. .., 1861 |
| 2 | I | McDermot, John | | May 13, 1863 |
| 2 | I | McRae, Wm. J | Union | |
| 5 | I | McClellan, Jas. L | | June 15, 1862 |
| 5 | I | McFarland, Sam. N | Waukesha, | July 7, 1863 |
| 5 | I | McCawley, Patrick | Manitowoc | July 16, 1861 |
| 5 | I | McDonell, Alexander M | | .., 1862 |
| 6 | I | McEwen, Bernard | | Nov. 16, 1863 |

| Reg't. | | Name. | Residence. | Date. |
|---|---|---|---|---|
| 6 | I | McDougal, Henry G | Prescott | Apr. 27, 1864 |
| 6 | I | McMiller, Michael | | July 27, 1865 |
| 8 | I | McLeod, Collins S | Eau Claire Co | |
| 8 | I | McDonald, Chester | R·pon | |
| 8 | I | McGuire, John | Bloomfield | |
| 11 | I | McCormick, John C. R | | Oct. 19, 1863 |
| 12 | I | McMonaugh, David | Wisconsin | Aug. .., 1863 |
| 12 | I | McGan, Geo | | Dec. 25, 1864 |
| 13 | I | McPherson, John | | June 29, 1865 |
| 13 | I | McGrath, Richard | | |
| 13 | I | McGilley, James | | |
| 14 | I | McLaughlin, Pat | | Nov. 30, 1864 |
| 14 | I | McLimans, John | | Jan. 18, 1863 |
| 17 | I | McMahon, Thos | | Mar. 20, 1862 |
| 17 | I | McNally, Thos | | Feb. 8, 1862 |
| 17 | I | McQueaney, Paul | | Apr. 6, 1862 |
| 17 | I | McKenzie, Wm | | |
| 17 | I | McMullen, Donald | Westford | Mar. 12, 1865 |
| 17 | I | McKennan, John | Wisconsin | May 14, 1864 |
| 17 | I | McDonald, Edward | | Apr. 18, 1864 |
| 17 | I | McNamara, John | | Dec. 5, 1863 |
| 17 | I | McDermol, Edward | Janesville | Apr. 18, 1862 |
| 52 | I | Morgan, Pat | | |
| 52 | I | Marshell, Pat | | |
| 52 | I | McCarty, Jas | | |
| 51 | I | McMann, Thos | Milwaukee | |
| 51 | I | Mahoney, Jno | Milwaukee | Feb. 28, 1865 |
| 51 | I | Murphey, Jno | Milwaukee | Feb. 28, 1865 |
| 51 | I | Marsh, Augustus | Milwaukee | Apr. 10, 1865 |
| 51 | I | Madden, Edward | Milwaukee | Apr. 28, 1865 |
| 51 | I | Martin, Henry | Milwaukee | |
| 51 | I | Monroe, Frank | Milwaukee | Mar. 28, 1865 |
| 51 | I | Murphy, James P | Appleton | Apr. 17, 1865 |
| 51 | I | McDonald, Jno | Milwaukee | May 9, 1865 |
| 50 | I | Marshal, Michael | Burke | Mar. 4, 1865 |
| 50 | I | Miller, Selucus C | Vernon Co | Aug. 25, 1865 |
| 50 | I | Meyers, Jno | Vernon Co | Sep. 3, 1865 |
| 50 | I | Madison, Rasmus | Denmark | Aug. 28, 1865 |
| 50 | I | Monroe, Frank | Hudson | Aug. 28, 1865 |
| 50 | I | Manes, Hanvelt | Prescott | July 9, 1865 |
| 50 | I | Makepeace, Sylvester | Sylvan | Aug. 27, 1865 |
| 50 | I | Martin, Joseph | Yankeetown | Aug. 30, 1865 |
| 50 | I | Murphy, Michael | | Mar. 31, 1865 |
| 50 | I | McGowen, Wm. H | | Aug. 25, 1865 |
| 50 | I | Muntner, Christian | Fond du Lac | Aug. 26, 1865 |
| 50 | I | McNish, Jas. B | Columbia Co | Aug. 1, 1865 |
| 50 | I | Moore, Andrew J | Prescott | Sep. 1, 1865 |
| 50 | I | Martin, Chas | Juneau Co | Aug. 31, 1855 |
| 49 | I | Murphy, Richard | Madison | |
| 49 | I | Mohr, Michael | Madison | |
| 48 | I | Miller, Chas | Milwaukee | Mar. 6, 1865 |
| 48 | I | McGrath, Dan'l | Milwaukee | Mar. 6, 1865 |
| 48 | I | Morgan, James | Janesville | Mar. 10, 1865 |
| 48 | I | McLeran, Chas | Milwaukee | Apr. 26, 1865 |
| 48 | I | McKarrman, Chas | Milwaukee | Mar. 1, 1865 |
| 48 | I | Murphy, Jerry | Milwaukee | Mar. 1, 1865 |
| 48 | I | Moeckl, Ernst | Fountain City | Nov. 18, 1865 |
| 47 | I | McCarty, Pat | | Feb. 22, 1865 |
| 47 | I | McDonald, Geo | | Feb. 22, 1865 |

| *Reg't.* | | *Name.* | *Residence.* | *Date.* |
|---|---|---|---|---|
| 47 | I | McMann, Wm | | Feb. 22, 1865 |
| 47 | I | Maloy, Martin | Madison | Feb. 22, 1865 |
| 45 | I | Mallins, Phillip | Hartford | Mar. 6, 1865 |
| 45 | I | Moser, Anton | Milwaukee | Dec. .., 1864 |
| 44 | I | McGinn, Jno | | Jan. 8, 1865 |
| 44 | I | McGuire, Pat | Milwaukee | Feb. 18, 1864 |
| 44 | I | Mahoney, Jno | | May 18, 1865 |
| 44 | I | Mallison, Jas. P | Fond du Lac | July 20, 1865 |
| 44 | I | Moore, Joseph | Janesville | July 4, 1865 |
| 43 | I | Morgan, Sam | Milwaukeee | Sep. 30, 1864 |
| 43 | I | Moore, Patrick | Milwaukee | |
| 43 | I | Meeker, Henry | Milwaukee | |
| 43 | I | Mack, James | Madison | |
| 43 | I | McDonald, Jno | Darlington | Oct. 2, 1864 |
| 43 | I | Murry, Patrick | Stoughton | Sep. 7, 1864 |
| 43 | I | McGuinas, Jno | Stoughton | Sep. 7, 1864 |
| 42 | I | McMann, Jno. M | Janesville | Oct. 30, 1864 |
| 41 | I | Mark, Joseph | Mauston | June 9, 1864 |
| 38 | I | Miller, Jno | Lisbon | July 19, 1864 |
| 38 | I | McCarthy, James | Milwaukee | Aug. 28, 1864 |
| 38 | I | Miller, Geo | Milwaukee | Aug. 20, 1864 |
| 38 | I | Moley, James | Milwaukee | Aug. 17, 1864 |
| 38 | I | Montgomery, James | Milwaukee | Aug. 25, 1864 |
| 38 | I | McCay, Jno | Milwaukee | Aug. 25, 1864 |
| 38 | I | Martin, James | Milwaukee | Aug. 17, 1864 |
| 37 | I | McCarty, Wm | Shullsburg | Apr. 22, 1864 |
| 37 | I | Moore, Abner M | | Aug. 19, 1864 |
| 37 | I | McCurdy, Thos | Eau Claire | June 25, 1864 |
| 37 | I | Mountford, Jno | Portage | Dec. 9, 1864 |
| 36 | I | Morse, Benj. W | Cataract | |
| 36 | I | Maxwell, Francis | Marion | |
| 35 | I | McCloud, Dudley D | Prairie du Chien | Feb. 26, 1864 |
| 35 | I | McMashen, James | Prairie du Chien | Feb. 26, 1864 |
| 35 | I | Miller, John | Milwaukee | Feb. 26, 1864 |
| 35 | I | Murphey, Barney | Janesville | Mar. 14, 1864 |
| 35 | I | Merritt, Henry H | Fond du Lac | |
| 35 | I | Murck, Joseph | Milwaukee | Feb. 27, 1866 |
| 35 | I | Metcalf, Wm. G | Janesville | Jan. 8, 1864 |
| 35 | I | McCann, John | Milwaukee | Apr. 18, 1864 |
| 35 | I | McFarland, Wm | | Mar. 7, 1866 |
| 34 | I | Miller, Geo | Mequon | Jan. 10, 1863 |
| 34 | I | Moldenhour, Chas | Cedarburg | Jan. 31, 1863 |
| 34 | I | Menette, Frantz | Belgium | Jan. 19, 1863 |
| 34 | I | Malley, Geo | Milwaukee | Jan. 19, 1863 |
| 34 | I | McGee, Wm | Germantown | Jan. 31, 1863 |
| 34 | I | Mann, Peter | Milwaukee | Feb. 18, 1863 |
| 34 | I | Meissner, Fred | Germantown | Feb. 20, 1863 |
| 34 | I | Mueller, Peter | Milwaukee | Feb. 1, 1863 |
| 34 | I | Miller, Frank | Ixonia | Jan. 31, 1863 |
| 34 | I | Mueller, Christopher | Herman | Dec. 17, 1862 |
| 34 | I | Mueller, Herman | Chicago | Dec. 17, 1862 |
| 34 | I | Mathes, Chas | Ephraim | Jan. 30, 1863 |
| 34 | I | Mark, Dan'l | Philadelphia | Dec. 28, 1862 |
| 34 | I | Monroe, John | Buffalo Co | Jan. 31, 1863 |
| 34 | I | Mequillet, Jacob | Milwaukee | Jan. 31, 1863 |
| 34 | I | Meirs, Fred'k | Sheboygan | Jan. 2, 1863 |
| 34 | I | Maufort, Gabriel | Kewaunee | Jan. 31, 1863 |
| 34 | I | McDermott, Jno | Beaver Dam | Jan. 31, 1863 |
| 34 | I | Miller, Henry | Rhine | Jan. 31, 1863 |

| *Reg't* | | *Name.* | *Residence.* | *Date.* |
|---|---|---|---|---|
| 34 | I | Miller, Fred'k | Hartford | Feb. 6, 1863 |
| 34 | I | Maloy, David | Lake Five | Jan. 31, 1863 |
| 34 | I | Malory Geo | Grafton | Dec. 28, 1862 |
| 34 | I | Mequillet, Jacob | Milwaukee | Feb. 2, 1863 |
| 34 | I | Macintyre, John | Douglas | Jan. 8, 1863 |
| 34 | I | Maisters, Henry | Mackford | Jan. 31, 1863 |
| 34 | I | Mittlestadt, Fred'k | Mecan | Jan. 19, 1863 |
| 34 | I | Meyer, Geo | Milwaukee | Dec. 23, 1862 |
| 33 | I | Meyers, Jno. B | California | Feb. 15, 1863 |
| 33 | I | McGrath, Thomas | St. Louis | Oct. 23, 1862 |
| 33 | I | Muer, Fritz | St. Louis | Sep. 12, 1862 |
| 33 | I | Miller, Adam | Jefferson City, Mo | Sep. 28, 1862 |
| 33 | I | Martin, Joseph | Tuscumbia, Mo | May 19, 1863 |
| 33 | I | Martin, Benj. C | Potosi, Mo | Oct. 14, 1862 |
| 33 | I | McCoy, Samuel | Trenton | Feb. 24, 1863 |
| 33 | I | McKee, Wm | Janesville | May 10, 1863 |
| 33 | I | McAvin, Wm | Shullsburg | May 16, 1863 |
| 32 | I | Martin, Samuel | Oshkosh | Oct. 7, 1862 |
| 32 | I | McKean, Jno | Oshkosh | Mar. 22, 1863 |
| 32 | I | Monigon, Peter | Westfield | Oct. 8, 1862 |
| 32 | I | McKeon, James | Packwaukee | Oct. 14, 1862 |
| 32 | I | Mcmillan, Wm | Columbus | Oct. 8, 1862 |
| 32 | I | Morrison, Rolla | | Aug. 21, 1863 |
| 32 | I | Morgan, Wm. C | Oxford | Oct. 10, 1862 |
| 32 | I | McGuire, James | Waupun | Mar. 25, 1864 |
| 32 | I | McGee, James | Waupun | Mar. 25, 1864 |
| 31 | I | Mines, Hugh | Prairie du Chien | Mar. 3, 1863 |
| 31 | I | Mayrand, Simon | Dodgeville | Mar 4, 1863 |
| 31 | I | Mack, Falconer T | | Mar. 2, 1863 |
| 31 | I | Marshall, Jno | Milwaukeee | Mar. 2, 1863 |
| 31 | I | Merrill, Samuel | Prairie du Chien | Mar. 2, 1863 |
| 31 | I | May, Wm | Fond du Lac | Apr. 29, 1864 |
| 31 | I | Maloney, Chas | | June 10, 1865 |
| 30 | I | McMellen, James | | Feb. 12, 1864 |
| 30 | I | Melville, Chas | | Feb. 12, 1864 |
| 30 | I | Moo e, Geo | | Mar. 28, 1864 |
| 30 | I | Marshall, Louis | | Mar. 25, 1864 |
| *30* | *I* | *McAnnally, Patrick* | Fond du Lac | Oct. 29, 1864 |
| 30 | I | McGarry, Michael | Fond du Lac | Oct. 29, 1864 |
| 30 | I | McElliott, Jeremiah | | Apr. 23, 1864 |
| 29 | I | McLaughlin, James | Watertown | Jan. 10, 1863 |
| 28 | I | McCausky, Patrick | Milwaukee | |
| 28 | I | Murphy, John | Milwaukee | |
| 28 | I | Martin, John | Milwaukee | |
| 27 | I | Mero, Joseph | Highland | Oct. 1, 1862 |
| 27 | I | McGovern, Patrick | Highland | Jan. 1, 1864 |
| 27 | I | Morley, James | Milwaukee | Dec. 4, 1862 |
| 27 | I | Munson, Chas | Milwaukee | Mar. 28, 1863 |
| 27 | I | Miller, Jno | Milwaukee | Mar. 20, 1863 |
| 27 | I | Miller, Chas | Milwaukee | Mar. 20, 1863 |
| 27 | I | Miller, Jos | Meeme | Mar. 7, 1863 |
| 27 | I | Myer, Frederick | | |
| 27 | I | Muller, Herman | | |
| 27 | I | Martins, Jno | Highland | May 18, 1864 |
| 27 | I | Marten, Adolph | Herman | Sep. 20, 1864 |
| 27 | I | Maker, Carl | Herman | Jan. 15, 1863 |
| 25 | I | Marshall, Samuel | Orion | Dec. 12, 1862 |
| 25 | I | Melvin, Jas | Irving | Feb. 18, 1863 |
| 25 | I | Melvin, Francis | Irving | Apr. 30, 1863 |

| Reg't. | | Name | Residence. | Date. |
|---|---|---|---|---|
| 25 | I | Mylerain, Thos | Fairplay | Jan. 22, 1862 |
| 24 | I | Murray, Theodore | Milwaukee | |
| 24 | I | Murray, Dan'l E | Milwaukee | |
| 24 | I | McCracker, Jas | Milwaukee | |
| 24 | I | McCormick, Jas. E | Milwaukee | |
| 24 | I | Murphy, Dan'l | Milwaukee | Aug. .., 1863 |
| 24 | I | Mayer, Fritz | Milwaukee | May 20, 1864 |
| 23 | I | Merrill, Rufus | West Point | Sep. 6, 1863 |
| 22 | I | Maxworthy, Albert | Beloit | Jan. 29, 1863 |
| 22 | I | McFarland, C. W | Rochester | Feb. 28, 1863 |
| 22 | I | Mukkleston, Allen | Waukesha | Sep. 15, 1863 |
| 22 | I | McCathsen, John | Janesville | Mar. 12, 1863 |
| 22 | I | McConnell, Jno | Monroe | Feb. 27, 1864 |
| 20 | I | Metz, Henry | Sheboygan | |
| 20 | I | McReal, Joseph | Sparta | June 4, 1862 |
| 20 | I | Murray, Hugh | | June 4, 1863 |
| 20 | I | Miller, Fred | Ripon | Aug. 8, 1863 |
| 20 | I | McKnight, Geo. W | Madison | Dec. 4, 1864 |
| 19 | I | McGary, Henry | Sparta | May 5, 1862 |
| 19 | I | Muggy, Thos | Kenosha | Apr. 1, 1862 |
| 19 | I | Miller, Henry | Kenosha | Apr. 2, 1862 |
| 19 | I | Magill, Sam'l | Kenosha | June 3, 1862 |
| 19 | I | Miller, Erasmus D | Westfield | June 3, 1862 |
| 19 | I | McKellen Duncan | Milwaukee | Feb. 10, 1862 |
| 19 | I | Max, Wm | Fox Lake | Apr. 13, 1862 |
| 19 | I | Michels, Alfred | Racine | June 10, 1862 |
| 19 | I | Meising, Chas | Milwaukee | |
| 18 | I | Milcake, Edy | Milwaukee | |
| 18 | I | Murphy, Dennis | Milwaukee | |
| 18 | I | Micheltree, Wm | Linwood | |
| 18 | I | Mayers, Jno | Milwaukee | Jan. 20, 1865 |
| 1 | C | Mc Elroy, Jno. H | Beaver Dam | Nov. 21, 1863 |
| 1 | C | Morton, Calvin C | Winneconne | |
| 1 | C | Myers, Wm | | Aug. 25, 1864 |
| 1 | C | Mc Clay, James | | Nov. 14, 1864 |
| 1 | C | Millins, David | | Dec. 14, 1864 |
| 1 | C | Mitchell, Wm jr | Janesville | Jan. 26, 1865 |
| 1 | C | Mc Cann, Sam'l | La Crosse | |
| 1 | C | Marray, Jas. H | Milwaukee | |
| 1 | C | Mills, Jno | Milwaukee | |
| 2 | C | Mc Fetisch, Jno | Oshkosh | Mar. 16, 1862 |
| 2 | C | Maloy, James | La Crosse | Oct. 10, 1865 |
| 2 | C | Meller, Eli | Mauston | Oct. 10, 1865 |
| 2 | C | Mills, Orson | Mauston | Oct. 11, 1865 |
| 2 | C | Miller, Fred'k | Fountain City | Oct. 14, 1865 |
| 2 | C | Masterson, James | Monroe | July 28, 1865 |
| 2 | C | Mercier, Nelson | | July 13, 1865 |
| 2 | C | Mosher, Jas. A | Steventown | July 13, 1865 |
| 3 | C | Mauxon, James B | Janesville | June 14, 1864 |
| 3 | C | Murray, Robt | Portage City | June 22, 1865 |
| 3 | C | Marsh, Willard P | | Aug 27, 1865 |
| 3 | C | Meyers, Frank | Platteville | Sep. 12, 1862 |
| 3 | C | Miller, Fred'k | Platteville | Dec. 31, 1862 |
| 3 | C | Merry, James H | Milwaukee | Mar. 26, 1863 |
| 3 | C | Mc Cormic, David | Appleton | .., 1862 |
| 3 | C | Madewell, Samuel | Carrolton | Apr. 30, 1864 |
| 3 | C | Morris, Luther | Oshkosh | Feb. 27, 1862 |
| 3 | C | Millard, Napoleon | Oshkosh | Jan. 21, 1863 |
| 3 | C | Miller, Jno | Leavenworth | Feb. 13, 1863 |

| *Reg't.* | *Name.* | *Residence.* | *Date.* |
|---|---|---|---|
| 3 C | Mc Donald, Wm | Madison | Mar. 10, 1863 |
| 3 C | Mc Kowan, Wm. T | Fond du Lac | June 13, 1863 |
| 3 C | Montgomery, Wm. H | Boscobel | Nov. 12, 1862 |
| 4 C | Moonle, M | Beloit | |
| 4 C | Moore, A. D | Madison | |
| 4 C | Marks, Chas | | Jan. 17, 1864 |
| 4 C | Muller, Fritz | Milwaukee | Mar. 20, 1864 |
| 4 C | Miller, Angus Mc Kay | Milwaukee | Mar. 30, 1864 |
| 4 C | Moon, Adelbert D | Summitt | April 1, 1864 |
| 4 C | Murray, Robt | Baton Rouge, La | April 1, 1865 |
| 1 H A | Monroe, Wm. M | New Berlin | |
| 1 H A | Mc Elroy, Edw'd | Alexandria, Va | Nov. 18, 1864 |
| 1 H A | Meck, Jno H | Alexandria, Va | Nov. 27, 1864 |
| 1 H A | Moore, James | Alexandria, Va | Feb. 8, 1865 |
| 1 H A | Merwin, Geo | Fulton | Aug. 6, 1865 |
| 1 L A | Morrow, Jno | La Crosse | Sept. 26, 1862 |
| 4 L A | Muski, Fred | Milwaukee | Oct. .., 1864 |
| 4 L A | Moyer, Josiah | Portsmouth | July 2, 1865 |
| 6 L A | Mc Mahon, Patrick | Lone Rock | June 27, 1862 |
| 7 L A | Miner, Edgar V | Milwaukee | Dec. 29, 1863 |
| 8 L A | Mc Auly, Dan'l | Stevens Point | May 10, 1862 |
| 8 L A | Mayheu, Truman | Eagle | May 17, 1862 |
| 9 L A | Machiea, Edward | Burlington | July 17, 1862 |

## N

| | | | |
|---|---|---|---|
| 1 I | Neldner, Fred | | |
| 1 I | Nelson, John R | | April 27, 1863 |
| 2 I | Noble, Franklin | Galena, Ill | April 21, 1862 |
| 2 I | Nealey, Horace | Springville | May 21, 1862 |
| 6 I | Nichols, Wm | | Sep. 14, 1862 |
| 6 I | Nichols, Lewis | Appleton | July 3, 1861 |
| 6 I | Nickerson, Andrew | | May 5, 1864 |
| 12 I | Neiser, Frank | | Dec. 25, 1864 |
| 14 I | Nom, John | | Jan. 18, 1863 |
| 15 I | Nerger, O. O | Sheldon, Minn | |
| 16 I | Nash, Chas. L | | Apr. 13, 1864 |
| 17 I | Noloran, Thos | | Mar. 20, 1862 |
| 17 I | Nelson, Fenton | | Aug. 17, 1862 |
| 51 I | Nelson, William | Milwaukee | April 6, 1862 |
| 50 I | Newton, Wm | Wiota | Sept. 5, 1862 |
| 47 I | Nelson, Frank | | Feb. 22, 1862 |
| 46 I | Nixon, Thos. J | Milwaukee | Mar. 6, 1862 |
| 37 I | Na-wa-ne-co-chin, Jno | Keshono | July 12, 1864 |
| 35 I | Nightingale, Nicholas | Janesville | Mar. 14, 1864 |
| 35 I | Nandsen, H. L | Brownville | Aug. 3, 1865 |
| 35 I | Nelson, Chas | Janesville | Jan. 4, 1864 |
| 34 I | Nelson, Gilbert | Dodgeville | Jan. 31, 1863 |
| 34 I | Nieland, Henry | Greenville | Jan. 17, 1863 |
| 34 I | Neville, Jaque | Sturgeon Bay | Jan. 30, 1863 |
| 34 I | Neville, Henry | Sturgeon Bay | Jan. 30, 1863 |
| 34 I | Nooks, H | | Dec. 16, 1862 |
| 34 I | Neimann, Carl | Washington | Jan. 31, 1863 |
| 34 I | Newtel, Francois | | |
| 33 I | Newson, Larey | Breckenridge, Mo | Feb. 24, 1863 |
| 33 I | Norvell, James | St. Louis | April 15, 1863 |
| 30 I | Nellis, Geo. B | Mineral Point | Mar. 11, 1863 |
| 27 I | Noth, Julius | Herman | |
| 27 I | Norton, Burdell R | Sheboygan | Mar. 12, 1863 |

| *Reg't.* | | *Name.* | *Residence.* | *Date.* |
|---|---|---|---|---|
| 27 | I | Nernberger, Fred'k | Sheboygan | Sept. 29, 1863 |
| 27 | I | Newmann, Theodore | Milwaukee | Dec. 30, 1862 |
| 27 | I | Nelson, W. F. | Lomira | Mar. 29, 1863 |
| 27 | I | Norwood, Cornelius | Sheb. Falls | Mar. 7, 1863 |
| 22 | I | Napp, Wm. F. | Delavan | Jan. 2, 1862 |
| 22 | I | Neal, Wm. F. | Beloit | May .., 1863 |
| 20 | I | Newnon, Jasper W. | Boscobel | Feb. 3, 1864 |
| 19 | I | Nace, A. G. | La Crosse | May 29, 1862 |
| 19 | I | Nicholds, Joseph | Sparta | May 5, 1862 |
| 18 | I | Nedry, Jno. | Berlin | |
| 3 | C | Nordyke, Jesse | Cazenovia | Mar. 26, 1862 |
| 3 | C | Norris, Geo. | St. Louis | June 29, 1862 |
| 4 | C | Nelson. Nels | Whitewater | May 21, 1864 |
| 1 | L A | Nicholson, Wm. | East Canada | Aug. 17, 1864 |
| 2 | L A | Nicholaus, Bold | Port Washington | Oct. 31, 1861 |
| 3 | L A | Nichols, Milo L. | Berlin | Dec. 20, 1861 |
| 4 | L A | Nesbie, James | Portsmouth | June 4, 1865 |
| 13 | L A | Norton, Frank | Baton Rouge, La | Mar. 11, 1865 |

## O

| | | | | |
|---|---|---|---|---|
| 1 | I | Otto, Chas. | | |
| 1 | I | Oleson, John | | |
| 1 | I | O'Connell, Jas. H. | | |
| 3 | I | Oleson, John | Milwaukee | |
| 3 | I | O'Rily, Thomas | | Dec. 4, 1861 |
| 5 | I | O'Neil, Hugh | | Sept. 17, 1863 |
| 5 | I | Osborne, John H. | | Oct. 18, 1863 |
| 6 | I | O'Neil, Lawrence | | Aug. 1, 1861 |
| 7 | I | Ogden, Wm. | Milwaukee | Dec. 17, 1864 |
| 10 | I | Odell, Fernando | Troy | Aug. 9, 1862 |
| 11 | I | Otter, James | Oneida | Aug. 27, 1863 |
| 15 | I | Olson, O. | Freeborn, Minn | |
| 15 | I | Olsin, Michael | Coon Prairie | |
| 15 | I | Olsin, Anrau | Koshkonong | |
| 15 | I | Olsin, Gustave | Colman, Iowa | |
| 17 | I | O'Connor, Jeremiah | | Mar. 19, 1862 |
| 17 | I | O'Connor, M. | | Mar. 19, 1862 |
| 17 | I | O'Leary, Timothy | | April 19, 1864 |
| 17 | I | Oakes, Chas. | Kendall | April 18, 1864 |
| 17 | I | O'Bermier, Samuel | Barton | Aug. 5, 1862 |
| 17 | I | Osburn, John, | Cedar | Nov. 1, 1863 |
| 51 | I | Orr, William | Milwaukee | Mar. 11, 1865 |
| 50 | I | O'Keefe, Dan'l | | |
| 49 | I | O'Brine, James | Madison | Mar. 12, 1865 |
| 48 | I | O'Brian, Pat | Milwaukee | Feb. 24, 1865 |
| 44 | I | O'Malloy, Jno. | | Jan. 7, 1865 |
| 39 | I | O'Brien, Michael | Milford | June 8, 1865 |
| 35 | I | O'Conner, Dennis | Milwaukee | Jan. 22, 1865 |
| 34 | I | O'Kieff, Thos. | | Jan. 3, 1863 |
| 34 | I | O'Neill, James | Mequon | Dec. 18, 1862 |
| 34 | I | Oehler, Ernst | Fillmore | Jan. 16, 1863 |
| 34 | I | Opp, John | Herman | Dec. 27, 1862 |
| 34 | I | Oestrich, Wm. | Princeton | Jan. 31, 1863 |
| 34 | 1 | Ohm, Frederick | Neshkoro | Dec. 19, 1862 |
| 34 | I | Olsen, Henry | Coon | Jan. 31, 1863 |
| 34 | I | Olsen, Hans | Hamburg | Jan. 31, 1863 |
| 33 | I | Odell, Louis F. | Breckenridge, Mo | Feb. 24, 1863 |
| 32 | I | Osborn, Jos. W. | Metomen | Jan. 1, 1863 |

| Reg't. | | Name. | Residence. | Date. |
|---|---|---|---|---|
| 32 | I | Ostrander, Chas | Oshkosh | Oct. 7, 1862 |
| 29 | I | O'Conner, Jeremiah | | Oct. 4, 1862 |
| 27 | I | O'Neil, Michael | Two Rivers | Mar. 30, 1863 |
| 24 | I | O'Brien, Kennedy | Milwaukee | July .., 1863 |
| 19 | I | Owens, J. J. | | Feb. 10, 1862 |
| 18 | I | Odell, Isaac H. | Springville | April 2, 1863 |
| 18 | I | Osborne, James, sr | Leon | Aug. .., 1863 |
| 1 | C | Oswald, Christian F | Oak Grove | June 1, 1863 |
| 2 | C | Owens, Wm. P. | Little Grant | Oct. 20, 1865 |
| 2 | C | Ohery, Michael | | July 22, 1864 |
| 2 | C | Oberst, Lorenz | Raymond | Oct. 3, 1864 |
| 3 | C | O'Harry, Michael | Geneva | June 12, 1862 |
| 3 | C | O'Gara, Jno | Clyman | Mar. 26, 1862 |
| 3 | C | Offenman, Leonard | Madison | May 1, 1863 |
| 4 | C | Osborn, Geo. L. | | Nov. 6, 1865 |
| 4 | C | Ober, Rich'd | Ripon | Apr. 27, 1866 |
| 4 | C | Osterlee, Conrad | Milwaukee | June 28, 1865 |
| 8 | L A | O'Brien, Jno | Chicago, Ill | Mar. 15, 1862 |

## P

| Reg't. | | Name. | Residence. | Date. |
|---|---|---|---|---|
| 1 | I | Parker, Geo | | |
| 1 | I | Pollock, Jas. K. | | |
| 1 | I | Putnam, Lafayette | | |
| 2 | I | Post, Peter | Waukesha | Jan. 14, 1861 |
| 3 | I | Peter, John | Ridgeway | |
| 3 | I | Pease, James | | Dec. 14, 1861 |
| 5 | I | Parrot, Isaac | | May 7, 1862 |
| 6 | I | Parker, Adelbert | Medina | July 4, 1861 |
| 7 | I | Phelps, Ambrose | | Sept. 17, 1862 |
| 7 | I | Preston, John | Milwaukee | Dec. 17, 1864 |
| 7 | I | Petty, James | | |
| 8 | I | Palmer, George | Eau Claire Co. | |
| 8 | I | Phillips, John W | Two Rivers | |
| 8 | I | Powderly, Wm. H | Bloomingfield | |
| 8 | I | Pooler, Albert | | Nov. 23, 1864 |
| 8 | I | Philips, Henry J | | |
| 10 | I | Pan, John W. | Manasha | Aug. 7, 1862 |
| 11 | I | Perry, John C | | Oct. 19, 1863 |
| 12 | I | Pierce, E. C. | Parks Corner | Sept. 18, 1863 |
| 12 | I | Park, John M | Stevens Point | Sep. 20, 1863 |
| 12 | I | Parker, Chas. H. | | June 27, 1865 |
| 13 | I | Peerce, Richard M | Maxonville | June 19, 1865 |
| 13 | I | Purdy, John W. | | |
| 14 | I | Parks, Nathaniel | Janesville | Dec. 1, 1863 |
| 14 | I | Parr, Thos. J | Onalaska | July 14, 1864 |
| 14 | I | Parks, Nathaniel | Janesville | Nov. 14, 1864 |
| 14 | I | Powers, Myron H | | Aug. 18, 1862 |
| 14 | I | Polas, Moses | Oneida | Nov. 18, 1864 |
| 14 | I | Phillips, Geo | Milwaukee | Feb. 10, 1865 |
| 14 | I | Powless, Henry | | Jan. 19, 1862 |
| 14 | I | Peters, Sterling | | Jan. 28, 1862 |
| 14 | I | Powles, Moses | Oneida | Nov. 19, 1864 |
| 14 | I | Place, Wm. S. | | Mar. 8, 1862 |
| 16 | I | Paul, Edward | Madison | Jan. 18, 1863 |
| 16 | I | Pulfort, Jonathan W | Plymouth | May 5, 1862 |
| 17 | I | Perry, Stephen S. | | Mar. 20, 1862 |
| 17 | I | Perry, Robt | | Feb. 15, 1862 |
| 17 | I | Porter, George | | Aug. 5, 1862 |

| *Reg't.* | | *Name.* | *Residence.* | *Date.* |
|---|---|---|---|---|
| 17 | I | Poiley Thos | | |
| 17 | I | Pegram, Hy J | Wisconsin | June .., 1864 |
| 17 | I | Purdy, William | Vicksburg | Nov. 11, 1864 |
| 17 | I | Pilson, Wilson | Beloit | July 1, 1865 |
| 17 | I | Porter, George, jr | Barton | Aug. 5, 1862 |
| 52 | I | Plummer, Ed | | |
| 50 | I | Perkinson, James | Vernon Co | Sept. 3, 1865 |
| 50 | I | Peacock, Thos | New Diggings | Aug. 27, 1865 |
| 50 | I | Parks, Joseph | Little Lake | Aug. 30, 1865 |
| 50 | I | Parkin, Christopher | New Diggings | Aug. 29, 1865 |
| 50 | I | Phelps, Ransom D | Darlington | Sept 5, 1865 |
| 48 | I | Porman, Wm | Milwaukee | Sept. 10, 1865 |
| 48 | I | Peterson, Gustavus | Milwaukee | Feb. 24, 1865 |
| 48 | I | Prublee, George | Milwaukee | Mar. .., 1865 |
| 48 | I | Pingrey, George | Omro | Sept 16, 1865 |
| 48 | I | Peck, Reuben | Ripon | Sept 19, 1865 |
| 48 | I | Peterson, Steen | Milwaukee | Sept. 6, 1865 |
| 43 | I | Picket, Seymour J | Milwaukee | Oct. 20, 1864 |
| 43 | I | Paul, Peter | Green Bay | Oct 1, 1864 |
| 40 | I | Phillips, Charles L | Jefferson | Aug. 13, 1864 |
| 38 | I | Pixley, | Milwaukee | Apr. 28, 1864 |
| 38 | I | Patterson, James | Milwaukee | Aug. 20, 1864 |
| 37 | I | Pearson, David | Reed's Landing | May .., 1864 |
| 36 | I | Perry, George W | Sun Prairie | Apr. 26, 1864 |
| 36 | I | Perry, Jno | Sun Prairie | Apr. 20, 1864 |
| 35 | I | Pasey, George W | Wauzeka | July 24, 1865 |
| 34 | I | Peters, Charles | Belgium | Dec. 18, 1862 |
| 34 | I | Parsons, Wm | Somers | Jan 31, 1863 |
| 34 | I | Praefke, Frans | Milwaukee | Jan. 28, 1863 |
| 34 | I | Persons, David | Dodgeville | Feb. 1, 1863 |
| 34 | I | Pagel, Albert | Wausau | Jan. 30, 1863 |
| 34 | I | Petitzian, Simon | Kewaunee | Jan. 31, 1863 |
| 34 | I | Perrlott, Antoine | Kewaunee | Jan. 29, 1863 |
| 34 | I | Paul, Joseph | Sturgeon Bay | Jan. 15, 1863 |
| 34 | I | Potter, Ludwig | Crystal Lake | Jan. 31, 1863 |
| 34 | I | Patterson, David | Holland | Dec. 20, 1862 |
| 34 | I | Peterson, John | | Jan. 10, 1863 |
| 33 | I | Patterson, James B | Tuscumbia, Mo | Feb. 22, 1863 |
| 33 | I | Pinkham, Cephas | | |
| 33 | I | Pinnette, Francis | St. Louis, Mo | Feb. 23, 1863 |
| 32 | I | Pierce, Amos | | Dec. 29, 1862 |
| 32 | I | Pickering, Isaac | Packwaukee | Dec. 31, 1862 |
| 32 | I | Pettit, Reuben L | Oshkosh | May 1, 1865 |
| 32 | I | Potter, George | | Jan. 1, 1863 |
| 31 | I | Polkinghorne, Wm | Dodgeville | Mar. 4, 1863 |
| 31 | I | Pease, George | Prairie du Chien | Nov 12, 1862 |
| 30 | I | Parker, Louis | Hancock | Aug. .., 1862 |
| 30 | I | Paige, Charles Titus | Auroraville | Nov. 10, 1862 |
| 30 | I | Parsons, John J | New Lisbon | Nov. 13, 1862 |
| 30 | I | Patterson, Charles H | Auroraville | July 20, 1863 |
| 30 | I | Patterson, Lysander | Auroraville | July 4, 1865 |
| 30 | I | Perry, Martin | Racine | May 13, 1864 |
| 29 | I | Pierce, Sidney | Portland | Jan. 23, 1863 |
| 29 | I | Powers, Elias M | Portland | Jan. 23, 1863 |
| 29 | I | Pollock, Ira | Horicon | Feb. 28, 1863 |
| 29 | I | Pratt, Edwin H | Hartford | Nov. 2, 1862 |
| 29 | I | Pierce, George | Oak Grove | Oct. 31, 1862 |
| 28 | I | Phillips, Charles | Waukesha | Jan. 25, 1863 |
| 28 | I | Price, George | Waukesha | Feb. 27, 1862 |

| Reg't. | | Name. | Residence. | Date. |
|---|---|---|---|---|
| 27 | I | Patterson, Fred'k | Milwaukee | Mar. 8, 1863 |
| 24 | I | Piersons, Jos. | Milwaukee | |
| 24 | I | Phelps, Chas. L. | Milwaukee | |
| 24 | I | Pfluger, Philip | Milwaukee | May 1, 1863 |
| 24 | I | Powell, Jno | Eagle | |
| 22 | I | Payne, Jno. S. | Magnolia | Jan. 28, 1863 |
| 21 | I | Penney, George | Waupaca | June 11, 1863 |
| 21 | I | Prince, Joel | Appleton | Oct. 8, 1862 |
| 19 | I | Payne, Maybourne | Sparta | Mar. 20, 1862 |
| 18 | I | Perkinson, Andrew | Readstown | |
| 18 | I | Payson, Jno. C. | Hampden | |
| 1 | C | Parkhurst, James | Delavan | Dec. 9, 1864 |
| 2 | C | Persons, Wm. | | Sep. 21, 1862 |
| 2 | C | Pratt, Jno. A. | | Mar. .., 1862 |
| 3 | C | Peskino, Myron J | Janesville | Aug. 26, 1865 |
| 3 | C | Prickett, Lewis | Appleton | 1862 |
| 3 | C | Prouty, Lyman | Oconto | 1862 |
| 3 | C | Preston, Willet C | Markesan | Oct. 1, 1864 |
| 3 | C | Packard, Joseph J | Kingston | 1862 |
| 3 | C | Palmer, George G | Milwaukee | June 12, 1863 |
| 3 | C | Payne, Thomas | Oshkosh | Mar. 27, 1862 |
| 3 | C | Power, John | Oshkosh | June 9, 1862 |
| 3 | C | Pohl, Wm. | Madison | Oct. .., 1862 |
| 4 | C | Pidgeon, Patrick | Oconto | May 25, 1863 |
| 4 | C | Perry, L. D | Dell Prairie | Feb. 4, 1862 |
| 4 | C | Pollard, J. W. | Baton Rouge, La | June 8, 1864 |
| 4 | C | Page, Newton | Chippewa Co. | |
| 1 | H A | Patterson, Jno | Alexandria, Va | Aug. 6, 1865 |
| 1 | L A | Paddock, Lorenzo A. | Salem | Sept. 12, 1862 |
| 4 | L A | Payson, Jno. C. | Racine | July 26, 1864 |
| 4 | L A | Peck, Daniel | Beloit | June 5, 1864 |
| 4 | L A | Powers, Wm. L. | Portsmouth | July 2, 1865 |
| 7 | L A | Pettey, David L | La Crosse | Feb. 5, 1864 |

## Q

| Reg't. | | Name. | Residence. | Date. |
|---|---|---|---|---|
| 6 | I | Quimby, Harris | | July 2, 1865 |
| 7 | I | Quinn, John | Milwaukee | Dec. 19, 1864 |
| 24 | I | Quinn, Hugh | Milwaukee | |

## R

| Reg't. | | Name. | Residence. | Date. |
|---|---|---|---|---|
| 1 | I | Robinson, Milo | | |
| 1 | I | Rickard, Leonard B. | Michigan | Aug 2, 1863 |
| 1 | I | Rodermasher, Franz | Sheboygan | May 12, 1864 |
| 2 | I | Raymond, Myron C. | La Crosse | Jan. 20, 1863 |
| 3 | I | Rod, Timothy | Green Bay | |
| 3 | I | Reed, Thomas | Franklin | |
| 5 | I | Rheinist, Ernst | | Sep. 27, 1861 |
| 5 | I | Rothschild, Max | | Dec. 14, 1862 |
| 5 | I | Raymond, Platt G | | Oct. 20, 1862 |
| 5 | I | Ridland, Albert | | |
| 5 | I | Rhine, Andrew | | Sep. 30, 1864 |
| 5 | I | Rablin Benj. T. | Virginia | July 13, 1864 |
| 5 | I | Reynolds, Thomas | Milwaukee | July 18, 1867 |
| 6 | I | Reed, Albert | | Sept. 18, 1861 |
| 6 | I | Ramsey, William | | July 28, 1861 |
| 6 | I | Rud, George W. | Beloit | April 14, 1862 |
| 7 | I | Rhines, Joseph R. | | Sep. 17, 1862 |
| 7 | I | Rogers, James H | Madison | May 2, 1863 |

| Reg't. | | Name. | Residence. | Date. |
|---|---|---|---|---|
| 7 | I | Robinson, James | Milwaukee | Dec. 19, 1864 |
| 8 | I | Russell, Wm. H. | Northport | |
| 8 | I | Reynolds, James H. | Oshkosh | |
| 8 | I | Rafferty, | | |
| 8 | I | Robinson, John | New York City | April 16, 1864 |
| 9 | I | Reiner, Fred. | | Feb. 21, 1863 |
| 9 | I | Ruefse, Bernard | | Feb. 11, 1863 |
| 10 | I | Rockwood, Delorina P. | Madison | July 10, 1862 |
| 11 | I | Riley, Barnard | | Nov. 18, 1861 |
| 12 | I | Randall, Henry | | Dec. 30, 1862 |
| 13 | I | Robinson, James | | |
| 14 | I | Ranson, Silas | Auburn | July 11, 1863 |
| 14 | I | Ranson, Bostic | | Jan. 18, 1863 |
| 14 | I | Robinson, James | Milwaukee | Feb. 10, 1865 |
| 14 | I | Roberts, Joseph | Stevens Point | July 17, 1864 |
| 14 | I | Rose, Nathan | | Nov. 29, 1862 |
| 14 | I | Ramsey, Samuel | | |
| 16 | I | Riley, Patrick | | Feb. 27, 1864 |
| 16 | I | Russell, Lee | Saxville | April .., 1862 |
| 16 | I | Rogers, L. C. | Indiana | Jan. 22, 1863 |
| 16 | I | Ross, Porter | | Feb. 20, 1862 |
| 16 | I | Robinson, James T | | |
| 17 | I | Reley, John | | Feb. 28, 1862 |
| 17 | I | Reynolds, C | | |
| 17 | I | Ready, Maurice | | Jan. 20, 1863 |
| 17 | I | Riley, Peter | | Jan. 20, 1863 |
| 17 | I | Roch, Michael | | Dec. 26, 1864 |
| 17 | I | Rousse, Louis | | June 16, 1864 |
| 17 | I | Rose, Marcus | | July 10, 1864 |
| 52 | I | Rivers, Lewis. | | Mar. 3, 1865 |
| 52 | I | Randall, E. F. | | |
| 52 | I | Raithbone, John C | | |
| 51 | I | Rice, Casper | Milwaukee | Mar. 28, 1865 |
| 51 | I | Rogers, Stephen | Milwaukee | Mar. 28, 1865 |
| 51 | I | Rush, Henry | Milwaukee | Apr. 18, 1865 |
| 51 | I | Raubkin, Wm | Cedarburg | |
| 50 | I | Rendahl, Elling J. | Jefferson | Mar. 6, 1865 |
| 50 | I | Roehrig, Robert | Appleton | Aug. 30, 1865 |
| 50 | I | Rush, John | Iowa Co | Aug. 29, 1865 |
| 50 | I | Reimer, Rudolph | Alma | Aug. 26, 1865 |
| 50 | I | Roever, Henry D. | Port Washington | Aug. 30, 1865 |
| 50 | I | Ran, George | Beaver Dam | Aug. 25, 1865 |
| 50 | I | Rowell, Jacob | Lima | |
| 50 | I | Rafferty, Patrick | Vernon Co | Aug. 31, 1865 |
| 48 | I | Ryan, John | | Sep. 8, 1865 |
| 48 | I | Reardon, John | Milwaukee | Feb. 28, 1865 |
| 48 | I | Rockefeler, R. M. | Waterloo | Aug. 18, 1865 |
| 48 | I | Ruffner, Peter | Milwaukee | Mar. 1, 1865 |
| 44 | I | Rivers, Frank | | Jan. 8, 1865 |
| 44 | I | Reas, Wm. H. | Waupaca | Aug. 5, 1864 |
| 43 | I | Russell, John | Milwaukee | Sep. 25, 1864 |
| 42 | I | Richardson, George A. A. | Hebron | Nov. 23, 1864 |
| 38 | I | Rodgers, James | Milwaukee | June 4, 1864 |
| 38 | I | Rowe, Wm | Milwaukee | June 15, 1864 |
| 38 | I | Reed, Rudolph | Milwaukee | Aug. 17, 1864 |
| 37 | I | Ruth, Thomas | Oshkosh | Apr. 28, 1864 |
| 37 | I | Right, George | Reed's Landing | May .., 1864 |
| 35 | I | Reily, John | Milwaukee | Apr. 28, 1864 |
| 35 | I | Rilling, John | Milwaukee | Apr. 9, 1865 |

| Reg't. | | Name. | Residence. | Date. |
|---|---|---|---|---|
| 35 | I | Rasey, Benjamin F. | Wautoma | Jan. 8, 1864 |
| 35 | I | Reed, Lucian W. | Milwaukee | Feb. 1, 1866 |
| 34 | I | Reiss, John | Belgium | Jan. 15, 1863 |
| 34 | I | Reik, John | Belgium | Jan. 16, 1863 |
| 34 | I | Runeau, Francois | West Bend | Jan. 8, 1863 |
| 34 | I | Reeve, Thomas | Dodgeville | Jan. 31, 1863 |
| 34 | I | Reiter, John | Milwaukee | Dec. 24, 1862 |
| 34 | I | Rippel, William | Arlington | Jan. 29, 1863 |
| 34 | I | Roskopf, Anton | Aurora | Feb. 2, 1863 |
| 34 | I | Reffen, Ludwig | | Jan. 3, 1863 |
| 34 | I | Roward, Jean Francois | Green Bay | Jan. 31, 1863 |
| 34 | I | Ryan, Thomas D. | Erin | Jan. 31, 1863 |
| 34 | I | Rohloff, Gottlieb | Germantown | Jan. 15, 1863 |
| 34 | I | Rosler, August | Shields | Mar. 7, 1863 |
| 34 | I | Rheinholdt, Victor | West Bend | Dec. 24, 1862 |
| 33 | I | Reynolds, William T | Linn Co., Mo | May 1, 1863 |
| 33 | I | Russell, George W. | Tuscumbia, Mo | Oct. 19, 1862 |
| 33 | I | Russell, James J. | Tuscumbia, Mo | Oct. 19, 1862 |
| 33 | I | Reed, Eri | Perry Co., Mo | Oct. 22, 1862 |
| 33 | I | Reinhardt, John | St. Joseph, Mo | Sept. 14, 1862 |
| 33 | I | Reese, James | Janesville | Apr. 20, 1863 |
| 33 | I | Ransom, R. D. | Springdale | Oct. 25, 1862 |
| 33 | I | Rogers, William | Racine | Oct. 25, 1862 |
| 33 | I | Ransom, R. B. | Springdale | Nov. 16, 1862 |
| 33 | I | Raynor, Nicholas | Jefferson City, Mo | Feb. 23, 1863 |
| 33 | I | Reynolds, George | Paris | Apr. 13, 1863 |
| 32 | I | Roberts, Edward F. | | Jan. 21, 1863 |
| 32 | I | Roberts, Thos. D. | | Oct. 1, 1862 |
| 32 | I | Reynolds, Louis | Menasha | Jan. 17, 1864 |
| 32 | I | Rabday, Andrew J. | Waupun | Nov. 16, 1864 |
| 31 | I | Raymond, Newton | Chicago | Jan. 23, 1863 |
| 30 | I | Rogers, Chas | Wautoma | Nov. 15, 1862 |
| 30 | I | Rogers, James | Madison | Dec. 10, 1863 |
| 30 | I | Riley, John | | Mar. 19, 1864 |
| 28 | I | Reily, Lawrence | East Troy | Oct. 10, 1862 |
| 28 | I | Riley, John | Milwaukee | |
| 28 | I | Rish, John | Milwaukee | |
| 28 | I | Riggs, James | Milwaukee | |
| 27 | I | Richlow, Fed'k | Herman | Mar. 30, 1863 |
| 27 | I | Randemacher, Peter | Wilson | Oct. 8, 1862 |
| 27 | I | Rummerfanger, Nicholas | Meeme | Mar. 7, 1863 |
| 27 | I | Richard, Jno. | | |
| 26 | I | Ritchie, Jno. | | Nov. 2, 1862 |
| 26 | I | Richenberg, Richard | Milwaukee | July 4, 1863 |
| 25 | I | Russell, Henry | Potosi | Jan. 27, 1863 |
| 25 | I | Rowe, Fred. S. | De Soto | Dec. 1, 1863 |
| 25 | I | Robinson, Clinton J. | Mitchell | Sept. 5, 1862 |
| 24 | I | Rine, Dan'l | Milwaukee | |
| 24 | I | Rabernard, ——— | Milwaukee | Nov. 1, 1863 |
| 23 | I | Robinson, Benj. R. | Madison | Feb. 24, 1863 |
| 22 | I | Raymond, Isaac | Union Grove | Jan. 24, 1863 |
| 22 | I | Roberts, Evan G. | Racine | Jan. 28, 1863 |
| 22 | I | Roache, Peter | Newark | June 12, 1863 |
| 21 | I | Roberts, Jas. B. | | Oct. 8, 1862 |
| 21 | I | Reardon, Jno. | | Sept 11, 1862 |
| 21 | I | Roberts, Robert | Nekimi | Dec. 31, 1862 |
| 20 | I | Roach, Chas. | La Crosse | |
| 20 | I | Rodgers, B. A. | Madison | |
| 20 | I | Rodgers, Seth W. | Wauzeka | |

| *Reg't.* | | *Name.* | *Residence.* | *Date.* |
|---|---|---|---|---|
| 19 | I | Root, Henry D | Reedsburg | May 17, 1862 |
| 19 | I | Reinbieb, Fre'k | Portage | June 4, 1862 |
| 19 | I | Renke, Frank | Racine | June 2, 1862 |
| 19 | I | Ramsdell, Dwight | Houston, Minn | May 31, 1862 |
| 18 | I | Rice, Truman | Plover | |
| 18 | I | Robbins, Rufus | Oshkosh | |
| 18 | I | Root, Almon R | Columbus | |
| 18 | I | Rowley, Henry | Ontario | Aug. 18, 1862 |
| 1 | C | Redlon, Leonard P | Plainfield | Feb. 22, 1863 |
| 1 | C | Ryan, Thomas | Beaver Dam | May 3, 1864 |
| 1 | C | Risk, James | Center | Dec. 3, 1864 |
| 1 | C | Rowe, Herbert | Palmyra | Oct. 1, 1862 |
| 2 | C | Riddall, Jno. W | Eau Claire | Oct. 12, 1865 |
| 2 | C | Rand, Martin V | La Crosse | July 13, 1865 |
| 2 | C | Rice, Jason B | Trempealeau | July 13, 1865 |
| 2 | C | Rice, Wm. E | Memphis | Apr. 23, 1864 |
| 2 | C | Rand, Andrew J | La Crosse | Sept 24, 1864 |
| 2 | C | Rudlen, David | Arlington | May 29, 1863 |
| 2 | C | Roberts, Robert | Oshkosh | Mar. .., 1862 |
| 2 | C | Riley, Jno | Vernonlee | Feb. 15, 1862 |
| 2 | C | Robins | Eau Claire | Sept. .., 1862 |
| 3 | C | Rand, James | Kingston | June 21, 1865 |
| 3 | C | Retty, Geo | Janesville | June 14, 1865 |
| 3 | C | Reiner, Geo | Madison | Sept 20, 1864 |
| 3 | C | Rose, Francis | Platteville | Apr. 22, 1864 |
| 3 | C | Rogers, William | Platteville | Mar. 25, 1862 |
| 3 | C | Ryan, Jno | Oshkosh | Feb. 7, 1863 |
| 4 | C | Reed, Ezra | Ft. Atkinson | Mar. 25, 1865 |
| 4 | C | Rahier, Peter | Madison | Sept 28, 1865 |
| 4 | C | Reed, Ezra | Ft. Atkinson | Sep. 29, 1865 |
| 4 | C | Robinson, William | Semormain | |
| 4 | C | Rockwood, Theodore H | Tomah | June 28, 1865 |
| 1 | H A | Rollings, Henry | Alexandria, Va | Apr. 1, 1865 |
| 1 | H A | Regan, Michael | Milwaukee | Sep. 11, 1863 |
| 1 | L A | Rumback, Gordian | Platteville | Jan. 23, 1862 |
| 1 | L A | Ray, Chas | Milwaukee | Sep. 30, 1863 |
| 4 | L A | Riley, Hugh | Beloit | Mar. 21, 1864 |
| 8 | L A | Ramney, Herman | Fountain | June 2, 1862 |
| 10 | L A | Rees, People | Prescott | Apr. .., 1864 |

## S

| | | | | |
|---|---|---|---|---|
| 1 | I | Savage, Horace D | | |
| 1 | I | Shaver Jas | | |
| 1 | I | Shofstall, Soloman | | |
| 1 | I | Schofield, Robt | | |
| 1 | I | Sprague, Oran | | Jan. 20, 1863 |
| 1 | I | Sexton John | Wisconsin | Aug. 2, 1863 |
| 2 | I | Strong, David | Lancaster | |
| 2 | I | Smith, Homer B | Marathon | Apr. 1, 1862 |
| 2 | I | Schroeppe, John | Roxbury | |
| 2 | I | Stone, John | Springfield | Aug. 5, 1863 |
| 3 | I | Steven, Austin | La Crosse | |
| 3 | I | School, John | Woodville | |
| 3 | I | String, Victor E | Wisconsin | Apr. 2, 1865 |
| 3 | I | Snyder, Peter | | July 2, 1865 |
| 3 | I | Smith, J. D | | |
| 5 | I | Smith, Michael | | Apr. 4, 1862 |
| 5 | I | Smith, Geo. A | | Oct. 20, 1862 |
| 5 | I | Scott, Peter A | Madison | Oct. 5, 1864 |

| Reg't. | | Name. | Residence. | Date. |
|---|---|---|---|---|
| 5 | I | Shoemaker, Wm | | May 1, 1863 |
| 5 | I | Smith, F. H | Waupaca | July 8, 1863 |
| 5 | I | Simmon, James P | Taycheedah | Dec. 28, 1863 |
| 5 | I | Smith, John | La Crosse | July 13, 1864 |
| 5 | I | Smith, Mathias | Milwaukee | June .., 1861 |
| 6 | I | Seany, John P | | Aug. 1, 1863 |
| 6 | I | Smith, Thomas | Beloit | June 18, 1864 |
| 6 | I | Shaw, John | | Aug. 2, 1862 |
| 6 | I | Sherwood, Isaac E | | July 27, 1862 |
| 6 | I | Schootey, John | | Sep. 14, 1862 |
| 6 | I | Scott, Geo. W | | Apr. .., 1863 |
| 6 | I | Spears, Francis M | Milwaukee | July 2, 1865 |
| 6 | I | Saunders, O. S | Strongs Prairie | |
| 7 | I | Stiles, Andrew | | Jan. 20, 1863 |
| 7 | I | Smith, Thomas | | Sep. 14, 1861 |
| 7 | I | Spears, Cassius | | Nov. 30, 1863 |
| 7 | I | Smith, Geo | Milwaukee | Dec. 19, 1864 |
| 7 | I | Storm, David W | Chippewa | Oct. 10, 1864 |
| 8 | I | Skenes, Thomas | | |
| 8 | I | Stoddard, James A | | Feb. 3, 1865 |
| 9 | I | Stemer, Joseph | | July 3, 1862 |
| 9 | I | Senne, Henry | | Feb. 11, 1863 |
| 9 | I | Stunn, Christian | | Aug. 4, 1863 |
| 10 | I | Sly, Jos. C | Plainsville | Aug. 4, 1862 |
| 10 | I | Singer, John | Little Grant | Mar. 4, 1864 |
| 11 | I | Swan, Chas A | | Feb. 19, 1863 |
| 11 | I | Stoner, John | Wisconsin | |
| 11 | I | Sharkey Hugh | | Oct. 24, 1864 |
| 11 | I | Swan, Chas A | Madison | Feb. 17, 1863 |
| 11 | I | Sianlan, James | Rutland | Nov. 20, 1861 |
| 12 | I | Sawyer, John | Green Bay | Dec. 25, 1864 |
| 12 | I | Starks, Wm | | June 27, 1865 |
| 13 | I | Sleaster, Charles | Milwaukee | Mar. 1, 1865 |
| 13 | I | Solway, Joseph | Milwaukee | Jan. 14, 1865 |
| 13 | I | Somersville, Thomas | Jefferson | July 24, 1865 |
| 13 | I | Simerson, Thomas J | Edgerton | Sept. 1, 1865 |
| 13 | I | Smith, John R | | |
| 13 | I | Stoner, John | | |
| 13 | I | Stickles, John | | |
| 13 | I | Smith, Calvin C | | |
| 13 | I | Smith, John R | | |
| 14 | I | Schmidt, Gerhart | | Jan. 12, 1863 |
| 14 | I | Smith. Alonzo | Black River Falls | July 2, 1861 |
| 14 | I | Schneider John | | Aug. 18, 1862 |
| 14 | I | Schneider, John | Vicksburg, Miss | Feb. 26, 1864 |
| 14 | I | Swamp, Anthony | | Aug. 19, 1865 |
| 14 | I | Slingerland, John | | Jan. 11, 1862 |
| 14 | I | Sellock, Wm | | Aug. 18, 1862 |
| 14 | I | Streeter, H. A | | Aug. 3, 1862 |
| 14 | I | Stoneson, Ole | | |
| 14 | I | Saul, Nils | | |
| 14 | I | Schorr, Christian | | |
| 16 | I | Sming, Wm | Mt. Morris | Aug. 18, 1862 |
| 16 | I | Sloyd, Silas | Fall River | Aug. 27, 1862 |
| 16 | I | Smith, William | | .., 1864 |
| 17 | I | Sullivan, Michael | | Mar. 20, 1862 |
| 17 | I | Stanley, Jonathan | | Mar. 20, 1862 |
| 17 | I | Sackett, Clifford | | Mar. 8, 1862 |
| 17 | I | Spicer, F. M | | July 7, 1862 |

| Regt. | | Name. | Residence. | Date. |
|---|---|---|---|---|
| 17 | I | Sheay, Thomas | | Mar. 20, 1862 |
| 17 | I | Sulliven, Owen | | Feb. 18, 1863 |
| 17 | I | Shelley, George | | Mar. 20, 1862 |
| 17 | I | Sherault, J. M | | Mar. 19, 1862 |
| 17 | I | Soplant, Octave | | Jan. 19, 1863 |
| 17 | I | Shields, John | | June 20, 1863 |
| 17 | I | Sinns, Charles | | Dec. 26, 1864 |
| 17 | I | Sorrel, Samuel | Vicksburg, Miss | May 1, 1865 |
| 17 | I | Schemirkom, John | Watertown | Nov. 12, 1864 |
| 17 | I | Shannon, Jas H | Vicksburg, Miss | Dec. 2, 1864 |
| 17 | I | St. Germain, O'Neal | Mauston | |
| 17 | I | Steinhausen, Frederick | Madison | May 19, 1863 |
| 17 | I | Scanlan, Pat | Madison | |
| 17 | I | Smith, Charles | | |
| 17 | I | Sherlrock, Victor | | July 2, 1865 |
| 17 | I | Sutherland, Wm | | Apr. 14, 1862 |
| 52 | I | Stillwell, Lewis | | |
| 52 | I | Stevens, Chas | | |
| 52 | I | Sharr, Francis | | |
| 52 | I | Schmidt, Jno | | |
| 52 | I | Smith, Geo | | |
| 52 | I | Starks, Eugene | | |
| 52 | I | Straus, Franz | | |
| 51 | I | Stearsis, Wm | Milwaukee | |
| 51 | I | Stanley, Edward P | Milwaukee | Mar. 28, 1865 |
| 51 | I | Schmidt, Geo | Milwaukee | Apr. .., 1865 |
| 51 | I | Snyder, Jno | Milwaukee | Apr. .., 1865 |
| 51 | I | Stark, Chas | Milwaukee | Apr. .., 1865 |
| 51 | I | Stewart, Wm | Madison | |
| 50 | I | Sohnes, Harvey | | Aug. .., .... |
| 50 | I | Schulze, Chas. F | Appleton | Aug. 30, 1865 |
| 50 | I | Seal, Dan'l W | Vernon Co | Aug. 25, 1865 |
| 50 | I | Side, Jno | New Diggings | Aug. 27, 1865 |
| 50 | I | Scott, Robt | New Diggings | Aug. 27, 1865 |
| 50 | I | Smith, Elisha | Darlington | Aug. 29, 1865 |
| 50 | I | Smith, Eugene | Darlington | Aug. 29, 1865 |
| 50 | I | Smith, Judson S | Bristol | Sep. 6, 1865 |
| 50 | I | St. John, Chas | Williamstown | Aug. 31, 1865 |
| 50 | I | Strong, Willis | Greenfield | Aug. 29, 1865 |
| 50 | I | Sweet, Jno | Lodi | Aug. 26, 1865 |
| 50 | I | Salesbury, Orsylon | | Aug. 27, 1865 |
| 50 | I | Schmidt, Fred | New London | Aug. 24, 1864 |
| 48 | I | Smith, James | | Sep. 7, 1865 |
| 48 | I | Schneider, Wm | Boscobel | Sep. 22, 1865 |
| 48 | I | Smith, Wm. G | Milwaukee | Feb. 19, 1865 |
| 48 | I | Sullivan, Wm | Milwaukee | Feb. 24, 1865 |
| 48 | I | Sweeney, James | Milwaukee | Feb. 24, 1865 |
| 48 | I | Slaser, S | Milwaukee | Sep. 6, 1865 |
| 48 | I | Stimpson, Samuel | Montello | Sep. 6, 1865 |
| 48 | I | Stafford, Darius B | Fox Lake | June 15, 1865 |
| 47 | I | Smith, Chas. F | | Feb. 22, 1865 |
| 47 | I | Swift, Fred'k | | Feb. 22, 1865 |
| 47 | I | Struthers, Enos | Mauston | Aug. 14, 1865 |
| 47 | I | Smith, Jno. F | Madison | Feb. 19, 1865 |
| 44 | I | Stewart, Chas | Milwaukee | Oct. 27, .... |
| 44 | I | Sopries, Rich'd | | Jan. 8, 1865 |
| 44 | I | Summers, Martin | La Crosse | Apr. 6, 1865 |
| 44 | I | Street, Geo. M | Hudson | Oct. 17, 1864 |
| 43 | I | Sam, Jacob | Green Bay | Oct. 5, 1864 |

| *Reg't.* | | *Name.* | *Residence.* | *Date.* |
|---|---|---|---|---|
| 43 | I | Smith, Thos | Milwaukee | Oct. 8, 1864 |
| 42 | I | Sims, Jno. M | Janesville | Oct. 30, 1864 |
| 40 | I | Seaver, Wm. H | Jeffersonville | Aug. 17, 1864 |
| 39 | I | Shurpf, Jno. J | Milford | June 8, 1864 |
| 38 | I | Skinner, Wm. F | Palmyra | Apr. 28, 1864 |
| 38 | I | Smith, Adam | Milwaukee | Aug. 27, 1864 |
| 38 | I | Swingle, Alex | Janesville | Sept. 12, 1864 |
| 38 | I | Sullivan, Timothy | Janesville | Sept. 3, 1864 |
| 37 | I | Smith, John | Madison | May .., 1864 |
| 36 | I | Stewart, James, C | Madison | May 7, 1864 |
| 35 | I | Smith, James | Milwaukee | Apr. 17, 1864 |
| 35 | I | Stevens, Reuben M | Fond du Lac | |
| 35 | I | Stafford, Melvin | Brownsville, Tex | Aug. 3, 1865 |
| 35 | I | Stowburner, Ezra T | Janesville | Jan. 17, 1866 |
| 35 | I | Sanborn, Solon F | Janesville | Jan. 8, 1864 |
| 34 | I | Schmitt, Henry | Cedarburg | Jan. 20, 1863 |
| 34 | I | Schulz, Thos | Milwaukee | Dec. 15, 1862 |
| 34 | I | Stuessi, Henry | Milwaukee | Dec. 31, 1862 |
| 34 | I | Schellhon, Franz | Grafton | Jan. 29, 1863 |
| 34 | I | Schmidt, Julius | Mequon | Jan. 24, 1863 |
| 34 | I | Schmidt, Aug | Mequon | Jan. 28, 1863 |
| 34 | I | Stroff, Mathias | Belgium | Jan. 5, 1863 |
| 34 | I | Steinback, Nicholas | Belgium | Jan. 15, 1863 |
| 34 | I | Sanburn, Jno. G | Kenosha | Jan. 28, 1863 |
| 34 | I | Stahl, Peter | Kenosha | Dec. 29, 1862 |
| 34 | I | Salsbury, Rich'd | Somers | Jan. 31, 1863 |
| 34 | I | Saueressy, Henry | Appleton | Feb. 1, 1863 |
| 34 | I | Scott, Isaaiah | Casco | Jan. 31, 1863 |
| 34 | I | Shelton, Patrick | Clyde | Feb. 1, 1863 |
| 34 | I | Schlick, Mathias | Reedsburg | Jan. 31, 1863 |
| 34 | I | Schild, Chas | Milwaukee | Jan. 31, 1863 |
| 34 | I | Schwnighamer, Jos | Hortonsville | Jan. 31, 1863 |
| 34 | I | Scott, Isaiah | Ellington | Jan. 31, 1863 |
| 34 | I | Simon, Pierre | Green Bay | Jan. 31, 1863 |
| 34 | I | Schmidt, Jacob | Milwaukee | July .., 1863 |
| 34 | I | Saueressig, Henry | West Bend | July 31, 1863 |
| 34 | I | Smith, John | Wayne | Dec. 28, 1862 |
| 34 | I | Savage, James | Richfield | Dec. 24, 1862 |
| 34 | I | Stebs, John, | Mecan | Jan. 29, 1863 |
| 34 | I | Stregle, George | Hamburg | Jan. 31, 1863 |
| 34 | I | Schieltzky, William | Newton | Jan. 29, 1863 |
| 34 | I | Scholl, Jacob | Grafton | Jan. .., 1863 |
| 34 | I | Sulms, Martin | Saukville | Dec. 10, 1862 |
| 34 | I | Smith, James | Morrison | Dec. 16, 1862 |
| 34 | I | Schmidt, John | Mequon | Dec. 16, 1862 |
| 34 | I | Schmidt, Fred'k | Greenfield | Dec. 16, 1862 |
| 34 | I | Schmidt, Frank | Milwaukee | Dec. 16, 1862 |
| 33 | I | Stephens, Alfred C | Missouri | Feb. 6, 1863 |
| 33 | I | Stephens, Elijah | Breckenridge, Mo | Sept. 23, 1862 |
| 33 | I | Schlinger, Fred | St. Louis, Mo | Dec. 23, 1862 |
| 33 | I | Stilson, Chas. W | Kenosha | July 28, 1865 |
| 32 | I | Schufelt, Orrin | Poygan | Oct. 24, 1864 |
| 32 | I | Sullivan, Michael | Fairfield | Oct. 30, 1862 |
| 32 | I | Stibbins, Orlando A | Harrisville | Jan. 31, 1862 |
| 32 | I | Stratten, A. M | Newton | Jan. 31, 1863 |
| 32 | I | Smith, Jno | Memphis, Tenn | Jan. 24, 1864 |
| 32 | I | Sheldon, Chas. O | | Feb. 12, 1864 |
| 32 | I | Simpson, Henry E | Calumus | July 20, 1863 |
| 32 | I | Summers, David | | July 29, 1863 |

| *Reg't.* | | *Name* | *Residence* | *Date.* |
|---|---|---|---|---|
| 31 | I | Schmidt, Jno | Milwaukee | Mar. 2, 1863 |
| 31 | I | Smith, Geo | Madison | Mar. 2, 1863 |
| 31 | I | Sharp, Cyrus | Prairie du Chien | Mar. 2, 1863 |
| 31 | I | Slatter, Jackson | | Mar. 2, 1863 |
| 31 | I | Smith, Geo. A | Prairie du Chien | Mar. 2, 1863 |
| 31 | I | Stevens, Jno. T | Monroe | Dec. 31, 1862 |
| 30 | I | Smith, Wm. G | Emerald | May 22, 1863 |
| 30 | I | Smith, Jno | Madison | Dec. 29, 1863 |
| 30 | I | Slattery, Jas | | Feb. 29, 1864 |
| 30 | I | Sullivan, Michael | | Mar. 6, 1864 |
| 30 | I | Shaw, Geo. M | | Dec. 26, 1863 |
| 30 | I | Smith, Jno | | Mar. 24, 1864 |
| 30 | I | Strahl, August | | Dec. 11, 1862 |
| 29 | I | Stephenson, Alpheus | Waterloo | Jan. 23, 1863 |
| 29 | I | Smith, Edwin | Waterloo | Jan. 23, 1863 |
| 29 | I | Stearns, Jno | Horicon | Feb. 10, 1863 |
| 29 | I | Sullivan, Daniel | Watertown | Nov. 2, 1862 |
| 29 | I | Shiners, Jno | Hartford | Oct. 12, 1862 |
| 29 | I | Schott, Fred'k | Deerfield | Nov. 15, 1863 |
| 29 | I | Sweeney, Jos | | Mar. 30, 1865 |
| 28 | I | Smith, Wester S | Waukesha, | May 10, 1863 |
| 28 | I | Smith, Frank | Milwaukee | |
| 28 | I | Smith, Geo | Milwaukee | |
| 27 | I | Schwartz, Henry | Milwaukee | Mar. 30, 1863 |
| 27 | I | Smith, Jno. A | Milwaukee | Mar. 9, 1863 |
| 27 | I | Smith, Solomon | Milwaukee | Mar. 28, 1863 |
| 27 | I | Standish, Henry H | Lindon | Mar. 7, 1863 |
| 27 | I | Sullivan, Dan'l | Madison | Mar. 24, 1863 |
| 27 | I | Schumacher, Geo. A | | |
| 27 | I | Spink, Albert | | |
| 27 | I | Searls, E. T | | |
| 26 | I | Schneer, Jno | | Dec. 15, 1862 |
| 26 | I | Slemmer, Geo | | |
| 26 | I | Salter, Wm | Milwaukee | Sep. 30, 1863 |
| 26 | I | Schmidt, Christian F | Milwaukee | |
| 26 | I | Schueler, Fritz | Ripon | May 20, 1863 |
| 26 | I | Smertcheck, Vincent | Racine | Apr. 30, 1862 |
| 25 | I | Sherland, Joel. E | Sparta | Feb. 17, 1863 |
| 25 | I | Stone, Sylvester | Sparta | Feb. 19, 1863 |
| 25 | I | Sanborn, Wm. W | Orion | Mar. 26, 1864 |
| 24 | I | Spahn, Franz | Port Washington | |
| 24 | I | Scheriff, Carl | Milwaukee | |
| 24 | I | Sexton, James | Milwaukee | |
| 24 | I | Steller, Maximilan | Milwaukee | |
| 24 | I | Shrelar, Jno | Milwaukee | Mar. 2, 1864 |
| 24 | I | Saull, Jno | Milwaukee | |
| 23 | I | Summerdale, Christoper | Prairie du Sac | Jan. 9, 1863 |
| 23 | I | Smith, Chas | Madison | Apr. 21, 1864 |
| 22 | I | Stanferd, David | Geneva | Jan. 31, 1862 |
| 22 | I | Sullivan, Dan'l | Delavan | Oct. 16, 1862 |
| 22 | I | Straw, Albert E | Richmond | Nov. 20, 1862 |
| 22 | I | Sullivan, Jno | Delavan | Feb. 10, 1863 |
| 21 | I | Snyder, Geo | | Oct. 8, 1862 |
| 21 | I | Sumner, Jas. P | | Nov. 3, 1862 |
| 21 | I | Snow, Isadore E | | Jan. |
| 19 | I | Sage, Marquis S | Houston, Minn | May 17, 1862 |
| 19 | I | Stephens, Henry | Elleotta, Minn | May 29, 1862 |
| 19 | I | Samble, Jno | Portage | Jan. 1, 1862 |
| 19 | I | Smith, C. P | Oxford | Jan. 1, 1862 |

| *Reg't.* | | *Name.* | *Residence.* | *Date.* |
|---|---|---|---|---|
| 19 | I | Schreier, Fred'k | Milwaukee | June 2, 1862 |
| 19 | I | Sabins, Rudd | Racine | June 3, 1862 |
| 19 | I | Shrieve, Ezekiel | Debello | July 2, 1862 |
| 19 | I | Skitzinger, Geo | Milwaukee | Mar. 15, 1862 |
| 19 | I | Skelknis, Wm | Milwaukee | Feb. 12, 1862 |
| 19 | I | Stephens, Henry E | Kenosha | Apr. 1, 1862 |
| 19 | I | Sherman, H. K | Prairie du Chien | May 15, 1862 |
| 19 | I | Studevous, Joseph | Milwaukee | July 7, 1862 |
| 19 | I | Sorrenson, Peter | Mukwonego | July 4, 1865 |
| 18 | I | Spaulding, R. W | Plover | |
| 18 | I | Smith, James | Plover | |
| 18 | I | Sherwin, W. H | Stockton | |
| 18 | I | Sheldon, Byron C | Milwaukee | |
| 18 | I | Sullivan, Michael | Oshkosh | |
| 18 | I | Slocum, A. H | Grand Rapids | |
| 18 | I | Singer, Philip | Viroqua | |
| 18 | I | Smith, Jesse | Jefferon | June 26, 1865 |
| 18 | I | Silas, Baptist | Freedom | Dec. .., 1864 |
| 18 | I | Sprout, Cummings N | Cataract | Aug. 18, 1862 |
| 18 | I | Smith, Wm. N | Grand Rapids | May .., 1862 |
| 1 | C | Smythe, Thos | Milwaukee | Apr. 29, 1863 |
| 1 | C | Sprague, Chas | La Crosse | Aug. .., 1862 |
| 1 | C | Smith, Chas. | | Nov. 8, 1864 |
| 1 | C | Spencer, Levi | Racine | Dec. 19, 1864 |
| 1 | C | Shave, Wm. T | Prairie du Chien | Dec. 2, 1864 |
| 1 | C | Seevy, James | St. Louis | Dec. 3, 1864 |
| 1 | C | Schiller, Fred'k | Prairie du Chien | Nov. 10, 1864 |
| 1 | C | Sanders Josiah P | Metomen | July 12, 1865 |
| 2 | C | Sharp, Aaron | | Oct. 10, 1865 |
| 2 | C | Swan, J. J | Eau Claire | Oct. 12, 1865 |
| 2 | C | Snow, Edwin, S | La Crosse | July 10, 1865 |
| 2 | C | Snow, Jno. W | La Crosse | July 10, 1865 |
| 2 | C | Sutton, Geo. W | Boscobel | July 22, 1865 |
| 2 | C | Shaw, Wm. H | Floyd | June 30, 1865 |
| 2 | C | Shipiman, Jno. G | | Aug. 1, 1864 |
| 2 | C | Smith, Frank D | Hudson | Oct. 19, 1864 |
| 2 | C | Sherman, Sylvester A | Eldorado | July 24, 1865 |
| 2 | C | Shaw, James | Rolla, Mo | May .., 1864 |
| 2 | C | Seibold, Geo | | Mar. 18, 1862 |
| 2 | C | Schmidt, Jno | | Dec. 11, 1862 |
| 2 | C | Stoker, John | Raymond | May 14, 1862 |
| 2 | C | Scott, Walter, M | Green Bay | Feb. 9, 1863 |
| 2 | C | Skerrs, Edward | Racine Co | Feb. 19, 1863 |
| 2 | C | Shehan, Thomas | | Oct. .., 1862 |
| 2 | C | Spinning, Wm. O | | Oct. 10, 1862 |
| 3 | C | Stolle, Carl F. W | Watertown | June 18, 1864 |
| 3 | C | Southerland, Zachariah | Van Buren, Ark | June 14, 1864 |
| 3 | C | Stray, Andrew J | Janesville | June 22, 1865 |
| 3 | C | Sandford, Esraol | Fort Scott | Apr. 5, 1865 |
| 3 | C | Smith, Joseph M | Oshkosh | Sept. 20, 1864 |
| 3 | C | Sweeney, James | Platteville | Sept. 12, 1862 |
| 3 | C | Smith, John | Chicago, Ill | Sept. 12, 1862 |
| 3 | C | Sullivan, ——— | | May .., 1862 |
| 3 | C | Stout, Thomas | Fort Scott | Dec. 21, 1864 |
| 3 | C | Safford, Aaron | Madison | Mar. 10, 1864 |
| 3 | C | Sibbold, Mark | Eau Claire | Jan. .., 1862 |
| 3 | C | Stein, Charles | Utica | Feb. 6, 1862 |
| 3 | C | Sullivan, Timothy | Eagle | June 4, 1862 |
| 3 | C | Stanton, Myron L | Waukesha | July 20, 1862 |

| Reg't. | | Name. | Residence. | Date. |
|---|---|---|---|---|
| 3 | C | Strong, Dan'l B | La Crosse | Sep. 2, 1864 |
| 3 | C | Smith, James | Pensaukee | May 21, 1862 |
| 3 | C | Seeder, Sam'l | Oshkosh | June 8, 1862 |
| 3 | C | Sanborn, Wm | Jefferson | Mar. .., 1862 |
| 4 | C | Smith, Wm | Oconto | Aug. 12, 1863 |
| 4 | C | Slee, Sam'l | Milwaukee | Mar. 6, 1864 |
| 4 | C | Saifeit, Julius | Madison | Feb. 15, 1864 |
| 4 | C | Switzer, Jno. C | Sparta | Apr. .., 1864 |
| 4 | C | Stroup, Joel | Albion | |
| 4 | C | Smith, Chas. H | Geneva | |
| 4 | C | Spaulding, Chas. D | Tomah | June .., 1864 |
| 4 | C | Sanford, Henry | Oconto | Aug 4, 1862 |
| 1 | H A | Smith, Henry | New York | |
| 1 | H A | Shain, Jno | Milwaukee | Sep. 15, 1863 |
| 1 | H A | Shawon, Patrick | Milwaukee | Sept. 11, 1863 |
| 1 | H A | Schafer, Thos | Milwaukee | Sept. 15, 1863 |
| 1 | H A | Smith, James | Alexandria, Va | Aug. 9, 1865 |
| 1 | L A | Stiltz, Joseph | La Crosse | Sept. 26, 1862 |
| 4 | L A | Sturtevant, C. L | | Mar. 27, 1862 |
| 7 | L A | Staymer, Frank S | Milwaukee | Mar. .., 1863 |
| 9 | L A | Schafer, Charles | Fort Lyon | Aug. 27, 1864 |
| 9 | L A | Schafer, Geo | Fort Lyon | Aug. 31, 1865 |
| 10 | L A | Sherman, Peter | Hartland | Apr. 30, 1862 |

## T

| Reg't. | | Name. | Residence. | Date. |
|---|---|---|---|---|
| 1 | I | Thomas, Samuel | | |
| 1 | I | Thomson, Thos | | Nov. .., 1862 |
| 2 | I | Turner, Wilber | Lodi | May 13, 1863 |
| 3 | I | Thrall, John | Milwaukee | |
| 3 | I | Tenson, Z. D | Wisconsin | Apr. 2, 1865 |
| 3 | I | Tucker, Daniel | Wisconsin | Apr. 2, 1865 |
| 5 | I | Thomson, Henry | Taycheeda | Sep. 30, 1863 |
| 5 | I | Truax, Isaac | | June 3, 1865 |
| 6 | I | Tuttle, Andrew M | | Mar. 21, 1862 |
| 6 | I | Tracey, Henry | | July 15, 1861 |
| 7 | I | Taber, Wm | | Aug. 30, 1862 |
| 7 | I | Thomas, James M | | Oct. 6, 1862 |
| 7 | I | Thomas, James | | Dec. 8, 1862 |
| 7 | I | Thompson, Jos. H | | |
| 8 | I | Truman, Eddy | Algoma | |
| 10 | I | Thurston, Alfred L | Lancaster | Aug. 7, 1862 |
| 10 | I | Thompson, David | Delavan | Dec. 1, 1862 |
| 11 | I | Thompson, Creighton | | Dec. 5, 1861 |
| 12 | I | Talbot, Daniel L | Bear Creek | Jan. 2, 1862 |
| 12 | I | Ticko, Samuel | Green Bay | June 27, 1865 |
| 12 | I | Turley, Joseph | Janesville | July 10, 1865 |
| 13 | I | Turner, Wm | Fond du Lac | Sept. 1, 1865 |
| 13 | I | Talmadge, Jas | | |
| 13 | I | Townsend, Daniel H | | |
| 14 | I | Taylor, Rob't | | Jan. 18, 1863 |
| 14 | I | Tuttle, John W | | Jan. 18, 1863 |
| 14 | I | Tuttle, Edwin R | | Aug. 12, 1862 |
| 15 | I | Thompson, Peter | Decorah, Iowa | |
| 15 | I | Thompson, John | | |
| 15 | I | Thompson, S | Mc Farland | |
| 17 | I | Thomas, Adolph | | Aug. 15, 1862 |
| 17 | I | Tinnon, Marks | | Apr. 20, 1862 |
| 17 | I | Trukey, John | | Mar. 19, 1862 |

| *Reg't.* | | *Name* | *Residence.* | *Date.* |
|---|---|---|---|---|
| 17 | I | Traynor, Jas | | Apr. 6, 1862 |
| 17 | I | Teague, Chas. R | Beloit | Feb. 10, 1864 |
| 17 | I | Tousley, Henry | | June 17, 1862 |
| 17 | I | Thompson, Samuel | | Jan. 16, 1863 |
| 52 | I | Turner, Wm | | |
| 51 | I | Taylor, Jno | Milwaukee | Mar. 8, 1865 |
| 51 | I | Thompson, Wm | Milwaukee | Apr. 20, 1865 |
| 50 | I | Turlson, Christopher | Crawford Co | Sep. 8, 1865 |
| 50 | I | Thatcher, Reuben H | Monroe Co | Sep. 9, 1865 |
| 50 | I | Tripp, Wm | Prescott | Aug. 1, 1865 |
| 50 | I | Thompson, Erwin | Madison | Aug. 28, 1865 |
| 49 | I | Terrill, Frank | West Point | Oct. 6, 1865 |
| 48 | I | Trage, Fred'k | Milwaukee | Feb. 28, 1865 |
| 48 | I | Thrall, Willis E | Omro | Sept. 16, 1865 |
| 48 | I | Thompson, Chas | Omro | Sep. 19, 1865 |
| 47 | I | Thompson, Jas | | Feb. 22, 1865 |
| 44 | I | Terry, James | | Jan. 7, 1865 |
| 44 | I | Tilletson, Jno. S | Madison | Feb. 15, 1865 |
| 43 | I | Trumbell, David | Milwaukee | Sep. 17, 1864 |
| 42 | I | Thompson, Thomas | Janesville | |
| 38 | I | Todd, David W | Janesville | Jan. 14, 1865 |
| 37 | I | Thomas, John | Janesville | Apr. 20, 1864 |
| 37 | I | Thompson, Wm | La Crosse | June 25, 1864 |
| 36 | I | Tinker, Geo. M | Madison | May 7, 1864 |
| 35 | I | Thirs, Jacob | Milwaukee | Jan. 29, 1866 |
| 34 | I | Thill, Franz | Belginm | Jan. 15, 1863 |
| 34 | I | Thurber, Dan'l | Clyde | Feb. 1, 1863 |
| 34 | I | Thegitz, Chrstof | Crystal Lake | Dec. 19, 1862 |
| 34 | I | Tschudi, Christian | Richfield | Dec. 31, 1862 |
| 34 | I | Travis, Geo | Kewaska | Dec. 28, 1862 |
| 34 | I | Theis, Mathias | Farmington | Jan. 8, 1863 |
| 34 | I | Tagatz, Ferdinand | Crystal Lake | Jan. 31, 1863 |
| 34 | I | Trafford, John | Kingston | Jan. 31, 1863 |
| 34 | I | Tim, Michael | Shields | Jan. 31, 1863 |
| 33 | I | Tennison, Joseph | Jefferson City, Mo | Oct. 7, 1862 |
| 33 | I | Thompson, Wm | Tuscumbia, Mo | Nov. 2, 1862 |
| 33 | I | Topperain, Wm | Muscoda | June 18, 1863 |
| 32 | I | Tyler, Benj | | Oct. 7, 1862 |
| 32 | I | Thomas, Joseph | Duck Creek | June 1, 1863 |
| 32 | I | Therber, Seth | Calamus | Dec. 16, 1864 |
| 31 | I | Thomson, Mat | | July 16, 1864 |
| 30 | I | Tubbs, Edward | Ridgeford | Aug. .., 1862 |
| 30 | I | Torpy, Mathew | Mineral Point | June 17, 1864 |
| 30 | I | Tuttle, Chester | Ft. Atkinson | Aug. 7, 1865 |
| 29 | I | Taylor, Jno | Waterloo | Jan 23, 1863 |
| 29 | I | Tadden, Orlando | Williamstown | Feb. 28, 1863 |
| 29 | I | Tompkins, Robert | Jefferson | Oct. 22, 1863 |
| 28 | I | Timlin, Patrick | Whitewater | Dec. 20, 1862 |
| 27 | I | Topliff, Libbeas | | |
| 26 | I | Trester, Herbert | Sheboygan | May .., 1863 |
| 26 | I | Tode, Adolph | Manitowoc | Aug. 27, 1863 |
| 24 | I | Theleman, Christ | Milwaukee | Jan. 8, 1863 |
| 23 | I | Thomas, Jno | | May 7, 1864 |
| 22 | I | Thomas, Sam'l. J | Berlin | Jan. 27, 1863 |
| 21 | I | Taylor, Abram | | Oct. 21, 1862 |
| 21 | I | Thomas, Peter | Oakfield | Apr. .., .... |
| 20 | I | Thrasher, C | Waukesha | |
| 19 | I | Thompson, Martin | La Crosse | May 29, 1862 |
| 19 | I | Turner, Luther | Rodolph | June 2, 1862 |

| *Reg't.* | | *Name.* | *Residence.* | *Date.* |
|---|---|---|---|---|
| 19 | I | Turner, Wm. | Pt. Andrew | Oct. 8, 1864 |
| 19 | I | Trousdale, Wm. J. | Pt. Andrew | Jan. 20, 1865 |
| 19 | I | Thilkie, Wm | Oshkosh | |
| 18 | I | Tucker, Chas. H. | Plover | |
| 18 | I | Tonlace, Marion E. | Columbus | |
| 18 | I | Taylor, Jasper | Plover | Aug. 3, 1862 |
| 1 | C | Ten Eyck, Chas. H. | Brodhead | Jan. 15, 1864 |
| 1 | C | Tubbs, John H. | Ripon | Nov. 21, 1863 |
| 1 | C | Thompson, Edward | | Nov. 1, 1861 |
| 1 | C | Towsley, Albert D. | Jefferson | Dec. 2, 1864 |
| 1 | C | Thomas, Edward J. | Cape Giradeau, Mo | |
| 2 | C | Terry, Albert | Janesville | Oct. 14, 1865 |
| 2 | C | Tracy, Jno. A. | Janesville | Oct. 16, 1865 |
| 2 | C | Truman, Jno | La Crosse | July 22, 1865 |
| 2 | C | Teague, Wm | Arkansas | Sep. 29, 1862 |
| 2 | C | Tompkins, Chas | Eldorado | June 23, 1865 |
| 3 | C | Thomas, Joseph | Janesville | Jan. 9, 1865 |
| 3 | C | Thomas, Edward N. | Platteville | Dec. 31, 1862 |
| 3 | C | Thielkee, Wm | Oshkosh | Feb. 27, 1862 |
| 4 | C | Thrasle, C. | Fond du Lac | |
| 4 | C | Thomas, Timothy | Jefferson | July 14, 1865 |
| 4 | C | Thompson, Michael | | Jan. 17, 1864 |
| 4 | C | Trempealeau, Joseph | Baton Rouge, La | July 23, 1865 |
| 1 | H A | Thomas, Wm | Racine | |
| 1 | L A | Thompson, Barnard | | July 19, 1864 |
| 1 | L A | Thompson, Wm | Racine | Jan. 26, 1862 |
| 7 | L A | Todd, Rob't | Milwaukee | Jan. .., 1863 |
| 7 | L A | Topliff, Edward A. | Milwaukee | Oct. 26, 1862 |
| 8 | L A | Turck, Albert | Madison | Apr. 7, 1863 |

## U

| | | | | |
|---|---|---|---|---|
| 17 | I | Ulrich, Julius W. | Milwaukee | Oct. 15, 1864 |
| 17 | I | Ulrich, Henry | Milwaukeee | Sep. 1, 1863 |
| 34 | I | Ulrich, Adolf | Montello | Jan. 31, 1863 |
| 26 | I | Uerling, Franz | Lamartine | May .., 1863 |
| 20 | I | Underwood, Jas. H. | Little Grant | Sep. 11, 1863 |
| 1 | C | Upson, Joseph B. | Richfield | May 11, 1864 |
| 1 | H A | Underkofler, James | | |

## V

| | | | | |
|---|---|---|---|---|
| 2 | I | Vantassel, John N. | Newville | Apr. 21, 1862 |
| 2 | I | Vollusweider, John | Grant Co | |
| 5 | I | Vreasy, Albert | Oshkosh | Sep. 16, 1864 |
| 5 | I | Vanetta, James E. | Milwaukee | Sep. 30, 1862 |
| 5 | I | Van Ett, James H. | | |
| 11 | I | Vosler, Geo. W. | | Feb. 8, 1863 |
| 17 | I | Vleit, Jasper | | Feb. 28, 1862 |
| 51 | I | Veneltie, Jacob | La Crosse | July 16, 1865 |
| 48 | I | Van Apps, Jas R. | Milwaukee | Mar. 5, 1865 |
| 43 | I | Vale, Ambrose | Milwaukee | Oct. 13, 1864 |
| 38 | I | Vaneltan, Wm. H. | Janesville | Sep. 18, 1864 |
| 35 | I | Vidal, Joseph | Portland | Apr. 11, 1864 |
| 35 | I | Veley, Henry | Delavan | Nov. 27, 1865 |
| 34 | I | Vantelet, Alex | Kewaunee | Jan. 31, 1863 |
| 33 | I | Vaughan, David | St. Louis | Sep. 25, 1862 |
| 32 | I | Van Ness, Moses | Oshkosh | Jan. 3, 1864 |
| 28 | I | Vanitten, Wm | Waukesha | Dec. 14, 1862 |
| 21 | I | Vaughn, Daniel W. | | Oct. 8, 1862 |

| Reg't. | | Name. | Residence. | Date. |
|---|---|---|---|---|
| 18 | I | Vaughn, Francis | Grand Rapids | |
| 18 | I | Vanderwort, Albert | Milwaukee | |
| 2 | C | Van Valkenberg, Myron | Darien | July 16, 1862 |
| 7 | L A | Valentine, Rowilla | Racine | Dec. 29, 1863 |
| 13 | L A | Vaughan, Mason D | Milwaukee | Nov. 24, 1863 |

## W

| Reg't. | | Name. | Residence. | Date. |
|---|---|---|---|---|
| 1 | I | Wattles, Delos M | | Sep. 28, 1862 |
| 1 | I | Williams, Samuel C | | Dec. 26, 1862 |
| 2 | I | Warsru, James | La Crosse | Oct. 10, 1862 |
| 2 | I | Webster, Drinnison | Canada East | May .., 1862 |
| 2 | I | Williams, George W | Cambria | Nov. 16, 1862 |
| 2 | I | Wilcox, Oramel | Harmony | |
| 2 | I | Wisor, Jerod | Portage | Jan. .., 1863 |
| 2 | I | Weatherby, Joseph | Westport | Dec. 8, 1862 |
| 3 | I | Wentworth, Amos A | | Sep. 16, 1863 |
| 3 | I | Williams, Albert J | | Feb. .., 1864 |
| 3 | I | Webb, James | | |
| 3 | I | Weidant Jacob | | |
| 3 | I | Wardsworth, R. J | | Feb. 26, 1862 |
| 3 | I | Whitney, Frank R | | Oct. 22, 1862 |
| 5 | I | Welty, Henry | | July 1, 1862 |
| 5 | I | White, Ceylon L | Fond du Lac | Mar. 15, 1865 |
| 5 | I | Welty, Henry | | |
| 5 | I | Whitman, George | Taycheedah | Dec. 28, 1863 |
| 6 | I | Wimple, Wyndot | Madison | |
| 6 | I | Will, Paul | | Aug. 7, 1861 |
| 6 | I | Wells, Samuel | | Nov. 28, 1861 |
| 6 | I | Warren, Almon G | | Nov. 28, 1861 |
| 6 | I | Whitewater, Thompson | | July 26, 1865 |
| 6 | I | Weatherby, George | Westfield | July 8, 1861 |
| 7 | I | Williams, Elyat | | Aug. 10, 1862 |
| 7 | I | Williams, Rolland | | Aug. 30, 1862 |
| 7 | I | Wraid, Harrison L | | Aug. 29, 1862 |
| 7 | I | Welch, John | Milwaukee | Dec. 19, 1864 |
| 7 | I | Watson, Frank O | Milwaukee | Feb. 11, 1865 |
| 7 | I | Whitham, Wm | | |
| 8 | I | Whitney, Seldon | | |
| 8 | I | Welland, Green | | July 15, 1864 |
| 9 | I | Weber, Frank | Milwaukee | Aug. 25, 1864 |
| 9 | I | Weilerman, Henry | Milwaukee | Aug. 5, 1864 |
| 9 | I | Wittmer, Charles | Prairie du Chien | |
| 9 | I | Wirth, Adam | Milwaukee | |
| 9 | I | Wozinack, Franz | Milwaukee | Dec. 28, 1865 |
| 10 | I | Winchell, Topping H | | |
| 11 | I | Waddle, George A | | Mar. 10, 1863 |
| 11 | I | Witcomb, Rufus | | Nov. 4, 1862 |
| 11 | I | Wilcox, George | New Orleans, La | Apr. 22, 1864 |
| 11 | I | White, Christian | | Aug. 1, 1865 |
| 11 | I | Wrought, Don. D | | Aug. 18, 1865 |
| 12 | I | Williams, John | Ridgeway | Jan. 5, 1861 |
| 12 | I | Wiley, Pratt J | Durand's Bluff | Aug. 1, 1864 |
| 13 | I | White, John | Milwaukee | Mar. 1, 1865 |
| 13 | I | Webster, Emmet A | Northville | June 15, 1865 |
| 13 | I | Wiley, Henry | Northville | June 24, 1865 |
| 13 | I | Winney, James R | Sugar Creek | June 15, 1865 |
| 13 | I | Weimms, Henderson | Pinney Factory | June 23, 1865 |
| 13 | I | West, Ralph | Leroy | July 20, 1865 |

| Reg't. | | Name. | Residence. | Date. |
|---|---|---|---|---|
| 13 | I | Wells, Edwin J. | | |
| 13 | I | Weed, Ulynn W | | |
| 13 | I | Watkins, John | | |
| 13 | I | Whipple, Ira E. | | |
| 13 | I | West, Alanson L. | | |
| 13 | I | Wright, Wm. M | La Prairie | Apr. 18, 1863 |
| 13 | I | Windsor, Philip | | Nov. 10, 1864 |
| 13 | I | Welch, Wm. H. | Milwaukee | Nov. 7, 1865 |
| 14 | I | Woodworth, George | Fort Howard | Nov. 19, 1864 |
| 14 | I | Whitney, George H. | | |
| 14 | I | Warren, Elijah T | | July 7, 1862 |
| 14 | I | Welch, Cyrus | | Jan. 11, 1862 |
| 14 | I | Walsh, Michael J | | June 30, 1862 |
| 14 | I | Wold, Ole | | |
| 14 | I | Wagener, George | Chicago, Ill | |
| 14 | I | Watts, William | Galeslig, Ind | |
| 16 | I | Wilson, George W | Leroy | Sep. 18, 1864 |
| 17 | I | Waunaka, William | | Mar. 20, 1862 |
| 17 | I | Woods, Thomas | | Apr. 10, 1862 |
| 17 | I | Walsh, John | | Aug. 9, 1862 |
| 17 | I | Warrick, J. | Vicksburg, Miss | Nov. 18, 1864 |
| 17 | I | Wilcox, John | | Apr. 20, 1862 |
| 17 | I | Whitaker, Jacob | | Apr. 14, 1862 |
| 52 | I | Williams, Charles | | Mar. 3, 1865 |
| 52 | I | Williams, James | | Mar. 3, 1865 |
| 52 | I | Wissendorf, Fritz | | |
| 52 | I | Walker, Henry | | |
| 51 | I | Wheeler, Charles H | Milwaukee | Mar. 4, 1865 |
| 51 | I | White, Frederick | Milwaukee | Apr. 20, 1865 |
| 51 | I | Warner, Charles | Milwaukee | Mar. 28, 1865 |
| 51 | I | Wilke, Charles | Cedarburg | |
| 50 | I | Wilson, Charles | Burke | Mar. 26, 1865 |
| 50 | I | Winters, Nelson W | Vernon Co | Aug. 25, 1865 |
| 50 | I | Walrack, Michael | La Fayette | Aug. 28, 1865 |
| 50 | I | Winchell, William | Prescott | Aug. 26, 1865 |
| 50 | I | Williams, John W | Ridgeway | April 1, 1865 |
| 50 | I | Williams, William J | Watertown | July 10, 1865 |
| 50 | I | Wilbur, Jewett | Ashton | Aug. 30, 1865 |
| 50 | I | Webber, Peter | Beaver Dam | Aug. 25, 1865 |
| 50 | I | Whitaker, Gaylord | Princeton | Aug. 28, 1865 |
| 50 | I | White, Horace F | Wonewoc | July 30, 1865 |
| 50 | I | Winderlich, John W | | Sep. 1, 1865 |
| 50 | I | Wey, William H | | Sep. 4, 1865 |
| 48 | I | Williams, Freeman | Eau Claire | Sep. 17, 1865 |
| 48 | I | Walthers, Bernhard | Belvidere | Sep. 7, 1865 |
| 48 | I | Westower, William | Milwaukee | Feb. 24, 1865 |
| 48 | I | Walfreen, P. H | Geneva | May 6, 1865 |
| 48 | I | Weed, John | Fox Lake | Sep. 7, 1865 |
| 47 | I | Welsch, John | | Feb. 22, 1865 |
| 47 | I | White, William | | Feb. 22, 1865 |
| 47 | I | Wilson, Charles | | Mar. 2, 1865 |
| 47 | I | Wing, George W | Jefferson | Jan. 28, 1865 |
| 44 | I | Wilson, William | | Jan. 7, 1865 |
| 44 | I | Wagner, Paul | | Jan. 7, 1865 |
| 44 | I | Wild, George | | Feb. 18, 1865 |
| 44 | I | Wade, Owen | Milwaukee | Feb. 21, 1865 |
| 44 | I | Wardell, M. R | Orion | Feb. 13, 1865 |
| 44 | I | Waterton, Phillip | Madison | June 22, 1865 |
| 44 | I | Wiley, John | Milwaukee | |

| Reg't. | | Name. | Residence. | Date. |
|---|---|---|---|---|
| 44 | I | Wilson, Edward | Milwaukee | |
| 43 | I | Warren, James | Hazel Green | Oct. 7, 1864 |
| 43 | I | Woods, Thomas J | La Crosse | Oct. 7, 1864 |
| 43 | I | West, James | Milwaukee | Sep. 7, 1864 |
| 39 | I | Wright, James H | Milford | June 10, 1864 |
| 38 | I | Wilson, George | Milwaukee | Aug. 20, 1864 |
| 38 | I | Wall, James | Milwaukee | Aug. 20, 1864 |
| 38 | I | Willow, James | Milwaukee | Aug. 20, 1864 |
| 38 | I | Weaver, Frederick | Milwaukee | Aug. 22, 1864 |
| 36 | I | Wilson, Charles J | Madison | April 6, 1864 |
| 36 | I | Wilson, Elijah D | Gilmanton | May .., 1864 |
| 35 | I | Webb, Jary B | Milwaukee | April 1, 1864 |
| 35 | I | Wittman, Herman | Theresa | Nov. 19, 1864 |
| 35 | I | Warer, Phillip | Milwaukee | Dec. 19, 1864 |
| 35 | I | Walroff, Jacob | Milwaukee | Feb. 18, 1866 |
| 35 | I | Wells, John M | Janesville | Jan. 8, 1864 |
| 34 | I | Weber, Peter | Mequon | Jan. 19, 1863 |
| 34 | I | Wait, V. H. B | Racine | Dec. 29, 1863 |
| 34 | I | Wylor, John | Paris | Jan. 31, 1863 |
| 34 | I | Wohl, Michael | Marathon | Feb. 5, 1863 |
| 34 | I | Wickbold, John | Marathon | Feb. 2, 1863 |
| 34 | I | Westerberg, Frederick | Greenville | Dec. 29, 1862 |
| 34 | I | Westerberg, William | Greenville | Dec. 29, 1862 |
| 34 | I | Wehlitz, Charles | Milwaukee | Dec. 31, 1862 |
| 34 | I | Wager, Peter | West Bend | Jan. 31, 1863 |
| 34 | I | Wart, Henry V | Racine | July 29, 1863 |
| 34 | I | Weis, Jacob | Milwaukee | Jan. 15, 1863 |
| 34 | I | Waterhouse, David | Clyman | Jan. 31, 1863 |
| 34 | I | Weldon, Smith | Hartford | Jan. 31, 1863 |
| 34 | I | Wickbold, John | Mishicott | Jan. 15, 1863 |
| 34 | I | Williams, John | Somers | |
| 34 | I | Werner, Ernst | Mecan | Jan. 31, 1863 |
| 34 | I | Welsch, Martin | Milwaukee | Dec. 16, 1862 |
| 33 | I | Whalen, P. | St. Louis | Nov. 26, 1862 |
| 33 | I | Wilson, Anthony | Kenosha | July 28, 1865 |
| 32 | I | Walker, William H | | Dec. 20, 1862 |
| 32 | I | Welch, James | | Oct. 31, 1862 |
| 32 | I | Warner, William E | Oshkosh | Feb. 22, 1864 |
| 32 | I | Worden, Charles E | | |
| 32 | I | Wood, Louis H. | Byron | Jan. 23, 1863 |
| 31 | I | Woodward, David | Dodgeville | Mar. 6, 1863 |
| 31 | I | Wright, William | Madison | Feb. 4, 1863 |
| 31 | I | Williams, Henry | Milwaukee | Feb. 18, 1863 |
| 31 | I | Williams, John | Waterford | Apr. 29, 1864 |
| 30 | I | Wars, James E | Plainfield | Nov. 2, 1862 |
| 30 | I | Weaver, David | Leon | Mar. 19, 1863 |
| 30 | I | Watery, Francis | Chippewa Falls | June 21, 1863 |
| 30 | I | Whitcome, James W | Milwaukee | Apr. 25, 1864 |
| 29 | I | Wallace, Jonas | Horicon | Mar. 14, 1863 |
| 29 | I | Wilson, James | | Feb. 5, 1865 |
| 28 | I | Wilber, David E | Delavan | Nov. 29, 1862 |
| 28 | I | Wallace, James | Horicon | Aug. 14, 1863 |
| 28 | I | White, Seymour | Spring Prairie | Apr. 30, 1864 |
| 28 | I | Wheeler, John C | Waukesha | Apr. 7, 1864 |
| 28 | I | Warsley, Jones | Milwaukee | |
| 28 | I | Williams, Harry | Milwaukee | |
| 28 | I | Woolfrom, Porter H | Waukesha | May 5, 1865 |
| 28 | I | Williams, Allen | Genessee | Nov. 30, 1863 |
| 27 | I | Weiers, William | Wilson | Oct. 8, 1862 |

| *Reg't.* | *Name.* | *Residence.* | *Date.* |
|---|---|---|---|
| 27 I | Worden, Milo | Scott | Mar. 18, 1863 |
| 27 I | Watson, Jackson W. | Milwaukee | Mar. 26, 1863 |
| 27 I | Welch, M | | |
| 26 I | Wenig, Oswald | Milwaukee | July 4, 1863 |
| 24 I | Wintzenberg, Henry F. | Milwaukee | |
| 24 I | Wright, Thomas | Milwaukee | Oct. 15, 1862 |
| 22 I | Walsh, Thomas | Geneva | May .., 1863 |
| 21 I | Wilson, Daniel E. | | Oct. 20, 1862 |
| 21 I | Woodards, James L. | Menasha | May 20, 1863 |
| 21 I | Walker, Charles A | Menasha | Aug. 7, 1863 |
| 21 I | Washburn, James E. | Oshkosh | Oct. 13, 1864 |
| 20 I | Willis, Ira A. | Waukesha | |
| 20 I | Welch, Edward | Milwaukee | Mar. 31, 1864 |
| 19 I | Waldron, Henry E | Reedsburg | May 29, 1862 |
| 19 I | Watch, Thomas | Waterford | Feb. 18, 1862 |
| 19 I | Weber, Philip | Oshkosh | June 2, 1862 |
| 19 I | Welkey, Frederick | La Crosse | 1862 |
| 18 I | Williams, Anson H. | Forrest | |
| 18 I | Woodruff, David C | Ripon | Aug. 18, 1862 |
| 18 I | White, John H. | Taycheedah | Mar. 30, 1862 |
| 1 C | Williams, Geo | Utica | |
| 1 C | Wood, Geo. B. | Madison, Ark. | Apr. 18, 1862 |
| 1 C | Watrona, Elish | Waupun | Dec. .., 1862 |
| 1 C | White, Jno. W. | Richford | Dec. 3, 1864 |
| 1 C | Wilson, Edward | Milwaukee | Mar. 14, 1864 |
| 2 C | Wood, M. W | Lancaster | |
| 2 C | White, Chas | Lancaster | Oct. 10, 1865 |
| 2 C | Warren, Elijah | Burke | July 25, 1865 |
| 2 C | Wilson, N. H. | Burke | July 25, 1865 |
| 2 C | Walsh, Francis | Lafayette Co. | June 17, 1865 |
| 2 C | Williams, Wm | Fond du Lac | Feb. 20, 1862 |
| 2 C | Wright, John | | Oct. 21, 1862 |
| 2 C | Wilstee, Ransom | Eau Claire | Oct. .., 1862 |
| 2 C | Wilkins, Chas | Memphis, Tenn. | |
| 3 C | Webb, Wardonies W. | | June 21, 1865 |
| 3 C | Wesh, Wm | | June 21, 1865 |
| 3 C | Wilkinson, Frank A. | Janesville | Aug. 26, 1865 |
| 3 C | Wetmore, Leander | Janesville | June 22, 1865 |
| 3 C | Williams, Richard | Janesville | June 22, 1865 |
| 3 C | Wright, Peter W. | Columbus | Apr. 25, 1862 |
| 3 C | Welch, Samuel | Fairplay. | Dec. 14. 1861 |
| 3 C | Williams, Wm | Van Buren, Ark. | Apr. 30, 1864 |
| 3 C | Warner, John J. | | Oct. 22, 1862 |
| 3 C | Whitney, Ezra W. | Oconto | June 13, 1864 |
| 3 C | Woodall, Marion | Appleton | Oct. 24, 1863 |
| 3 C | Withers, Stephen P. | | .., 1862 |
| 3 C | Withers, James | | .., 1862 |
| 3 C | Weeks, Wm. M. | Merton | Oct. 20, 1862 |
| 3 C | Waters, Joseph W. | Fort Smith | Mar. 4, 1864 |
| 4 C | Watson, Fred'k | Baton Rouge | |
| 4 C | Watch, James | Madison | |
| 4 C | Walker, F. M. | | Dec. 28, 1863 |
| 1 H A | Wilkins, Henry B. | East Troy | |
| 1 H A | Wilson, Albert C. | Milwaukee | Oct. 17, 1864 |
| 1 H A | Watson, Henry D. | Alexandria, Va. | Jan. 20, 1865 |
| 4 L A | Wallice, Albert | Portsmouth | July 2, 1865 |
| 8 L A | Ward, Chas. L. | Lindower | Oct. 30, 1862 |
| 13 L A | Walleck, Henry | Milwaukee | Nov. 10, 1863 |

| Reg't. | | Name. | Residence. | Date. |
|---|---|---|---|---|
| | | **Y** | | |
| 5 | I | Youmans, Richard N. | Stockbridge | .., 1861 |
| 16 | I | Young, Isaiah | Mauston | Aug. 18, 1862 |
| 17 | I | Young, Ja. K. | | Aug. 5, 1862 |
| 17 | I | Yeller, Valentine | | July 2, 1865 |
| 1 | C | Young, Daniel | Ripon | Dec. 15, 1863 |
| 2 | C | Young, Calvin | La Crosse | July 9, 1863 |
| 1 | H A | Yost, Wm | Elkhorn | Mar. 27, 1864 |
| 24 | I | Young, Benj. D | Milwaukee | Oct. 22, 1862 |
| 18 | I | Young, P. H | Berlin | |
| | | **Z** | | |
| 1 | C | Zenter, Rudolph | | Nov. 22, 1861 |
| 3 | C | Zollinger, Z. Joseph | La Crosse | Dec. 31, 1862 |
| 1 | H A | Zehner, Geo. W | Alexandria, Va | Aug. 6, 1865 |
| 34 | I | Zrunert, Wm | Cedarburg | July 30, 1863 |
| 34 | I | Zimmer, Wm | Menomonee | July 10, 1863 |
| 34 | I | Zome, Jacob | Milwaukee | Dec. 16, 1862 |
| 24 | I | Zarbocke, Henry | Milwaukee | |
| 21 | I | Zentner, Jacob | Fond du Lac | April .., 1864 |

---

STATE OF WISCONSIN  
OFFICE OF THE SECRETARY OF STATE, } SS.

I, Thomas S. Allen, Secretary of State of the State of Wisconsin, do hereby certify, that the foregoing list contains the names of all deserters from Wisconsin military organizations, together with the place of residence and date of desertion of each, as appears from the certified list of deserters procured from the War Department of the United States, pursuant to the provisions of section 1, of chapter 67, of the General Laws of 1867, corrected from the records of the office of the Adjutant General of the State of Wisconsin.

IN WITNESS WHEREOF, I have hereunto set my hand and affixed the Great Seal of the State of Wisconsin, at the capitol in Madison, this 9th day of July, A. D., 1857.

[L. S.]

THOS. S. ALLEN,  
Secretary of State.

# NON-REPORTING DRAFTED MEN AND DESERTERS AFTER REPORTING, UNDER VARIOUS DRAFTS.

## A

| *Name.* | *Residence.* | *Date.* |
|---|---|---|
| Astala, Johann | Milwaukee | Nov. 9, 1863 |
| Amerot, John | do | Nov. 9, 1863 |
| Ahern, Michael | do | Nov. 9, 1863 |
| Anderson, Hans | do | Nov. 9, 1863 |
| Allison, Thomas | do | Sep. 20, 1864 |
| Astor, Joseph | do | Sep. 20, 1864 |
| Allis, Thomas | do | Sept. 20, 1864 |
| Andrews, Wilbert | do | Sept. 20, 1864 |
| Anderson, Randall | do | Jan. 11, 1865 |
| Albert, J | do | Jan. 11, 1865 |
| Ahren, Thomas | do | Jan. 11, 1865 |
| Adams, Wm | do | Nov. 14, 1864 |
| Anderson, John | do | Nov. 10, 1863 |
| Allsop, John | do | Sep. 21, 1864 |
| Ainsworth, L | do | Nov. 10, 1863 |
| Anderson, John | do | Nov. 10, 1863 |
| Anderson, Olof | do | Nov. 10, 1863 |
| Ald, Charles | do | Nov. 10, 1863 |
| Albert, Henrich | do | Nov. 10, 1863 |
| Arnold, Samuel T | do | Sep. 21, 1864 |
| Ande, Stephen | do | Sep. 21, 1864 |
| Allis, L | do | Nov. 16, 1864 |
| Arestin, Gunison | do | Nov. 10, 1863 |
| Aolkey, Wm | do | Nov. 11, 1863 |
| Askmel, Charles | do | Nov. 25, 1864 |
| Andt, Ferdinand | do | Sep. 21, 1864 |
| Aeeken, Frederick | do | Nov. 25, 1864 |
| Ackerman, Joseph | do | Jan. 26, 1865 |
| Albrecht, Johann | do | Jan. 26, 1865 |
| Anderson, John | do | Sep. 22, 1864 |
| Algrim, Johann | do | Sep. 22, 1864 |
| Altring, John | Granville | Sep. 22, 1864 |
| Alias, Carl | | |
| Anthony, Joseph | Greenfield | Sep. 21, 1864 |
| Aadanes, Henry C | Lake | Sep. 22, 1864 |
| Abbott, Frederick | Oak Creek | Sep. 22, 1864 |
| Acher, Michael | do | Sep. 22, 1864 |
| Anderson, Warren C | Racine | Nov. 11, 1863 |
| Anderson, Elisha | do | Sept. 24, 1864 |
| Anderson, J. S | do | Sept. 24, 1864 |
| Anderson, David | do | Sept. 22, 1864 |

| *Name.* | *Residence.* | *Date.* |
|---|---|---|
| Anert, George | Racine, | Sept. 22, 1864 |
| Asperland, Henry | Dover | Nov. 11, 1864 |
| Airey, Nehemiah | do | Nov. 11, 1864 |
| Anderson, James | do | Dec. 10, 1864 |
| Alexander, Levi | Raymond | Sept. 23, 1864 |
| Anderson, Ole | do | Sept. 23, 1864 |
| Alf, William | Wheatland | Nov. 12, 1863 |
| Adamson, Martin | Bristol | Sep. 24, 1864 |
| Alden, John | Pleasant Prairie | Nov. 12, 1863 |
| Abbot, William | Whitewater | Nov. 12, 1863 |
| Altenburg, Henry | East Troy | Sep. 26, 1864 |
| Allison, William | Summit | Sep. 22, 1864 |
| Armstrong, Alexander | do | Nov. 30, 1864 |
| Allen, Dwin | Oconomowoc | Sep. 22, 1864 |
| Austin, John | Waukesha | Nov. 12, 1863 |
| Arlington, Wilhelm | Menomonee | Dec. 1, 1864 |
| Aswold, John | Brookfield | Sep. 23, 1864 |
| Annis, James | Fond du Lac | Nov. 19, 1863 |
| Adams, Hiram | Eden | Nov. 19, 1863 |
| Annis, Levi | Oakfield | Nov. 19, 1863 |
| Allen, Jason | Waupun | Nov. 19, 1863 |
| Anes, James | Emmett | Oct. 11, 1864 |
| Axley, David | Clyman | Nov. 20, 1863 |
| Armstrong, D. | Oak Grove | Nov. 20, 1863 |
| Achtenhagen, Fred | Watertown | Nov. 20, 1863 |
| Apfel, George | Leroy | Oct. 4, 1864 |
| Auner, George | do | Oct. 4, 1864 |
| Aust, John | do | Oct. 4, 1864 |
| Allerton, O. H. P | do | Dec. 1, 1864 |
| Ainsworth, Charles | Lomira | Dec. 1, 1864 |
| Arntonn, Conrad | Herman | Nov. 20, 1863 |
| Arnoldi, August | do | Oct. 18, 1863 |
| Anderson, Oliver | Erin | Dec. 1, 1864 |
| Albright, Charles | Barton | Oct. 12, 1864 |
| Abel, Henry | do | Dec. 1, 1864 |
| Abeliter, Christopher | do | Dec. 1, 1864 |
| Abbott, E | do | Dec. 1, 1864 |
| Aemberg, Engelbert | Richfield | Oct. 12. 1864 |
| Albright, Levi | Farmington | Oct. 18, 1864 |
| Asselman, Frank | do | Dec. 1, 1864 |
| Aunse, Joseph | Belgium | Nov. 21, 1863 |
| Ackerman, Anton | do | Dec. 1, 1864 |
| Algetg, Henry | Fredonia | Oct. 14, 1864 |
| Armbruster | Cedarburg | Nov. 23, 1863 |
| Anderson, Andros | Grafton | Oct. 13, 1864 |
| Arem, John | do | Dec. 1, 1864 |
| Anderson, Anson | do | Jan. 27, 1865 |
| Aurie, Henry | do | Jan. 27, 1865 |
| Athwart, Ernst | Saukville | Nov. 23, 1863 |
| Allen, Thomas | do | Oct. 14, 1864 |
| Ambsuster, Vincent | Sheboygan | Oct. 25, 1864 |
| Aveyer, Henry | do | Oct. 18, 1864 |
| Adam, Adam | do | Dec. 2, 1864 |
| Adams, Mich | do | .., 1864 |
| Arens, Henry | do | Oct. 18, 1864 |
| Alvis, Henry | Sheboygan Falls | Nov. 24, 1864 |
| Apley, Christian | do | Oct. 25, 1864 |
| Alder, Charles | do | Oct. 25, 1864 |
| Adams, Nicholas G | Holland | Oct. 21, 1864 |

| *Name.* | *Residence.* | *Date.* |
|---|---|---|
| Abbott, Jonathan G | Abbott | Oct. 18, 1864 |
| Amick, James | do | Dec. 2, 1864 |
| Allen, William | Lima | Nov. 12, 1863 |
| Adsit, Lucius S | Deerfied | Nov. 13, 1863 |
| Austin, A. C | Sun Prairie | Oct. 15, 1864 |
| Alson, John | do | Oct. 15, 1864 |
| Anderson, Andrew | Westport | Nov. 13, 1863 |
| Aspiarson, Andrew | Bristol | Nov. 13, 1863 |
| Adams, Rosolor C | Dekorra | Nov. 13, 1863 |
| Adams, Henry | Pacific | Nov. 16, 1863 |
| Aslackson, Arne | Perry | Feb. 27, 1865 |
| Aplit, Thomas | Watertown | Oct. 15, 1864 |
| Ash, Jas | Ridgeway | Nov. 19, 1864 |
| Anderson, John | Wilson | Sept. 26, 1864 |
| Anderson, Hanse | Highland | Sep. 28, 1864 |
| Anderson, Peter | do | Sept. 28, 1864 |
| Anderson, Andrew | do | Sep. 28, 1864 |
| Anding, Edward | do | Oct. 28, 1864 |
| Allen, Thos | Benton | Sept. 29, 1864 |
| Ashworth, Edmund | New Diggings | Sep. 29, 1864 |
| Archibald, Pat'k | Washington | Oct. 3, 1864 |
| Aucker, Herman | La Crosse Co | Nov. 13, 1863 |
| Allen, B. | Chippewa Co | Nov. 20, 1863 |
| Allen, Thos. I | Trempealeau Co | Nov. 18, 1863 |
| Andrews, Amos | Vernon Co | Nov. 18, 1863 |
| Anderson, Thos | do | Nov. 18, 1863 |
| Anderson, Peter | Hamburg | Sep. 21, 1864 |
| Allison, T | Harmony | Sep. 21, 1864 |
| Attikson, Elbridge | | Nov. 18, 1863 |
| Algers, Francis | Kildare | Sep. 19, 1864 |
| Allen, Wm | Lemonweir | Sep. 19, 1864 |
| Abrams, Franklin | Marion | Sep. 19, 1864 |
| Allen, Hiram | Lemonweir | Sep. 31, 1864 |
| Anderson, Andrew | Lanark | Sep. 22, 1864 |
| Adams (or Andrews,) Solomon O | Hull | Sep. 22, 1864 |
| Allen, Geo | Alma | Sep. 23, 1864 |
| Abbott, M. D | Pleasant Valley | Sep. 23, 1864 |
| Ames, Nelson | Trimbell | Sep. 23, 1864 |
| Anderson, Anders | Martell | Nov. 3, 1864 |
| Anderson, Alex | Eau Galle | Sep. 23, 1864 |
| Anderson, Knud | do | Sep. 23, 1864 |
| Anderson, Peter | do | Sep. 23, 1864 |
| Anderson, Gilbert | do | Nov. 3, 1864 |
| Allen, Alanson R | do | Nov. 3, 1864 |
| Anderson, Gilbert | Rush River | Sep. 23, 1864 |
| Aldridge, Alden J | Lincoln | Sep. 26, 1864 |
| Alvison, Thos. S | Easton | Nov. 14, 1864 |
| Ackerman, Wm | do | Sep. 26, 1864 |
| Ackerman, Albert | do | Sep. 26, 1864 |
| Alverson, Rich'd F | Leola | Sep. 26, 1864 |
| Anderson, Nelson | Eau Galle | Sep. 27, 1864 |
| Anderson, Andred | do | Sep. 27, 1864 |
| Anderson, Elling | do | Sep. 27, 1864 |
| Anderson, Helbert | do | Nov. 2, 1864 |
| Allen, Levi | Tomah | Nov. 10, 1864 |
| Anderson, Nels | Door Co | Nov. 20, 1863 |
| Aldrich, Ira C | Charlestown | Nov. 21, 1863 |
| Anderson, Peter | Winnebago Co | Nov. 24, 1863 |
| Atkinson, Thos | Mackford | Nov. 24, 1863 |

| *Name.* | *Residence.* | *Date.* |
|---|---|---|
| Annis, James | Mt. Morris | Nov. 25, 1863 |
| Albie, Ezra | Bloomfield | Nov. 2, 1865 |
| Andrews, Thos | Warren | Nov. 2, 1864 |
| Austin, Seldon | Deerfield | Nov. 2, 1864 |
| Appleton, Nathan | Plainfield | Dec. 29, 1864 |
| Amidon, Henry | Dayton | Nov. 25, 1863 |
| Alender, Chas | Bear Creek | Nov. 5, 1864 |
| A'Heam, Cornelius | Lebanon | Nov. 5, 1864 |
| Amice, Lawrence | Weyawega | Nov. 5, 1864 |
| Ames, E. B | Royalton | Nov. 5, 1864 |
| Anderson, Ole | St. Lawrence | Nov. 5, 1864 |
| Anderson, Hans | do | Nov. 5, 1864 |
| Aspinwall, Alfred | Kaukama | Nov. 27, 1863 |
| Allen, P. B | Appleton | Nov. 27, 1863 |
| Arnold, Edw'd | do | Nov. 27, 1863 |
| Arnold, Chas | Pensaukee | Nov. 28, 1863 |
| Anderson, Andrew | Peshtigo | Nov. 28, 1863 |
| Ansoege, Eugen | Newton | Dec. 29, 1864 |
| Ahlers, Fritz | do | Dec. 29, 1864 |
| Allvin, Joseph | Red River | Dec. 29, 1864 |
| Albert, Victor | Lincoln | Dec. 29, 1864 |
| Albert, Antoine | do | Dec. 29, 1864 |
| Abst, Peter | do | Dec. 29, 1864 |

## B.

| | | |
|---|---|---|
| Bullen, Mortimer | Farmington | Oct. 18, 1864 |
| Bull, George | do | Oct. 18, 1864 |
| Buchler, Leonard | do | Oct. 18, 1864 |
| Balman, Henry | do | Oct. 18, 1864 |
| Brutz, Henry | do | Oct. 18, 1864 |
| Beile, William | do | Dec. 1, 1864 |
| Beadly, John | do | Jan. 27, 1865 |
| Bublitz, August | Jackson | Oct. 11, 1864 |
| Bock, Jacob | do | Oct. 11, 1864 |
| Balelerrins, Henry | do | Oct. 11, 1864 |
| Brutz, John | do | Oct. 11, 1864 |
| Bader, Christian | Germantown | Nov. 21, 1863 |
| Biern, Peter | Belgium | Nov. 21, 1863 |
| Blong, Joseph | do | Nov. 21, 1863 |
| Bloer, Peter | do | Oct. 13, 1864 |
| Blong, Ambrosins | do | Oct. 13, 1864 |
| Brown, Mathias | do | Oct. 13, 1864 |
| Blick, John | do | Oct. 13, 1864 |
| Beser, Nicholas | do | Oct. 13, 1865 |
| Bartel, Peter | do | Oct. 13, 1865 |
| Besch, John | do | Oct. 13, 1864 |
| Berger, Anthony | do | Oct. 13, 1864 |
| Bautz, Michael | do | Oct. 13, 1864 |
| Bieker, Christopher | do | Oct. 13, 1864 |
| Bivier, Charles | do | Oct 13, 1864 |
| Becker, Joseph | do | Oct. 13, 1864 |
| Biever, Baptist | do | Dec. 1, 1864 |
| Borunsch, Michael | do | Dec. 1, 1864 |
| Becker, John | do | Dec. 1, 1864 |
| Bartol, Dronnius | do | Dec. 1, 1864 |
| Beder, David | Lomira | Jan. 27, 1865 |
| Bauer, John | Williamstown | Nov. 20, 1863 |
| Bundey, Smith | Trenton | Nov. 20, 1863 |

| *Name.* | *Residence.* | *Date.* |
|---|---|---|
| Barry, David | Erin | Oct. 12, 1864 |
| Barnes, John | do | Dec. 1, 1864 |
| Burk, Edward | do | Dec. 1, 1864 |
| Bastiam, D. E | Barton | Oct. 12, 1864 |
| Bordan, Peter | do | Oct. 12, 1864 |
| Ball, Julian | do | Oct. 12, 1864 |
| Boden, George | do | Dec. 1, 1864 |
| Brands, T | do | Dec. 1, 1864 |
| Bradford, Richard | do | Dec. 1, 1864 |
| Brehm, Anton | Polk | Oct. 12, 1864 |
| Buch, Jonothan | do | Dec. 8, 1864 |
| Brown, Peter | do | Dec. 8, 1864 |
| Back, Edward | Richfield | Oct. 12, 1864 |
| Bence, George | do | Oct. 12, 1864 |
| Braun, Arnold | do | Oct. 12, 1864 |
| Braun, Joseph | do | Oct. 12, 1864 |
| Becke, "Sec. 4" | do | Oct. 12, 1864 |
| Bock, Patrick | do | Oct. 12, 1864 |
| Bai, Joseph | do | Jan. 27, 1865 |
| Bartzen, Franz | do | Jan. 27, 1865 |
| Beskes, Jacob | do | Jan. 27, 1865 |
| Broker, Gotleip | do | Jan. 27, 1865 |
| Burchnard, John | do | Jan. 27, 1865 |
| Bauer, Fritz | do | Jan 27, 1865 |
| Burk, John | Sheboygan | Oct. 25, 1864 |
| Beths, John | do | Oct. 25, 1864 |
| Blande, Christian | do | Jan. 27, 1865 |
| Boo, Edward | do | Oct. 25, 1864 |
| Baumback, Carl | do | Oct. 18, 1865 |
| Bottz, Will | do | Oct. 18, 1864 |
| Baumert, Joseph | do | Dec. 2, 1864 |
| Betzold, Johan | do | Dec. 2, 1864 |
| Braun, Carol | do | Oct. 18, 1864 |
| Braun, Louis | do | Oct. 18, 1864 |
| Braun, Charles | do | Jan. 27, 1865 |
| Breminger, Jacob | Moselle | Oct. 18, 1864 |
| Battcher, August | do | Oct. 18, 1864 |
| Bauman, Lorenz | do | Oct. 18, 1864 |
| Braner, Fredrick | do | Dec. 2, 1864 |
| Bates, John | Sheboygan Falls | Oct. 25, 1864 |
| Bored, Druel | do | Oct. 25, 1864 |
| Brage, John A | do | Oct. 25, 1864 |
| Baumer, Fredrick | do | Oct. 25, 1864 |
| Balenstead, George | do | Dec. 2, 1864 |
| Buller, Fred | do | Dec. 2, 1864 |
| Brown, William | do | Dec. 2, 1864 |
| Buswell, Thomas | Lima | Nov. 24, 1863 |
| Brocter, H | do | Oct. 24, 1864 |
| Bailey, Francis | do | Oct. 24, 1864 |
| Brazum, Harvey | do | Oct. 24, 1864 |
| Bryan, W. H | do | Dec. 2, 1864 |
| Beran, Henry | do | Dec. 2, 1864 |
| Bernnleu, William | do | Dec. 2, 1864 |
| Buckman, John Crage | do | Dec. 2, 1864 |
| Buck, L. B | do | Dec. 2, 1864 |
| Bigleu, Theodore | do | Jan. 27, 1865 |
| Bellzink, A. T | Holland | Nov. 24, 1863 |
| Bartels, C | do | Oct. 21, 1864 |
| Ballam, J | do | Oct. 21, 1864 |

| *Name.* | *Residence.* | *Date.* |
|---|---|---|
| Brooks, William | Holland | Oct. 21, 1864 |
| Brendensihl, Charles | Abbott | Oct. 18, 1864 |
| Boer, Timothy | do | Oct. 18, 1864 |
| Berry, Thomas | do | Oct. 18, 1864 |
| Broadbertz, George | do | Oct. 18, 1864 |
| Brenderuhl, William | do | Oct. 18, 1864 |
| Brandmat, Fred'k | do | Dec. 2, 1864 |
| Brose, August | do | Dec. 2, 1864 |
| Botten, James, A | do | Dec. 2, 1864 |
| Beuffer, Peter | do | Dec. 2, 1864 |
| Bockhouse, Fredrick, | Scott | Oct. 21, 1864 |
| Bron, Ephriam | do | Jan. 27, 1865 |
| Blaushar, Mathew | do | Jan. 27, 1862 |
| Bannau, Edward | Plymouth | Dec. 6, 1864 |
| Becker, August | Fredonia | Oct. 14, 1864 |
| Bradskerder, August | do | Oct. 14, 1864 |
| Bromeuesko, Geraul | do | Oct. 14, 1864 |
| Bratt, Josep | do | Oct. 14, 1864 |
| Bromewasko, ——— | do | Oct. 14, 1864 |
| Brubb, Charles | do | Oct. 14, 1864 |
| Barch, Charles | do | Dec. 1, 1864 |
| Belger, Herman | do | Dec. 1, 1864 |
| Baker, Peter | do | Dec. 1, 1864 |
| Bruntz, William | Grafton | Nov. 23, 1863 |
| Bank, George | do | Oct. 13, 1864 |
| Blunth, Gustave | do | Oct. 13, 1864 |
| Bear, John Fergent | do | Oct. 13, 1864 |
| Brock, James | do | Oct. 13, 1864 |
| Bligh, Francis | do | Dec. 1, 1864 |
| Burgu, John | do | Dec. 1, 1864 |
| Bodier, Aug | do | Dec. 1, 1864 |
| Burkel, John | do | Dec. 1, 1864 |
| Burch, Math | do | Dec. 1, 1864 |
| Blank, George | do | Jan. 27, 1865 |
| Bruns, Dudrich | do | Jan. 27, 1865 |
| Beardley, James | do | Jan. 27, 1865 |
| Brady, John | Mequon | Nov. 23, 1863 |
| Berinn, Brasus | do | Nov. 23, 1863 |
| Barth, Anthon | do | Nov. 23, 1863 |
| Bradly, John P | Saukville | Oct. 14, 1864 |
| Bell, Nicholas | do | Oct. 14, 1864 |
| Burnett, John | Fond du Lac | Nov. 19, 1863 |
| Beaufort, Jo | do | Nov. 19, 1863 |
| Braun, Michael | do | Nov. 19, 1863 |
| Barker, William | do | Nov. 19, 1863 |
| Briggs, Henry J | Friendship | Nov. 19, 1863 |
| Banker, Zenia | Oakfield | Nov. 19, 1863 |
| Baukhanmer, Wm | Ashford | Nov 19, 1863 |
| Buedon, William | Auburn | Nov. 19, 1863 |
| Becker, Joseph | do | Oct 5, 1864 |
| Breed, Andrew | Empire | Oct. 5, 1864 |
| Bent, Joseph | Waupun Village | Oct. 5, 1864 |
| Bentley, Ward | Ripon | Oct. 5, 1864 |
| Birrety, Ambries | Eldorado | Oct. 5, 1864 |
| Bardensden, John | do | Oct. 5, 1864 |
| Bradley, John | do | Oct. 5, 1864 |
| Bunto, Anson | do | Oct. 5, 1864 |
| Blute, James | do | Oct. 5, 1864 |
| Benton, Charles | do | Oct. 5, 1864 |

| *Name.* | *Residence.* | *Date.* |
|---|---|---|
| Bell, Duncan | Eldorado | Oct. 5, 1864 |
| Baker Ira | Westford | Nov. 20, 1863 |
| Blake, Francis | Elba | Nov. 20, 1863 |
| Brockway, Stephen | Beaver Dam | Nov. 20, 1863 |
| Berbag, Edward | Emmett | Nov. 20, 1863 |
| Burtz, Gottlich | do | Nov. 20, 1863 |
| Brooks, Edward | do | Oct. 11, 1864 |
| Burtrett, Martin | do | Oct. 11, 1864 |
| Bulger, Thomas Jr | do | Oct. 11, 1864 |
| Bonetz, Founk | do | Nov. 20, 1863 |
| Boltz, Lions Jr | Clyman | Oct. 6, 1864 |
| Barette, A. C | Oak Grove | Nov. 20, 1863 |
| Belke, —— | Burnett | Nov 20, 1863 |
| Barnett, Frank | do | Nov. 20, 1863 |
| Buck, J J | Chester | Nov. 20, 1863 |
| Benke, Peter | Watertown | Nov. 20, 1863 |
| Bomgohn, Joseph | do | Oct. 6, 1864 |
| Barnett, Fred | do | Oct. 6, 1864 |
| Bork, August | do | Oct. 6, 1864 |
| Barkenhagen, Wm | do | Oct. 6, 1864 |
| Biesel, G | do | Oct. 6, 1864 |
| Budinger, Charles | do | Oct. 6, 1864 |
| Battis, Joseph | do | Dec. 1, 1864 |
| Brasier, Louis | Leroy | Oct. 4, 1864 |
| Bartes, John | do | Oct. 4, 1864 |
| Becker, Ornnil | do | Oct. 4, 1864 |
| Burnette, Allison C | do | Oct. 4, 1864 |
| Bowen, Philander | do | Dec. 1, 1864 |
| Buswitz, Frederick | Lomira | Nov. 20, 1863 |
| Barkhardt, Philip | do | Oct. 6, 1864 |
| Bockler, Joseph | do | Oct. 6, 1864 |
| Brown, John | do | Oct. 6, 1864 |
| Bauer, John | do | Oct. 6, 1864 |
| Buir, Thos | Milwaukee | Nov. 9, 1863 |
| Berger, Andrew | do | Nov. 9, 1863 |
| Bertram, Wm | do | Nov. 9, 1863 |
| Behmann, John | do | Nov. 9, 1863 |
| Balser, Geo | do | Nov. 9, 1863 |
| Barkhoff, Aug | do | Nov. 9, 1863 |
| Brandt, Herman | do | Nov. 9, 1863 |
| Brahon, Fritz | do | Nov. 9, 1863 |
| Blish, John | do | Nov. 9, 1863 |
| Bassitt, T N | do | Nov. 9, 1863 |
| Burns, David | do | Nov. 9, 1863 |
| Barnell, Carl | do | Nov. 9, 1863 |
| Blish, E | do | Nov. 9, 1863 |
| Burns, Jas | do | Sep. 19, 1864 |
| Boohan, Joseph | do | Sep. 19, 1864 |
| Brendt, Theo | do | Sep. 19, 1864 |
| Bramer, Geo | do | Sep. 19, 1864 |
| Banger, Michael | do | Sep. 19, 1864 |
| Berne, John | do | Sep. 19, 1864 |
| Beatser, Henry | do | Sep. 19, 1864 |
| Burger, John | do | Sep. 19, 1864 |
| Berner, Wm | do | Nov. 14, 1864 |
| Brebe, Fred | do | Nov. 14, 1864 |
| Brockhaska, Ignatz | do | Nov. 14, 1864 |
| Bates, Chas | do | Nov. 14, 1864 |
| Bertram, Wm | do | Nov. 14, 1864 |

| *Name.* | *Residence.* | *Date.* |
|---|---|---|
| Barnard, Wm | Milwaukee | Nov. 14, 1864 |
| Balluf, Conrad | do | Nov. 14, 1864 |
| Beltz, Jacob | do | Dec. 22, 1864 |
| Biernt, Fred | do | Dec. 22, 1864 |
| Back, Geo | do | Nov. 9, 1863 |
| Baley, T | do | Nov. 9, 1863 |
| Bailey, A | do | Nov. 9, 1863 |
| Becker, Adolph | do | Nov. 9, 1863 |
| Binner, Paul | do | Nov. 9, 1863 |
| Bahl, Bernard | do | Nov. 9, 1863 |
| Bachel, August | do | Nov. 9, 1863 |
| Bhles, Jacob | do | Sep. 20, 1864 |
| Baldwin, John | do | Sep. 20, 1864 |
| Bill, Willhelm | do | Sep. 20, 1864 |
| Byus, Jacob | do | Sep. 20, 1864 |
| Bursack, Chas | do | Sep. 20, 1864 |
| Berg, Jacob | do | Nov. 14, 1864 |
| Brandel, Franz | do | Nov. 14, 1864 |
| Brown, John | do | Nov. 14, 1864 |
| Binder, Franz | do | Nov. 14, 1864 |
| Best, Wm | do | Nov. 10, 1863 |
| Brennan, J | do | Nov. 10, 1863 |
| Brune, J | do | Nov. 10, 1863 |
| Blist, R. J | do | Nov. 10, 1863 |
| Baein, Chas | do | Nov. 10, 1863 |
| Bogle, W. N | do | Nov. 10, 1863 |
| Barth, Casper | do | Nov. 10, 1863 |
| Branth, T. H | do | Nov. 10, 1863 |
| Burns, John | do | Nov. 10, 1863 |
| Briggy, T | do | Nov. 10, 1863 |
| Bean, Joseph | do | Nov. 10, 1863 |
| Brugh, John or Richard | do | Sep. 20, 1864 |
| Bicknell, F, Wm | do | Sep. 20, 1864 |
| Bishop, L. J. | do | Sep. 20, 1864 |
| Beebe, L | do | Sep. 20, 1864 |
| Broeman, John | do | Sep. 20, 1864 |
| Burch, W | do | Sep. 20, 1864 |
| Blenk, Michael | do | Sep. 20, 1864 |
| Burke, John | do | Sep. 20, 1864 |
| Black, R. S | do | Sep. 20, 1864 |
| Boter, Wm | do | Nov. 15, 1864 |
| Bayton, Charles | do | Nov. 15, 1864 |
| Burk, Michael | do | Nov. 15, 1864 |
| Butler, John | do | Nov. 15, 1864 |
| Brady, T. C | do | Nov. 15, 1864 |
| Bagly, John | do | Nov. 15, 1864 |
| Benedict, Abraham | do | Nov, 15, 1864 |
| Brown, A. S | do | Nov. 15, 1864 |
| Brooks, —— | do | Nov. 15, 1864 |
| Brune, Thos | do | Nov. 51, 1864 |
| Bums, Thos | do | Nov. 15, 1864 |
| Bauvell, H. W | do | Nov. 15, 1864 |
| Brady, Hugh | do | Nov. 15, 1864 |
| Burkler, Martin | do | Jan. 19, 1865 |
| Bartell, Wm | do | Jan. 19, 1865 |
| Bladinger, Nick | do | Jan. 19, 1865 |
| Breuer, James | do | Jan. 19, 1865 |
| Butcher, Fritz | do | Nov 25, 1864 |
| Bizel, Charles | do | Nov. 25, 1864 |

| *Name.* | *Residence.* | *Date* |
|---|---|---|
| Bothely, S. | Milwaukee | Nov. 25, 1864 |
| Bauermann, —— | do | Nov. 25, 1864 |
| Bergermaster, John | do | Nov. 25, 1864 |
| Bergmuchl, Otto | do | Nov. 11, 1863 |
| Brasse, August | do | Nov. 11, 1863 |
| Bakler, Christian | do | Nov. 11, 1863 |
| Barth, Edmond | do | Nov. 11, 1863 |
| Bremmen, John | do | Sep. 21, 1864 |
| Bagemuhl, Michael | do | Sep. 21, 1864 |
| Beissensteine, Victus | do | Sep. 21, 1864 |
| Buchner, Nicholas | do | Sep. 21, 1864 |
| Barr, Frederick | do | Sep. 21, 1864 |
| Bening, John | do | Sep. 21, 1864 |
| Benz, Joseph | do | Sep. 21, 1864 |
| Breen, Conrad | do | Sep. 21, 1864 |
| Benz, Peter | do | Sep. 21, 1864 |
| Bitter, Frederick | do | Sep. 21, 1864 |
| Braasch, August | do | Sep. 21, 1864 |
| Bentner, Philip | do | Sep. 21, 1864 |
| Beyer, Anton | do | Sep. 21, 1864 |
| Balke, August | do | Sep. 21, 1864 |
| Beyer, Herman | do | Nov. 25, 1864 |
| Bissenger, Louis | do | Nov. 25, 1864 |
| Buchman, Heinrich | do | Nov. 25, 1864 |
| Berback, Fritz | do | Nov. 25, 1864 |
| Bartz, Frederick | do | Nov. 25, 1864 |
| Bennett, Wm. J. | do | Nov 25, 1864 |
| Becker, Johann | do | Nov. 10, 1863 |
| Bwiz, August | do | Sep. 21, 1864 |
| Bierns, Fred | do | Sep. 21, 1864 |
| Bunt, Charles | do | Sep. 21, 1864 |
| Barry, Henry | do | Sep. 21, 1864 |
| Boehme, Fred | do | Sep. 21, 1864 |
| Berneck, John | do | Sep. 21, 1864 |
| Bormeister, Ernest | do | Sep. 21, 1864 |
| Ballo, John | do | Nov. 15, 1864 |
| Broft, Carl | do | Nov. 16, 1864 |
| Becker, Edward | do | Nov. 16, 1864 |
| Beid, William | do | Nov. 16, 1864 |
| Behlos, Nicholas | do | Nov. 16, 1864 |
| Boint, Albert | do | Nov. 16, 1864 |
| Burke, Richard | do | Nov. 16, 1864 |
| Branch, Ernam | do | Nov. 10, 1863 |
| Brosens, Geo | do | Nov 10, 1863 |
| Bursche, Frank | do | Nov. 10, 1863 |
| Barrow, James | do | Nov. 10, 1863 |
| Baine, William | do | Nov. 10, 1863 |
| Burger, Jacob | do | Nov. 10, 1863 |
| Barr, Merza C | do | Nov. 11, 1863 |
| Behlan, John | do | Nov. 11, 1863 |
| Been, Avenauer Joseph | do | Nov. 11, 1863 |
| Burdick, Norman L. | do | Sep. 21, 1864 |
| Behuerck, Gotleib | do | Sep. 21, 1864 |
| Borchert, Ernst | do | Sep. 21, 1864 |
| Bihurs, Francis | do | Sep. 21, 1864 |
| Befil, Joseph | do | Jan. 11, 1865 |
| Brewset, J. H. | do | Jan. 11, 1865 |
| Bulger, P. W | do | Jan. 11, 1865 |
| Burke, John | do | Jan. 11, 1865 |

| *Name.* | *Residence.* | *Date.* |
|---|---|---|
| Bucher, Thomas | Milwaukee, | Nov. 10, 1863 |
| Buckley, Patrick | do | Nov. 10, 1863 |
| Ball, William | do | Nov. 10, 1863 |
| Bowers, James | do | Nov. 10, 1863 |
| Bone, William | do | Nov. 10, 1863 |
| Barney, John | do | Nov. 10, 1863 |
| Brownell, James | do | Sep. 21, 1864 |
| Baines, Richard | do | Sep. 21, 1864 |
| Burke, David | do | Sept. 21, 1864 |
| Baden, August | do | Nov. 10, 1863 |
| Bell, Robert | do | Nov. 10, 1863 |
| Brankman, Carl | do | Nov. 10, 1863 |
| Brown, John | do | Nov. 10, 1863 |
| Banson, Christian | do | Nov. 10, 1863 |
| Brouber, Henry | do | Nov. 10, 1863 |
| Braam, Lambert | do | Nov. 10, 1863 |
| Bryden, Robert | do | Nov. 10, 1863 |
| Bahn, Fred | do | Nov. 10, 1863 |
| Brown, Hiram | do | Nov. 10, 1863 |
| Ball, —— | do | Nov. 10, 1863 |
| Burke, Peter | do | Nov. 10, 1863 |
| Ballock, Amos | do | Nov. 10, 1863 |
| Bunger, Fritz | do | Nov. 10, 1863 |
| Boschen, —— | do | Nov. 10, 1863 |
| Bridges, M. L. | do | Nov. 10, 1863 |
| Brown, Jacob A. | do | Nov. 25, 1864 |
| Brady, Patrick | do | Nov. 30, 1864 |
| Bellman, Frederick | do | Nov. 30, 1864 |
| Berg, Jacob | do | Nov 30, 1864 |
| Bening, Bernard | do | Nov. 30, 1864 |
| Behren, Fred | do | Nov. 30, 1864 |
| Bromstadt, John | do | Nov. 11, 1863 |
| Baehr, Ernst | do | Sep. 22, 1864 |
| Bertram, Henry | do | Sep. 22, 1864 |
| Bohl, Ludwig | do | Sep. 22, 1864 |
| Bauer, Joseph | do | Dec. 7, 1864 |
| Bechta, John | do | Dec. 7, 1864 |
| Bartram, Werner | do | Dec. 7, 1864 |
| Becker, August | do | Dec. 7, 1864 |
| Brill, John | Granville | Sept. 22, 1864 |
| Brien, Henry | Wauwatosa | Nov. 11, 1863 |
| Base, Charles | Greenfield | Nov. 11, 1863 |
| Boss, Eberhart J | do | Sept. 22, 1864 |
| Breneer, John | do | Sep. 22, 1864 |
| Barney, James | do | Sep. 22, 1864 |
| Buenger, Carl | Lake | Nov. 11, 1863 |
| Butler, John | do | Nov. 11, 1863 |
| Bauer, Andrew | do | Sep. 22, 1864 |
| Brown, Charles | do | Sep. 22, 1864 |
| Benenk, Toeum | do | Dec. 13, 1864 |
| Bauer, Jacob | do | Dec. 13, 1864 |
| Beninger, Henry | Franklin | Nov. 11, 1863 |
| Brintz, John | do | Nov. 11, 1863 |
| Boonefeld, —— | Menomonee | Nov. 25, 1864 |
| Brill, Adam | do | Nov. 25, 1864 |
| Bredfeldt, Andrew | do | Nov. 25, 1864 |
| Brokenwaggon, E | Brookfield | Nov. 12, 1863 |
| Buell, Edward | do | Sep. 23, 1864 |
| Bell, James C | do | Sep. 23, 1864 |

| *Name.* | *Residence.* | *Date.* |
|---|---|---|
| Bundy, Freedon | New Berlin | Nov. 12, 1863 |
| Bubzer, George | do | Nov. 12, 1863 |
| Breyer, Valentine | Muskego | Nov. 12, 1863 |
| Brady, Michael | do | Nov. 12, 1863 |
| Brass, Fritz | do | Sep. 24, 1864 |
| Bull, Henry S. | do | Nov. 30, 1864 |
| Bloss, James | do | Nov. 30, 1864 |
| Bants, William | Oak Creek | Nov. 11, 1863 |
| Brockman, Charles | do | Sep. 22, 1864 |
| Becker, August | do | Sep. 22, 1864 |
| Bolden, Patrick | Racine | Nov. 11, 1863 |
| Brookman, Henry | do | Nov. 11, 1863 |
| Bums, Thomas | do | Nov. 11, 1863 |
| Branon, Christof | do | Sep. 24, 1864 |
| Boefel, Matthias | do | Sep. 24, 1864 |
| Byard, John | do | Sep. 24, 1864 |
| Balsky, Matthias | do | Sep. 24, 1864 |
| Buffell, Michael | do | Sep. 22, 1864 |
| Blish, Harvey | do | Sep. 22, 1864 |
| Buckley, William | do | Sep. 22, 1864 |
| Brown, Daniel | do | Sep. 22, 1864 |
| Boreman, William | do | Sep. 22, 1864 |
| Blake, Thomas | do | Sep. 22, 1864 |
| Beeheld, Jacob | do | Nov. 11, 1863 |
| Botsford, Ariah | do | Sep. 22, 1864 |
| Bowen, William D | do | Sep. 22, 1864 |
| Besel, Thomas | Mount Pleasant | Nov. 11, 1863 |
| Bonarr, William | do | Nov. 11, 1863 |
| Blackburn, Robert | Dover | Sep. 23, 1864 |
| Brook, James | do | Dec. 10, 1864 |
| Brice, Thomas | Raymond | Sep. 23, 1864 |
| Bristol, John | Caledonia | Nov. 11, 1863 |
| Baisady, John | do | Sep. 22, 1864 |
| Bowen, William | do | Dec. 7, 1864 |
| Beukenhagen, Albert | Kenosha | Nov. 12, 1863 |
| Bielm, Henry | Paris | Sep. 24, 1864 |
| Bruggeman, Henry | Wheatland | Sep. 24, 1864 |
| Burke, Martin | Salem | Nov. 12, 1863 |
| Bascom, Thomas | do | Nov. 12, 1863 |
| Booth, George H | do | Sep. 24, 1864 |
| Brinz, Henry | do | Sep. 24, 1864 |
| Bacon, Hiram | Bristol | Sep. 24, 1864 |
| Brogan, Hugh | Pleasant Prairie | Nov. 12, 1863 |
| Becker, Barney | do | Nov. 12, 1863 |
| Brown, Albert | Whitewater | Nov. 12, 1863 |
| Bundy, Charles | do | Nov. 12, 1863 |
| Bridge, John | do | Nov. 12, 1863 |
| Bear, Isaac | East Troy | Sep. 24, 1864 |
| Bungardy, Joseph | do | Dec. 2, 1864 |
| Byrne, Patrick | do | Dec. 2, 1864 |
| Bachalett, Peter | Hudson | Nov. 12, 1863 |
| Bodfish, J. L | Summit | Nov. 12, 1863 |
| Bulson, Henry H | do | Sep. 22, 1864 |
| Baile, Frederick | do | Sep. 22, 1864 |
| Baling, Fritz | do | Sep. 22, 1864 |
| Bolson, Timothy | do | Sep. 22, 1864 |
| Baartz, Henry | do | Nov. 30, 1864 |
| Baker, James | Oconomowoc | Sep. 22, 1864 |
| Bertlet, Charles | do | Sep. 22, 1864 |

| *Name.* | *Residence.* | *Date.* |
|---|---|---|
| Bartlet, August | Oconomowoc | Sep. 22, 1864 |
| Ballard, Herrick D | do | Sep. 22, 1864 |
| Bagley, Patrick | Mukwonego | Nov. 12, 1863 |
| Butler, John | Pewaukee | Nov. 12, 1863 |
| Busse, August | do | Sep. 22, 1864 |
| Brown, George | do | Dec. 2, 1864 |
| Benson, Louis W | do | Dec. 2, 1864 |
| Benson, Michael | do | Dec. 2, 1864 |
| Brain, Frank | do | Dec. 2, 1864 |
| Boh, John | Waukesha | Sep. 23, 1864 |
| Berry, Dominick | do | Sep. 23, 1864 |
| Barton, Richard | Vernon | Sep. 24, 1864 |
| Baker, John | Menomonee | Sep. 24, 1864 |
| Blande, Charles | do | Sep. 24, 1864 |
| Burke, Patrick | do | Sep. 24, 1864 |
| Barnes, Thomas | do | Sep. 24, 1864 |
| Braneer, John | do | Sep. 24, 1864 |
| Brahon, Aulara | do | Dec. 1, 1864 |
| Bland, Leonard | do | Dec. 1, 1864 |
| Bloddell, August | do | Dec. 1, 1864 |
| Bartlett, August | do | Dec. 1, 1864 |
| Barning, Fred | do | Nov. 25, 1864 |
| Bogermann, Daniel | do | Nov. 25, 1864 |
| Blaufusf, Valentine | do | Nov. 25, 1864 |
| Breitfeld, John | do | Nov. 25, 1864 |
| Biebe, Nicholas | do | Nov. 25, 1864 |
| Barsby, Henry | Rock | Nov. 12, 1863 |
| Burns, Lee | Janesville | Nov. 12, 1863 |
| Barron, William | Verona | Nov. 13, 1863 |
| Bottleson, Foster | Blue Mounds | Nov. 13, 1863 |
| Bartle, Gilbert | do | Sep. 19, 1864 |
| Brown, Henry Nelson | do | Sep. 19, 1864 |
| Baker, Charles | Cross Plains | Nov. 13, 1863 |
| Bimes, Jo. A | Madison | Nov. 13, 1863 |
| Bigelow, Thaddeus | Medina | Nov. 13, 1863 |
| Bailey, Nelson | Sun Prairie | Sep. 19, 1864 |
| Beers, Willie | do | Sep. 19, 1864 |
| Burns, Thomas | Westport | Nov. 13, 1863 |
| Blihle, Albert | Berry | Feb. 27, 1865 |
| Boling, Martin | Roxbury | Nov. 13, 1863 |
| Barrett, James | Jefferson | Nov. 13, 1863 |
| Benton, Warner | Farmington | Sep. 20, 1864 |
| Banke, Henry | do | Sep. 20, 1864 |
| Brinner, Frederick | do | Oct. 28, 1864 |
| Barrett, John | do | Nov. 13, 1863 |
| Buck, John | Watertown | Oct. 22, 1864 |
| Barrand, Ernst | do | Oct. 22, 1864 |
| Baldwin, Marvin M | Pacific | Nov. 16, 1863 |
| Brickwell, Joseph | Lewiston | Oct. 22, 1864 |
| Bakka, Ole Oleson | Perry | Feb. 27, 1865 |
| Bettcher, Frederick | Milford | Oct. 22, 1864 |
| Brink, Alexander H | do | Sep. 20, 1864 |
| Blair, William | do | Sep. 20, 1864 |
| Bemis, Cirus C | do | Oct. 22, 1864 |
| Bradbury, Warren | Watertown | Oct. 22, 1864 |
| Black, Godlip | do | Nov. 15, 1864 |
| Barker, Jacob | Ridgeway | Nov. 14, 1863 |
| Buckingham, John | do | Sep. 28, 1864 |
| Barnes, Burton | do | Sep. 28, 1864 |

| *Name.* | *Residence.* | *Date.* |
|---|---|---|
| Brewster, Chas | Dodgeville | Sep. 28, 1864 |
| Barey, Edward | do | Sep. 28, 1864 |
| Bell, Thos. | do | Oct. 28, 1864 |
| Bilkay, Jas | do | Oct. 28, 1864 |
| Bowers, John | Highland | Sep 28, 1864 |
| Bennett, Dan'l B. | do | Oct. 28, 1864 |
| Billings, Henry | do | Oct. 28, 1864 |
| Berry, Thos | do | Oct. 28, 1864 |
| Baker, Jacob | do | Oct. 28, 1864 |
| Braphy, Wm | do | Oct. 28, 1864 |
| Braphy, Jas | do | Sep. 28, 1864 |
| Buckley, Philip | do | Sep. 28, 1864 |
| Benoy, Wm | do | Nov. 19, 1864 |
| Baker Samuel | do | Dec. 7, 1864 |
| Beuhlman, Fred | do | Dec. 7, 1864 |
| Bowden, Wm. Hy | Linden or Mifflin | Nov. 14, 1863 |
| Breemin, Thos | Waldwick | Nov. 14, 1863 |
| Baylan, John | do | Oct. 4, 1864 |
| Burns, John | Kendall | Oct. 4, 1864 |
| Benson, Joseph jr. | Willow Springs | Oct. 4, 1864 |
| Burk, Wm | Wayne or Gratiot | Nov. 16, 1863 |
| Brown, John | Benton | Nov. 16, 1863 |
| Burns, Dan'l | do | Nov. 16, 1863 |
| Barkle, Wm | do | Sep. 29, 1864 |
| Baur, John | New Diggings | Nov. 16, 1863 |
| Blinkiron, Thos | do | Sep. 29, 1864 |
| Barrett, Barney | Utica | Sep. 30, 1864 |
| Bowen, E. F | Freeman or Lynxville | Nov. 18, 1863 |
| Beyer, Chas | Cassville, Beet'n or Watr'loo | Nov. 19, 1863 |
| Baker, J. T | Beetown | Oct. 1, 1864 |
| Berg, Geo | Harrison | Oct. 1, 1864 |
| Bird, Matthew | do | Oct. 1, 1864 |
| Brown, Thos | Hazel Green | Nov. 19, 1863 |
| Brooks, Allen | Reedsburg or Winfield | Nov. 20, 1863 |
| Badsuth, Leonard | Troy or Spring | Nov. 20, 1863 |
| Blakely, Philip | Bloom | Sep. 26, 1864 |
| Bird, Philip | Seneca | Sep. 30, 1864 |
| Blake, John | Scott | Sep. 30, 1864 |
| Black, Wm | do | Sep. 30, 1864 |
| Brown, Wm | Dellona | Oct. 3, 1864 |
| Barney, B. S | La Valle | Oct. 3, 1864 |
| Breen, Michael | do | Nov. 19, 1864 |
| Bray, Daniel | do | Nov. 19. 1864 |
| Boyes, Wm | Millville | Dec. 7, 1864 |
| Brofin, Wm | La Crosse city | Nov. 16, 1863 |
| Bottomby, Wm | La Crosse Co: | Nov. 16, 1863 |
| Brown, Patrick | Monroe Co | Nov. 17, 1863 |
| Bergman, Wm | Ridgeville | Sep. 20, 1864 |
| Bell, Geo | Tomah | Sep. 20, 1864 |
| Babcock, Elgin | do | Sep. 20, 1864 |
| Bishop, John | Portland | Sep. 20, 1864 |
| Brown, M |  | Sep. 20, 1864 |
| Brainard, B. F |  | Sep. 20, 1864 |
| Benson, Joseph |  | Sep. 20, 1864 |
| Bean, Peter | Chippewa Falls | Sep. 27, 1864 |
| Bailey, Eugene | do | Nov. 2, 1864 |
| Berthaume, Chas | do | Nov. 2, 1864 |
| Beanchame, Luzen | do | Sep. 27, 1864 |
| Benke, Christopher | Lafayette | Sep. 27, 1864 |

| *Name* | *Residence.* | *Date.* |
|---|---|---|
| Bozier, Frank | Lafayette | Sep. 27, 1864 |
| Brook, H. M | | Nov. 18, 1863 |
| Buckland, Geo | Northfield | Sep. 23, 1864 |
| Bickle, Wm | Manchester | Sep. 23, 1864 |
| Brooks, Henry R | do | Sep. 23, 1865 |
| Barnidon, Stephen | | Nov. 23, 1863 |
| Benson, Chas | | Nov. 23, 1863 |
| Blount, Wm. M | Richfield | Sep. 26, 1864 |
| Brosnehan, Dennis | New Haven | Sep. 26, 1864 |
| Round, Freeman F | Leola | Sep. 26, 1864 |
| Baldwin, Jno. W | Easton | Sep. 26, 1864 |
| Becke, David jr | Adams | Sep. 26, 1864 |
| Brusnehan, Corns | New Haven | Nov. 14, 1864 |
| Bonnett, Henry | Springville | Nov. 14, 1864 |
| Baker, Geo. H | Preston | Nov. 14, 1864 |
| Brush, Hobart | Portage Co | Nov. 23, 1863 |
| Bardon, Merett | Linwood | Sep. 22, 1864 |
| Bausherly, Onesine | Stockton | Oct. 31, 1864 |
| Baggo, James | Pine Grove | Sep. 22, 1864 |
| Baker, John W | do | Sep. 22, 1864 |
| Bradley, Jas. F | do | Sep. 22, 1864 |
| Barker, Chauncey | do | Sep. 22, 1864 |
| Bradt, James | Belmont | Sep. 22, 1864 |
| Blair, Henry | Lanark | Sep 22, 1864 |
| Bedell, Luther B | Hull | Sep. 22, 1864 |
| Banker, John | do | Sep. 22, 1864 |
| Bedell, Wm | do | Sep. 22, 1864 |
| Beedle, Jacob J J | do | Sep. 22, 1864 |
| Bran, Enock G. jr | do | Oct. 31, 1864 |
| Brown, Wm R | Eau Claire Co | Nov. 20, 1863 |
| Bradley, John | St. Croix Co | Nov. 20, 1863 |
| Barrett, James | Erin Prairie | Sep. 23, 1864 |
| Brown, Henry | do | Sep. 23, 1864 |
| Beebe, Sylvester | Ceylon | Oct. 5, 1864 |
| Buckley, Jo | Eau Galle | Nov. 3, 1864 |
| Bradshaw, Owen | do | Nov. 3, 1864 |
| Buttock, Wm. W | Springfield | Nov. 3, 1864 |
| Berlona, John | Vernon Co | Nov. 18, 1863 |
| Brown, Henry | do | Nov. 18, 1863 |
| Boyington, Chas | Bergen | Sep. 21, 1864 |
| Baker, Geo | Franklin | Sep. 21, 1864 |
| Bennett, Cyrus C | do | Sep. 21, 1864 |
| Benrad, Louis O | Hamburg | Nov. 15, 1864 |
| Bates, Judson | Whitestown | Nov. 15, 1864 |
| Butts, Marshall F | Sterling | Nov. 15, 1864 |
| Beverick, Adam | Buffalo Co | Nov. 18, 1863 |
| Baumann, Jno | Belvidere | Nov. 15, 1864 |
| Baker, John | Wilson | Sep. 26, 1864 |
| Brady, Nicholas | Kildare | Sep. 19, 1864 |
| Brinon, Michael | do | Sep. 19, 1864 |
| Bennett, G | do | Sep. 19, 1864 |
| Bond, W. R | Lemonweir | Sep. 19, 1864 |
| Bennett, Alfred | do | Sep. 19, 1864 |
| Byington, Geo | Summit | Sep 19, 1864 |
| Barstow, Wm | Lyndon | Sep. 19, 1864 |
| Burdick, Girard | do | Oct. 31, 1864 |
| Beedle, J. L | Seven Mile Creek | Oct. 31, 1864 |
| Brown, Thos | do | Oct. 31, 1864 |
| Brownell, Thos | Plymouth | Oct. 31, 1864 |

| Name. | Residence. | Date. |
|---|---|---|
| Bacon, Hiram | Plymouth | Oct. 31, 1864 |
| Bailey, Stephen W | do | Oct. 31, 1864 |
| Brainard, F E | do | Oct 31, 1854 |
| Brown, Oscar | Dexter | Sep. 22, 1864 |
| Behrens, Henry | Centralia | Nov. 15, 1864 |
| Brant, Peter | do | Nov. 15, 1864 |
| Bowers, John | Pleasant Valley | Sep. 23, 1864 |
| Breitinger, John | Martell | Sep. 23, 1864 |
| Bennett, Hiram | do | Sep. 23, 1864 |
| Bredahl, Hans | do | Nov. 3, 1864 |
| Borsbough, Jno. M | Pleasant Valley | Sep. 23, 1864 |
| Benett, Joel | Trumbell | Nov. 3, 1864 |
| Babcock, Lorenzo | Eau Galle | Nov. 2, 1864 |
| Bishop, Harrison | do | Sep. 27, 1864 |
| Birkel, Joseph | do | Sep. 27, 1864 |
| Bando, Fred | Berlin | Oct 14, 1864 |
| Babcock, G. W | Durand | Sep. 27, 1864 |
| Barry, Wm | Pepin | Sep. 27, 1864 |
| Balissie, Hubert | Door Co | Nov. 20, 1863 |
| Bossene, Clement | Brussels | Dec. 29, 1864 |
| Baugmet, Antonie | do | Dec. 29, 1864 |
| Boucher, Lewis | Red River | Nov. 20, 1863 |
| Bulton, Theodore | Ahnepee | Nov. 20, 1863 |
| Bonjean, Jo | Casco | Dec. 29, 1864 |
| Belk, Jno | Coryville | Dec. 29, 1864 |
| Belka, Jno | Montpelier | Dec. 29, 1864 |
| Butler, Ira | Franklin | Dec. 29, 1864 |
| Bronson, Joseph | Carlton | Dec. 29, 1864 |
| Beverard, Joseph | do | Dec. 29, 1864 |
| Bennett, Chauncey | do | Dec. 29, 1864 |
| Belin, Jno. B | Lincoln | Dec. 29, 1864 |
| Belin, Isadore | do | Dec. 29, 1864 |
| Bebo, Tilesford | Two Rivers | Nov 21, 1863 |
| Blong, Wm | do | Nov. 21, 1863 |
| Bitz, Carl | Manitowoc | Nov. 21, 1863 |
| Brown, J | do | Nov. 21, 1863 |
| Blackman, Loren | Cato | Nov. 21, 1863 |
| Bossman, Bernhard | Eaton | Nov. 24, 1863 |
| Broms, Patrick | Liberty | Nov. 21, 1863 |
| Brik, Peter | Meeme | Nov. 21, 1863 |
| Brand, Jno | do | Dec. 29, 1864 |
| Boutin, Edward | Two Creeks | Dec. 29, 1864 |
| Buknosky, Christoff | Mishicott | Dec. 29, 1864 |
| Barthels, Louis | do | Dec. 29, 1864 |
| Brodkerb, Jno | do | Dec. 29, 1864 |
| Buresch, Michael | Cooperstown | Dec. 29, 1864 |
| Brosken, Jno | Kossuth | Dec. 29, 1864 |
| Beachman, Peter | Newton | Dec. 29, 1864 |
| Backes, Johan | do | Dec. 29, 1864 |
| Bluhm, Carl | Stockbridge | Nov. 23, 1863 |
| Bowman, Job | do | Dec. 28, 1864 |
| Burke, Jno | do | Dec. 28, 1864 |
| Beckard, Jno | Harrison | Dec. 28, 1864 |
| Butler, Michael | Nekimi | Nov. 23, 1863 |
| Bartow, James V | do | Nov. 23, 1863 |
| Bushy, Chas | Clayton | Nov. 24, 1863 |
| Berthier, Jno | Utica | Nov. 24, 1863 |
| Bruesewitz, Dan'l | | Nov. 28, 1863 |
| Barker, Nathaniel J | Poygan | Dec. 31, 1864 |

| *Name.* | *Residence.* | *Date.* |
|---|---|---|
| Brogdon, Aaron | Poygan | Nov. 5, 1864 |
| Barker Curtis | do | Nov. 5, 1864 |
| Beal A. W | Berlin city | Nov. 24, 1863 |
| Brown, Thos. H | Mackford | Nov. 24, 1863 |
| Bollahan, Ludwig | Princeton | Nov. 24, 1863 |
| Burns, Wm. J | St. Marie | Nov. 24, 1863 |
| Baldwin, Wm | Marquette Co | Nov. 24. 1863 |
| Brugst, August | Mecan | Nov. 1, 1864 |
| Bowman, Wm. P | Buffalo | Nov. 1, 1864 |
| Busbee,, Jno. G | Crystal Lake | Nov. 1, 1864 |
| Burgess, M. H | Newton | Nov. 1, 1864 |
| Blyford, Jno | do | Nov. 1, 1864 |
| Boty, James | do | Dec. 31, 1864 |
| Boyden, James | do | Dec. 31, 1864 |
| Barton, Joseph | Moundville | Dec. 31, 1864 |
| Baxter, Henry D | Waushara Co | Nov. 24, 1863 |
| Benjamin, Ephraim G | Marion | Nov. 24, 1863 |
| Bauer, Peter | Bloomfield | Nov. 2, 1864 |
| Bauer, Henry | do | Nov. 2, 1864 |
| Brewster, Edward | do | Nov. 2, 1864 |
| Bauer, Christian | do | Nov. 2, 1864 |
| Blair, Joseph | Aurora | Nov. 2, 1864 |
| Bliss, Lester | do | Dec. 31, 1864 |
| Beaman, Alonzo | Warren | Nov. 2, 1864 |
| Bruce, Raswell Z | Springwater | Nov. 2, 1864 |
| Briggs, Silas L | do | Nov. 2, 1864 |
| Bartlet, Thos | Richford | Nov. 2, 1864 |
| Bacon, Roswell | do | Nov. 2, 1864 |
| Blane, Wm | do | Nov. 2, 1864 |
| Bassett, Wm. T | Coloma | Nov. 2, 1864 |
| Babcock, Hiram W | do | Dec. 31, 1864 |
| Bursell, Robt | Oasis | Nov. 2, 1864 |
| Burr, Ezra | do | Nov. 2, 1864 |
| Bray, Ransellaer | do | Nov. 2, 1864 |
| Buncom, Rich'd | Plainfield | Nov. 2, 1864 |
| Buggs, Franklin | do | Nov. 2, 1864 |
| Bound, Franklin | do | Nov. 2, 1864 |
| Bentley, Bethuel | do | Nov. 2, 1864 |
| Bender, Geo | do | Nov. 2, 1864 |
| Bardwell, Martin | do | Nov. 2, 1864 |
| Borden, Ephraim | do | Nov. 2, 1864 |
| Bullis, James | do | Nov. 2, 1864 |
| Barnes, Jeff | do | Dec. 31, 1864 |
| Brown, Edward | do | Dec. 31, 1864 |
| Burbank, Sidney H | Mukwa | Nov. 25, 1863 |
| Brogstrassen, Jacob | Weyauwega | Nov. 25, 1863 |
| Birdsall, James | do | Dec 31, 1864 |
| Barker, Joseph | Lind | Nov. 25, 1863 |
| Bierce, Austin A | Iola | Nov. 25, 1863 |
| Bailey, Paul C | do | Nov. 5, 1864 |
| Bailey, Melvin H | do | Dec. 31, 1864 |
| Bennetto, Jos. B | do | Dec. 31, 1864 |
| Baldwin, Aaron M | do | Nov. 25, 1863 |
| Brening, Chas | Bear Creek | Nov. 5, 1864 |
| Bailey, Jotham A | Royalton | Nov. 5, 1864 |
| Bowers, John | do | Nov. 5, 1864 |
| Bennett, Freeborn | St. Lawrence | Nov. 5, 1864 |
| Batcham, Eli D | do | Dec. 31, 1864 |

| *Name.* | *Residence.* | *Date.* |
|---|---|---|
| Bates, Wm. T | Freedom | Nov. 27, 1863 |
| Baum, Julius | do | Dec. 28, 1864 |
| Bushe, Nelson | Kaukama | Nov. 27, 1863 |
| Bloemer, Milo | Grand Chute | Nov. 27, 1863 |
| Brown, F | Appleton | Nov. 27, 1863 |
| Bowen, E | do | Nov. 27, 1863 |
| Berthier, Wilson | Center | Nov. 27, 1863 |
| Barrett, Henry | do | Nov. 27, 1863 |
| Barrett, Arthur | do | Nov. 27, 1863 |
| Becker, Henry | Black Creek | Dec. 28, 1864 |
| Brown, Chas | Maple Creek | Dec 28, 1864 |
| Badds, Adam | Brown Co | Nov. 27, 1863 |
| Brill, Jno | Morrison | Nov. 27, 1863 |
| Brogan, Jno | Holland | Nov. 27, 1863 |
| Burt, Wm | Lawrence | Nov. 27, 1863 |
| Brice, Lewis | Green Bay City | Nov. 27, 1863 |
| Bailey, Henry | Fort Howard | Nov. 27, 1863 |
| Brown, Alexander | Depere | Dec. 28, 1864 |
| Barker, Peter | Suamico | Dec. 28, 1864 |
| Burkhardt, Michael | Scott | Dec. 28, 1864 |
| Belawque, Edw'd | do | Dec. 28, 1864 |
| Berceau, Felician | Humboldt | Dec. 28, 1864 |
| Bincher, Constant | do | Dec. 28, 1864 |
| Burk, Dan'l | Marinette | Nov. 28, 1863 |
| Bishop, David | Oconto (village) | Nov. 28, 1863 |
| Brunette, Jesse | do | Nov. 28, 1863 |
| Bancross, Lewis | do | Nov. 28, 1863 |
| Brown, Wm. L | do | Nov. 28, 1863 |
| Burton, Rodger | Peshtigo | Nov. 28, 1863 |
| Brown, Jno | Stiles | Nov. 28, 1863 |
| Brown, Geo | do | Dec. 29, 1864 |
| Belzar, Fred | Pensaukee | Dec. 29, 1864 |
| Beauvcoek, Isaac | do | Dec. 29, 1864 |

## C

| | | |
|---|---|---|
| Colligan, Thomas | Emmett | Oct. 11, 1864 |
| Comer, Jacob L | Oak Grove | Nov. 20, 1863 |
| Clark, James | Burnett | Nov. 20, 1863 |
| Cherry, Edward W | Chester | Nov. 20, 1863 |
| Cibott, John | Watertown | Oct. 6, 1864 |
| Curley, Martin | do | Oct. 6, 1864 |
| Comer, Jacob | do | Dec. 1, 1864 |
| Cowls, T | Leroy | Nov. 20, 1863 |
| Clement, Jonathan F | do | Oct. 4, 1864 |
| Canter, Henry | do | Dec. 1, 1864 |
| Compton, Sylvester | Lomira | Nov. 20, 1863 |
| Cornelius, Benefeld | Herman | Jan. 27, 1864 |
| Carey, Henry S | Trenton | Nov. 20, 1863 |
| Courser, Wesley | do | Nov. 20, 1863 |
| Coughlin Cornelius | do | Nov. 20, 1863 |
| Cass, Richard | Hubbard | Nov. 21, 1863 |
| Cavanaugh, John | Rubicon | Nov. 21, 1863 |
| Connors, Thomas | Hartford | Nov. 21, 1863 |
| Clarey, Paul | Erin | Oct. 12, 1864 |
| Cooney, William | do | Oct. 12, 1864 |
| Curtin, John | do | Dec 1, 1864 |
| Connors, James | do | Dec. 1, 1864 |
| Cumbershau, W. R | Barton | Dec 1, 1864 |

| *Name* | *Residence* | *Date.* |
|---|---|---|
| Conrad, Adam | Polk | Oct. 12, 1864 |
| Cumm, John | Richfield | Nov. 21, 1863 |
| Curberry, Pat | Fond du Lac | Nov. 19, 1863 |
| Conroy, John | do | Nov 19, 1863 |
| Cayer, Nelson | Eden | Nov. 19, 1863 |
| Conley, John | do | Nov 19, 1863 |
| Casey, James | Oakfield | Nov. 19, 1863 |
| Cock n, John | Auburn | Nov. 19, 1863 |
| Carr, Frank | pringvale | Nov. 19, 1863 |
| Canary, Daniel | Ripon | Nov. 9, 1863 |
| Cloud, Cales | do | Nov. 19, 1863 |
| Catsam, Thomas | Elderado | Oct. 5, 1864 |
| Craker, William | do | Dec. 1, 1864 |
| Cowham, William | do | Dec. 1, 1864 |
| Connelly, James | Fox Lake | Dec. 1, 1864 |
| Coonan, John | do | Dec. 1, 1864 |
| Courser, George | do | Dec. 1, 1864 |
| Comelia, John | Westford | Nov 20, 1863 |
| Cobler, John | do | Nov 20, 1863 |
| Clue, Henry | Elba | Nov. 20, 1863 |
| Comstock, D. B. | P rtland | Nov. 20, 1863 |
| Cady, James | Shields | Nov 20, 1863 |
| Clason, Cyrus S. | Beaver Dam | Nov. 2 , 1863 |
| Cole, William | do | Nov. 20, 1863 |
| Cunningham, James | Emmett | Oct. 11, 1864 |
| Carley, Sylvester | do | Oct. 11, 1864 |
| Cartey, Groover | do | Oct. 11, 1864 |
| Casser Joseph | Richfield | Oct. 12, 1864 |
| Campbell, Charles | do | Oct. 12, 1864 |
| Campbell, John | do | Oct. 12, 1864 |
| Cosgrove, Michael | do | Oct. 12, 1864 |
| Callenbach, Gorhardt | do | Dec. 1, 1864 |
| Cum, Henry | do | Dec 1, 1864 |
| Ceronof, Thomas | do | Dec. 1, 1864 |
| Clump, Peter | do | Jan. 27, 1865 |
| Campbell, John | Farmington | Oct 18, 1864 |
| Clarke, Peter | do | Dec. 1, 1864 |
| Cristel, Mikel | do | Dec. 1, 1864 |
| Cranes, Godlip | do | Jan. 27, 1865 |
| Callaham, David | Jackson | Oct. 11, 1864 |
| Croil, William | Belgium | Oct. 13, 1864 |
| Carrols Nicholas | do | Oct. 13, 1864 |
| Carrols, Franz | do | Oct. 13, 1864 |
| Chapren, Hiram | do | Oct. 14, 1864 |
| Carntz, Ferdinand | do | Oct 14, 1864 |
| Cordell, Nicholas | Fredonia | Dec. 1, 1864 |
| Collins, A. | Grafton | Nov. 23, 1863 |
| Cole, George | do | Oct. 13, 1864 |
| Cronor, Timothy | do | Oct. 13, 1864 |
| Claty, Francis | do | Oct. 13, 1864 |
| Clu-, August | do | Oct. 13, 1864 |
| Clark, Melvin | do | Oct 13, 1864 |
| Cole, John | Plymouth | Oct. 21, 1864 |
| Crockett H. W | do | Oct. 21, 1864 |
| Crues, Geo | Milwaukee | Nov. 9, 1863 |
| Caaterr, Geo | do | Nov. 9, 1863 |
| Cox, Geo | do | Nov 9, 1863 |
| Coe, David | do | Nov. 9, 1863 |
| Celarer, Dan'l C | do | Sep. 19, 1864 |

| *Name.* | *Residence.* | *Date.* |
|---|---|---|
| Cocklin, August | Milwaukee | Sep. 19, 1864 |
| Clinton, Fred | do | Sep. 19, 1864 |
| Caltux, Jacob | do | Sep. 19, 1864 |
| Cunningham M | do | Sep. 19, 1864 |
| Charles, Thos | do | Sep. 19, 1864 |
| Caleman, Lawrence | do | Sep. 19, 1864 |
| Clark, J. B | do | Nov. 14, 1864 |
| Connalley, Michael | do | Nov. 14, 1864 |
| Casper, Dan'l | do | Nov. 14, 1864 |
| Carr, Pat | do | Nov. 14, 1864 |
| Cassell, Jacob | do | Nov. 14, 1864 |
| Conrad, Baft | do | Nov. 14, 1864 |
| Cough, Christian | do | Dec. 22, 1864 |
| Castron, Barnt | do | Dec. 22, 1864 |
| Cuttler, Chas | do | Nov. 9, 1863 |
| Cleason, John | do | Nov. 9, 1863 |
| Clark, Wm | do | Nov. 9, 1863 |
| Conner, Jas | do | Sep. 20, 1864 |
| Cortzen, Lewis | do | Sep. 20, 1864 |
| Cohn, Geo | do | Sep. 20, 1864 |
| Cary, P | do | Nov. 10, 1863 |
| Cowan, W | do | Nov. 10, 1863 |
| Caliman, John | do | Nov. 10, 1863 |
| Carrol, Thos | do | Nov. 10, 1863 |
| Chamberlain, C. T | do | Nov. 10, 1863 |
| Callahan, Pat | do | Nov. 10, 1863 |
| Caswell, Geo | do | Nov. 10, 1863 |
| Collow, W | do | Nov. 10, 1863 |
| Crilly, Nick | do | Nov. 10, 1863 |
| Conners, Jas | do | Nov. 10, 1863 |
| Callihan, ——— | do | Nov. 10, 1863 |
| Cassin, Thos | do | Nov. 10, 1863 |
| Carter, W | do | Nov. 10, 1863 |
| Carroll, P | do | Nov. 10, 1863 |
| Cassidy, Peter | do | Nov. 10, 1863 |
| Cinroy, Patrick | do | Nov. 10, 1863 |
| Coveneran, John | do | Nov. 10, 1863 |
| Connell, Jerry | do | Nov. 10, 1863 |
| Clark, John | do | Nov. 10, 1863 |
| Cathrine, G | do | Nov. 10, 1863 |
| Cinlan, John | do | Nov. 10, 1863 |
| Clark, James | do | Nov. 10, 1863 |
| Collins, E. D | do | Nov. 10, 1863 |
| Coin, Maton | do | Sep. 20, 1864 |
| Clark, John | do | Sep. 20, 1864 |
| Cooper, Thomas | do | Sep. 20, 1864 |
| Crocket, E. R | do | Sep. 20, 1864 |
| Campbell, Thomas | do | Sep. 20, 1864 |
| Camel, James | do | Sep. 20, 1864 |
| Cline, John | do | Sep. 20, 1864 |
| Conriff, Henry | Milwaukee | Sep. 20, 1864 |
| Carey, J | do | Sep. 20, 1864 |
| Cratz, L | do | Sep. 20, 1864 |
| Coyne, Patrick William | do | Sep. 20, 1864 |
| Carsey, Thomas | do | Sep. 20, 1864 |
| Clary, Patrick | do | Sep. 20, 1864 |
| Cole, Henry | do | Sep. 20, 1864 |
| Cahal, ——— | do | Sep. 20, 1864 |
| Cogan, J | do | Sep. 20, 1864 |

| *Name.* | *Residence.* | *Date.* |
|---|---|---|
| Carey, Jerry | Milwaukee | Sep. 20, 1864 |
| Crout, J. S. | do | Sep. 20, 1864 |
| Collimer, Jerry | do | Sep. 20, 1864 |
| Crouch, Mark | do | Nov. 15, 1864 |
| Coleman, Richard | do | Nov. 15, 1864 |
| Crilby, I. J. | do | Nov. 15, 1864 |
| Craivan, J. | do | Nov. 15, 1864 |
| Cammer, Thomas | do | Nov. 15, 1864 |
| Coin, William | do | Nov. 15, 1864 |
| Connel, Jerry | do | Nov. 15, 1864 |
| Calow, Michael | do | Nov. 15, 1864 |
| Coughlin, David | do | Nov. 15, 1864 |
| Chase, Egbert | do | Nov. 15, 1864 |
| Coffee, Daniel | do | Nov. 15, 1864 |
| Connell, John | do | Nov. 15, 1864 |
| Colshirers, F. | do | Nov. 15, 1864 |
| Cuttle, H. C. | do | Nov. 15, 1864 |
| Camble, B. | do | Nov. 15, 1864 |
| Cadding, A. H. | do | Jan. 11, 1865 |
| Conners, Thomas | do | Jan. 11, 1865 |
| Curtin, M. | do | Jan. 11, 1865 |
| Collocks, Daniel | do | Jan. 11, 1865 |
| Curdike, J. | do | Jan. 11, 1865 |
| Carl, Martin | do | Jan. 11, 1865 |
| Curley, J | do | Jan. 11, 1865 |
| Cannon, John | do | Jan. 11, 1865 |
| Connolly, Dennis | do | Jan. 11, 1865 |
| Carroll, Martin | do | Jan. 11, 1865 |
| Crilley, Edward | do | Jan. 11, 1865 |
| Carroll, Daniel | do | Jan. 11, 1865 |
| Clancey, James | do | Nov. 10, 1863 |
| Connell, James | do | Nov. 10, 1863 |
| Curlly, Thomas | do | Nov. 10, 1863 |
| Cary, Timothy | do | Nov. 10, 1863 |
| Cochran, Timothy | do | Nov. 10, 1863 |
| Conklin, Oscar | do | Nov. 10, 1863 |
| Clancy, Patrick | do | Nov. 10, 1863 |
| Cocklin, Timothy | do | Nov. 10, 1863 |
| Crouch, Gideon | do | Nov. 10, 1863 |
| Cary, Jerry | do | Nov. 10, 1863 |
| Curlly, John | do | Nov. 10, 1863 |
| Clarke, W. G. | do | Nov. 10, 1863 |
| Collins, Thomas | do | Sep. 21, 1864 |
| Connell, Patrick | do | Sep. 21, 1864 |
| Casson, Michael | do | Sep. 21, 1864 |
| Cohill, James | do | Sep. 21, 1864 |
| Carey, George H. | do | Nov. 10, 1863 |
| Carnell, William V. | do | Nov. 10, 1863 |
| Crumb, Joseph | do | Nov. 10, 1863 |
| Cooney, William | do | Nov. 10, 1863 |
| Cricky, Charles | do | Nov. 10, 1863 |
| Casterly, Conrad | do | Nov. 10, 1863 |
| Cromvell, J. B. | do | Nov. 10, 1863 |
| Christianson, Dan. | do | Nov. 10, 1863 |
| Cory, Truman | do | Nov. 10, 1863 |
| Crockept, E. R | do | Nov. 10, 1863 |
| Comode, James | do | Sep. 21, 1864 |
| Carter, James M. | do | Sep. 21, 1864 |
| Clay, Henry | do | Sep. 21, 1864 |

| *Name* | *Residence.* | *Date.* |
|---|---|---|
| Clock, John | Milwaukee | Sep. 21, 1864 |
| Coeln, Frederick | do | Sep. 21, 1864 |
| Carley, Erastus | do | Nov. 10, 1863 |
| Crosier, Jarvis | do | Nov. 10, 1863 |
| Christman, Philip | do | Nov. 10, 1863 |
| Casper, Peter | do | Nov. 11, 1863 |
| Cramer, John | do | Nov. 11, 1863 |
| Collett, Peter | do | Nov. 25, 1864 |
| Cold, Jenkins | do | Nov. 11, 1863 |
| Caspar, Heinrich | do | Nov. 11, 1863 |
| Christianson, James | do | Nov. 11, 1863 |
| Cold, Harper | do | Nov. 11, 1863 |
| Crawford, James | do | Nov. 30, 1864 |
| Chishoim, William | do | Jan. 26, 1865 |
| Christiansen, Thomas | do | Jan. 19, 1865 |
| C[illegible]urn, Thomas | do | Jan. 19, 1865 |
| Cutterburgh, William | do | Jan. 19, 1865 |
| Conrad, William H. | do | Dec. 7, 1864 |
| Crayling, Gustaff | Granville | Sep. 22, 1864 |
| Caspary, Simon | Wauwatosa | Nov 11, 1863 |
| Camlin, Thomas | Greenfield | Sep. 22, 1864 |
| Crounse, Silas H | do | Sep. 22, 1864 |
| Conrad, John | do | Sep. 21, 1864 |
| Copetsky, John | Lake | Nov. 11, 1863 |
| Cleveland, Mahlon W | do | Sep. 22, 1864 |
| Carey, Charles | Oak Creek | Sep. 22, 1864 |
| Clough, J | Racine | Nov. 11, 1863 |
| Crowe, Patrick | do | Nov. 11, 1863 |
| Clock, William | do | Nov. 11, 1863 |
| Cooper, Hugh G. | do | Sep. 24, 1864 |
| Cramer, Matthias | do | Sep. [illegible]4, 1864 |
| Cartman, Frank | do | Sep. 24, 1864 |
| Clinick, Anton | do | Nov. 11, 1863 |
| Cram, Frederick | do | Nov. 11, 1863 |
| Chauncy, Daniel | do | Sep. 22, 1864 |
| Coleman, Frederick | do | Sep. 22, 1864 |
| Calbroun, Richard | Mount Pleasant | Sep. 23, 1864 |
| Cheesemore, D | Dover | Nov. 11, 1863 |
| Crane, William | do | Sep 23, 1864 |
| Crane, Walter | do | Dec. 10, 1864 |
| Chsach, ——— | Rochester | Sep. 23, 1864 |
| Carpenter, William | do | Sep. 23, 1864 |
| Collahan, Patrick | do | Sep. 23, 1864 |
| Coin, Thomas | do | Sep. 23, 1864 |
| Colburn, Allen | Raymond | Nov. 11, 1863 |
| Christenson, Niels | do | Sep. 23, 1864 |
| Compte, Henry | do | Sep. 23, 1864 |
| Cross, William | do | Sep. 23, 1864 |
| Carney, Thomas | Caledonia | Sep. 22, 1864 |
| Cook, Joseph | do | Sep. 22, 1864 |
| Collins, Daniel W | do | Dec. 7, 1864 |
| Calligan, Michael | do | Dec. 7, 1864 |
| Cresser, Nicholas | Somers | Nov. 12, 1863 |
| Crane, George B | do | Nov. 12, 1863 |
| Carpenter, Joseph | Wheatland | Dec. 14, 1864 |
| Cottrea, C. F. | do | Dec. 14, 1864 |
| Clapp, Jessie J. | do | Dec. 14, 1864 |
| Case, Anson D. | Paris | Sep. 24, 1864 |
| Christian, William | Randall | Sep. 24, 1864 |

| *Name.* | *Residence.* | *Date.* |
|---|---|---|
| Capol, Charles | Randall | Sep. 24, 1864 |
| Cottrell, Larned | do | Sep. 24, 1864 |
| Chase, Charles E. | Bristol | Nov. 12, 1863 |
| Crousay, Daniel | Delavan | Nov. 12, 1863 |
| Chambers, James | do | Nov. 12, 1863 |
| Clark, George L. | do | Nov. 12, 1863 |
| Cook, Joseph | Sugar Creek | Nov. 12, 1863 |
| Colman, Walter | Richmond | Nov. 12, 1863 |
| Clarke, Edward F. | Whitewater | Nov. 12, 1863 |
| Clinton, James | do | Nov. 12, 1863 |
| Coyne, Thomas | La Fayette | Nov. 12, 1863 |
| Connotly, John | Geneva | Nov. 12, 1863 |
| Connell, Thomas | East Troy | Sep. 24, 1864 |
| Cretes, George C. | do | Sep. 24, 1864 |
| Crane, Charles | do | Sep. 24, 1864 |
| Clark, P. M. | do | Sep. 24, 1864 |
| Cobeliske, August | do | Sep. 24, 1864 |
| Cox, Daniel | Spring Prairie | Nov. 12, 1863 |
| Cramer, Martin | Summit | Sep. 22, 1864 |
| Clark, Bryan | do | Sep. 22, 1864 |
| Campbell, L. A. | Oconomowoc | Sep. 22, 1864 |
| Carney, Michael | do | Sep. 22, 1864 |
| Coleman, Martin | do | Dec. 5, 1864 |
| Carson, George | Delafield | Nov. 12, 1863 |
| Couton, Daniel | Pewaukee | Sep. 22, 1864 |
| Cadwell, John | do | Sep. 22, 1864 |
| Cook, Emanuel | do | Dec. 2, 1864 |
| Connelly, Edward | Waukesha | Sep. 23, 1864 |
| Coonay, John | do | Sep. 23, 1864 |
| Cole, John | do | Sep. 23, 1864 |
| Costigan, Dennis | Menomonee | Sep. 24, 1864 |
| Cacy, Thomas | do | Sep. 24, 1864 |
| Cailey, Peter | do | Sep. 24, 1864 |
| Clark, John | do | Sep 24, 1864 |
| Clucheser, Peter | do | Sep. 24, 1864 |
| Cook, James | do | Dec. 1, 1864 |
| Cleveland, George | do | Dec. 1, 1864 |
| Cady, Nicholas | do | Dec. 1, 1864 |
| Crogan, Barney | Brookfield | Sep. 23, 1864 |
| Cleveland, Marcus M | New Berlin | Nov. 12, 1863 |
| Carroll, Thomas | do | Nov. 12, 1863 |
| Crosby, John | Muskego | Sep. 24, 1864 |
| Cless, John J. | do | Nov. 30, 1864 |
| Carr, Jacob | do | Dec. 1, 1864 |
| Comes, James | Delafield | Sep. 22, 1864 |
| Christeinson, Niels P. | do | Sep. 22, 1864 |
| Campbell, Jerome W | Avon | Nov. 12, 1863 |
| Clement, A. | Beloit | Nov. 12, 1863 |
| Ceefort, Charles | do | Nov. 12, 1863 |
| Casey, John | Rock | Nov. 12, 1863 |
| Croak, Michael | Magnolia | Nov. 12, 1863 |
| Carey, Samuel | Janesville | Nov. 12, 1863 |
| Coyle, Henry | do | Nov. 12, 1863 |
| Collins, John | do | Nov. 12, 1863 |
| Coburn, Philip | do | Nov. 12, 1863 |
| Cargill, Thomas E | Harmony | Nov. 12, 1863 |
| Cramb, A. C. | Milton | Nov. 12, 1863 |
| Connor, Daniel | do | Nov. 12, 1863 |
| Caneen, Michael | Vermont | Sep. 19, 1864 |

| *Name.* | *Residence.* | *Date.* |
|---|---|---|
| Cunningham, John | Madison | Nov. 13, 1863 |
| Cambergger, Mat | do | Nov. 13, 1863 |
| Capper, William | do | Nov. 12, 1863 |
| Conner, Patrick | Deerfield | Nov. 13, 1863 |
| Christopher, Martin | do | Nov. 13, 1863 |
| Conley, Philip | do | Nov. 13, 1863 |
| Clark, Thomas | Sun Prairie | Sep. 19, 1864 |
| Corlie, Henry A | do | Sep. 19, 1864 |
| Cotton, Charles | Westport | Nov. 13, 1863 |
| Coles, John | Windsor | Nov. 13, 1863 |
| Crandall, Russel W | Farmington | Oct. 28, 1864 |
| Curtis, F. C | Watertown | Sep. 20, 1864 |
| Conrad, F. W | Columbus | Nov. 16, 1863 |
| Crowley, Daniel | Pacific | Sep. 21, 1864 |
| Crowley, John | Lewiston | Sep. 21, 1864 |
| Christianson, Christian | Perry | Sep. 19, 1864 |
| Cistelson, Johan | do | Sep. 19, 1864 |
| Caughey, William M | Springdale | Sep. 19, 1864 |
| Cashem, Frank | Watertown | Oct. 15, 1864 |
| Casey, William | Fort Winnebago | Sep. 21, 1864 |
| Cotter, Edward | do | Sep. 21, 1864 |
| Cook, Wm. J | Rockb'dg, Henri'ta or Will'w. | Nov. 14, 1863 |
| Cook, John | Henrietta | Sept. 26, 1864 |
| Carpenter, Jonathan | Arena or Wyoming | Nov. 14, 1863 |
| Casady, Alex | Ridgeway | Nov. 14, 1863 |
| Casady, John | do | Sep. 28, 1864 |
| Conly, Wm | do | Sep. 28, 1864 |
| Canan, Jas | do | Sep. 28, 1864 |
| Crassin, Philip | do | Oct. 28, 1864 |
| Christienson, Ole | Dodgeville | Sept. 28, 1864 |
| Clymore, Richard | do | Sep. 28, 1864 |
| Curnow, John | do | Oct. 28, 1864 |
| Christapherson, Michael | Highland | Sep. 28, 1864 |
| Cauch, John W | do | Oct. 28, 1864 |
| Cullin, Thos | do | Dec. 7, 1864 |
| Crowley, Michael | Linden or Mifflin | Nov. 14, 1863 |
| Ching, Thos | Waldwick | Oct. 4, 1864 |
| Callins, Jas | do | Oct. 4, 1864 |
| Christopherson, Hans | Moscow | Sep. 28, 1864 |
| Carroll, Martin | do | Sep. 28, 1864 |
| Chesterfield, John Jr | Willow Springs | Nov. 16, 1863 |
| Carty, Pat | Benton | Sep. 29, 1864 |
| Carter, Edward | do | Sep. 29, 1864 |
| Charles, Richard | New Diggings | Nov. 16, 1863 |
| Conagen, Owen | do | Nov. 16, 1863 |
| Conley, Andrew | do | Nov. 16, 1863 |
| Crawford, Thos | do | Sep. 29, 1864 |
| Cook, David | Beetown | Oct. 1, 1864 |
| Chapman, Thos | Platteville | Nov. 19, 1863 |
| Cribban, John | Bloom | Sep. 26, 1864 |
| Chitwood, Wm | Sylvan | Sep. 26, 1864 |
| Cruice, Pat | Westford | Sep. 26, 1864 |
| Crowley, John | Seneca | Sep. 30, 1864 |
| Craw, Harmon E | do | Oct. 29, 1864 |
| Crawley, Ed | Eastman | Sep. 30, 1864 |
| Cavenaugh, Owen | do | Sep. 30, 1864 |
| Crowley, Pat | do | Sep. 30, 1864 |
| Cumisky, Philip jr | do | Nov. 19, 1864 |
| Carmody, Pat | Millville | Oct. 1, 1864 |

| *Name.* | *Residence.* | *Date.* |
|---|---|---|
| Carral, Pat | La Valle | Oct. 3, 1864 |
| Cannon, Wm | Woodland | Oct. 3, 1864 |
| Clark, David | Bear Creek | Oct. 3, 1864 |
| Cull, Michael | Millville | Oct. 28, 1864 |
| Cady, Pat | Blue River | Oct. 29, 1864 |
| Cooper, Thos. J | Franklin | Oct. 29, 1864 |
| Cafron, Thomas | Blue River | Nov. 19, 1864 |
| Canula, Peter | do | Nov. 19, 1864 |
| Carrol, John | do | Nov. 19, 1864 |
| Campbell, P. M | Lavalle | Nov. 19, 1864 |
| Connell, Theodore | La Crosse City | Nov. 13, 1863 |
| Cheshire, John L | La Crosse Co | Nov. 13, 1863 |
| Carter, John | Campbell | Nov. 18, 1863 |
| Carter, John | do | Nov. 19, 1863 |
| Cooper, Lewis | Irving | Sep. 23, 1864 |
| Clark, Marcus | Manchester | Sep. 23, 1864 |
| Curtis, Robert | Portage Co | Nov. 23, 1863 |
| Chamberlin, Frank | do | Nov. 23, 1863 |
| Clark, Michael | do | Nov. 23, 1863 |
| Clark, James | Linwood | Oct. 31, 1864 |
| Conner, John | do | Oct. 31, 1864 |
| Corey, Aaron | Sharon | Oct. 31, 1864 |
| Coleman, Henry | Linwood | Sep. 22, 1864 |
| Coleman, Geo. E | do | Sep. 22, 1864 |
| Collins, Wm | Belmont | Sep. 22, 1864 |
| Collier, David | do | Sep. 22, 1864 |
| Cooney, Martin | Lanark | Sep. 22, 1864 |
| Chamberlin, James | Hull | Sep. 22, 1864 |
| Collier, Arthur | Belmont | Nov. 15, 1864 |
| Collier, John | do | Nov. 15, 1864 |
| Champion, Thos | St. Croix Co | Nov. 20, 1863 |
| Costigan, John | Emerald | Sep. 23, 1864 |
| Caesley, Horace | Rush River | Sep. 23, 1864 |
| Clendenninng, Robert | St. Croix Co | Sep. 23, 1864 |
| Connolly, Thos | do | Sep. 23, 1864 |
| Carafelle, Chas | Somerset | Oct. 5, 1864 |
| Cuttneau, Joseph | do | Oct. 5, 1864 |
| Cuttenu, Chas | do | Oct. 5, 1864 |
| Cuttenu, Peter | do | Nov. 3, 1864 |
| Collins, Samuel | Eau Galle | Nov. 3, 1864 |
| Christiansen, Christopher | do | Nov. 3, 1864 |
| Carpenter, Jesse | Dunn Co | Nov. 23, 1863 |
| Clark, Chas | Weston | Sep. 23, 1864 |
| Chase, Edward | Eau Galle | Sep. 27, 1864 |
| Clouson, Tobias | do | Sep. 27, 1864 |
| Chase, J. A | do | Nov. 2, 1864 |
| Cullman, John A | do | Nov. 2, 1864 |
| Chisin, Murdock | Clam River | Nov. 20, 1863 |
| Chabino, Clement | Wood county | Nov. 18, 1863 |
| Carrier, Leon D | Centralia | Sep. 22, 1864 |
| Carting, Nicholas | do | Sep. 22, 1864 |
| Carroll, Jeremiah | Kildare | Sep. 19, 1864 |
| Conway, Dennis | do | Sep. 19, 1864 |
| Clermen, Martin | do | Sep. 19, 1864 |
| Coalbum, Michael | do | Sep. 19, 1864 |
| Casey, James | do | Oct. 31, 1864 |
| Coalbum, Patrick | do | Oct. 31, 1864 |
| Conway, Lawrence | do | Oct. 31, 1864 |
| Caughlin, James | do | Oct. 31, 1864 |

| Name | Residence | Date. |
|---|---|---|
| Claffin, C. C | Lemonweir | Sep. 19, 1864 |
| Claffin Lorenzo S | do | Sep. 19, 1864 |
| Camp, Robert | do | Oct. 31, 1864 |
| Case, Harvey | Summit | Sep. 19, 1864 |
| Calkins, Levi | do | Sep. 19, 1864 |
| Clark, Geo | do | Oct. 31, 1864 |
| Cowen, James | Lyndon | Sep. 20, 1864 |
| Carrick, Jerry | do | Sep. 20, 1864 |
| Clark, Henry | do | Sep. 20, 1864 |
| Capstick, Geo | do | Sep. 20, 1864 |
| Clark, Henry | do | Sep. 20, 1864 |
| Clark, Horace | do | Oct. 31, 1864 |
| Cornish, Joel | Germantown | Sep. 20, 1864 |
| Collahan, Daniel | Tomah | Sep. 20, 1864 |
| Cassidy, Jno | do | Nov. 10, 1864 |
| Cary, H | Clifton | Sep. 20, 1864 |
| Corkin, Jas | Ettrick | Sep. 21, 1864 |
| Christonson, Ole | do | Sep. 21, 1864 |
| Colburn, Frans S | Bergen | Sep. 21, 1864 |
| Conner, James | Greenwood | Sep. 21, 1864 |
| Colbington, S. H | Franklin | Nov. 15, 1864 |
| Carey, David | do | Nov. 15, 1864 |
| Chohoon, Thos | Naples | Sep. 26, 1864 |
| Couley, Jno | do | Nov. 16, 1864 |
| Creese, Joseph, | Wilson | Sep. 26, 1864 |
| Collins, Wm | Lincoln | Sep. 26, 1864 |
| Coleby, Jno | Easton | Sep. 26, 1864 |
| Casey, Jas | do | Sep. 26, 1864 |
| Campbell, Jno | do | Sep. 26, 1864 |
| Carter, Wm | Adams | Sep. 26, 1864 |
| Champlin, Chas. M | do | Sep. 26, 1864 |
| Caverhell, Enoch | Monroe | Sep. 26, 1864 |
| Corey, Roswell R | Springville | Nov. 14, 1864 |
| Cummings, Benj | Preston | Sep. 26, 1864 |
| Crawford, Robert | Leola | Nov. 14, 1864 |
| Clark, J | New Haven | Nov. 14, 1864 |
| Crosby, Alden | Durand | Sep. 27, 1864 |
| Carpenter, Horace | do | Sep. 27, 1864 |
| Callihan, Jas | Pepin | Sep. 27, 1864 |
| Cannon, Nelson | Lima | Sep. 27, 1864 |
| Carpenter, —— | do | Sep. 27, 1864 |
| Coffe, Jno | Chippewa Falls | Sep. 27, 1864 |
| Clark, James jr | do | Nov. 2, 1864 |
| Clements, Geo | La Fayette | Sep. 27, 1864 |
| Campbell, Jas | Trumbull | Nov. 3, 1864 |
| Champion, Joseph | Waubeek | Nov. 16, 1864 |
| Cenger, Samuel | Lima | Nov. 16, 1864 |
| Cooper, John | Door Co | Nov. 20, 1863 |
| Choudoin, Autoine | Brussells | Dec. 29, 1864 |
| Cordier, Eugene | do | Dec. 29, 1864 |
| Champion, Jno | Kewaunee | Nov. 20, 1863 |
| Cunningham, Jno | do | Nov. 20, 1863 |
| Chaleck, Louis | do | Nov. 20, 1863 |
| Conrad, Mathias | Montpelier | Dec. 29, 1864 |
| Coon, Joseph | Red River | Dec. 29, 1864 |
| Cuzick, Joseph | Franklin | Dec. 29, 1864 |
| Coleman, Bernhard | Carlton | Dec. 29, 1864 |
| Chully, Jas. Pierre | Lincoln | Dec. 29, 1864 |
| Culve, Jno. J | do | Dec. 29, 1864 |

| *Name.* | *Residence.* | *Date* |
|---|---|---|
| Connell, Michael | Maple Grove | Nov. 21, 1863 |
| Caflish, David | do | Dec. 29, 1864 |
| Caga, Joseph | Two Rivers | Nov. 21, 1863 |
| Carr, Martin | Newton | Nov. 21, 1863 |
| Camfert, Albert | Gibson | Dec. 29, 1864 |
| Cizeck, Wenzel | Kossuth | Dec. 29, 1864 |
| Clark, Michael | Cato | Dec 29, 1864 |
| Cuish, John | Calumet Co | Nov. 21, 1863 |
| Cummings, Francis R | Charleston | Nov. 21, 1863 |
| Connell, Patrick | Chilton | Nov. 23, 1863 |
| Connelly, James | do | Dec. 28, 1864 |
| Coleman, John | do | Dec. 28, 1864 |
| Crompart, Napoleon | Brothertown | Nov. 23, 1863 |
| Collin, James | Rantoul | Dec. 28, 1864 |
| Chrissey, James | Woodville | Dec. 28, 1864 |
| Conroy, Patrick | Harrison | Dec. 28, 1864 |
| Canady, Timothy | Stockbridge | Dec. 28, 1864 |
| Coats, Noel C. | Vinland | Nov. 23, 1863 |
| Cox, Henry C | Oshkosh city | Nov. 23, 1863 |
| Cusick, Hiram G | Algoma | Nov. 23, 1863 |
| Crays, Jno. F | do | Nov. 23, 1863 |
| Campbell, Thos. J | Omro | Nov. 23, 1863 |
| Comstock, Mark J | Rushford | Nov. 24, 1863 |
| Cleveland, Clark | Clayton | Nov. 24, 1863 |
| Colton, Thos | Utica | Nov. 24, 1863 |
| Cain, James | Poygan | Dec. 29, 1863 |
| Case, Walter | do | Dec. 29, 1863 |
| Crandall, Samuel H | Berlin | Nov. 24, 1864 |
| Cornnif, Chas | Berlin city | Nov. 24, 1864 |
| Conner, Gahagan | Green Lake | Nov. 24, 1864 |
| Chapel, James M | Kingston | Nov. 24, 1864 |
| Crumwell John | St. Marie | Nov. 24, 1864 |
| Callahan, John | Marquette Co | Nov. 24, 1864 |
| Clark, Henry | do | Nov. 24, 1864 |
| Clelland, Hugh | do | Nov. 24, 1864 |
| Callaghan, Owen | Neshkora | Nov. 1, 1864 |
| Callahan, Jeremiah | Mecan | Nov. 1, 1864 |
| Chambe lain, L. E | Buffalo | Nov. 1, 1864 |
| Cockle, Dan'l | Crystal Lake | Nov. 1, 1864 |
| Collins, James | Shields | Nov. 1, 1864 |
| Camlets, Ferdinand | do | Nov. 1, 1864 |
| Caldwell, Chas | Springfield | Nov. 1, 1864 |
| Cummings, Patrick | Douglas | Dec. 31, 1864 |
| Coplen, Chas | Newton | Dec. 31, 1864 |
| Clum, Ambrose | Waushara Co | Nov. 25, 1863 |
| Clapper, David A | Wautoma | Nov. 25, 1863 |
| Coggins, David | | Nov. 25, 1863 |
| Crows, Richard | | Nov. 25, 1863 |
| Chafee, Calvin | Plainfield | Nov. 25, 1863 |
| Crosby, Wm | do | Nov. 25, 1863 |
| Clement, Horace | do | Nov. 2, 1864 |
| Clement, A. | do | Dec. 31, 1864 |
| Cook, Ralph | do | Dec. 31, 1864 |
| Cartwright, H. W | do | Dec. 31, 1864 |
| Cannien, Phillip | Poysippl | Nov. 2. 1864 |
| Crimming, John | Aurora | Nov. 2, 1864 |
| Crimming, Jackson | do | Nov. 2, 1864 |
| Culver, Sylvester C | do | Nov. 2, 1864 |
| Clark, James | do | Dec. 31, 1864 |

| *Name.* | *Residence.* | *Date.* |
|---|---|---|
| Crimmings, M | Aurora | Dec. 31, 1864 |
| Cary, Richard | do | Dec. 31, 1864 |
| Covill, Geo. W | Warren | Nov. 2, 1864 |
| Cartwright, Alounsy | Richford | Nov. 2, 1864 |
| Chatwood, Wm | do | Nov. 2, 1864 |
| Chatwood, Geo | do | Nov. 2, 1864 |
| Chatwood, Thomas | do | Nov. 2, 1864 |
| Clark, Benj | do | Nov. 2, 1864 |
| Curtis, John S | do | Dec. 31, 1864 |
| Cook, S G | Deerfield | Nov. 2, 1864 |
| Coleman, Henry | do | Nov. 2, 1864 |
| Carey, Joseph C | do | Nov. 2, 1864 |
| Crowe, Eyre | Oasis | Nov. 2, 1864 |
| Crowe, Gideon | do | Dec. 31, 1864 |
| Calkins, Andrew | Lebanon | Nov. 25, 1863 |
| Collier, James | do | Nov. 5, 1864 |
| Cary, Nathan | Mukwa | Nov. 25, 1863 |
| Colborn, Z. C | Royalton | Nov. 25, 1863 |
| Carroll, Samuel | do | Nov. 5, 1864 |
| Cleary, Dennett | | Nov. 25, 1863 |
| Chambers, Wm. H | Weyauwega | Nov. 5, 1864 |
| Christianson, Claus | St. Lawrence | Nov. 5, 1864 |
| Collier, Hiram | do | Dec. 31, 1864 |
| Chandler, Kimball T | Iola | Nov. 5, 1864 |
| Cram, Luther | do | Nov. 5, 1864 |
| Christopherson, Ole | do | Dec. 31, 1864 |
| Christiansen, Cristin | do | Dec. 31, 1864 |
| Christiansen, Jacob | do | Dec. 31, 1864 |
| Champion, Samuel | Matteson | Nov. 25, 1864 |
| Carafousel Frank | Kaukama | Nov. 27, 1864 |
| Cottnigan, Thos | Buchanan | Nov. 27, 1864 |
| Commd, Tona | Grand Chute | Nov. 27, 1864 |
| Cary, Jno. B | Appleton | Nov. 27, 1864 |
| Craft, Fred | Center | Nov. 27, 1864 |
| Cannon, Patrick | do | Dec. 28, 1864 |
| Curley, Bernard | do | Dec. 28, 1864 |
| Colter, Patrick | do | Dec. 28, 1864 |
| Carter, Arnold | Osborn | Dec. 28, 1864 |
| Crake, Mason S | | Nov. 27, 1864 |
| Cannon, Morgan | Hortonia | Dec. 28, 1864 |
| Collins, James | Morrison | Dec. 28, 1864 |
| Choennett, Jôseph | do | Dec. 28, 1864 |
| Cain, Thos | do | Dec. 28, 1864 |
| Cocklin, Francis | Holland | Nov. 27, 1864 |
| Coughlin, Bernard | do | Nov. 27, 1864 |
| Caverney, Patrick | do | Dec. 28, 1864 |
| Carroll, James | do | Dec. 28, 1864 |
| Claney, Wm | do | Dec. 28, 1864 |
| Cain, Flan S | do | Dec. 28, 1864 |
| Clabots, Wm | Humboldt | Dec. 28, 1864 |
| Coney, Barney | Glenmore | Dec. 28, 1864 |
| Carlton, Geo | Depere | Dec. 28, 1864 |
| Couillard, Chas | Oconto | Nov. 28, 1863 |
| Champlain, Frank | do | Nov. 28, 1863 |
| Colynhornn, Robt | Peshtigo | Nov. 28, 1863 |
| Convery, James | Stiles | Nov. 28, 1863 |
| Clancey, Patrick | do | Dec. 29, 1863 |
| Clancey, Thomas | do | Dec. 29, 1863 |
| Coleman, Michael | Little | Nov. 28, 1863 |

| *Name.* | *Residence.* | *Date.* |
|---|---|---|
| Coahy, Stephen | Little | Nov. 28, 1863 |
| Clary, Timothy | do | Nov. 28, 1863 |
| Coughlin, Hugh | do | Nov. 28, 1863 |
| Cramer, Henry D. | do | Nov. 28, 1863 |
| Cudall, Lewis | do | Nov. 28, 1862 |
| Collins, James | Grafton | Dec. 1, 1864 |
| Clausen, Charles | Mequon | Nov. 23, 1863 |
| Colens, John | Saukville | Nov. 23, 1863 |
| Coriom, James | do | Oct. 14, 1864 |
| Cronenberg, Joseph | do | Oct. 14, 1864 |
| Cane, Morison | Sheboygan | Nov. 23, 1863 |
| Couchin, Henry | do | Dec. 2, 1864 |
| Cole, Edward | do | Jan. 27, 1865 |
| Carry, James | do | Dec. 2, 1864 |
| Canitz, Louis | do | Oct. 18, 1864 |
| Clanst, Wilhelm | do | Oct. 18, 1864 |
| Colenberg, Louis | Sheboygan Falls | Dec. 2, 1864 |
| Capeller, Anton | do | Jan. 27, 1864 |
| Chapman, Edwin | Lima | Dec. 2, 1864 |
| Clark, L. C. | do | Jan. 27, 1865 |
| Corden, William | Holland | Nov. 24, 1863 |
| Cain, Albert | do | Oct. 21, 1864 |
| Clark, James | Abbott | Jan. 27, 1865 |
| Caraker, Jacob | Scott | Dec. 2, 1864 |
| Cemei, John | do | Dec. 2, 1864 |
| Cross, Perry | do | Dec. 2, 1862 |
| Crotsgner, Henry | do | Jan. 27, 1865 |
| Croker Nicholas | do | Jan. 27, 1865 |

## D

| Name | Residence | Date |
|---|---|---|
| Decke, S. | Lima | Nov. 24, 1863 |
| Ducks, John | do | Oct. 24, 1864 |
| Dye, Andrew | do | Oct. 24, 1864 |
| Donnelson, Geo | do | Dec. 2, 1864 |
| Dulison, Jacob | do | Dec. 2, 1864 |
| Delands, John | do | Jan. 27, 1865 |
| DeGrauf, Lunees | Holland | Oct. 21, 1864 |
| DeGraft, James | do | Oct. 21, 1864 |
| Dekker, Peter | do | Oct. 21, 1864 |
| Dillon, John | do | Oct. 21, 1864 |
| DeGrotz, D | do | Oct. 21, 1864 |
| Dragodorf, Herman | Abbott | Oct. 18, 1864 |
| Doolan, John | do | Oct. 18, 1864 |
| Doyle, Jeremiah | do | Jan. 27, 1865 |
| Dayner, Ferdinand | Grafton | Oct. 13, 1865 |
| Drope, John | do | Dec. 1, 1864 |
| Dimarod, Mathias | do | Dec. 1, 1864 |
| Decker, Peter Joseph | do | Jan. 27, 1865 |
| Deitzen, Jacob | do | Jan. 27, 1865 |
| Dedic, Nicholas | Port Washington | Nov. 23, 1863 |
| Dempsey, Anthony | Saukville | Oct. 14, 1864 |
| Daly, Edward | do | Oct. 14, 1864 |
| Dempsey, John | do | Oct. 14, 1864 |
| Donahoe, William | do | Oct. 14, 1864 |
| Daly, Jeremiah | do | Oct. 14, 1864 |
| Demsey, Patrick | do | Oct. 14, 1864 |
| Dempsey, Michael | do | Oct. 14, 1864 |
| Detsh, Andrew | Sheboygan | Nov. 25, 1863 |
| Dyke, Alexander | do | Jan. 27, 1865 |

| *Name.* | *Residence* | *Date* |
|---|---|---|
| Dykes, Edward | Sheboygan | Oct. 25, 1864 |
| Denn, Simon | do | Dec. 2, 1864 |
| Detsch, John | do | Oct. 18, 1864 |
| Deekeman, Peter | do | Jan. 27, 1865 |
| Dann, Thomas | Moselle | Oct. 18, 1864 |
| Dumrol, Christian | Sheboygan Falls | Nov. 24, 1863 |
| Drus, Herman | do | Oct. 25, 1864 |
| Dale, John | do | Oct. 25, 1864 |
| Dawson, Jacobin | do | Dec. 2, 1864 |
| Drope, James | do | Dec. 2, 1864 |
| Delaney, Thomas H | Hubbard | Nov. 21, 1863 |
| Dye, Ruel | Hustisford | Nov. 21, 1863 |
| Donahoe, Michael | Erin | Nov 21, 1863 |
| Dunlap, John | do | Dec. 1, 1864 |
| Donahoe, Andrew O | do | Dec. 1, 1864 |
| Dora, Michael | do | Dec. 1, 1864 |
| Douglas, W. F | Barton | Oct. 12, 1864 |
| Davis, William | do | Oct. 12, 1864 |
| Dutcher, H | do | Oct. 12, 1864 |
| Darling, Otis | West Bend | Nov. 21, 1863 |
| Deifenback, Peter | Polk | Jan. 27, 1863 |
| Donnaho, Thomas | Richfield | Oct. 12, 1864 |
| Dillan, John | do | Oct. 12, 1864 |
| Dunn, Thomas | do | Dec. 1, 1864 |
| Danehu, Thomas | do | Dec. 1, 1864 |
| Dreekman, John | do | Jan. 27, 1865 |
| Diedrich, Joseph | Belgium | Oct. 13, 1864 |
| Delles, Peter R | do | Oct. 13, 1864 |
| Dries, John | do | Dec. 1, 1864 |
| Diesch, Nicholas | do | Dec. 1, 1864 |
| Domback, Peter | do | Dec. 1, 1864 |
| Dressler, William | Grafton | Oct. 13, 1864 |
| Doherty, Michael | Fond du Lac | Nov. 19, 1863 |
| Dencey, Ruben S | Lamartine | Nov. 19, 1863 |
| Davis, Rensaler | do | Nov. 19, 1863 |
| Delong, Charles | do | Nov. 19, 1863 |
| Daley, Timothy | Rosendale | Nov. 19, 1863 |
| Danigan, John | Eldorado | Oct. 5, 1864 |
| Dedʃoff, William | do | Oct. 5, 1864 |
| Dav rson, Robert | do | Dec. 1, 1864 |
| Dunham, George W | do | Dec 1, 1864 |
| Devine, James | Fox Lake | Nov. 19, 1863 |
| Doug erty, Patrick | Shields | Nov. 20, 1863 |
| Dewire, Edward | Emmett | Oct. 11, 1864 |
| Davis, William | do | Oct. 11, 1864 |
| Dorsey, James | Clyman | Nov. 20, 1863 |
| Dobraty, William | Watertown | Oct. 6, 1864 |
| Dagan, Albert | Leroy | Dec. 1, 1864 |
| Dagan, John | do | Jan. 27, 1865 |
| Dublard, John | Lomira | Oct. 6, 1864 |
| Doyt, Henry | do | Oct. 6, 1864 |
| Deifenback, Peter | do | Oct. 6, 1864 |
| Des Larger, Morris | Theresa | Nov. 20, 1863 |
| Dobbenpfuhl, Carl | do | Nov. 20, 1863 |
| Dickman, Frederick | Herman | Nov. 24, 1863 |
| Dickman, Arnold | do | Nov. 24, 1863 |
| Decher, Fritz | do | Oct. 18, 1864 |
| Duprey, Jr | Milwaukee | Jan. 11, 1865 |
| Daniels, John | do | Jan. 11, 1865 |

| *Name.* | *Residence.* | *Date.* |
|---|---|---|
| Douglass, Peter | Milwaukee | Jan. 11, 1865 |
| Dally, Barney | do | Jan. 11, 1865 |
| Duggan, Edward | do | Nov. 10, 1863 |
| De Claire, ——— | do | Nov. 10, 1863 |
| Darby. Patrick | do | Nov. 10, 1863 |
| Daltor, Edward | do | Sept. 21, 1864 |
| Dowers, John | do | Sept. 21, 1864 |
| Dean, William | do | Sept. 21, 1864 |
| Duggan, ——— | do | Sept. 21, 1864 |
| Donahue, M | do | Nov. 10, 1863 |
| Dalley, Charles | do | Nov. 10, 1863 |
| Dally, Larry | do | Nov. 10, 1863 |
| Dykeman, John W | do | Nov. 10, 1863 |
| Dan H | do | Nov. 10, 1863 |
| Deich, ——— | do | Nov. 10, 1863 |
| Dunning, Thomas | do | Sep. 21, 1864 |
| Dossin, Charles | do | Sep. 21, 1864 |
| Doyle, Thomas | do | Nov. 25, 1864 |
| Dimming, William | do | Nov. 25, 1864 |
| Dyesket, John | do | Nov. 25, 1864 |
| Duering, John | do | Nov. 11, 1863 |
| Drake, P | do | Nov. 11, 1863 |
| Delius, Christian | do | Sep. 21, 1864 |
| Diesf, Charley | do | Sep. 21, 1864 |
| Deltmar, Martin | do | Sep. 21, 1864 |
| Diessing, Frederick | do | Sep. 21, 1864 |
| Dobler, Jno | do | Jan. 19, 1865 |
| Dodge, Job | do | Nov. 9, 1863 |
| Dundas, John | do | Nov. 9, 1863 |
| Dan, Fred | do | Nov. 9, 1863 |
| Dellin, Wm | do | Nov. 9, 1863 |
| Dullenty, Wm | do | Nov. 9, 1863 |
| Daggett, ——— | do | Nov. 9, 1863 |
| Dame, Chas | do | Nov. 9, 1863 |
| Dreusze, Jacob | do | Nov. 9, 1863 |
| Dumbe, Richard | do | Sept. 19, 1864 |
| Danford, Jas | do | Nov. 14, 1864 |
| Doyle, Michael | do | Nov. 14, 1864 |
| Dellion, Michael | do | Nov. 14, 1864 |
| Delany, Jas | do | Nov. 14, 1864 |
| Dillon, John | do | Nov. 14, 1864 |
| Donnelly, John | do | Dec. 22, 1864 |
| Dominick, Joseph | do | Nov. 9, 1863 |
| Diede, Henry, | do | Nov. 9, 1863 |
| Dewey, Harton H | do | Nov. 9, 1863 |
| Deltmann, Gotlieb | do | Sep. 21, 1864 |
| Drustel, Albert | do | Sep. 21, 1864 |
| Doughworth, Wm | do | Nov. 14, 1864 |
| Devine, Jas | do | Nov. 10, 1863 |
| Doyle. Joseph | do | Nov. 10, 1863 |
| Daniel, Thomas | do | Nov. 10, 1863 |
| Doherty, John | do | Nov. 10, 1868 |
| Durdy, J | do | Nov. 10, 1863 |
| Daley, John | do | Nov. 10, 1863 |
| Dunn, John | do | Nov. 10, 1863 |
| Donohue, James | do | Sep. 20, 1864 |
| Difle, W. S | do | Sep. 20, 1864 |
| Duprey, Jen'r | do | Sep. 20, 1864 |
| Duyre, C | do | Sep. 20, 1864 |

| *Name.* | *Residence.* | *Date.* |
|---|---|---|
| Diffey, Orien | Milwaukee | Sep. 20, 1864 |
| Dudley, J. | do | Sep. 20, 1864 |
| Delahanty, Pat'k | do | Sep. 20, 1864 |
| Dibble, William | do | Sep. 20, 1864 |
| Dimsey, James | do | Nov. 15, 1864 |
| Dearby, J. | do | Nov. 15, 1864 |
| Dutzer, Robert | do | Nov. 15, 1864 |
| Delany, Mathew | do | Nov. 15, 1862 |
| Donely, L. J. | do | Nov. 15, 1864 |
| Doyle, F. | do | Nov. 15, 1864 |
| Dickinson, Samuel | do | Nov. 15, 1864 |
| Davis, Rowland | do | Nov. 15, 1864 |
| Douney, Frank | do | Nov. 15, 1864 |
| Dorcan, C. | do | Nov. 15, 1864 |
| Denoville, Eugene | do | Jan. 11, 1865 |
| Dally, Edward | do | Jan. 11, 1865 |
| Duffee, Michacl | Racine | Sep. 22, 1864 |
| Decker, Samuel | do | Jan. 19, 1865 |
| Dayley, John | do | Sep. 22, 1864 |
| Decker, Peter | Mount Pleasant | Nov. 11, 1863 |
| Doctor, John | do | Nov. 11, 1863 |
| Dibble, Richard | Dover | Sep. 23, 1864 |
| Donald, John | do | Sep. 23, 1864 |
| Drake, John | Rochester | Sep. 24, 1864 |
| Dawson, James | Raymond | Sep. 23, 1864 |
| Dyer, John | Caledonia | Nov. 11, 1863 |
| Donlan, John | do | Dec. 7, 1864 |
| Dee, Michael | Salem | Sep. 24, 1864 |
| Dronst, John | do | Sep. 24, 1864 |
| Dabins, Egbert | Randall | Sep. 24, 1864 |
| Duffey, James | do | Sep. 24, 1864 |
| Dalton, Thomas | do | Dec. 16, 1864 |
| Dunn, Boyd | Sharon | Nov. 12, 1863 |
| Davis, John | Darien | Nov. 12, 1863 |
| Ducy, Thomas L. | Whitewater | Nov. 12, 1863 |
| Deverits, M. | East Troy | Sep. 24, 1864 |
| Drake, Charles P. | do | Sep. 24, 1864 |
| Darion, Juhau Y. | Bloomfield | Nov. 12, 1864 |
| Dodge, William | Summit | Sep. 22, 1864 |
| Draves, Henry | do | Sep. 22, 1864 |
| Dickens, Abel | Oconomowoc | Sep. 22, 1864 |
| Daly, Owen | do | Sep. 22, 1864 |
| Dedman, Christian | Milwaukee | Nov. 25, 1864 |
| Deiring, Valentine | do | Nov. 25, 1864 |
| Dapper, Peter | do | Nov. 25, 1864 |
| Duttenhafer, Francis | do | Nov. 30, 1864 |
| Dreis, Johann | do | Jan. 26, 1865 |
| Dant, Tobias | do | Nov. 11, 1865 |
| Deckman, Wilhelm | do | Dec. 7, 1864 |
| Dresen, Hubert | Granville | Nov. 11, 1863 |
| Donahue, John. | do | Nov. 11, 1863 |
| Donavan, Demas | do | Nov. 11, 1863 |
| David, William | do | Sep. 22, 1864 |
| Donavan, Dennis | do | Sep. 22, 1864 |
| Dulig, Peter | Greenfield | Nov. 11, 1863 |
| Doff, John | do | Nov. 11, 1863 |
| Dumphey, Owen | do | Sep. 22, 1864 |
| Deville, George H. | do | Sep. 21, 1864 |
| Dona, Henry | Franklin | Nov. 11, 1863 |

| *Name.* | *Residence* | *Date.* |
|---|---|---|
| Dimsay, Anthony | Oak Creek | Sep. 22, 1864 |
| Diedrich, Peter | do | Sep. 22, 1864 |
| Dean, George | Racine | Nov. 11, 1863 |
| Dorrick, Frank | do | Nov. 11, 1863 |
| Dickson, John | do | Nov. 11, 1863 |
| Davis, Joseph W | do | Sep. 24, 1864 |
| Davis, Thomas | do | Sep. 24, 1864 |
| Duff, Michael | do | Nov. 11, 1863 |
| Dworack, Frank | do | Sep. 22, 1864 |
| Duffe, Martin | do | Sep. 22, 1864 |
| Duffee, Martin | do | Sep. 22, 1864 |
| Dewire, Thomas | Pewaukee | Nov. 12, 1863 |
| Doe, Fred | do | Sep. 22, 1864 |
| Daniels, Winthrop | Vernon | Sep. 24, 1864 |
| Deveraux, Nicholas | do | Sep. 24, 1864 |
| Dredman, Franz | Menomonee | Sep. 24, 1864 |
| Dahlman, Frank | do | Sep. 24, 1864 |
| Dritchen, Michael | do | Dec. 1, 1864 |
| Dobexs, John D. | do | Nov. 25, 1864 |
| Dropper, Johannes | do | Nov. 25, 1864 |
| Drehmel, William | Brookfield | Sep. 23, 1864 |
| Daws, Samuel | New Berlin | Nov. 12, 1863 |
| Dougherty, Peter | Muskego | Sep. 24, 1864 |
| Danielson, Chris | do | Sep. 24, 1864 |
| Dunn, Robert | do | Dec. 1, 1864 |
| Dwyer, Michael | Janesville | Nov. 12, 1863 |
| Drake, Mortimer | Fitchburg | Nov. 13, 1863 |
| Dunn, Michael | Verona | Nov. 13, 1863 |
| Davis, David A | Madison | Nov. 13, 1863 |
| Dunn, John | do | Nov. 12, 1863 |
| Davis, John H | Sun Prairie | Sep. 19, 1864 |
| Dodge, H. F | do | Nov. 15, 1864 |
| Dimint, Edward | Berry | Nov. 15, 1864 |
| Dallurau, Hiram | Farmington | |
| Dallman, Christian | do | Sep 20, 1864 |
| Dufer, Philip | do | Sep 20, 1864 |
| Dwarak, Mathias | Watertown | Sep. 20, 1864 |
| Dickerson, Joseph H | Courtland | Nov 16, 1863 |
| Dee, James | Randolph | Nov. 16, 1863 |
| Derosie, Nelson | Scott | Nov. 16, 1863 |
| Devine, Byron | Lewiston | Nov. 16, 1863 |
| Donely, John | do | Sep. 27, 1864 |
| Davidson, Thomas | Perry | Feb 27, 1865 |
| Dew, William | Concord | Sep. 20, 1864 |
| Drisbeck, Persha | Milford | Sep 20, 1864 |
| Daffy, Thomas | Watertown | Sep. 20, 1864 |
| Dricurt, John | do | Sep. 20, 1864 |
| Deamond, John | do | Sep. 20, 1864 |
| Drinkwater, Ephram | Fort Winebago | Sep 21, 1864 |
| Doyle, Joseph | Ridgeway | Sep. 28, 1864 |
| Davis, Sam'l J | do | Oct. 28, 1862 |
| Donely, Barney | Clyde | Sep. 27, 1864 |
| Doyle, Wm | do | Sep. 27, 1864 |
| Demby, Rob't | Dodgeville | Nov 14, 1864 |
| Deyol, Stephen | do | Sep. 28, 1864 |
| Dolan, Patrick | Highland | Nov. 14, 1863 |
| Driscol, Dan'l | do | Sep. 28, 1864 |
| Davis, Edward | do | Sep. 28, 1864 |

| *Name.* | *Residence.* | *Date.* |
|---|---|---|
| Drury, Joseph | Highland | Sep. 28, 1864 |
| Delaney, Wm | do | Oct. 28, 1864 |
| Dolphin, Geo | do | Oct. 28, 1864 |
| Dernon, Thos | do | Nov. 19, 1864 |
| Delaney, Martin | do | Dec. 7, 1864 |
| Devlin, Simon | Kendall or Belmont | Nov. 16, 1863 |
| Doran, Patrick | Kendall | Oct. 4, 1864 |
| Dickson, George | Benton | Nov. 16, 1863 |
| Dougherty, Michael | do | Sep. 29, 1864 |
| Dougherty, John | do | Sep. 29, 1864 |
| Doyle, Garrett | do | Sep. 29, 1864 |
| Duffey, Thomas | do | Sep. 29, 1864 |
| Donavan. John | New Diggings | Sep. 29, 1864 |
| Dunleavy, John | do | Sep. 29, 1864 |
| Dunleavy, Patrick | do | Sep. 29, 1864 |
| Downs, Michael | Elk Grove | Nov. 16, 1863 |
| Durst, Daniel | New Glarus or Exeter | Nov. 17, 1863 |
| Delamater, Barney | Cadiz | Sep. 27, 1864 |
| Dulon, Timothy | Jefferson | Sep. 27, 1864 |
| Dolan, Michael | Utica | Sep. 30, 1864 |
| Denin, Michael | do | Sep. 30, 1864 |
| Denin, James | do | Sep. 30, 1864 |
| Dickson, William | Beetown | Oct. 1, 1864 |
| Daily, John | Waterloo | Oct. 1, 1864 |
| Driscol, Daniel | Jamestown | Nov. 19, 1863 |
| Devers, Hugh | Baraboo | Nov. 20, 1863 |
| Deckert, Joseph | Sylvan | Sep. 26, 1864 |
| Devine, James | Spring Grove | Oct. 5, 1864 |
| Dunne, Arthur | Eastman | Sep. 30, 1864 |
| Dagnon, Michael | do | Sep. 30, 1864 |
| Dowling, Jeremiah | Haney | Sep. 30, 1864 |
| Dunn, Edward | Millville | Oct. 1, 1864 |
| Day, John | Blue River | Oct. 1, 1864 |
| Deihler, Christian | La Valle | Oct. 3, 1864 |
| Durall, Henry | Bear Creek | Oct. 3, 1864 |
| Derig, William | Franklin | Oct. 29, 1864 |
| Donahoe, Patrick | Bear Creek | Nov. 19, 1864 |
| Dunn, Thomas | La Crosse city | Nov. 13, 1863 |
| Ditrick, Paul | do | Nov. 13, 1863 |
| Downs, Joseph | La Crosse Co | Nov. 13, 1863 |
| Davis, Edward | Juneau Co | Nov. 17, 1863 |
| Daten, Edward | Kildare | Sep. 19, 1864 |
| Daten, Elijah | do | Oct. 31, 1864 |
| Donahan, Richard | Seven Mile Creek | Sep. 19, 1864 |
| Davenport, Patrick | do | Sep. 19, 1864 |
| Davenport, James | do | Sep. 19, 1864 |
| Darr, Patrick | do | Sep. 19, 1864 |
| Donovan, Richard | do | Oct 31, 1864 |
| Dubig, John | Plymouth | Sep. 19, 1864 |
| Downing, Henry | do | Oct. 31, 1864 |
| Dea, John O | Summit | Sep 19, 1864 |
| Darrow, Dempster | do | Sep. 19, 1864 |
| Dulanty, James | Lynden | Sep. 20, 1864 |
| Deneen, James | do | Oct. 31, 1864 |
| Day, Alanson I. | St. Croix Co | Nov. 20, 1863 |
| Dillon, Michael | Erin Prairie | Sep. 23, 1864 |
| Dixon, Thomas, Jr. | do | Sep. 23, 1864 |
| Dillon, James | do | Nov. 3, 1864 |
| Dixon, Thomas (2nd) | do | Nov. 3, 1864 |

| *Name.* | *Residence.* | *Date.* |
|---|---|---|
| Decker, Stillman | Eau Galle | Nov. 3, 1864 |
| Dunbar, Michael | Ceylon | Oct. 5, 1864 |
| Donahue, Daniel | Dunn Co | Nov. 23, 1863 |
| Douglass, John | Eau Galle | Sep. 27, 1864 |
| Dehler, Edward | Spring Brook | Nov. 2, 1864 |
| Duvall, Joseph | Wood Co | Nov. 18, 1863 |
| Dolan, John | Seneca | Sep. 20, 1864 |
| Dyer, John | Jefferson | Sep. 19, 1864 |
| Dwire, James | do | Sep. 19, 1864 |
| Duyer, Thomas | do | Sep. 19, 1864 |
| Devane, Pat | Wellington | Sep. 20, 1864 |
| Daine, Daniel | Oak Dale | Sep. 20, 1864 |
| Doyle, John | Ettrick | Sep. 21, 1864 |
| Dudley, E. C | Bergen | Sep. 21, 1864 |
| Drake, Phineas | Franklin | Sep. 21, 1864 |
| Delap, Thomas | Whitestown | Sep. 21, 1864 |
| Dutton, Oscar E | Pine Grove | Sep. 22, 1864 |
| Dutton, George H | do | Sep. 22, 1864 |
| Dutton, Rufus W | do | Nov. 15, 1864 |
| Derozier, Liseum | Stockton | Sep. 22, 1864 |
| Dumfrey, Thomas | Linwood | Oct. 31, 1864 |
| Denney, Charles | Sharon | Sep. 22, 1864 |
| Dunnigan, James | Belmont | Sep. 22, 1864 |
| Dunnigan, Edward | do | Nov. 15, 1864 |
| Dunnigan, John | Irving | Sep. 23, 1864 |
| Dittman, Henry | Newark Valley | Sep. 26, 1864 |
| Dawes, James | Monroe | Sep. 26, 1864 |
| Davidson, James | Adams | Nov. 14, 1864 |
| Davidson, Thomas | do | Nov. 14, 1864 |
| Dawson, Larnes | New Haven | Nov. 14, 1864 |
| Dagon, Christopher | Chippewa Falls | Nov. 2, 1864 |
| Dennis, Henry | Door Co | Nov. 20, 1863 |
| Degraganage, Alexander | Brussells | Dec. 29, 1864 |
| Dram, James | Little Suamico | Dec. 29, 1864 |
| Dewan, James | Franklin | Nov. 20, 1863 |
| Donim, Fred | do | Dec. 29, 1864 |
| Dam, Jacob | do | Dec. 29, 1864 |
| Davern, James | do | Dec. 29, 1864 |
| Delvet, Charles | Lincoln | Nov. 20, 1863 |
| Devillers, Charles | do | Dec. 29, 1864 |
| Denis, Justmer | do | Dec. 29, 1864 |
| Donhue, Daniel | Kewaunee | Dec. 29, 1864 |
| Decamps, Jean | Red River | Dec. 29, 1864 |
| Debouch, Felician | do | Dec. 29, 1864 |
| Degreve, Joseph | do | Dec. 29, 1864 |
| Decremes, Henry | do | Dec. 29, 1864 |
| Delouf, August | Casco | Dec. 29, 1864 |
| Doyle, Frence | Maple Grove | Nov. 21, 1863 |
| Dennis, John | Franklin | Nov. 21, 1863 |
| Dugan, Jeremiah | do | Nov. 21, 1863 |
| Dunn, Emmett | Eaton | Nov. 24, 1863 |
| Dunn, Daniel O. C | do | Nov. 24, 1863 |
| Decorah, Matzlof | Gibson | Dec. 29, 1863 |
| Dworzach, Joseph | do | Dec. 29, 1863 |
| Dehir, Michael | Meeme | Dec. 29, 1863 |
| Dietrich, John Frederick | Newton | Dec. 29, 1863 |
| Dennison, Englebert | Charlestown | Nov. 21, 1863 |
| Davidson, M | Stockbridge | Dec. 28, 1864 |
| Davids, Daniel | do | Dec. 28, 1864 |

| *Name.* | *Residence.* | *Date.* |
|---|---|---|
| Duffey, Martin | Stockbridge | Dec. 28, 1864 |
| Deet, Lloyd, Jr. | Menasha | Nov. 23, 1864 |
| Daylehas, E. | Oshkosh city | Nov. 23, 1864 |
| Dwore, Gideon F | Nepeuskin | Nov. 23, 1864 |
| Dent, William | Rushford | Nov. 24, 1864 |
| Durkee, James H | Clayton | Nov. 24, 1864 |
| Doege, Leopold | | Nov. 24, 1864 |
| Dolan, Michael | Poygan | Nov. 5, 1864 |
| Davis, Elliot | Berlin city | Nov. 24, 1863 |
| Davis, Thomas J. | Mackford | Nov. 24, 1863 |
| Donahue, John | do | Nov. 24, 1863 |
| Darrow, Alfred | Saxeville | Nov. 25, 1863 |
| Donley, James | Warren | Nov. 2, 1864 |
| Daniels, Leonard | do | Nov. 2, 1864 |
| Davies, Ellis | Springwater | Nov. 2, 1864 |
| Davies, Daniel | do | Nov. 2, 1864 |
| Davies, John H | do | Nov. 2, 1864 |
| Dalziel, Andrew | do | Nov. 2, 1864 |
| Davis, William | Deerfield | Nov. 2, 1864 |
| Drew, Ezra | Plainfield | Nov. 2, 1864 |
| Drake, Aaron | do | Nov. 2, 1864 |
| Douglas, Absalom | do | Nov. 2, 1864 |
| Davids, E. B | do | Dec. 31, 1864 |
| Daniels, Theodore | Aurora | Dec. 31, 1864 |
| Durgin, Hiram | Richford | Dec. 31, 1864 |
| Delong, Merritt C | Weyawega | Nov. 25, 1863 |
| Douglas, Theodore | Dayton | Nov. 25, 1863 |
| Devand, Louis | Union | Nov. 5, 1864 |
| Doty, Peter | do | Nov. 5, 1864 |
| Dean, Benjamin | do | Nov. 5, 1864 |
| Dawson, John | Lebanon | Nov. 5, 1864 |
| Doud, Thomas | do | Nov. 5, 1864 |
| Danielson, Christopher | St. Lawrence | Nov. 5, 1864 |
| Damon, Icheal | do | Dec. 31, 1864 |
| Dimmock, John | Iola | Dec. 31, 1864 |
| Dixon, Daniel | Matteson | Nov. 5, 1864 |
| Deborad, Veruches | Freedom | Nov. 27, 1863 |
| Dodge, Philip | do | Dec. 28, 1864 |
| Dorsey, James | Center | Dec. 28, 1864 |
| Dallas, L. D | do | Dec. 28, 1864 |
| Dressent, Joseph | Kaukama | Nov. 27, 1863 |
| Darley, John | Appleton | Nov. 27, 1863 |
| Dessirie, O. B | do | Nov. 27, 1863 |
| Dorsey, Patrick | Morrison | Nov. 27, 1863 |
| Dailey, Patrick | do | Nov. 27, 1863 |
| Daley, James | do | Dec. 28, 1864 |
| Durer, Phillip | Lawrence | Nov. 27, 1864 |
| Dunn, M. H | Green Bay city | Nov. 27, 1864 |
| Danuze, John J | Green Bay | Dec. 28, 1864 |
| Duville, John B | Scott | Dec. 28, 1864 |
| Datiene, John Baptist | do | Dec. 28, 1864 |
| Debois, Peter | Eaton | Dec. 28, 1864 |
| Dockery, Patrick | Holland | Dec. 28, 1864 |
| Donohue, Dennis | Marinette | Nov. 28, 1863 |
| Duffimi, Lewis | Oconto | Nov. 28, 1863 |
| Darling, Daniel | Peshtigo | Nov. 28, 1863 |
| Dailey, John | Packwaukee | Nov. 1, 1864 |
| Day, August | Crystal Lake | Nov. 1, 1864 |
| Donevan, Florence | Shields | Nov. 1, 1864 |

| *Name.* | *Residence.* | *Date.* |
|---|---|---|
| Devaney, John | Shields | Nov. 1, 1864 |
| Duncan, Michael | Neshkora | Dec. 31, 1864 |
| Dawson, James | Douglas | Dec. 31, 1864 |

## E

| | | |
|---|---|---|
| Evers, John | Fond du Lac | Nov. 19, 1863 |
| Ellis, William | Oakfield | Nov. 19, 1863 |
| Ellers, George | Auburn | Oct. 5, 1864 |
| Eddy, A. | Springvale | Nov. 19, 1863 |
| Ennis, William | Eldorado | Oct. 5, 1864 |
| Evens, James | Fox Lake | Nov. 19, 1863 |
| Evans, Thomas B. | Beaver Dam | Nov. 20, 1863 |
| Eving, David | Emmett | Oct. 11, 1864 |
| Evans, Davis | do | Oct. 11, 1864 |
| Everett, Charles | Clyman | Oct. 6, 1864 |
| Eldridge, Robert | Barton | Oct. 12, 1864 |
| Emwalter, Frederick | Polk | Oct. 12, 1864 |
| Elliott, Thomas | do | Oct. 12. 1864 |
| Ernst, Gotleib | do | Dec. 8, 1864 |
| Eben, Philip | Richfield | Oct. 12, 1864 |
| Eastinger, Antoni | do | Oct. 12, 1864 |
| Eichler, Charles | Farmington | Nov. 21, 1863 |
| Engle, Anton | do | Dec. 1, 1864 |
| Ezel, John | do | Dec. 1, 1864 |
| Enright, David | do | Jan. 27, 1865 |
| Ehmke, Theodore | Jackson | Oct. 11, 1864 |
| Erdmann, August | do | Oct. 11, 1864 |
| Ettes, Nicholas | Belgium | Oct. 13, 1864 |
| Ernester, Peter | do | Oct. 13, 1864 |
| Ellenbecker, Theodore | do | Oct. 13, 1864 |
| Eckers, George | do | Oct. 13, 1864 |
| Ellenbecker, Nicholas | do | Dec. 1, 1864 |
| Eckel, Charles | Grafton | Oct. 13, 1864 |
| Evans, John | do | Dec. 1, 1864 |
| Englehardt, Engle | Sheboygan Falls | Nov. 24, 1863 |
| Eastwood, M. J. | do | Oct. 25, 1864 |
| Eurich, J. | do | Dec. 2, 1864 |
| Eastman, Levi | Plymouth | Oct. 21, 1864 |
| Emkah, Wm. | Milwaukee | Nov. 9, 1863 |
| Ehless, Louis | do | Sep. 19, 1864 |
| Esterbrook, Wm | do | Nov. 9, 1863 |
| Ellis, Theo | do | Nov. 9, 1863 |
| Eiters, Frederick | do | Nov. 9, 1863 |
| Ellis, Henry | do | Nov. 9, 1863 |
| Ellerson, Richard | do | Nov. 9, 1863 |
| Ellmann, Adam | do | Sep. 20, 1864 |
| Elli, Nicholas | do | Nov. 14, 1864 |
| Ellsby, T. S. | do | Sep. 20, 1864 |
| Ernags, W. S. | do | Sep. 20, 1864 |
| Edmunds, John | do | Sep. 20, 1864 |
| Eaton, James | do | Nov. 15, 1864 |
| Evans, Samuel | do | Nov. 15, 1864 |
| Eaves, John | do | Nov. 15, 1864 |
| Eke, E. W | do | Nov. 15, 1864 |
| Ellerton, George | do | Nov. 15, 1864 |
| Erwart, John | do | Nov. 15, 1864 |
| Ellis, George | do | Nov. 15, 1864 |
| Eschman, Henry | do | Jan. 11, 1864 |
| Ellsworth, William H. | do | Jan. 11, 1864 |

| *Name.* | *Residence.* | *Date.* |
|---|---|---|
| Egan, Gilbert | Milwaukee | Jan. 11, 1864 |
| Edwards, John | do | Sep. 21, 1864 |
| Edwin, Charles | do | Sep. 21, 1864 |
| Edmondson, John | do | Sep. 21, 1864 |
| Ehlers, Fred | do | Nov. 10, 1863 |
| Eckman, ——— | do | Nov. 10, 1863 |
| Ehrml, Oast | do | Jan. 19, 1865 |
| Esser, John | Menomonee | Sep. 24, 1864 |
| Evert, Christoph | do | Nov. 25, 1864 |
| Erdmann, Johann | do | Nov. 25, 1864 |
| Eckhart, William | Brookfield | Nov. 12, 1863 |
| Eyer, George | do | Sep. 23, 1864 |
| Elliott, Mathew jr | Muskego | Sep. 24, 1864 |
| Eckles, James | do | Nov. 30, 1864 |
| Esterlee, Conrad | Milwaukee | Nov. 11, 1863 |
| Emse, Christian | do | Sep. 21, 1864 |
| Ebal, Frederick | do | Nov. 25, 1864 |
| Elliott, Thomas | do | Nov. 30, 1864 |
| Elliott, Andrews | do | Nov. 30, 1864 |
| Ehlers, ——— | do | Dec. 7, 1864 |
| Ebal, Charles | do | Dec. 7, 1864 |
| Ewer, Lawrence | Granville | Sep. 22, 1864 |
| Evans, Thomas | Franklin | Nov. 11, 1863 |
| Evans, James | do | Nov. 11, 1863 |
| Erscheus, Michael | Oak Creek | Sep. 22, 1864 |
| Ehreufels, Philip | Racine | Sep. 24, 1864 |
| Evans, Thomas R | do | Sep. 24, 1864 |
| Evans, Jim | Mount Pleasant | Nov. 11, 1863 |
| Ellis, J. I. F. | Raymond | Sep. 23, 1864 |
| Echley, Frank | Caledonia | Sep. 22, 1864 |
| Enrich, Charles | do | Sep. 22, 1864 |
| Easlman, Harvey | Kenosha | Nov. 12, 1863 |
| Eddy, Ozro | Wheatland | Sep. 24, 1864 |
| Englehart, John | Paris | Sep. 24, 1864 |
| Emmory, David | Sharon | Nov. 12, 1863 |
| Emerson, Charles | Whitewater | Nov. 12, 1863 |
| Emery, John | Bloomfield | Nov. 12, 1863 |
| Eastmond, Charles | Summit | Sep. 22, 1864 |
| Enke, Charles | Oconomowoc | Sep. 22, 1864 |
| Eustis, John | do | Dec. 5, 1864 |
| Essex, Frederick | do | Sep. 22, 1864 |
| Everson, Holstine | Vermont | Sep. 19, 1864 |
| Erickson, Samuel | Otsego | Nov. 16, 1863 |
| Eaves, James | Portage City | Sep. 21, 1864 |
| Edwards, Eran H | Spring Vale | Nov. 16, 1863 |
| Egan, Michael | Lewiston | Sep. 21, 1864 |
| Egan, William | do | Sep. 21, 1864 |
| Erickson, Lurs | Perry | Sep. 19, 1864 |
| Erenson, Christian | do | Feb. 27, 1865 |
| Engelbrachts, Henry | Milford | Oct. 22, 1864 |
| Egleston, Almon | Marcelon | Sep. 21, 1864 |
| Eagan, Barney | Clyde | Sep. 27, 1864 |
| Euson, Tolive | Dodgeville | Sep. 28, 1864 |
| Erickson, Lewis | do | Nov. 19, 1864 |
| Edwards, Thomas | Highland | Sep. 28, 1864 |
| Egan, Nicholas | do | Sept. 28, 1864 |
| Egan, Patrick | do | Oct. 28, 1864 |
| Egan, Patrick (2d) | do | Oct. 28, 1864 |
| Edwards, Henry | do | Nov. 19, 1864 |

| *Name* | *Residence.* | *Date* |
|---|---|---|
| Emerson, A. | Moscow | Sep. 28, 1864 |
| Edwards, Thos | Benton | Sept. 29, 1864 |
| Edwards, James H | do | Sep. 29, 1864 |
| Eustace, William | do | Sep. 29, 1864 |
| Evans, William | New Diggings | Sept. 29, 1864 |
| Erstenson, Tars | Utica | Sep. 30, 1864 |
| Edwards, William | Prairie du Chien | Nov. 18, 1863 |
| Eagy, Andrew | Bloom | Sep. 26, 1864 |
| Eder, Adam | Lavalle | Oct. 29, 1864 |
| Emerson, Martial | Chippewa Co | Nov. 20, 1863 |
| Elmer, A. J | Dunn Co | Nov. 23, 1863 |
| Elins, Henry | do | Nov. 23, 1863 |
| Elsenpeter, Henry | do | Nov. 23, 1863 |
| Empter, Frederick | Spring Brook | Sep. 27, 1864 |
| Elson, Hubert | Washington | Sep. 19, 1864 |
| Ensch, John | Marion | Sep. 19, 1864 |
| Ellsworth, Frank | Kildare | Oct. 31, 1864 |
| Elliot, Thos | Adrain | Sep. 20, 1864 |
| Elwell, Webster | Tomah | Sep. 20, 1864 |
| Estabrook, Benjamin R. | Sheldon | Sep. 20, 1864 |
| Edwards, John | Portland | Nov. 10, 1864 |
| Eychauer, Milton | Hamburgh | Sep. 21, 1864 |
| Everson, Ever | Coon | Sep. 21, 1864 |
| Eiden, Mathias | Sharon | Sep. 22, 1864 |
| Elbach, Michael | do | Oct. 31, 1864 |
| Edwards, John | Pine Grove | Nov. 15, 1864 |
| Eaton, John S | Hull | Sep. 22, 1864 |
| Eardman, Carl | Berlin | Sep. 22, 1864 |
| Early, Michael | Erin Prairie | Sep. 23, 1864 |
| Eaton, Urias R | Easton | Sep. 26, 1864 |
| Ely, E. M | Monroe | Nov. 14, 1864 |
| Emerson, Embeck | Waubeek | Nov. 16, 1864 |
| Enocksen, Enoch | Manitowoc | Nov. 21, 1863 |
| Elliot, Stephen jr | Two Creeks | Dec. 28, 1864 |
| Evenson, Christoff | Gibson | Dec. 29, 1864 |
| Ereckson, Ereck | Manitowoc Rapids | Dec. 29, 1864 |
| Ehrenich, Julius | Newton | Dec. 29, 1864 |
| Evans, William | Nepeuskin | Nov. 23, 1863 |
| Elms, Cornelius G | Clayton | Nov. 24, 1863 |
| Edson, Alonzo | Berlin City | Nov. 24, 1863 |
| Early, D. W | Waupaca | Nov. 25, 1863 |
| Eagan, Jerry | Lebanon | Nov. 2, 1864 |
| English, Jno | do | Dec. 31, 1864 |
| Erickson, Hermon | St. Lawrence | Dec. 5, 1864 |
| Erickson, Knud | Iola | Dec. 5, 1864 |
| Ettinger, Adam | Appleton | Nov. 27, 1863 |
| Erickson, Peter | Peshtigo | Nov. 28, 1863 |
| Eddy, John | Little Suamico | Dec. 29, 1864 |
| Erdman, August | Crystal Lake | Nov. 1, 1864 |
| Emerick, Warren | Douglas | Dec. 31, 1864 |
| Evening, Henry | Bloomfield | Nov. 2, 1864 |
| Eursy, August | do | Dec. 31, 1864 |
| Engle, Gothez | do | Dec. 31, 1864 |
| Evans, Morris G | Springwater | Nov. 2, 1864 |
| Engel, John | Deerfield | Nov. 2, 1864 |
| Eager, Daniel | Oasis | Nov. 2, 1864 |
| Engel, Edward | Humboldt | Dec. 28, 1864 |
| Elser, Joseph | Preble | Dec. 28, 1864 |
| Eaton, Henry | Carlton | Dec. 29, 1864 |

| *Name.* | *Residence.* | *Date.* |
|---|---|---|
| Everard, Francois | Brussells | Dec. 29, 1864 |

## F

| *Name.* | *Residence.* | *Date.* |
|---|---|---|
| Frey, Heinrich | Richfield | Dec. 1, 1864 |
| Fries, Peter | do | Dec. 1, 1864 |
| Fray, Martin | do | Dec. 1, 1864 |
| Flemming, Michael | do | Jan. 27, 1865 |
| Flynn, Michael | do | Jan. 27, 1865 |
| Fry, —— | do | Jan. 27, 1865 |
| Farrell, Peter | do | Jan. 27, 1865 |
| Ficks, William | Farmington | Jan. 27, 1865 |
| Fircher, G. | Jackson | Oct. 11, 1864 |
| Flanigan, John | do | Oct. 11, 1864 |
| Fullweiler, Eli | do | Oct. 11, 1864 |
| Fellbaum, Martin | do | Oct. 11, 1864 |
| Flies, Frank | Belgium | Nov. 21, 1863 |
| Falm, Simon | do | Nov. 21, 1863 |
| Foltz, Michael | do | Oct. 13, 1864 |
| Fritz, Nicholas | do | Oct. 13, 1864 |
| Fahler, John | do | Oct. 13, 1864 |
| Farber, Michael | do | Oct. 13, 1864 |
| Fleppchan, John | do | Oct. 13, 1864 |
| Farber, Peter | do | Oct. 13, 1864 |
| Federspaid, T. | do | Dec. 1, 1864 |
| Fritz, John | do | Dec. 1, 1864 |
| Fenereisew, John | do | Dec. 1, 1864 |
| Fichler, Nicholas | Fredonia | Oct. 14, 1864 |
| Firk, John | do | Nov. 21, 1863 |
| Franker, Keitel | do | Nov. 21, 1863 |
| Fohley, Patrick | Cedarburg | Nov. 21, 1863 |
| Fitzke, Frederick | do | Nov. 23, 1863 |
| Frunklen, Charles | Grafton | Nov. 23, 1863 |
| Flanagan, John | do | Oct. 13, 1864 |
| Frost, Fritz | do | Oct. 13, 1864 |
| Fleischman, Andrew | do | Oct. 13, 1864 |
| Frost, Peter | do | Oct. 13, 1864 |
| Fennis, Peter | do | Oct. 13, 1864 |
| Frank, Joseph | Saukville | Oct. 14, 1864 |
| Fissing, Charles | Sheboygan | Oct. 18, 1864 |
| Federer, George | do | Oct. 18, 1864 |
| Frink, Frederich | do | Dec. 2, 1864 |
| Frulger, George | do | Dec. 2, 1864 |
| Fischer, Herman | Moselle | Oct. 18, 1864 |
| Febig, August | Sheboygan Falls | Dec. 2, 1864 |
| Frayr, S. | Lima | Oct. 24, 1864 |
| Fritz, Patrick | do | Jan. 27, 1865 |
| Fifer, William | Abbott | Oct. 18, 1864 |
| Frederick, Charles | Hermon | Nov. 20, 1863 |
| Friske, Charles | do | Nov. 24, 1863 |
| Franz, August | do | Dec. 2, 1864 |
| Frank, John | Hartford | Nov. 21, 1863 |
| Fungar, Frank | Addison | Nov. 21, 1863 |
| Featherston, John | Erin | Oct. 12, 1864 |
| Fitzpatrick, James | do | Dec. 1, 1864 |
| Fitzpatrick, Francis | do | Dec. 1, 1864 |
| Fenstermacker, William | Barton | Oct. 12, 1864 |
| Frontgons, Victor | do | Dec. 1, 1864 |
| Finnegan, Jas. | do | Dec. 1, 1864 |
| Filner, Louis | Polk | Nov. 21, 1863 |

| *Name.* | *Residence.* | *Date.* |
|---|---|---|
| Freulweck, Ludwick | Polk | Oct. 12, 1864 |
| Foreman, Almon | do | Oct. 12, 1864 |
| Farrington, Marble | do | Oct. 12, 1864 |
| Fox, Thomas | do | Dec. 8, 1864 |
| Frier, David | do | Dec. 8, 1864 |
| Ferrier, John | do | Dec. 8, 1864 |
| Fitzsinger, Francis | Richfield | Nov. 21, 1863 |
| Fank, Bernard | do | Oct. 12, 1864 |
| Fuller, Ames | do | Oct. 12, 1864 |
| Funk, George | do | Oct. 12, 1864 |
| Farell, Thomas | do | Oct. 12, 1864 |
| Fross, Peter | do | Oct. 12, 1864 |
| Fuller, A. B | do | Oct. 12, 1864 |
| Farrel, Thomas | do | Dec. 1, 1864 |
| Flynn, John | do | Dec. 1, 1864 |
| Flynn, Thomas | Fond du Lac | Nov. 19, 1863 |
| Flynn, John | do | Nov. 19, 1863 |
| Floss, Charles | do | Nov. 19, 1863 |
| Freeman, Dennis | Friendship | Nov. 19, 1863 |
| Forward, William | Oakfield | Nov. 19, 1863 |
| Frank, William | Auburn | Oct 5, 1864 |
| Fellenz, Hubbard | do | Oct. 5, 1864 |
| Filoke, Henry | do | Oct. 5, 1864 |
| Foths, Frederick | do | Oct. 5, 1864 |
| Flint, Michael | do | Oct. 5, 1864 |
| Fuller, David | Lamartine | Nov. 19, 1863 |
| Fairbank, John W | Waupun Village | Nov. 19, 1863 |
| Flavin, Peter | Elba | Nov. 20, 1863 |
| Foot, Charles H | Beaver Dam | Nov. 20, 1863 |
| Fenton, Dennis | Clyman | Oct. 6, 1864 |
| Freber, Henry | do | Oct. 6, 1864 |
| Frank, John H | do | Oct. 6, 1864 |
| Fisell, James | Burnett | Nov. 20, 1863 |
| Folson, Carl | Watertown | Oct. 6, 1864 |
| Fuket, Anton | do | Oct. 6, 1864 |
| Freske, Ludwig | do | Oct. 6, 1864 |
| Feudt, Alloicus | do | Oct. 6, 1864 |
| Freske, Ludwig | do | Oct. 6, 1864 |
| Frockling, Felix | do | Dec. 1, 1864 |
| Furlong, John A | Leroy | Oct. 4, 1864 |
| Felner, Joseph | do | Oct. 4, 1864 |
| Fidgman, John | do | Oct. 4, 1864 |
| Fidgman, Thomas | do | Oct. 4, 1864 |
| Fisker, Carl | Lomira | Jan. 27, 1865 |
| Friend, Joseph | Granville | Nov. 11, 1863 |
| Fahey, Patrick | do | Sep. 22, 1864 |
| Felsing, Henry | do | Sep. 22, 1864 |
| Freyberg, Ferdinand | do | Sep. 22, 1864 |
| Furlong, George | Greenfield | Nov. 11, 1863 |
| Fischer, Antonio | do | Sep. 22, 1864 |
| Femefeden, William | Lake | Nov. 11, 1863 |
| Forbes, William | Oak Creek | Nov. 11, 1863 |
| Forbes, Michael | do | Sep. 22, 1864 |
| Finnegan, James | Racine | Sep. 24, 1864 |
| Foster, James | do | Sep. 22, 1864 |
| Field, James | do | Sep. 22, 1864 |
| Fergason, Clarus | do | Sep. 22, 1864 |
| Fahey, Charles | do | Sep. 22, 1864 |
| Finch, Charles E | do | Sep. 22, 1864 |

| *Name.* | *Residence.* | *Date* |
|---|---|---|
| Flynn, Thomas | Racine | Nov. 11, 1863 |
| Foat, Charles, | Dover | Sep. 23, 1864 |
| Flint, Martin, | Waterford | Nov. 11, 1863 |
| Ferris, Alfred | Raymond | Nov. 11, 1863 |
| Farley, Thomas | Caledonia | Nov. 11, 1863 |
| Fey, John | Paris | Nov. 12, 1863 |
| Fritz, Peter | do | Nov. 12, 1863 |
| Fulton, Osgood | Salem | Sep. 24, 1864 |
| Fray, Edward | do | Sep. 24, 1864 |
| Farmer, Thomas | Randall | Dec. 16, 1864 |
| Frank, Henry | Bristol | Nov. 12, 1863 |
| Flemming, Wm O | Milwaukee, | Nov. 10, 1863 |
| Folin, Wm | do | Nov. 10, 1863 |
| Furlong, James | do | Nov. 10, 1863 |
| Flood, Chris | do | Sep. 20, 1864 |
| Forsyth, John | do | Sep. 20, 1864 |
| Faulkner, C | do | Sep. 20, 1864 |
| Fahey, Michael | do | Sep. 20, 1864 |
| Fitch, Samuel | do | Sep. 20, 1864 |
| Foley, John | do | Sep. 20, 1864 |
| Fanning, Frank | do | Nov. 15, 1864 |
| Finch, Joshua | do | Nov. 15, 1864 |
| Fisher, F. | do | Nov. 15, 1864 |
| French, August | do | Nov. 15, 1864 |
| Foley, E. H. | do | Nov. 15, 1864 |
| Forsyth, George | do | Nov. 15, 1864 |
| Farrell, Patrick | do | Jan. 11, 1865 |
| Fielding, John | do | Jan. 11, 1865 |
| Folly, G. B. | do | Jan. 11, 1865 |
| Franein, John | do | Jan. 11, 1865 |
| Flavin, M. | do | Jan. 11, 1865 |
| Flaus, Christopher | do | Jan. 11, 1865 |
| Fitzgoold, David | do | Nov. 10, 1863 |
| Fox, James | do | Sep. 21, 1864 |
| Felman, A. | do | Sep. 21, 1864 |
| Franzman, John | do | Sep. 21, 1864 |
| Ford, John | do | Sep. 21, 1864 |
| Frenzle, Anton | do | Sep. 21, 1864 |
| Fitzgerald, Morris | do | Nov. 9, 1863 |
| Frenaff, Charles | do | Nov. 9, 1863 |
| Fryer, Peter | do | Nov. 9, 1863 |
| Fagan, Patrick | do | Sep. 19, 1864 |
| Freeman, William | do | Sep. 19, 1864 |
| Fire, Jacob | do | Sep. 19, 1864 |
| Frank, Julius | do | Nov. 14, 1864 |
| Fesky, John | do | Nov. 9, 1863 |
| Fuller, A. | do | Nov. 9, 1863 |
| Fisher, Christ | do | Nov. 9, 1863 |
| Fisch, John | do | Nov. 9, 1863 |
| Franz, Gottlieb | do | Nov. 9, 1863 |
| Forth, Chas | do | Nov. 9, 1863 |
| Fouzen, Richard | do | Sep. 20, 1864 |
| Fink, Philip | do | Sep. 20, 1864 |
| Frederick, Aug | do | Nov. 14, 1864 |
| Frederick, Joseph | do | Nov. 14, 1864 |
| Fitzhugh, Ed | do | Nov. 14, 1864 |
| Franklin, Robert | do | Nov. 14, 1864 |
| Fawler, J. H | do | Nov. 10, 1863 |
| Fay, Michael | do | Nov. 10, 1863 |

| *Name.* | *Residence.* | *Date.* |
|---|---|---|
| Forastell, Nich | Milwaukee | Nov. 10, 1863 |
| French, J. C. | do | Nov. 10, 1863 |
| Faulks, J. W. | do | Nov. 10, 1863 |
| Frits, J | do | Nov. 10, 1863 |
| Frank, Louis | do | Sep. 21, 1864 |
| Filtz, Richard | do | Sep. 21, 1864 |
| Faith, Anton | do | Nov. 16, 1864 |
| Forb, Joshua | do | Nov. 10, 1863 |
| Forestel, Ed | do | Nov. 25, 1864 |
| Fosle, George | do | Nov. 25, 1864 |
| Flood, James | do | Nov. 25,1 964 |
| Ferry Clark | do | Nov. 25, 1864 |
| Fritscher, Joseph | do | Nov. 11, 1863 |
| Famer, Simon | do | Nov. 11, 1863 |
| Fritsche, Gordeke | do | Sep. 21, 1864 |
| Fritz, Martin | do | Sep. 21, 1864 |
| Fritsch, Joseph | do | Sep. 21, 1864 |
| Fischer, John Geo | do | Sep. 21, 1864 |
| Frederick, August | do | Sep. 21, 1864 |
| Fraze, Fritz | do | Nov. 25, 1864 |
| Fusch, Franz | do | Nov. 25, 1864 |
| Freedy, Chas. | do | Nov. 30, 1864 |
| Fess, William | do | Nov. 30, 1863 |
| Freedy, William | do | Nov. 30, 1864 |
| Fennescheit, Joseph | do | Jan. 26, 1865 |
| Fels, William | do | Jan. 26, 1865 |
| Frana, Lorenz | do | Jan. 26, 1865 |
| Freidenburg, Fred | do | Nov. 11, 1863 |
| Freidenburg, Fred | do | Nov. 11, 1863 |
| Frana, Charles | do | Nov. 11, 1863 |
| Fraud, Wenzel | do | Sep. 22, 1864 |
| Fink, F | do | Dec. 7, 1864 |
| Farley, Jno | do | Jan. 19, 1865 |
| Finn, Michael | Delavan | Nov. 12, 1863 |
| Flemming, Patsey | do | Nov. 12, 1863 |
| Ferry, David | Richmond | Nov. 12, 1863 |
| Fisher, A. C | East Troy | Sep. 24, 1864 |
| Foss, Wm. A | do | Dec. 2, 1864 |
| Friedler, Chris. John | Summit | Sept. 22, 1864 |
| Folckheimer, Barnst | do | Sep. 22, 1864 |
| Fiedler, George | do | Sep. 22, 1864 |
| Frederickson, Andrew | Oconomowoc | Sept. 22, 1864 |
| Frary, August | do | Dec. 5, 1864 |
| Feehan, Patrick | do | Dec. 5, 1864 |
| Fields, William | Pewaukee | Sep. 22, 1864 |
| Frier, August | do | Sep. 22, 1864 |
| Frazen, William | Vernon | Sep. 24, 1864 |
| Foley, Michael | do | Sep. 24, 1864 |
| Fuhr, Jacob | Menomonee | Sep. 24, 1864 |
| Fitchenburg, Valentine | do | Sep. 24, 1864 |
| Freitsingen, John | do | Dec. 1, 1864 |
| Felsinger, Henry | do | Dec. 1, 1864 |
| Farber, John | Brookfield | Sep. 23, 1864 |
| Flynn, Robert | Muskego | Sep. 24, 1864 |
| Fleming, Peter | do | Nov. 30, 1864 |
| Farrar, C. S | Janesville | Nov. 12, 1863 |
| Farham, G. M | Milton | Nov. 12, 1863 |
| Flanagan, Thomas | Union | Nov. 12, 1863 |
| Fannig, Martin | Oregon | Nov. 12, 1863 |

| *Name.* | *Residence.* | *Date.* |
|---|---|---|
| Faller, William B. | Pleasant Spring | Nov. 13, 1863 |
| Fisher, Bernard | Berry | Sep. 19, 1864 |
| Fohsen, Antonie | do | Sep. 19, 1864 |
| Frunzer, Weinard | do | Feb. 27, 1865 |
| Fitchen, Amot | Roxbury | Nov. 13, 1863 |
| Flemming, John | Palmyra | |
| Ford, John | Lewiston | Nov. 16, 1863 |
| Fitzgeral, Edward | do | Sep. 21, 1864 |
| Ford, Michael | do | Nov. 15, 1864 |
| Foy, Stephen | Springdale | Sep. 19, 1864 |
| Fritz, Ferdinand | Watertown | Dec. 15, 1864 |
| Flory, Corn. P. | Pulaski or Clyde | Nov. 14, 1863 |
| Flynn, Michael | Clyde | Oct. 28, 1864 |
| Fling, Michael | Ridgeway | Nov. 14, 1863 |
| Freden, Nick | do | Sep. 28, 1864 |
| Fitzsimons, Thos | Dodgeville | Sep. 28, 1864 |
| Fieldsend, John | do | Sep. 28, 1864 |
| Ford, John | Highland | Nov. 14, 1863 |
| Fox, Jas. | do | Sep. 28, 1864 |
| Ford, Michael | do | Sep. 28, 1864 |
| Farrager, John | do | Nov. 19, 1864 |
| Finkel, Chas. M. | do | Dec. 7, 1864 |
| Flynn, Dan'l | Waldwick | Oct. 4, 1864 |
| Flannegan, John | do | Oct. 4, 1864 |
| Fay, Patrick | Kendall | Oct. 4, 1864 |
| Fisher, Daniel | do | Oct. 4, 1864 |
| Fitzsimmons, Chris. | do | Nov. 19, 1864 |
| French, Chas | Willow Springs | Nov. 16, 1863 |
| Flagerty, Jas | Benton | Sep. 29, 1864 |
| Funk, Geo | do | Sep. 29, 1864 |
| Fawcett, Thos | New Diggings | Sep. 29, 1864 |
| Foust, G. L. | Albany | Nov. 17, 1863 |
| Flanigan, Philip | Prairie du Chein | Nov. 18, 1863 |
| Foley, John | Bloom | Sep. 26, 1864 |
| Fitzgibbons, Micheal | Seneca | Sep. 30, 1864 |
| Flannigan, John | Eastman | Sep. 30, 1864 |
| Flannigan, Wm | do | Oct. 29, 1864 |
| Fowler, Thos | Millville | Oct. 1, 1864 |
| Fordan, John | Bear Creek | Oct. 3, 1864 |
| Flaherty, John | Millville | Oct. 28, 1864 |
| French, Sam'l | La Crosse Co | Nov. 16, 1863 |
| Flin, Michael | Chippewa Co | Nov. 20, 1863 |
| Frett, Frank | do | Nov. 20, 1863 |
| Flinn, Thos | do | Nov. 23, 1863 |
| Frink, Henry | Chippewa Falls | Sep. 27, 1864 |
| Forcier, Michael | La Fayette | Nov. 2, 1864 |
| Fitch, Newell | St. Croix Co | Nov. 20, 1863 |
| Flemmine, Wm | Emerald | Sep. 23, 1864 |
| Fasdick, Dan'l W | Vernon Co | Nov. 18, 1863 |
| Fennelta, Peter | do | Nov. 18, 1863 |
| Finely, Martin | Franklin | Sep. 21, 1864 |
| Finnely, Jas | do | Nov. 15, 1864 |
| Ferguson, John | Kildare | Sep. 19, 1864 |
| Finnegan, Dan | do | Sep. 31, 1864 |
| Francis, Hiram | do | Sep. 31, 1864 |
| Fitzgerald Jno | do | Sep. 31, 1864 |
| Frey, Warren | Plymouth | Sep. 31, 1864 |
| Flood, Jno | do | Sep. 19, 1864 |
| Farley, Patrick | Clearfield | Sep. 19, 1864 |

| *Name.* | *Residence.* | *Date.* |
|---|---|---|
| Fine, Godfrey | Marion | Sep. 19, 1864 |
| Fawcett, Miles | Lyndon | Sep. 19, 1864 |
| Fogle, Rob't | Summit | Sep. 31, 1864 |
| Frosbinger, Carl | Ridgeville | Sep. 20, 1864 |
| Foley, Timothy | Tomah | Sep. 20, 1864 |
| Faeker, Lloyd | do | Nov. 10, 1863 |
| Freer, John J | Glendale | Nov. 10, 1864 |
| Field, Wm | Centralia | Sep. 22, 1864 |
| Fuller, Hosea | Linwood | Sep. 22, 1864 |
| Fate, Wm. C | Stockton | Sep. 22, 1864 |
| Ferguson, Francis | Hull | Sep. 31, 1864 |
| Foley, Michael | Eau Galle | Sep. 27, 1864 |
| Fuller, Herman | do | Nov. 2, 1864 |
| Fulton, James | do | Nov. 2, 1864 |
| Fairfield, Wm | Easton | Nov. 14, 1864 |
| Feiats, Chas | Kewaunee Co | Nov. 20, 1863 |
| Flarity, Wm | do | Nov. 20, 1863 |
| Fick, Jno | do | Dec. 31, 1864 |
| Frawley, Jno | Franklin | Dec. 31, 1864 |
| Frawley, Michael | do | Nov. 20, 1863 |
| Frisque, Herbert | Casco | Dec. 31, 1864 |
| Frisque, David | do | Dec. 31, 1864 |
| Fase, Albert | do | Dec. 31, 1864 |
| Fountain, Adam | Carlton | Dec. 29, 1864 |
| Felicean, Louis | Lincoln | Dec. 29, 1864 |
| Felory, P. M | Two Rivers | Nov. 21, 1863 |
| Furebacker, Paul | Eaton | Nov. 21, 1863 |
| Fielden, Donald | Maple Grove | Dec. 29, 1864 |
| Fielden, John | do | Dec. 29, 1864 |
| Fricke, George | Manitowoc Rapids | Dec. 29, 1864 |
| Frisch, Peter | Newton | Dec. 29, 1864 |
| Fischer, Andreas | Calumet Co | Nov. 21, 1863 |
| Friden, Julius | Stockbridge | Dec. 28, 1864 |
| Forkins, Martin | Brothertown | Dec. 28, 1864 |
| Forest, Wm | Neenah | Nov. 25, 1863 |
| Fields, M. C | Oshkosh city | Nov. 23, 1863 |
| Fulsom, Jno. H | do | Nov. 23, 1863 |
| Fiddis, Jno | do | Nov. 23, 1863 |
| Fish, Dan'l E | Omro | Nov. 24, 1863 |
| Fitzpatrick, James, jr | Rushford | Nov. 24, 1863 |
| Flynn, James | Winnebago Co | Nov. 24, 1863 |
| Fagan, Jno. P | Mackford | Nov. 24, 1863 |
| Flemming, Jno | St. Marie | Dec. 31, 1864 |
| Fratzke, Jno. August | Marquette Co | Nov. 24, 1863 |
| Fransisco, Chas | Crystal Lake | Nov. 1, 1864 |
| Farnham, Dan'l | do | Dec. 31, 1864 |
| Forbes, S. D | Springfield | Nov. 1, 1864 |
| Fratzke, August | Newton | Nov. 1, 1864 |
| Fitzgerald, Stephen | Waupaca Co | Nov. 24, 1864 |
| Fox, Wm | Lind | Nov. 24, 1864 |
| Fitzgerald, Jno | Lebanon | Nov. 5, 1864 |
| Fitzgerald, Martin | do | Nov. 5, 1864 |
| Fife, John R | Caledonia | Nov. 5, 1864 |
| Frambauer, Herman | do | Dec. 31, 1864 |
| Fisher, Anton | Outagamie Co | Nov. 27, 1863 |
| Fisher, Carl | Greenfield | Nov. 28, 1863 |
| Fisher, Antonie | do | Nov. 27, 1863 |
| Farmer, Joseph B | Dale | Nov. 27, 1863 |
| Felie, Joseph | Black Creek | Dec. 28, 1864 |

| *Name.* | *Residence.* | *Date.* |
|---|---|---|
| Fingher, August | Maple Creek | Dec. 28, 1864 |
| Frelost, Anton | do | Dec. 28, 1864 |
| Fitzpatrick, Patrick | Brown Co | Nov. 27, 1863 |
| Fitzgerald, Edward | Depere | Nov. 27, 1863 |
| Francart, Francis | Green Bay | Dec. 28, 1864 |
| Flyn, Edmund | Holland | Dec. 28, 1864 |
| Finegan, Bernard | do | Dec. 28, 1864 |
| Fox, P. A | do | Dec. 28, 1864 |
| Farlum. Horlehen | do | Dec. 28, 1864 |
| Farlichon, James | Bellville | Dec. 28, 1864 |
| Frawley, Wm | Oconto Village | Nov. 28, 1863 |
| Ferguson, Geo | do | Nov. 28, 1863 |
| Fitzsimmons, Thos | do | Nov. 28, 1863 |
| Farley, Patrick | Pensaukee | Nov. 28, 1863 |
| Filch, John | Peshtigo | Nov. 28, 1863 |
| Ferguson, James | Stiles | Nov. 28, 1863 |
| Farrell, Wm | do | Nov. 28, 1863 |
| Follet, Suther | Richford | Nov. 2, 1864 |
| Fireman, Jacob | Deerfield | Nov. 2, 1864 |
| French, B B | Plainfield | Nov. 2, 1864 |
| Fergison, George | do | Nov. 2, 1864 |

## G

| *Name.* | *Residence.* | *Date.* |
|---|---|---|
| Graves, Myron G | Leroy | Jan. 27, 1865 |
| Grigget, Charles | do | Jan. 27, 1865 |
| Gunther, Louis | Lomira | Jan 27, 1865 |
| Galligan, Senor | do | Oct. 6, 1864 |
| Goodrich, Oscar | Trenton | Nov. 20, 1863 |
| Gerber, John | Rubicon | Nov. 21, 1863 |
| Grady, James | Erin | Oct. 12, 1864 |
| Geary, Edward | do | Dec. 1, 1864 |
| Gueuther, Henry | Barton | Dec. 1, 1864 |
| Gerhardt, Martin | do | Dec. 1, 1864 |
| Gross, Jacob | Polk | Oct. 12, 1864 |
| Germuuden, Henry | do | Dec. 8, 1864 |
| Greiner, Gotfried | do | Dec. 8, 1864 |
| Geison, Hubbard | Richfield | Nov. 21, 1863 |
| Gasser, Joseph | do | Oct. 12, 1863 |
| Gatz, William | do | Oct. 12, 1863 |
| Gould, Don Carlos | do | Dec. 1, 1864 |
| Gotz, Stephen | do | Dec. 1, 1864 |
| Good, Malacha | do | Dec. 1, 1864 |
| Geil, John | do | Jan. 27, 1865 |
| Goldarnmer, Juluis | Farmington | Oct. 18, 1864 |
| Gerhard, Ferdinand | do | Dec. 1, 1864 |
| Grop John | do | Dec. 1, 1864 |
| Gotsek, Herman | Jackson | Oct. 11, 1864 |
| Gerhard, Philip | do | Oct. 11, 1864 |
| Gentleinau, Jacob | Germantown | Nov. 21, 1863 |
| Graff, Christian | do | Nov. 21, 1863 |
| Greif, John | do | Nov. 21, 1863 |
| Grotz, John | Belgium | Dec. 1, 1864 |
| Gelesur, Jacob | do | Dec. 1, 1864 |
| Grotz, Nicholas | do | Dec. 1, 1864 |
| Gasche, Peter | do | Oct. 13, 1864 |
| Gasper, John | do | Oct. 13, 1864 |
| Griller, Henry | do | Oct. 13, 1864 |
| George, John | do | Oct. 13, 1864 |
| Gelsen, John W | do | Oct. 13, 1864 |

| *Name.* | *Residence.* | *Date.* |
|---|---|---|
| Gretten, John, Peter | do | Oct. 13, 1864 |
| Graff, John | do | Oct. 13, 1864 |
| Geters, Anton | do | Oct. 13, 1864 |
| Gallez, Jacob | do | Dec. 1, 1864 |
| Gruen, Peter | do | Dec. 1, 1864 |
| Grof, Michael | do | Dec. 1, 1864 |
| Grinitz, Gotleib | do | Dec. 1, 1864 |
| George, John | do | Dec. 1, 1864 |
| Giebler, Jacob | Fredonia | Oct. 14, 1864 |
| Gribeler, Peter | do | Oct. 14, 1854 |
| Geihu, John | do | Dec. 1, 1864 |
| Geiss, George | do | Dec. 1, 1864 |
| Geiss, Peter or John | do | Dec. 1, 1864 |
| Gmseldinzer, Michael | do | Nov. 21, 1863 |
| Geifler, August | Grafton | Oct. 13, 1864 |
| Gall, John | do | Oct. 13, 1864 |
| Geitzen, Joseph | do | Dec. 1, 1864 |
| Gatley, Michael | do | Dec. 1, 1864 |
| Goggin, John | Saukville | Oct. 14, 1864 |
| Ghall, Carl | do | Oct. 14, 1864 |
| Goregh, Thomas | do | Oct. 14, 1864 |
| Grusser, Carl | Sheboygan | Nov. 23, 1863 |
| Gray, Robert | do | Nov. 23, 1863 |
| Gruman, Frank | do | Nov. 23, 1863 |
| Grantts, Owen | do | Nov. 24, 1863 |
| Gilseclerf, Peter | do | Oct. 25, 1864 |
| Gundeson, James | do | Oct. 25, 1864 |
| Grumann, John | do | Oct. 25, 1864 |
| Gertson, Lars | do | Oct. 25, 1864 |
| Gildner, Henry | do | Jan. 27, 1865 |
| Gehr, Gottl | do | Oct. 25, 1864 |
| Grosser, Paul | do | Dec. 2, 1864 |
| Glanzer, Henry | do | Jan. 27, 1865 |
| Goldsmith, Sanford B | Sheboygan Falls | Nov. 24, 1863 |
| Greabner, Henry | do | Oct. 25, 1864 |
| Green, John | Lima | Nov. 24, 1863 |
| Granar, Henry O | do | Oct. 24, 1864 |
| Garice, Henry | do | Oct. 24, 1864 |
| George, William | do | Oct. 24, 1864 |
| Gibbs, L. R | Lima | Oct. 24, 1864 |
| Gates, M. A | do | Oct. 21, 1864 |
| Gurhais, Howard | do | Oct. 21, 1864 |
| Gargan, William | do | Dec. 2, 1864 |
| Gromfeld, C. C | do | Dec. 2, 1864 |
| Gilligan, William | Holland | Nov. 24, 1863 |
| Gasten, James | do | Oct. 21, 1864 |
| Greweldinger, Philip | Abbott | Oct. 18, 1864 |
| Galligan, James | do | Oct. 18, 1864 |
| Gersch, Mortz | do | Jan. 27, 1865 |
| Gill, Nicholas | Scott | Jan. 27, 1865 |
| Gates, Delos | Plymouth | Oct. 21, 1864 |
| Green, William | Fond du Lac | Nov. 19, 1863 |
| Gardner, George | Friendship | Nov. 19, 1863 |
| Gohkey, Eugene | Byron | Nov. 19, 1863 |
| Golback, Michael | Ashford | Nov. 19, 1863 |
| Gribley, Edward | Auburn | Oct. 5, 1864 |
| Gable, Frederick | Forest | Oct. 5, 1864 |
| Greeny, Joseph | Springvale | Oct. 5, 1864 |
| Graham, Andrew | Alto | Oct. 5, 1864 |

| *Name.* | *Residence.* | *Date.* |
|---|---|---|
| Galager, John | Waupun Village | Oct. 5, 1864 |
| Gowin, Soloman J | do | Oct. 5, 1864 |
| Griffith, Thomas D | Eldrado | Oct. 5, 1864 |
| Greena, Joseph | Metomen | Nov. 19, 1863 |
| Gee, Darius | Fox Lake | Nov. 19, 1863 |
| Gilmore, M. G | Portland | Nov. 20, 1863 |
| Grover, Thomas | Beaver Dam | Nov. 20, 1863 |
| Gardell, Charles | Emmett | Oct. 11, 1864 |
| Gahlman, Joseph | Clyman | Oct. 6, 1864 |
| Gowen, John | Chester | Nov. 20, 1863 |
| Gruling, Fred | Watertown | Oct. 6, 1864 |
| Gamm, Christian | do | Oct. 6, 1864 |
| Garmnon, Ferdinand | do | Oct. 6, 1864 |
| Gruntz, Henry | do | Oct. 6, 1864 |
| Gubig, Charles | do | Oct. 6, 1864 |
| Glanner, Carl | do | Dec. 1, 1864 |
| Guetzloff, Christopher | do | Dec. 1, 1864 |
| Granitz, William | do | Dec. 1, 1864 |
| Grimis, Richard | Summit | Sep. 22, 1864 |
| Guernsey, Reuben P | do | Sep. 22, 1864 |
| Graham, John | Oconomowoc | Sep. 22, 1864 |
| Gallagher, James | do | Sep. 22, 1864 |
| Goatlet, Charles | Pewaukee | Sep. 22, 1864 |
| Groff, Nicholas | do | Sep. 22, 1864 |
| Griswold, —— | do | Sep. 22, 1864 |
| Goldfinch, John | Waukesha | Sep. 23, 1864 |
| Growdy, William | Vernon | Sep. 24, 1864 |
| Grode, Peter | Menomonee | Sep 24, 1864 |
| Gillery, Bernard | do | Sep. 24, 1864 |
| Gray, William | do | Dec. 1, 1864 |
| Groot, Simon | Brookfield | Sep. 23, 1864 |
| Gradler, John | do | Sep. 23, 1864 |
| Gradler, Leonard | do | Sep. 23, 1864 |
| Gamble, Edward | New Berlin | Nov. 12, 1863 |
| Gaskin, Thomas | Muskego | Sep. 24, 1864 |
| Gross, William | do | Sep. 24, 1864 |
| Gasner, Christ | do | Sep. 24, 1864 |
| Grunde, Carl | do | Dec. 1, 1864 |
| Greenway, John | do | Dec. 1, 1864 |
| Gross, Philip | Milwaukee | Sep. 21, 1864 |
| Grechger, Leonhardt | do | Nov. 25, 1864 |
| Gravenstin, Carl | do | Nov. 25, 1864 |
| Gurker, Gottleib | do | Nov. 25, 1864 |
| Gewatt, John W | do | Nov. 25, 1864 |
| Goedcke, Frederick | do | Nov. 25, 1864 |
| Guetsen, Wilhelm | do | Nov. 25, 1864 |
| Gutzlaff, Johann | do | Jan. 26, 1865 |
| Geyer, Frederick | do | Nov. 11, 1863 |
| Goks, August | do | Dec. 7, 1864 |
| Gaul, Gottleib | do | Dec. 7, 1864 |
| Glossenapp, August | Granville | Sep. 22, 1864 |
| Garfast, John | Greenfield | Sep. 22, 1864 |
| Graney, John | do | Sep. 22, 1864 |
| Gshmesett, Frederick | do | Sep. 22, 1864 |
| Goefurth, Charles | do | Sep. 21, 1864 |
| Gorman, John | do | Sep. 21, 1864 |
| Glancey, Thomas | Lake | Dec. 13, 1864 |
| Gerlinger, Henry | Oak Creek | Sep. 22, 1864 |
| Gillien, Emile | Racine | Nov. 11, 1863 |

| *Name.* | *Residence.* | *Date.* |
|---|---|---|
| Gilday, Owen | Racine | Nov. 11, 1863 |
| Gildchrist, Louis | do | Nov. 11, 1863 |
| Graham, James | do | Sep. 24, 1864 |
| Gottsacker, Jacob | do | Sep. 24, 1864 |
| Grey, James | do | Sep. 22, 1864 |
| Gillon, John | do | Sep. 22, 1864 |
| Gorman, Patrick | do | Sep. 22, 1864 |
| Giff, John | do | Sep. 22, 1864 |
| Gottschalk, Charles | Milwaukee | Nov. 9, 1863 |
| Grindler, John | do | Nov. 9, 1863 |
| Gatze, Carl | do | Nov. 9, 1863 |
| Goodman, George | do | Nov. 9, 1863 |
| Gallain, Herman | do | Sep. 19, 1864 |
| Geller, Lewis | do | Sep. 19, 1864 |
| Green, August | do | Sep. 19, 1864 |
| Glesokof, Fred | do | Nov. 14, 1864 |
| Ginsmore, John | do | Nov. 14, 1864 |
| Griffiths, John | do | Dec. 22, 1864 |
| Galligan, Thomas | do | Dec. 22, 1864 |
| Galloway, William | do | Dec. 22, 1864 |
| Gomry, John | do | Dec. 22, 1864 |
| Goodhue, Peter | do | Nov. 9, 1863 |
| Gottschalk, —— | do | Nov. 9, 1863 |
| Gasper, William | do | Nov. 9, 1863 |
| Gipson, Isaac | do | Sep. 20, 1864 |
| Gray, H. C | do | Sep. 20, 1864 |
| Gunn, Lope | do | Sep. 20, 1864 |
| Galloway, George | do | Nov. 14, 1864 |
| Grierser, Henry | do | Nov. 14, 1864 |
| Gross, Fred | do | Nov. 14, 1864 |
| Grey, B | do | Nov. 10, 1863 |
| Gounn, Benjamin | do | Nov. 10, 1863 |
| Griffit, A. R | do | Nov. 10, 1863 |
| Gillett, Augustus | do | Nov. 10, 1863 |
| Gramschester, J | do | Jan. 19, 1865 |
| Genslar, Frederick | do | Nov. 10, 1863 |
| Goch, Anson | do | Nov. 10, 1863 |
| Groll, William V | do | Nov. 10, 1863 |
| Golman, John | do | Nov. 10, 1863 |
| Gallagher, Patrick | do | Nov. 10, 1863 |
| Grasse, William | do | Nov. 10, 1863 |
| Gentsch, Mathew | do | Sep. 27, 1864 |
| Guhrs, Johann | do | Sep. 27, 1864 |
| Gorders, James | do | Sep. 27, 1864 |
| Guth, Ernst | do | Sep. 27, 1864 |
| Grioisel, August | do | Sep. 27, 1864 |
| Geeseler, —— | do | Nov. 15, 1864 |
| Gier, Charles | do | Nov. 16, 1864 |
| Griessel, August | do | Nov. 16, 1864 |
| Grossenly, William | do | Nov. 16, 1864 |
| Gesler, Albert | do | Nov. 16, 1864 |
| Gargle, Patrick Ross | do | Nov. 16, 1864 |
| Gray, G. H. jr | do | Nov. 10, 1863 |
| Greenwald, —— | do | Nov. 10, 1863 |
| Gabrihon, Otta | do | Nov. 11, 1863 |
| Good, John | do | Nov. 11, 1863 |
| Gadger, Charles | do | Sep. 21, 1864 |
| Giedsker, Carl | do | Nov. 25, 1864 |
| Grollkey, Joseph | do | Nov. 11, 1863 |

| *Name.* | *Residence.* | *Date.* |
|---|---|---|
| Guber, Johann | Milwaukee | Nov. 11, 1863 |
| Galler, Carl | do | Sep. 21, 1864 |
| Gross, Johann | do | Sep. 21, 1864 |
| Gade, Frederick | do | Sep. 21, 1864 |
| Gates, J. L. W | do | Nov. 10, 1863 |
| Gilman, Nicholas | do | Nov. 10, 1863 |
| Gilmore, Nicholas | do | Nov. 10, 1863 |
| Green, Patrick | do | Sep. 20, 1864 |
| Ginerly, P | do | Sep. 20, 1864 |
| Grant, Patrick | do | Sep. 20, 1864 |
| Gairnly, M | do | Sep. 20, 1864 |
| Griffith, W. R | do | Sep. 20, 1864 |
| Ginskey, M | do | Sep. 20, 1864 |
| Gerrety, J | do | Nov. 15, 1864 |
| Goff, Patrick | do | Nov. 15, 1864 |
| Gabb, J. H | do | Nov. 15, 1864 |
| Green, C | do | Nov. 15, 1864 |
| Goodrich, E | do | Nov. 15, 1864 |
| Gintz, Michael | do | Nov. 15, 1864 |
| Guims, J | do | Nov. 15, 1863 |
| Grier, Warren | do | Nov. 15, 1863 |
| Griffin, J | do | Jan. 11, 1865 |
| Genety, J. M | do | Jan. 11, 1865 |
| Gentz, P | do | Jan. 11, 1865 |
| Gabriel, Jonas | do | Nov. 10, 1863 |
| Green, John | do | Nov. 10, 1863 |
| Gwine, Waldo | do | Nov. 10, 1863 |
| Guendlthwaitt, G | do | Nov. 10, 1863 |
| Gildemlyer, Joseph | do | Nov. 10, 1863 |
| Gargeart, A | do | Nov. 10, 1863 |
| Garvey, Thomas | do | Sep. 21, 1864 |
| Griswold, Edward | do | Sep. 21, 1864 |
| Green, George F | Racine | Jan. 19, 1865 |
| Glass, Homer | do | Sep. 22, 1864 |
| Golmann, Frederick E | Mount Pleasant | Sep. 23, 1864 |
| Gaffrey, David | Dover | Dec. 10, 1864 |
| Garity, John | Rochester | Sep. 24, 1864 |
| Gepson, Theodore E | do | Sep. 24, 1864 |
| Gansel, Charles | Waterford | Nov. 11, 1863 |
| Gammer, Isang | Caledonia | Nov. 11, 1863 |
| Gettle, George | do | Nov. 11, 1863 |
| Galien, P | do | Sep. 22, 1864 |
| Garagthy, William | do | Sep. 22, 1864 |
| Gable, Joseph | do | Sep. 22, 1864 |
| Gable, Mathew | do | Sep. 22, 1864 |
| Greaves, Adelmer | Summers | Nov. 12, 1863 |
| Glass, Michael | Paris | Nov. 12, 1863 |
| Gratz, John P | do | Nov. 12, 1863 |
| Gallagher, Thomas | Wheatland | Sep. 24, 1864 |
| Gallagher, John | Salem | Nov. 12, 1863 |
| Gollaghan, Edward | do | Sep. 24, 1864 |
| Grant, William | do | Sep. 24, 1864 |
| Gardner, James | Randall | Dec. 16, 1864 |
| Getty, Robert | Delavan | Nov. 12, 1864 |
| Gun, Henry H | Whitewater | Nov. 12, 1864 |
| Green, John | do | Nov. 12, 1864 |
| Gross, Martin | Geneva | Nov. 12, 1864 |
| Gaskill, James | East Troy | Sep. 24, 1864 |
| Goff, S. C | do | Sep. 24, 1864 |

| *Name.* | *Residence* | *Date.* |
|---|---|---|
| Gastner, Henry | Spring Prairie | Nov. 12, 1863 |
| Good, James | Blue Mounds | Sep. 19, 1864 |
| Gutzman, William | York | Nov. 13, 1863 |
| Grindler, John | Farmington | .., .... |
| Grupper, Frederick | do | Sep. 20, 1864 |
| Grace, John | Pacific | Nov. 16, 1864 |
| Golden, Patrick | Lewiston | Oct. 22, 1864 |
| Gill, Joel W | Clyde | Oct. 28, 1864 |
| Griffiths, David | Dodgeville | Sep. 28, 1864 |
| Goodwin, John | do | Sep. 28, 1864 |
| Goodlad, Samuel | do | Sep. 28, 1864 |
| Goldtrap, William | Highland | Sep. 28, 1864 |
| Galligan, Phillip | do | Sep. 28, 1864 |
| Gunderson, Ole | do | Sep. 28, 1864 |
| Greenash, Christian | do | Oct. 28, 1864 |
| Gulbertson, Andrew | do | Oct. 28, 1864 |
| Grace, Patrick | do | Nov. 19, 1864 |
| Griffin, Michael | do | Jan. 6, 1865 |
| Gottheart, Joseph | Waldwick | Nov. 14, 1863 |
| Gilbank, John | Kendall or Belmont | Nov. 16, 1863 |
| Gilbank, Thomas | do | Nov. 16, 1863 |
| Grigon, Matthew | Kendall | Oct. 4, 1864 |
| Griffen, James | Willow Springs | Nov. 16, 1863 |
| Glenville, Thomas | Benton | Nov. 16, 1863 |
| Gray, William Jr | do | Sep. 29, 1864 |
| Goldsworthy, William | do | Sep. 29, 1864 |
| Geehan, John | New Diggings | Sep. 29, 1864 |
| Gordchild, William R | Clayton | Sep. 30, 1864 |
| Gale, Frank | Prairie du Chien | Nov. 18, 1863 |
| Glennings, Robert | Waterloo | Oct. 1, 1864 |
| Gilmore, Sandford | do | Oct. 1, 1864 |
| Grarahh, Simeon | Dayton | Sep. 26, 1864 |
| Garvey, Peter | Seneca | Sep. 30, 1864 |
| Gainer, Patrick | do | Sep. 30, 1864 |
| Garvey, Christopher | do | Oct. 29, 1864 |
| Garvey, Patrick | do | Oct. 29, 1864 |
| Granest, Michael | Eastman | Sep. 30, 1864 |
| Grimm, Henry | Blue River | Oct. 1, 1864 |
| Glynn, Patrick | Millville | Oct. 28, 1864 |
| Gray, J H | Washington | Oct. 29, 1864 |
| Gallander, Charles | La Crosse Co | Oct. 13, 1864 |
| Gordon, Daniel | do | Oct. 13, 1864 |
| Gammon, John | do | Oct. 13, 1864 |
| Gordon, Moses | Campbell | Sep. 19, 1864 |
| Gotha, Adolph | Chippewa Co | Nov. 20, 1863 |
| Gilbert, Wright | do | Nov. 23, 1863 |
| Goolet, Prosser | Chippewa Falls | Sep. 27, 1864 |
| Godni, Felix | do | Nov. 2, 1864 |
| Goodell, Charles | do | Nov. 2, 1864 |
| Griffin, Alvan N | Juneau Co | Nov. 17, 1863 |
| Garwin, Patrick | Kildare | Sep. 19, 1864 |
| Griffith, George | do | Sep. 31, 1864 |
| Galvin, Edward | Lemonweir | Sep. 19, 1864 |
| Geyan, Christian | Marion | Sep. 19, 1864 |
| Godfrey, Bartholomew | Germantown | Sep. 20, 1864 |
| Gleason, John | St. Croix Co | Nov. 20, 1863 |
| Gerraghty, Michael | Erin Prairie | Nov. 3, 1864 |
| Ginnam, David | Somerset | Nov. 3, 1864 |
| Groom, George W | Dunn Co | Nov. 23, 1864 |

| *Name.* | *Residence.* | *Date.* |
|---|---|---|
| Green, Reuben | Eau Galle | Sep 27, 1864 |
| Gehrson, Gehr | Ettrick | Sep. 21, 1864 |
| Gibson, Milo B | Chase | Sep. 21, 1864 |
| Gillerand, Barney | Tomah | Sep. 20, 1864 |
| Graham, Michael | do | Nov. 3, 1864 |
| Goody, John | do | Nov. 10, 1864 |
| Gamick, James | do | Nov. 10, 1864 |
| Garder, Isaac | Webster | Sep. 20, 1864 |
| Gumsrud, John | Hamburg | Nov. 15, 1864 |
| Gibson, Orrin | Springfield | Sep. 22, 1864 |
| Grinnell, Samuel | Linwood | Sep. 22, 1864 |
| Grannis, Eli | Pine Grove | Sep. 22, 1864 |
| Gardner, Benjamin | do | Nov. 15, 1864 |
| Gould, Albert S | Belmont | Nov. 15, 1864 |
| Gray, Church | Lanark | Sept. 22, 1864 |
| Gibson, Nelson | Naples | Sept. 26, 1864 |
| Green, Obadiah | Lincoln | Sept. 26, 1864 |
| Galliger, Patrick | Door Co | Nov. 20, 1863 |
| Gilles Emanuel | Lincoln | Nov. 20, 1863 |
| Grover, Henry | Kewaunee | Dec. 29, 1864 |
| Gay, William | Coryville | Dec. 29, 1864 |
| Getch, William | Montpelier | Dec. 29, 1864 |
| Giermier, John | Franklin | Dec. 29, 1864 |
| Grissell, Jacob | Carlton | Dec. 29, 1864 |
| Gray, Stephen M | Franklin | Nov. 21, 1863 |
| Gleason, John | Manitowoc | Nov. 21, 1863 |
| Gunderson, Ole | do | Nov. 21, 1863 |
| Groshaus, Bolthsas | Eaton | Nov. 24, 1863 |
| Gesler, Scharlis | Cooperstown | Dec. 29, 1864 |
| Gammon, John | Maple Grove | Dec. 29, 1864 |
| Guihean, Patrick | do | Dec. 29, 1864 |
| Guihean, John | do | Dec. 29, 1864 |
| Green, Thomas | Rockland | Dec. 29, 1864 |
| Groh, Peter | Meeme | Dec. 29, 1864 |
| Gurley, Andrew | Calumet Co | Nov 21, 1863 |
| Gamiger, Felix | Rantoul | Dec. 28, 1864 |
| Green, Filo | Brothertown | Dec. 28, 1864 |
| Griswold, John | Oshkosh city | Nov. 23, 1863 |
| Griffith, William | do | Nov. 23, 1863 |
| Gordon, Benjamin F | Omro | Nov. 23, 1863 |
| Gregory, A. C. | Poygan | Nov. 5, 1864 |
| Gilbert, Peter | Manchester | Nov. 24, 1863 |
| Gustin, James H | Wautoma | Nov. 25, 1863 |
| Gerrma, Apperson | Plainfield | Nov. 25, 1863 |
| Grow, J. D | do | Nov. 2, 1864 |
| Gadrian, Julian | Bloomfield | Nov. 2, 1864 |
| Grimes, William | Warren | Nov. 2, 1864 |
| Griffett, Charles | do | Nov. 2, 1864 |
| Goodrich, Chauncey | Richford | Nov. 2, 1864 |
| Giles, Darius | Oasis | Nov. 2, 1864 |
| Ghanis, Christopher | Aurora | Dec. 31, 1864 |
| Griffin, Michael | Union | Nov. 5, 1864 |
| Gibson, Gilbert | Scandinavia | Nov. 5, 1863 |
| Gudmanson, Ammie | St. Lawrence | Nov. 5, 1864 |
| Gregerson, Peter | Iola | Nov. 5, 1864 |
| Gunderson, Hans | do | Dec. 31, 1864 |
| Gunderson, Knud | do | Dec. 31, 1864 |
| Gregorsen, Gregor | do | Dec. 31, 1864 |
| Gouthore, Frederick | Appleton | Nov. 27, 1863 |

| *Name.* | *Residence.* | *Date.* |
|---|---|---|
| Gravel, Joseph | Appleton | Nov. 27, 1863 |
| Gallagher, Frank | do | Nov. 27, 1863 |
| Gazer, Anton | do | Nov. 27, 1863 |
| Gauterbeni, Rudolph | do | Nov. 27, 1863 |
| Groht, Christopher Jr | Center | Nov. 27, 1863 |
| Garvin, James | do | Nov. 27, 1863 |
| Grotte, Christin | do | Dec. 28, 1864 |
| Garvey, John Jr | Freedom | Dec. 28, 1864 |
| Greely, Paul A | | Nov. 27, 1863 |
| Gilder, William | Stiles | Nov. 28, 1863 |
| Gray, Nathan | do | Dec. 29, 1864 |
| Gulkie, John | Little Suamico | Dec. 29, 1864 |
| Gamon, James | Neshkoro | Nov. 1, 1864 |
| Gilgamon, William | do | Dec. 31, 1864 |
| Gusert, Ludwig | Mecan | Nov. 1, 1864 |
| Ganke, John | do | Dec. 31, 1864 |
| Golken, Gottlep | do | Dec. 31, 1864 |
| Gordon, Patrick | Shields | Nov. 2, 1864 |
| Gray, Ira | Douglas | Dec. 31, 1864 |
| Goderson, James | do | Dec. 31, 1864 |
| Grover, L. G | Newton | Dec. 31, 1864 |
| Gragg, Hiram | Osborn | Dec. 28, 1864 |

## H

| | | |
|---|---|---|
| Hilton, Jacob | Polk | Dec. 8, 1864 |
| Hall, John | do | Dec. 8, 1864 |
| Hammel, Johann L | do | Dec. 8, 1864 |
| Haser, Carl | Richfield | Oct. 12, 1864 |
| Herby, Bartollmais | do | Oct. 12, 1864 |
| Hartleman, Whilhelm | do | Oct. 12, 1864 |
| Harbley, Dieter | do | Oct. 12, 1864 |
| Ham, Charles | do | Dec. 1, 1864 |
| Hartzog, Mathew | do | Dec. 1, 1864 |
| Hagerty, William | do | Dec. 1, 1864 |
| Hagerty, Wilhelm | do | Dec. 1, 1864 |
| Heber, Bartholomew | do | Jan. 27, 1865 |
| Hacy, Michael | Farmington | Nov. 21, 1863 |
| Harta, Ant | do | Oct. 18, 1864 |
| Hide, Peter | do | Dec. 1, 1864 |
| Hoehme, Gaffred | do | Dec. 1, 1864 |
| Herida, Frederick | do | Dec. 1, 1864 |
| Hickendorf, Frederick | Jackson | Oct. 11, 1864 |
| Huberty, Anton | Germantown | Nov. 21, 1863 |
| Heugel, Franz | Belgium | Oct. 13, 1864 |
| Hehack, John | do | Oct. 13, 1864 |
| Hemmen, John | do | Oct. 13, 1864 |
| Heman, John | do | Oct. 13, 1864 |
| Hemmen, Nich | do | Dec. 1, 1864 |
| Hemmen, John | do | Dec. 1, 1864 |
| Harrington, John | Fredonia | Oct. 14, 1864 |
| Hinkers, John P | Leroy | Dec. 1, 1864 |
| Hammel, Johann L | do | Jan. 27, 1864 |
| Hulbert, Luciers | Lomira | Oct. 6, 1864 |
| Hall, John | do | Jan. 27, 1864 |
| Hay, Henry | Williamstown | Nov. 20, 1863 |
| Higgins, W. E | do | Nov. 20, 1863 |
| Hinning, Carl | Herman | Nov. 24, 1863 |
| Herzog, John | do | Nov. 24, 1863 |
| Heideman, Wilhelm | do | Jan. 27, 1865 |

| *Name.* | *Residence.* | *Date.* |
|---|---|---|
| Hagen, Hugo | Trenton | Nov. 20, 1863 |
| Haubrick, Peter | do | Nov. 20, 1863 |
| Heuser, George | do | Nov. 20, 1863 |
| Haight, G. L. | Hubbard | Nov. 21, 1863 |
| Hamilton, Thomas | Rubicon | Nov. 21, 1863 |
| Haggra, August | Addison | Nov. 21, 1863 |
| Hausen, J | Erin | Nov. 21, 1863 |
| Hines, John | do | Oct. 12, 1864 |
| Healey, John | do | Oct. 12, 1864 |
| Heberlin, Jacob | Barton | Oct. 12, 1864 |
| Huntington, William | do | Oct. 12, 1864 |
| Hargis, Philip | do | Oct. 12, 1864 |
| Hall, John | do | Dec. 1, 1864 |
| Hoos, Mathias | West Bend | Nov. 21, 1863 |
| Haas, Frederick | do | Nov. 21, 1863 |
| Heifenbuck, Philip | Polk | Oct. 12, 1864 |
| Hard, Conrad | do | Oct. 12, 1864 |
| Horn, Henry | Richfield | Oct. 12, 1864 |
| Harles, Tillip | Fredonia | Oct. 14, 1864 |
| Hanan, James | do | Oct. 14, 1864 |
| Holtz, Welhen | do | Oct. 14, 1864 |
| Hartman, Emtz | do | Oct. 14, 1864 |
| Hopel, Wilhelm | do | Dec. 1, 1864 |
| Hoffman, John | do | Dec. 1, 1864 |
| Huras, Andreas | do | Dec. 1, 1864 |
| Haman, Henry | do | Nov. 21, 1863 |
| Helm, John | Cedarburg | Nov. 23, 1863 |
| Hurley, Michael | do | Nov. 23, 1863 |
| Hiner, Ferdinand | Grafton | Nov. 23, 1863 |
| Han, John | do | Oct. 13, 1864 |
| Heuer, Ferdinand | do | Jan. 27, 1865 |
| Houff, Samuel | do | Jan. 27, 1865 |
| Haper, P | Mequon | Nov. 23, 1863 |
| Hadcom, Mathias | Port Washington | Nov. 23, 1863 |
| Hall, Michael | Saukville | Oct. 14, 1864 |
| Habermeyer, Michael | do | Oct. 14, 1864 |
| Hagerty, John | do | Oct. 14, 1864 |
| Hanington, Michael | do | Oct. 14, 1864 |
| Hansen, Thomas | Sheboygan | Nov. 23, 1863 |
| Hobart, Clement | do | Dec. 2, 1864 |
| Hyer, Martin | Holland | Dec. 2, 1864 |
| Hause, William | Abbott | Oct. 18, 1864 |
| Henry, Barney | do | Oct. 18, 1864 |
| Hand. Patrick | do | Oct. 18, 1864 |
| Hohlfeld, Harmm | do | Oct. 18, 1864 |
| Hand, Mathew | do | Jan. 27, 1865 |
| Hanel, Philip | do | Jan. 27, 1865 |
| Haskins, Patrick | do | Jan. 27, 1865 |
| Harden, Coon L | Scott | Nov. 24, 1863 |
| Haines, Samuel | do | Dec. 2, 1864 |
| Heren, John O | do | Dec. 2, 1864 |
| Hanney, Them | do | Dec. 2, 1864 |
| Hoffman, John G | Plymouth | Dec. 6, 1864 |
| Haigh, George | do | Dec. 6, 1864 |
| Henry, Edward | Sheboygan | Jan. 27, 1865 |
| Hem, Heinrich | do | Oct. 18, 1864 |
| Hath, Jenken | do | Oct. 18, 1864 |
| Herman, John | do | Oct. 18, 1864 |
| Hartman, Christian | do | Dec. 2, 1864 |

| *Name.* | *Residence.* | *Date.* |
|---|---|---|
| Heidezenthal, Joseph | Sheboygan | Dec. 2, 1864 |
| Hartman, Christopher | do | Oct. 18, 1864 |
| Hist, Johann | do | Oct. 18, 1864 |
| Heiligenthal, George | do | Oct. 18, 1864 |
| Hinz, John | do | Oct. 18, 1864 |
| Haffer, Ernst | Moselle | Oct. 18, 1865 |
| Herzog, Henrich | do | Oct. 18, 1864 |
| Hausen, August | do | Dec. 2, 1864 |
| Hildebrand, Ferdinand | do | Dec. 2, 1864 |
| Huper, Philip | do | Dec. 2, 1864 |
| Honey, George W | Sheboygan Falls | Nov. 24, 1863 |
| Hanford, William | do | Nov. 24, 1863 |
| Haine, John A | do | Dec. 2, 1864 |
| Haudki, Henry | do | Dec. 2, 1864 |
| Hike, Robert | Lima |  |
| Hatter, B | do | Nov. 24, 1863 |
| Hahn, John | do | Oct. 24, 1864 |
| Halzruth, K | do | Oct. 24, 1864 |
| Holshuh, Casper | do | Oct. 21, 1864 |
| Hall, Martin | do | Dec. 2, 1864 |
| Hale, Chas. H | Fond du Lac | Nov. 19, 1863 |
| Haden, John | do | Nov. 19, 1863 |
| Hutchinson, —— | do | Nov. 19, 1863 |
| Hauss, Charles | do | Nov. 19, 1863 |
| Holmes, John | do | Nov. 19, 1863 |
| Hawk, Simeon | Osceola | Nov. 19, 1863 |
| Hale, John | Oakfield | Nov. 19, 1863 |
| Hendricke, Benj. F | Ashford | Nov. 19, 1863 |
| Heller, John | Auburn | Oct. 5, 1864 |
| Henriques, Peter | do | Oct. 5, 1864 |
| Harder, John | do | Oct. 5, 1864 |
| Harris, John B | Lamartine | Nov. 19, 1863 |
| Hill, George H | do | Nov. 19, 1863 |
| Harmer, Thomas | Springvale | Nov. 19, 1863 |
| Hillebert Spencer M | Waupun village | Nov. 19, 1863 |
| Hall, B. B | Ripon | Nov. 19, 1863 |
| Hinkley, Oren D | Rosendale | Nov. 19, 1863 |
| Hughes, John J | Eldorado | Oct. 5, 1864 |
| Hummel, Joseph | Westford | Nov. 20, 1863 |
| Hagerty, Edward | Shields | Nov. 20, 1863 |
| Hickey, D | do | Nov. 20, 1863 |
| Hillins, Jasper | Emmett | Nov. 20, 1863 |
| Hanrahan, Patrick | do | Oct. 11, 1864 |
| Hackert, Patrick | do | Oct. 11, 1864 |
| Hause, Christian | Burnett | Nov. 20, 1863 |
| Haulon, James | Chester | Nov. 20, 1863 |
| Halie, Daniel | Watertown | Oct. 6, 1864 |
| Henke, Carl | do | Dec. 1, 1864 |
| Hauser, John | Leroy | Oct. 4, 1864 |
| Hart, Albert | do | Oct. 4, 1864 |
| Hostert, John | do | Oct. 4, 1864 |
| Holstein, Albert | Milwaukee | Nov. 9, 1863 |
| Hoffman, William | do | Nov. 9, 1863 |
| Horn, William | do | Nov. 9, 1863 |
| Heuler, Carl | do | Nov. 9, 1863 |
| Heneig, Joseph | do | Nov. 9, 1863 |
| Hareal, John | do | Nov. 9, 1863 |
| Highland, L | do | Nov. 9, 1863 |
| Horst, Philip | do | Nov. 9, 1863 |

| Name. | Residence. | Date. |
|---|---|---|
| Heidmann, Wm | Milwaukee | Nov. 9, 1863 |
| Harmuth, Anton | do | Nov. 9, 1863 |
| Hasten, Wm | do | Nov. 9, 1863 |
| Hagneroe, Heinrich | do | Nov. 9, 1863 |
| Hartman, John | do | Sep. 19, 1864 |
| Hubbert, Rob't | do | Sep. 19, 1864 |
| Hayes, James | do | Sep. 19, 1864 |
| Hoyd, Wm | do | Sep. 19, 1864 |
| Holksphuls, Jas | do | Sep. 19, 1864 |
| Heiden, Jaachim | do | Nov. 14, 1864 |
| Hafer, Johann | do | Nov. 14, 1864 |
| Hulin, Andrew | do | Nov. 14, 1864 |
| Hartung, Anton | do | Dec. 22, 1864 |
| Herring, Chas | do | Dec. 22, 1864 |
| Harter, John | do | Nov. 9, 1863 |
| Hunt, D | do | Nov. 9, 1863 |
| Hausworth, John | do | Nov. 9, 1863 |
| Hubert, F. C | do | Nov. 9, 1863 |
| Halger, Nicholas | do | Nov. 9, 1863 |
| Hoffman, Hinrich | do | Nov. 9, 1863 |
| Halt, Frederick | do | Sep. 20, 1864 |
| Hallena, Ed | do | Nov. 14, 1864 |
| Hathman, Henry | do | Nov. 14, 1864 |
| Hosmer, J. H | do | Nov. 10, 1863 |
| Halearan, M | do | Nov. 10, 1863 |
| Harris, Robert | do | Nov. 10, 1863 |
| Heman, H. B | do | Nov. 10, 1863 |
| Histan, Edward | do | Nov. 10, 1863 |
| Hughs, Martin | do | Nov. 10, 1863 |
| Herp, W | do | Nov. 10, 1863 |
| Hakum, M | do | Nov. 10, 1863 |
| Hallibock, J. S | do | Nov. 10, 1863 |
| Hayden, S | do | Nov. 10, 1863 |
| Hagar, Walter | do | Nov. 10, 1863 |
| Harm, Michael | do | Nov. 10, 1863 |
| Hassedy, L | do | Nov. 10, 1863 |
| Hayes, Michael | do | Nov. 10, 1863 |
| Hickey, W | do | Nov. 10, 1863 |
| Heley, Wm | do | Nov. 10, 1863 |
| Hannon, John | do | Nov. 10, 1863 |
| Hamlin, Thos | do | Nov. 10, 1863 |
| Heay, W | do | Nov. 10, 1863 |
| Haunts, P | do | Nov. 10, 1863 |
| Hockmire, Henry | do | Nov. 10, 1863 |
| Harey, W | do | Nov. 10, 1863 |
| Higgins, Pat | do | Sept. 20, 1864 |
| Hillard, H | do | Sep. 20, 1864 |
| Hamsn, John | do | Sep. 20, 1864 |
| Hollin, E. V | do | Sep. 20, 1864 |
| Hortel, J | do | Sep. 20, 1864 |
| Harper, Robert | do | Sep. 20, 1864 |
| Heany, W. J | do | Sep. 20, 1864 |
| Horn, F. J | do | Sep. 20, 1864 |
| Homes, John | do | Sep. 20, 1864 |
| Holland, Toney | do | Sep. 20, 1864 |
| Hertin, M | do | Sep. 20, 1864 |
| Hopkins, Dennis | do | Sep. 20, 1864 |
| Hobsback, C | do | Sep. 20, 1864 |
| Horan, Thomas | do | Sep 20, 1864 |

| *Name.* | *Residence.* | *Date.* |
|---|---|---|
| Harlick, A. | Milwaukee | Sep. 20, 1864 |
| Hinds, W. H. | do | Sep. 20, 1864 |
| Hally, Michael | do | Nov. 15, 1864 |
| Hurly, Patrick | do | Nov. 15, 1864 |
| Herbert, John | do | Nov. 15, 1864 |
| Hansen, P. | do | Nov. 15, 1864 |
| Higgins, J. C | do | Nov. 15, 1864 |
| Hughs, Joshua | do | Nov. 15, 1864 |
| Him, A. jr | do | Nov. 15, 1864 |
| Higgins, Joseph | do | Nov. 15, 1864 |
| Hamlin, —— | do | Nov. 15, 1864 |
| Harkman, Moses | do | Nov. 15, 1864 |
| Harty, A. | do | Nov. 15, 1864 |
| Hisford, P. | do | Nov. 15, 1864 |
| Horn, William | do | Nov. 15, 1864 |
| Hockhart, Richard | do | Nov. 10, 1863 |
| Holme, Wm. | do | Nov. 11, 1863 |
| Harrison, Geo. B | do | Nov. 11, 1863 |
| Henner, Gregor | do | Nov. 11, 1863 |
| Hein, Christian | dd | Nov. 11, 1863 |
| Hager, Stephen | do | Nov. 11, 1863 |
| Haefen, Anie | do | Sep. 21, 1864 |
| Hine, August | do | Sep. 21, 1864 |
| Halens, Daniel | do | Sep. 21, 1864 |
| Humbold, August | do | Sep. 21, 1864 |
| Hepert, Henry | do | Sep. 21, 1864 |
| Hermester, Wenzel | do | Sep. 21, 1864 |
| Hacker, John | do | Sep. 21, 1864 |
| Hranoosta, Wenzel | do | Sep. 21, 1864 |
| Harris, Christian | do | Sep. 21, 1864 |
| Henister, John | do | Nov. 25, 1864 |
| Hotz, Charles | do | Nov. 25, 1864 |
| Hierber, Michael J | do | Nov. 25, 1864 |
| Heinrich, Emil | do | Nov. 11, 1863 |
| Horst, Stephen | do | Nov. 11, 1863 |
| Haisch, Fred'k Wm | do | Sep. 21, 1864 |
| Hees, Heinrich | do | Sep. 21, 1864 |
| Henning, Carl | do | Sep. 21, 1864 |
| Helback, Michael | do | Sep. 21, 1864 |
| Happ, Wilhelm | do | Nov. 25, 1863 |
| Heinke, Carl | do | Nov. 25, 1863 |
| Hait, Casper | do | Nov. 25, 1863 |
| Hatfill, Carl | do | Nov. 25, 1863 |
| Hurske, Johann | do | Nov. 25, 1863 |
| Hill, Royal | do | Sep. 21, 1864 |
| Hadly, Chas. W | do | Sep. 21, 1864 |
| Hanson, Hans | do | Nov. 10, 1863 |
| Hempe, Fred | do | Nov. 10, 1863 |
| Hasting, Alfred | do | Nov. 10, 1863 |
| Hailmans, Henry | do | Nov. 10, 1863 |
| Heartwell, Horace | do | Nov. 10, 1863 |
| Hine, —— | do | Nov. 10, 1863 |
| Himstradt, Jacob | do | Nov. 10, 1863 |
| Hople, Anton | do | Sep. 21, 1864 |
| Heiden, John | do | Sep. 21, 1864 |
| Hall, P. F | do | Sep. 21, 1864 |
| Hanes, Alfred | do | Sep. 21, 1864 |
| Holin, Martin | do | Sep. 21, 1864 |
| Hafinmeister, Louis | do | Sep. 21, 1863 |

| *Name* | *Residence.* | *Date.* |
|---|---|---|
| Hoenig, Fred | Milwaukee | Nov. 15, 1864 |
| Hass, ——— | do | Nov. 15, 1864 |
| Heiss, Ludwig | do | Nov. 16, 1864 |
| Hinkfass, Johann | do | Nov. 16, 1864 |
| Hochstein, Math | do | Nov. 16, 1864 |
| Horn, Fritz | do | Nov. 16, 1864 |
| Hahn, Michael | do | Nov. 16, 1864 |
| Herring, Charles | do | Nov. 16, 1864 |
| Hoffman, Louis | do | Nov. 10, 1863 |
| Hufschmidt, John M | do | Nov. 10, 1863 |
| Harlind, A. C | do | Nov. 10, 1863 |
| Huntington, C. P | do | Nov. 10, 1863 |
| Havish, Adolph A | do | Nov. 10, 1863 |
| Harmuth, Anton | do | Nov. 10, 1863 |
| Herbert, R. B | Milwaukee | Nov. 15, 1864 |
| Hoehstein, Mathias | do | Jan. 11, 1865 |
| Hammon, Thomas | do | Jan. 11, 1865 |
| Hifferan, James | do | Jan. 11, 1865 |
| Hanning, B | do | Jan. 11, 1865 |
| Hall, Henry | do | Jan. 11, 1865 |
| Hulburt, H. G | do | Jan. 11, 1865 |
| Hartzel, F | do | Jan. 11, 1865 |
| Haberstroh, John | do | Jan. 11, 1865 |
| Haapa, Morris | do | Jan. 11, 1865 |
| Hass, Christian | do | Jan. 11, 1865 |
| Hausberg, C | do | Jan. 11, 1865 |
| Harbeck, Anton | do | Jan. 11, 1865 |
| Harenstvauss, John | do | Jan. 11, 1865 |
| Hill, Ogden | do | Jan. 11, 1865 |
| Halloran, ——— | do | Jan. 11, 1865 |
| Hayworth, Wm | do | Jan. 11, 1865 |
| Hueffner, John | do | Nov. 10, 1863 |
| Henskel, C. W | do | Nov. 10, 1863 |
| Higgins, Wm. E | do | Nov. 10, 1863 |
| Holey, Fredrick | do | Nov. 10, 1863 |
| Hennessey, Mathen | do | Nov. 10, 1863 |
| Haley, Peter | do | Sep. 21, 1864 |
| Howe, Frank | do | Sep. 21, 1864 |
| Hawley, James | do | Sep. 21, 1864 |
| Horn, Ezra | do | Sep. 21, 1864 |
| Huttersley, William | do | Sep. 21, 1864 |
| Hagan, James | do | Sep. 21, 1864 |
| Huepmore, Chas | do | Sep. 21, 1864 |
| Harrington, John | Waukesha | Sep. 23, 1864 |
| Harte, Retsa | do | Sep. 23, 1864 |
| Hudson, John | Vernon | Nov. 12, 1863 |
| Hannebeny, Patrick | do | Sep. 24, 1864 |
| Honlzbore, Joseph | Menomonee | Sep. 24, 1864 |
| Hudt, William | do | Sep. 24, 1864 |
| Higgins, Peter | do | Sep. 24, 1864 |
| Holding, William | do | Sep. 24, 1864 |
| Hintz, Frederick | do | Nov. 25, 1864 |
| Hamann, Wilhelm | do | Nov. 25, 1863 |
| Hallendoff, John | Muskego | Sep. 24, 1864 |
| Herring, Henry | do | Nov. 30, 1864 |
| Hart, Henry | do | Nov. 30, 1864 |
| Hensberry, Richard | do | Nov. 30, 1864 |
| Humper, Conrad | do | Dec. 1, 1864 |
| Hughes, Hugh | Delafield | Sep. 22, 1864 |

| *Name* | *Residence.* | *Date* |
|---|---|---|
| Harkins, Daniel | Pleasant Prairie | Nov. 12, 1863 |
| Hay, John | Delavan | Nov. 12, 1863 |
| Hind, James | do | Nov. 12, 1863 |
| Hames, John | do | Nov. 12, 1863 |
| Horen, Daniel | Whitewater | Nov. 12, 1863 |
| Heart, George | East Troy | Sep. 24, 1864 |
| Hill, Pride | do | Sep. 24, 1864 |
| Hamlin, David B | Bloomfield | Nov. 12, 1863 |
| Hahn, Adam | Summit | Sep. 22, 1864 |
| Higgins, Henry | do | Sep. 22, 1864 |
| Hosmer, John | do | Sep. 22, 1864 |
| Holdoll, Charles | do | Nov. 30, 1864 |
| Howell, Howell | do | Nov. 30, 1864 |
| Hogan, Lawrence | Oconomowoc | Nov. 12, 1863 |
| Hall, Philip W | do | Nov. 12, 1863 |
| Halverson, Ole | do | Sep. 22, 1864 |
| Hurd, David | do | Sep. 22, 1864 |
| Henry, Thomas | do | Sep. 22, 1864 |
| Hawes, J. M | do | Dec. 5, 1864 |
| Hartung, Gottleib | do | Dec. 5, 1864 |
| Hunhaltz, Frederick | do | Dec. 5, 1864 |
| Houes, James | Genesee | Nov. 12, 1863 |
| Hanser, Vincint | do | Nov. 12, 1863 |
| Hudson, Albert | Mukwanego | Nov. 12, 1863 |
| Hanifin, Jeremiah | Lisbon | Nov. 12, 1863 |
| Horton, Charles B | Pewaukee | Dec. 2, 1864 |
| Harland, Wm. | do | Dec. 2, 1864 |
| Horn, Soloman, jr | do | Dec. 2, 1864 |
| Huebschen, John | Milwaukee | Jan. 26, 1865 |
| Hegle, F. B | do | Jan. 26, 1865 |
| Hasbestion, Wm | do | Nov. 11, 1863 |
| Haefer, George | do | Nov. 11, 1863 |
| Haas, Frederick | do | Sep. 22, 1864 |
| Hegelin, Adolph | do | Dec. 7, 1864 |
| Harback, Henry | do | Dec. 7, 1864 |
| Hamnrann, Johann | do | Dec. 7, 1864 |
| Hill, Moses B | Granville. | Sep. 22, 1864 |
| Hurlbey, John | Wauwatosa | Nov 11, 1863 |
| Hennessey, John | Greenfield | Nov. 11, 1863 |
| Hass, John | do | Nov. 11, 1863 |
| Haack, John | Lake | Nov. 11, 1863 |
| Hess, Joseph | do | Sep. 22, 1864 |
| Hendrichson, P. D | do | Sep. 22, 1864 |
| Hocker, Uackinn | do | Dec. 13, 1864 |
| Hulsbeck, Peter J | do | Dec. 13, 1864 |
| Holden, Edward | do | Dec. 13, 1864 |
| Hogan, Thomas, jr | Franklin | Nov. 11, 1863 |
| Hechel, John | do | Nov. 11, 1863 |
| Hughs, William | Oak Creek | Nov. 11, 1863 |
| Hauch, Jacob | do | Sep. 22, 1864 |
| Howley, James | do | Sep. 22, 1864 |
| Hewit, Edward | Racine | Nov. 11, 1863 |
| Hays, William | do | Nov. 11, 1863 |
| Hasting, John | do | Nov. 11, 1863 |
| Herzel, Fred | Racine | Nov. 11, 1863 |
| Haines, Peter | do | Nov. 11, 1863 |
| Harris, John | do | Nov. 11, 1863 |
| Hantske, Frederick | do | Sep. 24, 1864 |
| Hiller, Mathias | do | Sep. 24, 1864 |

| *Name.* | *Residence.* | *Date.* |
|---|---|---|
| Hieneta, Christian | Racine | Nov. 11, 1863 |
| Henry, James | do | Sep. 22, 1864 |
| Hiler, William | do | S p. 22, 1864 |
| Hagres, Martin | do | Jan. 19, 1865 |
| Han, Farden | do | Jan. 19, 1865 |
| Horst, Elijah | Mount Pleasant | Sep. 23, 1864 |
| Hockin, George | do | Sep. 23, 1864 |
| Harrison, John W | Dover | Sep. 23, 1864 |
| Hartmann, Theodore | Burlington | Nov. 11, 1863 |
| Hely, William | Rochester | Sep. 24, 1864 |
| Healy, William J | do | Sep. 24, 1864 |
| Holm, Henry | Raymond | Nov. 11, 1863 |
| Haver, John | do | Sep. 23, 1864 |
| Hanson, Knutt | do | Dec 9, 1864 |
| Humas, Nathan | Caledonia | Dec. 7, 1864 |
| Henry, William | do | Dec. 7, 1864 |
| Hanners, George | do | Dec. 7, 1864 |
| Hern, Patrick | Kenosha | Nov. 12, 1863 |
| Hall, William | Somers | Nov. 12, 1863 |
| Hauey, Mathias | Brighton | Nov. 12, 1863 |
| Helms, Ira | Salem | Sep. 24, 1864 |
| Hogan, Thomas jr | do | Sep. 24, 1864 |
| Haase, William | do | Sep. 24, 1864 |
| Heath, Sherban | Center | Nov. 12, 1863 |
| Hulberg, Thomas | Dunkirk | Nov. 13, 1863 |
| Halderson, Neils | Blue Mounds | Oct. 22, 1864 |
| Higgins, Th | Madison | Nov. 13, 1863 |
| Haskins, James J | Medina | Nov. 13, 1863 |
| Harmer, Henry | Sun Prairie | Oct. 15, 1864 |
| Hanson, K | Burke | Nov. 13, 1863 |
| Harlof, Christian | Berry | Nov. 13, 1863 |
| Hanson, John | do | Sep. 19, 1864 |
| H., F. Otto | Dane | Nov. 13, 1863 |
| Hogan, James | Vienna | Nov. 13, 1863 |
| Hunt, C. P | Cold Spring | |
| Halstein, Henry | Farmington | Sep. 20, 1864 |
| Haniter, George | do | Sep. 20, 1864 |
| Hager, John | do | Sep. 20, 1864 |
| Homer, Christopher | Watertown | Sep. 20, 1864 |
| Hazelman, John | do | Sep. 20, 1864 |
| Hartwell, John | do | Sep. 20, 1864 |
| Hays, John | Ridgeway | Sep. 28, 1864 |
| Halderson, Ole | do | Sep. 28, 1864 |
| Hamilton, John | do | Nov. 19, 1864 |
| Hollister, Niles | do | Nov. 19, 1864 |
| Hart, Albert | Willow | Sep. 26, 1864 |
| Haxie, Thomas | Clyde | Sep. 27, 1864 |
| Hollister, James | Dodgeville | Oct. 28, 1864 |
| Hays, Jacob | Highland | Nov. 14, 1863 |
| Hanson, Hans Andrew | do | Sept. 28, 1864 |
| Herbig, Christian | do | Sep. 28, 1864 |
| Holmes, Geo | do | Sep. 28, 1864 |
| Hugill, Henry | do | Sep. 28, 1864 |
| Heiser, H. H | do | Sep. 28, 1864 |
| Hanson, Jacob | do | Sep. 28, 1864 |
| Holmes, Joseph | do | Oct. 28, 1864 |
| Halland, Peter | do | Oct. 28, 1864 |
| Halman, John | do | Oct. 28, 1864 |
| Hall, James | do | Oct. 28, 1864 |

| *Name.* | *Residence.* | *Date.* |
|---|---|---|
| Hayes, Thomas | Highland | Jan. 6, 1865 |
| Huler, George | do | Jan. 6, 1865 |
| Hartert, John W | Waldwick | Oct. 4, 1864 |
| Haverson, George | Moscow | Nov. 14, 1863 |
| Hupperts, William | Kendall or Belmont | Nov. 16, 1863 |
| Hurd, James | Benton | Sep. 29, 1864 |
| Hawkins, J. H | do | Sep. 29, 1864 |
| Hawkins, James | do | Sep. 29, 1864 |
| Hull, Jackson | do | Sep. 29, 1864 |
| Hines, Thomas | do | Sep. 29, 1864 |
| Halkney, Godlip | Watertown | Oct. 22, 1864 |
| Hughs, John | do | Oct. 22, 1864 |
| Hoag, Levi G | Lodi | Nov. 16, 1863 |
| Hall, Elijah | Dekorrah | Nov. 16, 1863 |
| Hurd, Z. G | do | Sep. 21, 1864 |
| Haldorson, Niles | Perry | Sep. 19, 1864 |
| Heller, Peter | do | Sep. 19, 1864 |
| Halverson, Ole | do | Sep. 19, 1864 |
| Hanson, Hanson | do | Sep. 19, 1864 |
| Holstenson, Arne | do | Nov. 17, 1864 |
| Hanson, Anders | do | Feb. 27, 1865 |
| Hughs, James | Milford | Sep. 20, 1864 |
| Hans, Walthew | Watertown | Nov. 15, 1864 |
| Hudson, R | Fort Winnebago | Sep. 21, 1864 |
| Harrington, Jerry | New Diggings | Nov. 16, 1863 |
| Hailey, John | do | Sep. 29, 1864 |
| Harrington, James | do | Sep. 29, 1864 |
| Hackworth, Thomas | Clarno | Nov. 17, 1863 |
| Hartwett, William | Cassville, Beet'n or Waterloo | Nov. 19, 1863 |
| Hall, Isaac | Waterloo | Oct. 1, 1864 |
| Hannon, Mark | Clifton | Nov. 19, 1863 |
| Henkel, Martin | Potosi | Nov. 19, 1863 |
| Hare, Jacob | Harrison | Oct. 1, 1864 |
| Harelson, Nathaniel | do | Oct. 1, 1864 |
| Hayden, Charles H | Franklin or Bear Creek | Nov. 20, 1863 |
| Harris, Samuel | Bloom | Sep. 26, 1864 |
| Henthorn, George W | Sylvan | Sep. 26, 1864 |
| Hutzel, Jacob | Spring Green | Oct. 5, 1864 |
| Hogaboom, James | Dellona | Oct. 3, 1864 |
| Hays, John | do | Oct. 3, 1864 |
| Hawlett, William | Franklin | Oct. 3, 1864 |
| Hilberry, Laban | Sylvan | Oct. 28, 1864 |
| Hawlett, Patrick | Franklin | Oct. 29, 1864 |
| Hecock, Ezar | Monroe Co | Nov. 17, 1863 |
| Hall, Archibald | Jefferson | Sept. 19, 1864 |
| Henry, John | Tomah | Sep. 20, 1864 |
| Helms, Daniel | do | Sep. 20, 1864 |
| Heath, Monson G | Clifton | Sep. 20, 1864 |
| Henderly, Joseph | do | Sep. 20, 1864 |
| Harlson, C | Portland | Sep. 20, 1864 |
| Henry, Michael | Sheldon | Sep. 20, 1864 |
| Hubbard, William | do | Sep. 20, 1864 |
| Hollins, William | Glendale | Nov. 10, 1864 |
| Haskins, Truman | Oak Dale | Nov. 10, 1863 |
| Hammil, James | do | Nov. 10, 1863 |
| Hendrickson, Henry | Portland | Nov. 10, 1863 |
| Herick, George | Adams Co | Nov. 19, 1863 |
| Hogan, Michael | do | Nov. 19, 1863 |
| Hayes, Phillip | New Haven | Sep. 26, 1864 |

| *Name.* | *Residence.* | *Date.* |
|---|---|---|
| Hall, J. F | Leola | Sep. 26, 1864 |
| Hicks, Levi A. | Easton | Sep. 26, 1864 |
| Hicks, Edward W | do | Sep. 26, 1864 |
| Harris, Caleb C | Springville | Sep. 26, 1864 |
| Haskins, Dwelly | Preston | Sep. 26, 1864 |
| Hastings, Alvin | St. Croix Co | Nov. 20, 1863 |
| Hanson, Christian | Eau Galle | Sep. 23, 1864 |
| Humphrey, John | do | Sep. 23, 1864 |
| Hennessy, William | Erin Prairie | Sep. 23, 1864 |
| Humphrey, John | Ceylon | Oct. 5, 1864 |
| Hanson, Ole | do | Oct. 5, 1864 |
| Hunter, Joshua | Springfield | Nov. 15, 1863 |
| Hyatt, N. B. | Pierce Co | Nov. 23, 1863 |
| Holcomb, E. C | do | Nov. 23, 1863 |
| Howard, Marshall | Pleasant Valley | Sep. 23, 1864 |
| Hayward, C. G. N. | Perry | Sep. 23, 1864 |
| Hambleton, William | Trimbell | Sep. 23, 1864 |
| Hampton, J. C | Martell | Nov. 3, 1863 |
| Healy, John | Vernon Co | Nov. 18, 1863 |
| Hart, Seth | Franklin | Sept. 21, 1864 |
| Harding, Sydney | do | Nov. 15, 1863 |
| Herron, William A | do | Nov. 15, 1863 |
| Hull, Moses | Webster | Sept. 21, 1864 |
| Hyslass, Robert | Polk Co | Nov. 20, 1863 |
| Hemmingway, John B | do | Nov. 20, 1863 |
| Hurley, Michael | do | Nov. 20, 1863 |
| Hagerty, John | Wood Co. | Nov. 18, 1863 |
| Hossier, Frederick | Dexter | Sep. 22, 1864 |
| Haynes, Berry | Centralia | Nov. 15, 1864 |
| Hempsen, John | do | Sep. 22, 1864 |
| Hocksmier, George | Campbell | Sep. 19, 1864 |
| Hallegan, Thomas | Kildare | Sep. 19, 1864 |
| Haygan, Tom | do | Oct. 31, 1864 |
| Howell, Thomas | Seven Mile Creek | Sep. 19, 1864 |
| Hays, William | do | Sep. 19, 1864 |
| Howard, Tim | do | Oct. 31, 1864 |
| Hutchings, Dwight | Lemonweir | Sep. 19, 1864 |
| Hervson, Benjamin | do | Oct. 31, 1864 |
| Hill, O. R | Wonewoc | Sep. 19, 1864 |
| Hill, L. P | do | Sep. 19, 1864 |
| Hindman, William | Lyndon | Sep. 19, 1864 |
| Heaty, Dennis | do | Sep. 19, 1864 |
| Hawes, Elijah L | do | Oct. 31, 1864 |
| Harrison, John | do | Oct. 31, 1864 |
| Huntley, William | Summit | Oct. 31, 1864 |
| Hammil, Patrick | do | Oct. 31, 1864 |
| Hebbins, Rein | Marion | Oct. 31, 1864 |
| Hurks, Frederick | do | Oct. 31, 1864 |
| Huff, Bruce | Linwood | Sep. 22, 1864 |
| Halladay, Edwin | do | Sep. 22, 1864 |
| Hebert, Tennis | do | Oct. 31, 1864 |
| Henry, Welcome | Pine Grove | Sep. 22, 1864 |
| Havens, We lington | do | Nov. 15, 1864 |
| Howard, Hiram | Lanark | Sep. 22, 1864 |
| Hopkins, Michael | do | Nov. 15, 1864 |
| Haman, Henry | Berlin | Sep. 22, 1864 |
| Hoviell, Elisha | Alma | Sep. 23, 1864 |
| Helmer, Joseph | do | Nov. 16, 1864 |
| Hayes, W. E | Durand | Sep. 27, 1864 |

| *Name.* | *Residence.* | *Date.* |
|---|---|---|
| Hogne, Henry | Pepin | Sep. 27, 1864 |
| Hill, Walter | Waubeek | Sep. 27, 1864 |
| Hammond, James | do | Nov. 16, 1864 |
| Holbrook, George F | Eau Galle | Sep. 27, 1864 |
| Hebert, Samuel | do | Sep. 27, 1864 |
| Haley, John | do | Sep. 27, 1864 |
| Hawley, Michael | do | Sep. 27, 1864 |
| Harrington, Tim | do | Sep. 27, 1864 |
| Huber, Peter | do | Nov. 2, 1864 |
| Hess, Henry | do | Nov. 2, 1864 |
| Holm, Wayne | Spring Brook | Sep. 27, 1864 |
| Hogan, John Jr | Chippewa Falls | Sep. 27, 1864 |
| Holstein, S. P | do | Sep 27, 1864 |
| Hogan, Mike | do | Sep. 27, 1864 |
| Halbert, S | do | Nov. 2, 1864 |
| Hall, Ira | La Fayette | Sep. 27, 1864 |
| Hawkins, John | do | Nov. 2, 1864 |
| Hamilton, Gavin | do | Nov. 2, 1864 |
| Horst, Christian | Belvidere | Nov. 16, 1864 |
| Herbegeaux, Antoine | Door Co | Nov. 20, 1863 |
| Hale, S. W. A | Ahnepee | Nov. 20, 1863 |
| Hancey, Peter W | Kewaunee | Nov. 20, 1863 |
| Heraly, M | Casco | Dec. 29, 1864 |
| Hefferman, Michael | Franklin | Dec. 29, 1864 |
| Hequit, Isadore | Lincoln | Dec. 29, 1864 |
| Hequit, Dundonie | do | Dec 29, 1864 |
| Hick, Frank | Manitowoc | Nov. 21, 1863 |
| Hunter, James T | do | Nov. 21, 1863 |
| Hoye, Wm. E | do | Nov. 21, 1863 |
| Hope, George | Cato | Nov. 21, 1863 |
| Hopper, Thomas | Eaton | Nov. 21, 1863 |
| Hecker, Jno | Liberty | Nov. 21, 1863 |
| Henzel, Ernst | Schleswig | Nov. 21, 1863 |
| Hudson, Adolphus | Gibson | Dec. 29, 1864 |
| Huletz, Jacob | Kossuth | Dec. 29, 1864 |
| Harris, Wm | Manitowoc Rapids | Dec. 29, 1864 |
| Hoffman, Nicholas | Meeme | Dec. 29, 1864 |
| Herr, Adam | do | Dec. 29, 1864 |
| Hoben, Patrick | Newton | Dec. 29, 1864 |
| Huber, John | Stockbridge | Nov. 23, 1863 |
| Hurs, John | Brothertown | Nov. 23. 1863 |
| Hatty, Andrew | do | Dec. 28, 1864 |
| Hues, Patrick | do | Dec. 28, 1864 |
| Hught, Hayward | do | Dec. 28, 1864 |
| Holland, Phillip | Menasha | Nov. 23, 1863 |
| Hanly, Timothy | do | Nov. 23, 1863 |
| Hillman, Henry | Neenah | Nov. 23, 1863 |
| Hink, Hiram | Vinland | Nov. 23, 1863 |
| Hile, F. B | Oshkosh city | Nov. 23, 1863 |
| Hart, John | Utica | Nov. 24, 1863 |
| Hickerman, Jeremiah | | Nov. 24, 1863 |
| Huntington, B. B | | Nov. 28, 1863 |
| Herbst, Mathias | Poygan | Nov. 5, 1864 |
| Herbst, Ludwig | do | Nov. 5, 1864 |
| Hart, Theodore | do | Dec. 31, 1864 |
| Hughes, Wm. E | Berlin | Nov. 24, 1863 |
| Hall, Joseph | Mackford | Nov. 24, 1863 |
| Herrick, Patrick C | Seneca | Nov. 24, 1863 |
| Husselman, Marcus | Marquette Co | Nov. 24, 1863 |

| *Name.* | *Residence.* | *Date.* |
|---|---|---|
| Haney, James | Marquette Co | Nov. 24, 1863 |
| Hopwood, George | do | Nov. 24, 1863 |
| Heft, Edward | Neshkora | Nov. 24, 1863 |
| Hayes, Henry | do | Nov. 1, 1864 |
| Hayes, Benjamin | do | Nov. 1, 1864 |
| Hayes, Joseph | do | Nov. 1, 1864 |
| Holtz, Lewis | Shields | Nov. 1, 1864 |
| Hamilton, Jno. H | Springfield | Nov. 1, 1864 |
| Hill, Stephen | Moundville | Dec. 31, 1864 |
| House, Wm | do | Dec. 31, 1864 |
| Hermon, Louis | Douglas | Dec. 31, 1864 |
| Hyer, Frederick W | Crystal Lake | Dec. 31, 1864 |
| Holtz, Ferdinand | Newton | Dec. 31, 1864 |
| Harrison, James | Waushara Co | Nov. 25, 1863 |
| Huffman, James B | Saxeville | Nov. 25, 1863 |
| Hodgson, Chas. H | Aurora | Nov. 2, 1864 |
| Hall, Thomas | do | Nov. 2, 1864 |
| Hansen, Daniel | Aurora | Nov. 2, 1864 |
| Hollenbeck, Jno | do | Nov. 2, 1864 |
| Hall, Benjamin F | do | Dec. 31, 1864 |
| Hughs, John J | Springwater | Nov. 2, 1864 |
| Hall, Otis | Richford | Nov. 2, 1864 |
| Haskins, Daniel | Coloma | Nov. 2, 1864 |
| Howze, Gottheilb | Deerfield | Nov. 2, 1864 |
| Hubbell, Petmeir | Oasis | Nov. 2, 1864 |
| Harisk, James | do | Dec. 31, 1864 |
| Havens, Laurons | Plainfield | Nov. 2, 1864 |
| Havens, Victorus | do | Nov. 2, 1864 |
| Ham, Cornelius | do | Dec. 31, 1864 |
| Hill, W. S | do | Dec. 31, 1864 |
| Hurd, Albert | do | Dec. 31, 1864 |
| Harkey, Wm | Waupaca Co | Nov. 25, 1863 |
| Hensi, E | Lebanon | Nov. 25, 1863 |
| Hays, J. M | do | Nov. 5, 1864 |
| Hunt, Cornelius | do | Nov. 5, 1864 |
| Healy, John | do | Nov. 5, 1864 |
| Hearn, Michael A | do | Nov. 5, 1864 |
| Hunt, Dennis | do | Nov. 5, 1864 |
| Hurley, John | do | Dec. 31, 1864 |
| Hermanson, Hermon | | Nov. 25, 1863 |
| Harris, Isaac | Waupaca | Nov. 25, 1863 |
| Hubner, John | Caledonia | Nov. 5, 1864 |
| Haley, John | Weyawega | Nov. 5, 1864 |
| Howard, Lyman | do | Nov. 5, 1864 |
| Haley, Martin | do | Dec. 31, 1864 |
| Hopkins, Henry | St. Lawrence | Nov. 5, 1864 |
| Hermonson, Gjirt | do | Nov. 5, 1864 |
| Hughes, Jno. H | do | Dec. 31, 1863 |
| Hermonsen, Soren | do | Dec. 31, 1864 |
| Howell, Hans | Iola | Nov. 5, 1864 |
| Hanson, Christian | do | Dec. 31, 1864 |
| Halverson, Ole | do | Dec. 31, 1864 |
| Herb, Mike | Outagamie Co | Nov. 27, 1863 |
| Hartman, Daniel F | Freedom | Nov. 27, 1863 |
| Hickok, F. M | Appleton | Nov. 27, 1863 |
| Horn, Frederick | Center | Nov. 27, 1863 |
| Hilson, Wm. Edwin | | Nov. 27, 1863 |
| Hanagan, Michael | Greenville | Nov. 27, 1863 |
| Holmes, Gilmore | Maple Creek | Dec. 28, 1863 |

| *Name.* | *Residence.* | *Date.* |
|---|---|---|
| Hemming, Michael | Morrison | Nov. 28, 1863 |
| Hummel, Isaac | Suamico | Dec. 28, 1864 |
| Hubbard, Samuel P | do | Dec. 28, 1864 |
| Hugart, John | Marinette | Nov. 28, 1863 |
| Harmon, Alonzo | do | Nov. 28, 1863 |
| Hainers, Edward | Stiles | Nov. 28, 1863 |
| Hendricks, Cornelius | do | Dec. 29, 1864 |
| Hawk, John | do | Dec. 29, 1864 |
| Hendricks, Annis | do | Dec. 29, 1864 |
| Hall, Albert | Peshtigo | Nov. 28, 1863 |
| Heltranorso, John | Pensaukee | Dec. 29, 1864 |
| Hower, George | Little Suamico | Dec. 29, 1864 |

## I.

| | | |
|---|---|---|
| Iaeger, Joseph | Watertown | Dec. 1, 1864 |
| Illian, Phillip | Barton | Nov. 27, 1863 |
| Inglehard, Jacob | Polk | Nov. 27, 1863 |
| Inglisch, August | do | Oct. 12, 1864 |
| Illig, ——— | Moselle | Dec. 2, 1864 |
| Idlebush, John | Scott | Oct. 21, 1864 |
| Ikner, George | Milwaukee | Nov. 10, 1863 |
| Ide, Charles | Rochester | Sep. 24, 1864 |
| Inden, Paul | Menomonee | Dec. 1, 1864 |
| Inglebritson, Ole | Dodgeville | Sep. 28, 1864 |
| Inglebreitson, Ole | do | Oct. 28, 1864 |
| Ingerbretson, Kenuts | Highland | Sep. 28, 1864 |
| Iverson, Chas | Eastman | Sep. 30, 1864 |
| Irtmore, Nelson | Oshkosh city | Nov. 23, 1863 |
| Ingatzby, Henry | Marinette | Nov. 28, 1863 |
| Ingraham, Jay D | Springfield | Nov. 1, 1864 |
| Iselin, Augustus | Adams Co | Nov. 19, 1863 |
| Ingalls, E. J | Kildare | Nov. 19, 1864 |
| Ingerwalsen, Tolf | Eau Galle | Nov. 2, 1864 |

## J

| | | |
|---|---|---|
| Joyce, James | Portland | Nov. 20, 1863 |
| Joslyn, James | Lowell | Nov. 20, 1863 |
| Justin, Joseph | Lomira | Nov. 20, 1863 |
| Jarrot, John | Williamstown | Nov. 20, 1863 |
| Jop, Rudolph | Trenton | Nov. 20, 1863 |
| Judd, Edward | Hubbard | Nov. 21, 1863 |
| James, Harvey | do | Nov. 21, 1863 |
| Johnnick, Jacob | Hartford | Nov. 21, 1863 |
| Jeffarts, Michael | Erin | Dec. 1, 1864 |
| Jansen, Al | Barton | Oct. 12, 1864 |
| Jansen, George | do | Oct. 12, 1864 |
| Just, William | West Bend | Nov. 21, 1863 |
| Jochem, Jacob | Polk | Oct. 12, 1864 |
| Jones, Joseph | Richfield | Oct. 12, 1864 |
| Jahn, William | Farmington | Dec. 1, 1864 |
| John, Thomas | Belgium | Oct. 13, 1864 |
| Jonker, Fredrick | Fredonia | Oct. 14, 1864 |
| Janish, Gregory | Port Washington | Nov. 23, 1863 |
| Johnson, Ole | Sheboygan | Oct. 25, 1864 |
| John, Gottlieb | Moselle | Oct. 18, 1864 |
| Jager, Ferdinand | do | Dec. 2, 1864 |
| Jessert, Hr | Wilson | Nov. 24, 1864 |

| *Name.* | *Residence.* | *Date.* |
|---|---|---|
| Jonas, Michael | Sheboygan Falls | Oct. 25, 1864 |
| Jones, Calvin | Lima | Dec. 2, 1864 |
| Jasse, James | Holland | Nov. 24, 1863 |
| Jager, William | Milwaukee | Nov. 10, 1863 |
| Johrs, Fritz | do | Sep. 21, 1864 |
| Johnson, ——— | do | Nov. 15, 1864 |
| Joers, Charles | do | Nov. 16, 1864 |
| Johnson, John | do | Sep. 21, 1864 |
| Johnson, Theodore | do | Sep. 21, 1864 |
| Junk, Wilhelm | do | Sep. 21, 1864 |
| Junu, Julius | do | Sep. 21, 1864 |
| Jlket, Wilhelm | do | Sep. 21, 1864 |
| Jecks, Fritz | do | Sep. 22, 1864 |
| Johnson, George | Wauwatosa | Nov. 11, 1863 |
| Johnson, Philip | Greenfield | Nov. 11, 1863 |
| Jake, William | do | Sep. 22, 1864 |
| Jager, M chael | Lake | Sep. 22, 1864 |
| Jansen, Mathias | | |
| Jones, Robert | Racine | Nov. 11, 1863 |
| Jones, Griffith P. | do | Sep. 24, 1864 |
| Jones, Hugh | do | Sep. 24, 1864 |
| James, John | Mount Pleasant | Nov. 11, 1863 |
| Johnson, ——— | do | Sep. 23, 1864 |
| Johnson, Samuel | Dover | Sep. 23, 1864 |
| Jordson, Hans | Raymond | Nov. 11, 1863 |
| Jones, Res | Caledonia | Dec. 7, 1864 |
| Jennil, Emil | Bristol | Sep. 24, 1864 |
| Jones, Americus W. | Sugar Creek | Nov. 12, 1863 |
| Jones, Henry L. | La Grange | Nov. 12, 1863 |
| Janon, Pat | Milwaukee | Nov. 9, 1863 |
| Jansen, Nicholas | do | Nov. 14, 1864 |
| James, Stephen | do | Dec. 22, 1864 |
| Jarles, Johann | do | Nov. 9, 1863 |
| Jacobus, Jacob | do | Nov. 9, 1863 |
| Jones, Samuel | do | Sep. 20, 1864 |
| Jassinger, Martin | do | Nov. 10, 1863 |
| Jones, Stephen | do | Nov. 10, 1863 |
| Jones, H R | do | Sep. 20, 1864 |
| Johnson, Lawrence | do | Sep. 20, 1864 |
| Jones, Joshua | do | Sep. 20, 1864 |
| Jones, J. B. | do | Sep. 20, 1864 |
| Johnson, Oliver | do | Sep. 20, 1864 |
| Jones, H. | do | |
| Jessepts, K. | do | Nov. 15, 1864 |
| Jhmig, Jacob | do | Nov. 15, 1864 |
| Jones, David | do | Nov. 15, 1864 |
| Jones, Davis | do | Nov. 15, 1864 |
| Jones, Charles | do | Nov. 15, 1864 |
| Jones, D. D | do | Jan. 11, 1865 |
| Jones, Enoch | do | |
| Jones, Jonathan | do | |
| Jabes, John | do | Nov. 10, 1863 |
| Judd, Eli | do | Nov. 10, 1863 |
| Jordan, Thomas | do | Sep. 21, 1864 |
| Johnson, Wm. R. | do | Sep. 21, 1864 |
| Jacobs, Abraham | Geneva | Nov. 12, 1863 |
| Jones, Robert R. | Summit | Nov. 30, 1864 |
| James, Thomas | do | Nov. 30, 1864 |
| Jensen, Claus | Marton | Nov. 12, 1863 |

| *Name* | *Residence.* | *Date.* |
|---|---|---|
| James, William | Genesee | Nov. 12, 1863 |
| Johnson, Joseph | Waukesha | Nov. 12, 1863 |
| Jameman, John | Brookfield | Nov. 12, 1863 |
| Johns, Julius | Muskego | Nov. 12, 1863 |
| Johnson, Andrew | do | Nov. 30, 1864 |
| Jefferson S. C. | Janesville | Nov. 12, 1863 |
| Johnson James | Rutland | Nov. 12, 1863 |
| Johnson Andrews | Blooming | Nov. 13, 1863 |
| Julius, Fred | Sun Prairie | Nov. 15, 1864 |
| Johnson, William | Westport | Nov. 15, 1864 |
| Jordon, Michael | Lewiston | Sep. 21, 1864 |
| Jones, Thomas | Springdale | Sep. 19, 1864 |
| Jones, John | do | Sep. 19, 1864 |
| Jones, Wm. | Ridgeway | Oct. 28, 1864 |
| Jones, Thos. B. | Dodgeville | Nov. 14, 1863 |
| Jones, Wm. H. | do | Nov. 14, 1863 |
| Jones, Wm. | do | Sep. 28, 1864 |
| Jones, Robt. | do | Sep. 28, 1864 |
| James, Wm. | do | Sep. 28, 1864 |
| James, Wm. | do | Oct. 28, 1864 |
| Jones, David | do | Nov. 19, 1864 |
| Jones, Hugh | do | Nov. 19, 1864 |
| Jewell, Henry | do | Nov. 19, 1864 |
| Jameson, Ole | do | Nov. 19, 1864 |
| James, Thos. | do | Nov. 19, 1864 |
| Johnstone, Melse | Highland | Nov. 14, 1863 |
| Johnston, Andrew | do | Sep. 28, 1864 |
| Jones, John R. | do | Sep. 28, 1864 |
| Jacob, Hary | do | Sep. 28, 1864 |
| Javginson, Toker | Moscow | Sep. 28, 1864 |
| Jackson, John | Benton | Sep. 29, 1864 |
| Jackson, Joseph | do | Sep. 29, 1864 |
| Johnson, Galleton | Ellenboro | Oct. 1, 1864 |
| Jackson, David | Lavalle | Oct. 29, 1864 |
| Jackson, Henry | Juneau Co | Nov. 17, 1863 |
| Johnson, Jno. | Pierce Co | Nov. 23, 1863 |
| Jolly, Wm. | Wood Co | Nov. 18, 1863 |
| Jizell, Mitchell | Centralia | Sep. 22, 1864 |
| Jones, W. W. | Rodolph | Sep. 21, 1864 |
| Jordan, Jerome | Campbell | Sep. 19, 1864 |
| Jones, D. E. | Portland | Sep. 20, 1864 |
| Johnson, Ole | do | Nov. 10, 1864 |
| Jiles, Geo. | Tomah | Nov. 10, 1864 |
| Johnson, Michael | Ettrick | Sep. 21, 1864 |
| Johnson, Peter | Hamburg | Sep. 21, 1864 |
| Juneau, John S. | Webster | Sep. 21, 1864 |
| Jones, Henry | Harmony | Nov. 15, 1864 |
| Johnson, G. O. | Sharon | Sep. 22, 1864 |
| Jordan, John | Lanark | Sep. 22, 1864 |
| Janke, James | Lynn | Sep. 23, 1864 |
| Johnson, Lewisse | Eau Galle | Sep. 27, 1864 |
| Jorgenson, Johanos | Spring Brook | Sep. 27, 1864 |
| Jenson, Ole | Martell | Sep. 23, 1864 |
| Johnson, Willard | Rush River | Sep. 23, 1864 |
| James, Geo. | Springville | Sep. 26, 1864 |
| Jones David | Chippewa Falls | Sep 27, 1864 |
| Jackson, Sam'l | do | Nov. 2, 1864 |
| Johnson, Lewis | Alma | Nov. 15, 1864 |
| Johnson, Joseph | Rockland | Nov. 21, 1863 |

| *Name.* | *Residence.* | *Date.* |
|---|---|---|
| Juno, Maximilian | Gibson | Dec. 29, 1864 |
| Jermain, John | Meeme | Dec. 29, 1864 |
| Jenkins, Thos | do | Dec. 29, 1864 |
| Jacobs, Ernest | do | Dec. 29, 1864 |
| Jones, John C | Oshkosh city | Nov. 23, 1863 |
| Johnson, Sam'l B | Poygan | Nov. 5, 1864 |
| John—(works for Ed. Steers) | Green Lake | Nov. 24, 1863 |
| Jeffers, Melan, D | Waushara Co | Nov. 25, 1863 |
| Johnson, Carter | Plainfield | Nov. 2, 1864 |
| Jones, Jno. D | Springwater | Dec. 31, 1864 |
| Jones, Robt. H | do | Dec. 31, 1864 |
| Johnson, Almon R | Deerfield | Dec. 31, 1864 |
| Jooseter, Francis | Kaukama | Nov. 27, 1863 |
| Jennings, John | Hortonia | Dec. 28, 1864 |
| Jinner, L. W | Ft. Howard | Nov. 28, 1863 |
| Johnson, Sam'l, W | Preble | Dec. 28, 1864 |
| Jasone, Peter | Eaton | Dec. 28, 1864 |
| Jucker, John | Holland | Dec. 28, 1864 |
| Johnson, Martin | Oconto | Nov. 28, 1863 |
| Jordan, Chas | Peshtigo | Nov. 28, 1863 |
| Jarvey, m. J | Stiles | Nov. 28, 1863 |
| John, Wm | do | Dec. 29, 1864 |
| Jones, Thomas | Buffalo | Nov. 1, 1864 |
| Johnson, Andreas | Iola | Nov. 5, 1864 |
| Johnson, Gjert | do | Nov. 5, 1864 |
| Johnson, Neil | do | Nov. 5, 1864 |
| Jacobson, Peter | do | Nov. 5, 1864 |
| Jac bsen, Errick | do | Nov. 5, 1864 |
| Johnson, Jno | St. Lawrence | Dec. 31, 1864 |
| Johnson, Hermon | Iola | Dec. 31, 1864 |
| Jadin Batise | Casco | Dec. 29, 1864 |
| Jander, Jno | Franklin | Dec. 29, 1864 |

## K

| *Name.* | *Residence.* | *Date.* |
|---|---|---|
| Keserman, Joseph | Sheboygan | Dec. 2, 1864 |
| Ka serman ——— | do | Dec. 2, 1864 |
| Klahoust, Wilhelm | do | Dec. 2, 1864 |
| Karsteel, Carl | do | Oct. 18, 1864 |
| Konrad, Peter | Moselle | Dec. 2, 1864 |
| Kemby, Simon | Sheboygan Falls | Oct. 25, 1864 |
| Kimball, George | do | Oct. 25, 1864 |
| Koffel, Godfrey | do | Oct. 25, 1864 |
| Koffman, Fred | do | Oct. 25, 1864 |
| Klobs, John | do | Oct. 25, 1864 |
| Kaffer, Godfrey | do | Dec. 2, 1864 |
| Keppen, Herman | Lima | Nov. 24, 1863 |
| Knowles, S J | do | Oct. 24, 1864 |
| Kewberg, John | do | Dec. 2, 1864 |
| Klugg, John | Holland | Oct. 21, 1864 |
| Kies, Peter | Abbott | Nov. 24, 1863 |
| Kies, Valentine | do | Oct. 18, 1864 |
| Kogan, Michael | do | Oct. 18, 1864 |
| Kease, Henry | Scott | Oct. 21, 1864 |
| Kuskee, William | do | Oct. 21, 1864 |
| Krigg, Henry | do | Dec. 2, 1864 |
| Kelps, Frasis | do | Jan. 27, 1865 |
| Kirrch, Peter | Plymouth | Oct. 21, 1864 |
| Kleuker, William | do | Dec. 6, 1864 |

| *Name.* | *Residence.* | *Date.* |
|---|---|---|
| Klop, Martin | Fredonia | Oct. 14, 1864 |
| Kotch, Tretrig | do | Oct. 14, 1864 |
| Kilps, Joseph | do | Dec. 1, 1864 |
| Klans, Adolph | do | Dec. 1, 1864 |
| Kalter, Jacob | do | Dec. 1, 1864 |
| Kertz, Linard | do | Dec. 1, 1864 |
| Kertz, Christopher | do | Dec. 1, 1864 |
| Kronen, Danes | do | Nov. 21, 1863 |
| Kuntzer, Jacob | Grafton | Oct. 13, 1864 |
| Klug, Heman | do | Oct. 13, 1864 |
| Kelley, John | do | Dec. 1, 1864 |
| Keisler, William | do | Dec. 1, 1864 |
| Keinger, Bapt | do | Jan. 27, 1865 |
| Kloetz, August | do | Jan 27, 1865 |
| Kuzer, Franz | Mequon | Nov. 23, 1863 |
| Kopp, George | do | Nov 23, 1863 |
| Klausing, Gustave | do | Nov. 23, 1863 |
| Krause, Dederick | do | Nov. 23, 1863 |
| Kronenburg, Jacob | Saukville | Oct. 14, 1864 |
| Kester, Adam alias John Zimar | do | Oct. 14, 1864 |
| Keug, Richard | Sheboygan | Nov. 23, 1863 |
| Kohner, Louis | do | Nov. 24, 1863 |
| Kaeswerter, Wilhelm | do | Oct. 25, 1864 |
| Kanable, Thomas | do | Jan. 27, 1865 |
| Kollner, ——— | do | Oct. 18, 1864 |
| Koenic, Domine | Polk | Oct. 12, 1864 |
| Kissinger, Jacob | do | Oct. 12, 1864 |
| Kuebuck, Heinrich | do | Oct. 12, 1864 |
| Kock, John | do | Oct. 12, 1864 |
| Kissling, Jacob | do | Oct. 12, 1864 |
| Klop, John | do | Dec. 8, 1864 |
| Kelley, Thomas | Richfield | Nov. 21, 1863 |
| Kelley, Thomas | do | Oct. 12, 1864 |
| Koler, John | do | Oct. 12, 1864 |
| Klaus, Jacob | do | Oct. 12, 1864 |
| Kan, Hubbard | do | Oct. 12, 1864 |
| Kain, Mathew O. | do | Oct. 12, 1864 |
| Keeper, Henry | do | Dec. 1, 1864 |
| Kous, Jacob | do | Dec. 1, 1864 |
| Kohler, Augustine | do | Dec. 1, 1864 |
| Kiehle, Joseph | do | Dec. 1, 1864 |
| Kafling, Peter | do | Dec. 1, 1864 |
| Kichel, Jonathan | do | Dec. 1, 1864 |
| Kohlenburgg, Gerhard | do | Dec. 1, 1864 |
| Keren, John | do | Dec. 1, 1864 |
| Keder, Antz | do | Jan. 27, 1865 |
| Kaser, Joseph | do | Jan. 27, 1865 |
| Kenny, James M | do | Jan. 27, 1865 |
| Krill, John | Farmington | Oct. 18, 1864 |
| Krill, Peter | do | Oct. 18, 1864 |
| Kahn, G | do | Oct. 18, 1864 |
| Krell, Mathias | do | Dec. 1, 1864 |
| Kessel, John | do | Dec. 1, 1864 |
| Krell, Nicholas | do | Jan. 27, 1865 |
| Krell, Peter | do | Jan. 27, 1865 |
| Kurth, Carl | Jackson | Nov. 21, 1863 |
| Klump, Jacob | do | Oct. 11, 1864 |
| Kaller, Albert | do | Oct. 11, 1864 |
| Kaleiba, August | do | Oct. 11, 1864 |

| *Name.* | *Residence.* | *Date.* |
|---|---|---|
| Kanenberg, August | Jackson | Oct. 11, 1864 |
| Kollein, John | do | Oct. 11, 1864 |
| Koepsel, Charles | do | Oct. 11, 1864 |
| Kerressin, Fred | do | Oct. 11, 1864 |
| Knusbel, Carl | do | Oct. 11, 1864 |
| Kniskel, Godfried | do | Oct. 11, 1864 |
| Kniger, Carl, No. 1 | do | Oct. 11, 1864 |
| Kuttchen, Lambert | Belgium | Nov. 21, 1863 |
| Keifer, Thomas | do | Oct. 13, 1864 |
| Klaus, John | do | Oct. 13, 1864 |
| Krick, Peter | do | Oct. 13, 1864 |
| Krier, Nicholas | do | Oct. 13, 1864 |
| Kirch, Bernard | do | Oct. 13, 1864 |
| Krick, Frank | do | Oct. 13, 1864 |
| Karteiser, Nicholas | do | Dec. 1, 1864 |
| Klein, Martin | do | Dec. 1, 1864 |
| Kauthen, Nicholas | do | Dec. 1, 1864 |
| Kusch, Mathias | do | Dec. 1, 1864 |
| Kutchen, Anton | do | Dec. 1, 1864 |
| Kline, John | Fredonia | Oct. 14, 1864 |
| Kelman, Michael | do | Oct. 14, 1854 |
| Koon, Samuel | do | Oct 14, 1864 |
| Klaus, Jacob | do | Oct. 14, 1864 |
| Kelten, John | do | Oct. 14, 1864 |
| Kelly, Thomas | do | Oct. 14, 1864 |
| Ketzer, George | do | Oct. 14, 1864 |
| Kelden, Sepel | do | Oct. 14, 1864 |
| Kaunter, Nicholas | Leroy | Nov. 20, 1863 |
| Kesten, Christian | do | Oct. 4, 1864 |
| Keiley, James | do | Oct. 4, 1864 |
| Kalhammer, Jacob | do | Dec. 1, 1864 |
| Kefer, Martin | Lomira | Oct. 6, 1864 |
| Kinney, William | Trenton | Nov. 20, 1863 |
| Kennedy, Lawrence | Hubbard | Nov. 21, 1863 |
| Kamb, Julius | do | Nov. 21, 1863 |
| Kennemann, William | do | Nov. 21, 1863 |
| Kroutz, Henry | Lebanon | Nov. 21, 1863 |
| Kenigan, William | Hartford | Nov. 21, 1863 |
| Kruser, John | do | Nov. 21, 1863 |
| Kriezer, Peter | Erin | Nov. 21, 1863 |
| Kennedy, John | do | Oct. 12, 1864 |
| Kinney, John | do | Oct. 12, 1864 |
| Kersovum, Michael | do | Oct. 12, 1864 |
| Kean, Stephen | do | Dec. 1, 1864 |
| Kelch, Lorenzo | Kewaskum | Nov. 21, 1863 |
| Kircher, Henry | Barton | Nov. 21, 1863 |
| Knoeck, Peter | do | Oct. 12, 1864 |
| Koger, Martin | do | Oct. 12, 1864 |
| Knapps, John | do | Oct. 12, 1864 |
| Knapp, Martin | do | Oct. 12, 1864 |
| Ketchum, Henry | do | Oct 12, 1864 |
| Kleyoer, Fred | do | Oct. 12, 1864 |
| Kunn, Franz | do | Dec. 1, 1864 |
| Konings, John | do | Dec. 1, 1864 |
| Krahm, Anton | Auburn | Oct. 5, 1864 |
| Kanhy, Jacob | do | Oct. 5, 1864 |
| Kelmer, Ansel | Alto | Nov. 19, 1863 |
| Kelly, John | Ripon | Nov. 19, 1863 |
| Koeing, Frederick | Eldorado | Oct. 5, 1864 |

| *Name.* | *Residence.* | *Date.* |
|---|---|---|
| Kemp, Thomas | Eldorado | Dec. 1, 1864 |
| King, Frederick | do | Dec. 1, 1864 |
| Kiend, August | Elba | Nov. 20, 1863 |
| Keegood, John | Shields | Nov. 20, 1863 |
| Keller, August | Lowell | Nov. 20, 1863 |
| Karr, William | Emmett | Nov. 20, 1863 |
| Koeff, Christian | do | Nov. 20, 1863 |
| Klug, William | do | Oct. 11, 1864 |
| King, Herman | do | Oct. 11, 1864 |
| Kinney, William | do | Oct. 11, 1864 |
| Kakhan, Ferdinand | do | Oct. 11, 1864 |
| Kleus, Charles | do | Oct. 11, 1864 |
| Kachten, August | Burnett | Nov. 20, 1863 |
| Kircher, John | Watertown | Nov. 20, 1863 |
| Kroennig, Herman | do | Nov. 20, 1863 |
| Kaaht, Julius | do | Oct. 6, 1864 |
| Kripps, John | do | Oct. 6, 1864 |
| Kurtz, Ferdinand | do | Oct. 6, 1864 |
| Kruger, August | do | Oct. 6, 1864 |
| Kreton, John | do | Oct. 6, 1864 |
| Kirlow, John | do | Oct. 6, 1864 |
| Koch, Charles | do | Dec. 1, 1864 |
| Kahell, John | Milwaukee | Nov. 9, 1863 |
| Koniff, Peter | do | Nov. 9, 1863 |
| Kelley, Timothy | do | Nov. 9, 1863 |
| Kirchner, J. A | do | Nov. 9, 1863 |
| Kiehr, Christian | do | Nov. 9, 1863 |
| Kego, Fred | do | Nov. 9, 1863 |
| Keman, Geo | do | Nov. 9, 1863 |
| Kernan, Geo | do | Sep. 19, 1864 |
| Knipper, Louis | do | Sep. 19, 1864 |
| Kossack, Joel | do | Sep. 19, 1864 |
| Kocherinks, John | do | Sep. 19, 1864 |
| Kelliker, Daniel | do | Sep. 19, 1864 |
| Klumt, Peter | do | Nov. 14, 1864 |
| Klinebile, Henry | do | Nov. 14, 1864 |
| Kosak, Wm | do | Nov 14, 1864 |
| Kossack, Gustave | do | Nov. 14, 1864 |
| Kumil, Andrew | do | Nov. 14, 1864 |
| Kreuse, George | do | Nov. 14, 1864 |
| Krutze, Frank | do | Dec. 2, 1864 |
| Knutler, Nicholas | do | Nov. 9, 1863 |
| Katen, Anton | do | Nov. 9, 1863 |
| Kroenig, August | do | Dec. 2, 1864 |
| Karrmasting, Wm | do | Nov. 9, 1863 |
| Kurringer, Charles | do | Sep. 20, 1864 |
| Koeber, Michael | do | Sep. 20, 1864 |
| Klumb, Philip | do | Sep. 20, 1864 |
| Kurtz, George | do | Nov. 14, 1864 |
| Karlicki, Charles | do | Nov. 25, 1864 |
| Kaune, John | do | Nov. 25, 1864 |
| Kelil, John | do | Nov. 25, 1864 |
| Kaum, John | do | Nov 25, 1864 |
| Kelil, John | do | Nov 11, 1863 |
| Krinz, August | do | Nov. 11, 1863 |
| Kringle, Nicholas | do | Nov. 11, 1863 |
| Koerner, August | do | Nov. 11, 1863 |
| Kerschner, Johann | do | Nov. 11, 1863 |
| Kaiser, Henry | do | Nov. 11, 1863 |

| *Name.* | *Residence.* | *Date.* |
|---|---|---|
| Klier, Andreas | Milwaukee | Nov. 11, 1863 |
| Kritz, Joseph | do | Nov. 11, 1863 |
| Kewant, Frederick | do | Sep. 21, 1864 |
| Kuhr, Adam | do | Sep. 21, 1864 |
| Kewent, Wilhelm | do | Sep. 21, 1864 |
| Kirchman, Frederick | do | Sep. 21, 1864 |
| Kitzmann, August | do | Sep. 21, 1864 |
| Khunt, Frederick | do | Sep. 21, 1864 |
| Koch, William | do | Sep. 21, 1864 |
| Kennedy, Patrick | do | Sep. 21, 1864 |
| Knuschild, Nicholas | do | Sep. 21, 1864 |
| Kempts, Anton | do | Sep. 21, 1864 |
| Kaneman, Franz | do | Sep. 21, 1864 |
| Kaster, Christopher | do | Sep. 21, 1864 |
| Kirchman, August | do | Sep. 21, 1864 |
| Krettow, Albert | do | Sep. 21, 1864 |
| Kinskech, Wilhelm | do | Sep. 21, 1864 |
| Kruskech, Frederick | do | Sep. 21, 1864 |
| Kaspar, Jacob | do | Jan. 26, 1865 |
| Kloeser, Matthias | do | Nov. 16, 1864 |
| Kego, W | do | Nov. 16, 1864 |
| Kranz, William | do | Nov. 16, 1864 |
| Krantschneider, Louis | do | Nov. 16, 1864 |
| Kuhn, A. C. | do | Nov. 10, 1863 |
| Kliman, David | do | Nov. 10, 1863 |
| Kline, Joseph | do | Nov. 11, 1863 |
| Kelees, John | do | Sep. 21, 1864 |
| Kuna, Joseph | do | Sep. 21, 1864 |
| Krey, Charles | do | Sep. 21, 1864 |
| Kroeger, August | do | Sep. 21, 1864 |
| Keehler, Andrew, | do | Sep. 21, 1864 |
| Klen, George | do | Sep. 21, 1864 |
| Kleiblack, Frederick | do | Sep. 21, 1864 |
| Koelch, Thomas | do | Sep. 21, 1864 |
| Kom, Charles | do | Sept. 21, 1864 |
| Krieger, Fritz | do | Sept. 21, 1864 |
| Kleberg, Mathias | do | Sep. 21, 1864 |
| Keepner, Johann | do | Sep. 21, 1863 |
| Kriger, Leonard | do | Sep. 21, 1864 |
| Kraack, John | do | Sep. 21, 1864 |
| Kroeger, Stephen | do | Sep. 21, 1864 |
| Koecher, Carl | do | Nov. 25, 1864 |
| Kernan, Frederick | do | Nov. 25, 1864 |
| Kline, Thomas | do | Nov. 25, 1864 |
| Klein, William | do | Nov. 25, 1864 |
| Klampa, Henry | do | Nov. 25, 1864 |
| Kuble, John | do | Nov. 25, 1864 |
| Klace, John | do | Nov. 25, 1864 |
| Kellogg, H. W | do | Jan. 11, 1865 |
| Kingsbury, Joseph | do | Nov. 10, 1863 |
| Kaylor, Cornelius | do | Nov. 10, 1863 |
| Kenaugh, Thomas | do | Sep. 21, 1864 |
| Kelly, James | do | Sep. 21, 1864 |
| Keys, John | do | Sep. 21, 1864 |
| Kinney, Michael | do | Sep. 21, 1864 |
| Kelly, John | do | Sep. 21, 1864 |
| Kirby, Thomas | do | Sep. 21, 1864 |
| Kenney, Michael | do | Nov. 10, 1863 |
| Kanhall, Charles | do | Nov. 10, 1863 |

| Name. | Residence. | Date. |
| --- | --- | --- |
| Kelly, James | Milwaukee | Nov. 10, 1863 |
| Kimball, A. H | do | Nov. 10, 1863 |
| Knox, James | do | Nov. 10, 1863 |
| Krant, John | do | Nov. 10, 1863 |
| Krug, Frederick | do | Nov. 10, 1863 |
| Krieger Charles | do | Nov. 10, 1863 |
| Knock, Henry | do | Nov 10, 1863 |
| Kruger, Carl | do | Sep. 21, 1864 |
| Kruger, Joachim | do | Sep. 21, 1864 |
| Kummush, Fritz | do | Sep. 21, 1864 |
| Kammer, William | do | Sep. 21, 1864 |
| Kulsh, Charles | do | Sep. 21, 1864 |
| Kuch, Frederich | do | Sep. 21, 1864 |
| Kochlen, Fritz | do | Sep. 21, 1864 |
| Kurth, Frederick | do | Nov. 15, 1864 |
| Krasse, Wm | do | Nov. 15, 1864 |
| Kuntz, Adam | do | Nov. 16, 1864 |
| Krug, Fred | do | Nov. 16, 1864 |
| Kruest, Adam | do | Nov. 16, 1864 |
| Keyes, Joseph | do | Nov. 10, 1863 |
| Kearney, N | do | Nov 10, 1863 |
| Kensla, P | do | Nov. 10, 1863 |
| Kingsley, —— | do | Nov. 10, 1863 |
| Kerby, F | do | Nov. 10, 1863 |
| Kassas, Henry | do | Sep. 20, 1864 |
| Karem, J | do | Sep. 20, 1864 |
| Kelty, Michael | do | Sep. 20, 1864 |
| Kelley, L | do | Sep. 20, 1864 |
| Kelley, Theodore | do | Sep. 20, 1864 |
| Keely, Mark | do | Sep. 20, 1864 |
| Kenan, A | do | Sep 20, 1864 |
| Kenney, J | do | Sep. 20, 1864 |
| Keating, Thomas | do | Sep. 20, 1864 |
| Kellogg, Edson | do | Sep. 20, 1864 |
| Ketchen, —— | do | Sep. 20, 1864 |
| Krausser, August | do | Nov. 15, 1864 |
| Keyes, J. C | do | Nov 15, 1864 |
| Keeling, Frank | do | Nov. 15, 1864 |
| Kennedy, Pierce | do | Nov. 15, 1864 |
| Keams, Patrick | do | Nov. 15, 1864 |
| Keff, S | do | Nov. 15, 1864 |
| Keeper, F | do | Nov. 15, 1864 |
| Kenney, Neil | do | Jan. 11, 1865 |
| Kenely, Charles | do | Jan. 11, 1865 |
| Kraker, Daniel | do | Jan. 11, 1865 |
| Kenedy, William | do | Jan. 11, 1865 |
| Kite, Charles | do | Jan. 19, 1865 |
| Kolzrols, John | do | Jan. 19, 1865 |
| Kuck, Charles | do | Jan. 19, 1865 |
| Kretky, Weclew | do | Jan. 19, 1865 |
| Klaus, Nicholas | do | Jan. 19, 1865 |
| Kesterling, Martin | do | Jan. 26, 1865 |
| Klier, Andreas | do | Jan. 26, 1865 |
| Kerring, Frederick | do | Jan. 26, 1865 |
| Kruskeck, Gustav | do | Jan. 26, 1865 |
| Krocher, Oswald | do | Jan. 26, 1865 |
| Kelley, Peter | do | Nov. 11, 1863 |
| Kisopf, Joseph | do | Nov. 11, 1863 |
| Koss, Charles | do | Nov. 11, 1863 |

| *Name.* | *Residence.* | *Date* |
|---|---|---|
| Kassell, Anton | Milwaukee | Dec. 7, 1864 |
| Kruger, Wilhelm | do | Dec. 7, 1864 |
| Kratschoil, Franz | do | Dec. 7, 1864 |
| Kessner, Gottleib | Granville | Sep. 22, 1864 |
| Kramer, Frederick | do | Sep. 22, 1864 |
| Kelley, James | Wauwatosa | Nov. 11, 1863 |
| Kran, August | do | Nov. 11, 1863 |
| Kitskow, Albert | Greenfield | Nov. 11, 1863 |
| Kasmer, Otto | do | Sep. 22, 1864 |
| Kravenger, Henry | Lake | Nov. 11, 1863 |
| Kruber, "alias" George | do | Nov. 11, 1863 |
| Kroch r, John | Oak Creek, | Nov. 11, 1863 |
| Kneeland, John | do | Sep. 22, 1864 |
| Kleber, G. J. | Racine | Nov 11, 1863 |
| Keisler, Jacob | do | Sep. 24, 1864 |
| Kleason, Mathias | do | Sep. 24, 1864 |
| Kesilka, Wencel | do | Nov. 11, 1863 |
| Keffa, John | do | Sep. 22, 1864 |
| Knely, Michael | do | Sep. 22, 1864 |
| Kupper, Anthony (or Andrew) | do | Sep. 22, 1864 |
| Kiha, Joseph | Muskego | Dec. 1, 1864 |
| Kohn, August | do | Dec. 1, 1864 |
| Kelly, John | Delafield | Sep. 22, 1864 |
| Kuman, Frederick | Racine | Sep. 22, 1864 |
| Keeper, George F. | do | Jan. 19, 1865 |
| Kenetels, W. H. | Mount Pleasant | Nov. 11, 1863 |
| Krossig, Martin | Caledonia | Nov. 11, 1863 |
| Kaber, Nicholas | do | Sept. 22, 1864 |
| Kertz, Leonard | do | Dec. 7, 1864 |
| Kruckman, —— | Wheatland | Sep. 24, 1864 |
| Ketterhagen, G. | do | Sep. 24, 1864 |
| Kotis, John | Salem | Sep. 24, 1864 |
| Kelley, Patrick | Pleasant Prairie | Nov. 12, 1863 |
| King, William | Delavan | Nov. 12, 1863 |
| Kerrigan, John | East Troy | Sep. 24, 1864 |
| Kelley, C. W. | Summit | Nov. 30, 1864 |
| Knable, Magnus | Pewaukee | Sep. 22, 1864 |
| Keefer, Daniel | do | Dec. 2, 1864 |
| Kilpatrick, Samuel | Waukesha | Nov. 12, 1863 |
| Kavanaugh, Hugh | do | Sep. 23, 1864 |
| Kelly, Bernard | Vernon | Sep. 24, 1864 |
| Kecham, Merits | Menomonee | Nov. 12, 1863 |
| Kedyee, Peter | do | Sep. 24, 1864 |
| Klepsten, Peter | do | Sep. 24, 1864 |
| Kieren, Anthony | do | Sep. 24, 1864 |
| Keiffer, Michael | do | Dec. 1, 1864 |
| Keht, Jacob | do | |
| Kelly, Theodore | do | |
| Klebenow, Johann | do | Nov. 25, 1864 |
| Kuntzman, Fred | Brookfield | Sep. 23, 1864 |
| Killer, Andrew | Muskego | Nov. 12, 1863 |
| Kelly, John | Beloit | Nov. 12, 1863 |
| Kelly, Henry | Janesville | Nov. 12, 1863 |
| Kinney, Thomas | Milton | Nov. 12, 1863 |
| Kliner, John | Sun Prairie | Sep. 19, 1864 |
| Kabb, Martin | Berry | Sep. 19, 1864 |
| Kenig, Joseph | do | Feb. 27, 1865 |
| Kennedy, John | Mazomanie | Nov. 13, 1863 |
| Kelm, Peter | Farmington | Sep. 20, 1864 |

| *Name.* | *Residence* | *Date* |
|---|---|---|
| Kurtz, Henry | Waterloo | Nov. 13, 1863 |
| Kinshel, Julius | Watertown | Sep. 20, 1864 |
| Kurch, Frederick | do | Sep. 20, 1864 |
| Kramny, Henry | do | Oct. 22, 1864 |
| Knough, Charles | Ixonia | Nov. 13, 1863 |
| Knough, Henry | do | Nov. 13, 1863 |
| Kugn, Caleb | Randolph | Nov. 13, 1863 |
| Krouitz, Henry | Watertown | Sep. 20, 1864 |
| Kelly, Thomas | do | Sep. 20, 1864 |
| Ketler, John | do | Nov. 15, 1864 |
| Kocher, ——— | do | Nov. 15, 1864 |
| Kirst, Frock | Ridgeway | Sep. 28, 1864 |
| Knootson, Ole | do | Oct. 28, 1864 |
| Kerrin, William | Dodgeville | Nov. 19, 1864 |
| Kelley, Thomas | Highland | Sep. 28, 1864 |
| Kneutson, Nelse | do | Sep. 28, 1864 |
| Kartz, George | do | Oct. 28, 1864 |
| Krier, Matthias | Waldwick | Oct. 4, 1864 |
| King, Thomas | do | Oct. 4, 1864 |
| Kober, Herman | Moscow | Sep. 28, 1864 |
| Kelley, James | White Oak Springs | Oct. 4, 1864 |
| Kelley, James | Benton | Sep. 29, 1864 |
| Kempthorne, James | do | Sep. 29, 1864 |
| Keenan, John | do | Sep. 29, 1864 |
| Kelley, John L. | New Diggings | Sep. 29, 1864 |
| Kelley, John D. | do | Sep. 29, 1864 |
| Kenney, Thomas | Albany | Nov. 17, 1863 |
| Kitchell, Milton | Cadiz | Nov. 17, 1863 |
| Killbride, Thomas | Utica | Sep. 30, 1864 |
| Kibbe, William H. | Fairfield or New Buffalo | Nov. 20, 1863 |
| Keenan, Frank | La Valle | Oct. 3, 1864 |
| Kesinch, Peter | Washington | Oct. 3, 1864 |
| Kelly, Patrick | Marshall | Oct. 28, 1864 |
| Keating, Michael | Millville | Oct. 28, 1864 |
| Kilpatrick, William | La Crosse | Nov. 16, 1863 |
| Kair, John | Campbell | Sep. 19, 1864 |
| Keel, Henry | Monroe Co | Nov. 17, 1863 |
| Kelley, Patrick, No. 2. | Adrian | Sep. 20, 1864 |
| Kranner, William | Sheldon | Sep 20, 1864 |
| Keyhole, John | Genoa | Sep 20, 1864 |
| Kellicut, Erastus | Portland | Nov. 10, 1864 |
| Keys, Sidney | Jackson Co | Nov. 18, 1863 |
| Kellum, John | Adams Co. | Nov. 23, 1863 |
| Kinney, James | New Haven | Sep. 26, 1864 |
| Kane, Timothy | do | Sep. 26, 1864 |
| Knudson, Ole | do | Sep. 26, 1864 |
| Knapp, Harrison | Lincoln | Nov. 14, 1864 |
| Keil, Godfrey | Dunn Co. | Nov 23, 1863 |
| Kennedy, Jerry | do | Nov. 23, 1863 |
| Kramer Lewis | Eau Galle | Sep 27, 1864 |
| Knute, Oleson | do | Sep. 27, 1864 |
| Kirkland Hiram | do | Sep. 27, 1864 |
| Kelley, William | do | Nov. 14, 1864 |
| Knott, Edward | Seven Mile Creek | Sep. 19, 1864 |
| Kelley, Tebedee | Lyndon | Sep. 20, 1864 |
| Kowan, James | do | Sep. 20, 1864 |
| Kelly, Patrick, No. 2 | Germantown | Sep. 20, 1864 |
| Keena, Patrick | Kildare | Oct. 31, 1864 |
| Keena, Matthew | do | Oct. 31, 1864 |

| *Name.* | *Residence.* | *Date.* |
|---|---|---|
| Kernon, Amos | Kildare | Oct. 31, 1864 |
| Kennedy, Patrick | Lemonweir | Oct. 31, 1864 |
| Kingsley, Seth | Summit | Oct. 31, 1864 |
| Kingsley, Elias | do | Oct. 31, 1864 |
| Kesler, Peter | Rodolph | Sep. 22, 1864 |
| Kimball, Nathaniel | Stockton | Sep. 22, 1864 |
| Kozoskoski, Frank | Sharon | Sep. 22, 1864 |
| Klaven, August | Linwood | Sep. 22, 1864 |
| Kinney, Edmund | Martell | Sep. 22, 1864 |
| Kelly, Edward | Erin Prairie | Sep. 23, 1864 |
| Kelly, Michael | do | Sep. 23, 1864 |
| King, Banzelia | Somerset | Oct. 31, 1864 |
| King, Frank | do | Oct. 31, 1864 |
| Kiemon, Eugene | Rush River | Nov 2, 1864 |
| Kellone, Elisha | Naples | Sep. 26, 1864 |
| Kinle, Henry | Modena | Sep. 26, 1864 |
| Kenyon, A. B. | Waterville | Sep. 27, 1864 |
| Kean, Thomas | Chippewa Falls | Sep. 27, 1864 |
| Kingsbury, Edward | Bloomer Prairie | Sep 27, 1864 |
| Kennedy, Joseph | Chippewa Falls | Nov. 2, 1864 |
| Kreb, Mathias | Mishicott | Nov. 20, 1863 |
| Kurbar, John | Cooperstown | Nov. 24, 1863 |
| Kaufman, William | Kossuth | Nov. 24, 1863 |
| Knudson, Knud S. | Liberty | Nov. 24, 1863 |
| Knudson, Ole | do | Nov. 24, 1863 |
| Kniger, August | Schleswig | Nov, 24, 1863 |
| Kesler, August | Oshkosh city | Nov. 23, 1863 |
| Keuffert, Peter | do | Nov. 23, 1863 |
| Kies, Emanuel | Nepeuskin | Nov. 23, 1863 |
| Knapp, James | Omro | Nov. 23, 1863 |
| Kilmarten, James | Winnebago Co | Nov. 24, 1863 |
| Kline, Ernst | do | Nov. 28, 1863 |
| Kenyon, Elisha | Poygan | Nov. 5, 1864 |
| Keller, Matthew | do | Nov. 5, 1864 |
| Kock, Charles | Gibson | Dec. 29, 1864 |
| Kavanaugh, Arthur | Maple Grove | Dec. 29, 1864 |
| Kelley, Miles | do | Dec. 29, 1864 |
| Kodoertitz, ——— | Manitowoc Rapids | Dec. 29, 1864 |
| Koplitz, Anton | do | Dec. 29, 1863 |
| Kabat, Franz | Rockland | Dec. 29, 1863 |
| Karbatsch, Carl | Newton | Dec. 29, 1863 |
| Klein, Nicholas | do | Dec. 29, 1863 |
| Klein, Jno | do | Dec. 29, 1864 |
| Kelley, Thomas | Dayton | Nov. 24, 1863 |
| Kisner, August | Marquette Co | Nov 24, 1863 |
| Kisner, Chas. | do | Nov. 24, 1863 |
| Klatt, Michael | Mecan | Nov. 1, 1864 |
| Kelley, Michael | Buffalo | Nov. 1, 1864 |
| King, Charles | Crystal Lake | Nov. 1, 1864 |
| Konkey, Lewis | do | Nov. 1, 1864 |
| King, Charles | do | Nov. 1, 1864 |
| Kadden, Jno | Shields | Nov. 1, 1864 |
| Kinney, Randall | do | Nov. 1, 1864 |
| Kirth, Louis | Waupaca Co | Nov. 25, 1863 |
| Klinkoph, Louis | Larabee | Nov. 5, 1864 |
| Klennan, Charles | Bear Creek | Nov. 5, 1864 |
| Karney, Thomas | Lebanon | Nov. 5, 1864 |
| Kerrigan, Michael | do | Nov. 5, 1864 |
| Karney, Robert | do | Dec. 31, 1864 |

| *Name.* | *Residence.* | *Date.* |
|---|---|---|
| Kerr, Samuel | Lebanon | Dec. 31, 1864 |
| Knudson, Ole | Iola | Dec. 31, 1864 |
| Knudson, K ud | do | Nov. 5, 1864 |
| Knudson, Lars | do | Nov. 5, 1864 |
| Koma, Andrew | Grand Chute | Nov. 27, 1863 |
| Kort, Andrew | do | Dec. 28, 1864 |
| Kellogg, Ezra | Hortonia | Dec. 28, 1864 |
| Koffend, Antone | Appleton | Nov. 27, 1863 |
| Kohl, Jacob | Center | Nov. 27, 1863 |
| Killeen, Michael | Aurora | Nov. 2, 1864 |
| Kelly, Herman | Plainfield | Nov. 2, 1864 |
| Kroley, Michael | Harrison | Dec. 28, 1864 |
| Keating, Patrick | Stockbridge | Dec. 28, 1864 |
| Krepsor, Jno | Chilton | Dec. 28, 1864 |
| Kisner, ——— | Brothertown | Dec. 28, 1864 |
| Kartlin, William | Montpelier | Dec. 29, 1864 |
| Knudson, Mads | Franklin | Dec. 29, 1864 |
| Knudson, Ole | do | Dec. 29, 1864 |
| Kukl, Thomas | do | Dec. 29, 1864 |
| Kinick, Casper | do | Dec. 29, 1864 |
| Kenard, John B. | Lincoln | Dec. 29, 1864 |
| Kave, Flane | Stiles | Dec. 29, 1864 |
| Kelly John | do | Dec. 29, 1864 |
| Kereven, Jno | do | Dec. 29, 1864 |
| Kelso, William | Wrightstown | Nov. 28, 1863 |

## L

| Name | Residence | Date |
|---|---|---|
| Lary, Daniel | Fond du Lac | Nov. 19, 1863 |
| Ladare, Eugene | do | Nov 19, 1863 |
| Lawry, Charles | do | Nov. 19, 1863 |
| Laughlin, William | do | Nov. 19, 1863 |
| Louery, William | do | Nov. 19, 1863 |
| Leuting, John | Ashford | Nov. 19, 1863 |
| Lumbeg, William | Lamartine | Nov. 19, 1863 |
| Lane Augustus C. | Waupun Village | Nov. 19, 1863 |
| Lowery, William | Eldrado | Nov. 19, 1863 |
| Lept, Charles | do | Nov. 19, 1863 |
| Lants, August | do | Nov. 19, 1863 |
| Leonard, Michael | do | Nov. 19, 1863 |
| Lang, Patrick | do | Nov. 19, 1863 |
| Lantz, John | do | Nov. 19, 1863 |
| Lilly, Sike | Lowell | Nov. 20, 1863 |
| Lyons, Thomas | Clyman | Oct. 6, 1864 |
| Leia, Octave | Oak Grove | Nov. 20, 1863 |
| Lenstater, Conrad | Watertown | Oct. 6, 1864 |
| Lentz, David | do | Oct. 6, 1864 |
| Lepke, Fred | do | Dec. 21, 1864 |
| Lambricht, August | do | Dec. 1, 1864 |
| Leach, Martin | Lomira | Jan. 27, 1865 |
| Ludwig, John | do | Oct. 6, 1864 |
| Lyman, James O. | Hartford | Nov. 21, 1863 |
| Leurce, Jacob | Erin | Oct. 12, 1864 |
| Lynch, John | do | Dec. 1, 1864 |
| Linch, Charles | do | Dec. 1, 1864 |
| Leibert, Frederick | Polk | Oct. 12, 1864 |
| Liebend, John | do | Oct. 12, 1864 |
| Liver, Lemanual | do | Dec. 8, 1864 |
| Lopey, George | Richfield | Oct. 12, 1864 |
| Luman, Philip | do | Oct. 12, 1864 |

| *Name.* | *Residence.* | *Date.* |
|---|---|---|
| Lofi, George | Richfield | Oct. 12, 1864 |
| Leonhaul, Henry | do | Dec. 1, 1864 |
| Lehman, Philip | do | Dec. 1, 1864 |
| Limback, Christ. | do | Jan. 27, 1865 |
| Lambricht, John | Farmington | Oct. 18, 1864 |
| Lord, Edward | do | Dec. 1, 1864 |
| Long, James | do | Jan. 27, 1865 |
| Livetman, George | Jackson | Oct. 11, 1864 |
| Lubknow, Frederick | do | Oct. 11, 1864 |
| Lecher, John | Belgium | Dec. 1, 1864 |
| Ludvig, Peter | do | Dec. 1, 1864 |
| Lowin, Frank | do | Dec. 1, 1864 |
| Lafoulain, Joseph | do | Dec. 1, 1864 |
| Lidcam, George | Fredonia | Oct. 14, 1864 |
| Libet, John | do | Oct. 14, 1864 |
| Linzer, John | do | Nov. 21, 1863 |
| Lightner, Samuel | Grafton | Dec. 1, 1864 |
| Lightner, Gideon | do | Dec. 1, 1864 |
| Larron, Lane | Grafton | Jan. 27, 1865 |
| Lauge, John | Port Washington | Nov. 23, 1863 |
| Lonereutz, Charles | Saukville | Nov. 23, 1863 |
| Lobenstein, John | do | Oct. 14, 1864 |
| Louitz, Charles | do | Oct. 14, 1864 |
| Lambeck, Michael | do | Oct. 14, 1864 |
| Louitz, Louis | do | Oct. 14, 1864 |
| Lutto, Hiram | Sheboygan | Jan 27, 1865 |
| Linden, John | do | Oct. 25, 1864 |
| Lschetzsche, August | do | Dec. 2, 1864 |
| Lindewthall, Dormick | do | Dec. 2, 1864 |
| Lubinkey, Henry | do | Dec. 2, 1864 |
| Landaner, John | do | Oct. 18, 1864 |
| Lotz, Charles | do | Oct. 18, 1864 |
| Lefurge, James | do | Oct. 18, 1864 |
| Lind, Johannes | Moselle | Oct. 18, 1864 |
| Leeman, Pat | Wilson | Nov. 24, 1864 |
| Lusbink, John | Lima | Nov. 24, 1863 |
| Land, Peter | do | Nov. 24, 1863 |
| Lams, Lawrence | Holland | Oct. 21, 1864 |
| Lams, M. | do | Oct. 21, 1864 |
| Lee, Elmore | Abbott | Dec. 2, 1864 |
| Loneg, John | do | Dec. 2, 1864 |
| Laughlin, Charley | Scott | Oct. 21, 1864 |
| Laville, John | Granville | Sep. 22, 1864 |
| Lanzondorf, Henry | do | Sep. 22, 1864 |
| Leirick, Henry | do | Sep. 22, 1864 |
| Leidolph, Carl | do | Sep. 22, 1864 |
| Lorche, August | do | Sep. 22, 1864 |
| Linn, William | do. | Sep. 22, 1864 |
| Linsley, Thomas | Greenfield | Sep. 22, 1864 |
| Lobel, Frederick | do | Sep. 22, 1864 |
| Leonard, William | do | Sep. 22, 1864 |
| Lamar, William | do | Sep. 21, 1864 |
| Lavin, Charles | Lake | Nov. 11, 1863 |
| Linn nkamp, Chris | do | Nov. 11, 1863 |
| Lenthner, Michael | Franklin | Nov. 11, 1863 |
| Long, Theodore | Oak Creek | Nov. 11, 1863 |
| Longfellow, John | Racine | Nov. 11, 1863 |
| Longfield, Richard | do | Nov. 11, 1863 |
| Lavin, Patrick | do | Nov. 11, 1863 |

| *Name.* | *Residence.* | *Date.* |
|---|---|---|
| Lyons, John | Racine | Sep. 22, 1864 |
| Lanson, Jacob | do | Sep. 22, 1864 |
| Larvin, Patrick | Mount Pleasant | Nov. 11, 1863 |
| Levit, Joseph | do | Sep. 23, 1864 |
| Luber Ader | do | Sep. 23, 1864 |
| Langmaid, Albert S | Rochester | Sep. 24, 1864 |
| Lompe, Valentine | Waterford | Nov. 11, 1863 |
| Lularius, John | Raymond | Sep. 23, 1864 |
| Leonard, Henry | Caledonia | Sep. 22, 1864 |
| Lovjoy, Charles | do | Sep. 22, 1864 |
| Liedhoff, Bennett | Randall | Nov. 12, 1863 |
| Lawrence, Wm | do | Nov. 9, 1863 |
| Larkin, Martin | do | Nov. 9, 1863 |
| Laidlaw, Walter | do | Sep. 19, 1864 |
| Licher, Geo | do | Nov. 9, 1863 |
| Langenberger, J | do | Nov. 9, 1863 |
| Lenike, Gottleib | do | Nov. 9, 1863 |
| Laherty, Jas | do | Nov. 9, 1863 |
| Ludwig, Johann | do | Nov. 14, 1864 |
| Luckan, David | do | Nov. 10, 1863 |
| Lavin, Jas | do | Nov. 10, 1863 |
| Leonard, P. H | do | Nov. 10, 1863 |
| Laudercraft, Andrs | do | Nov. 10, 1863 |
| Lahakee, J. L | do | Nov. 10, 1863 |
| Lower, R. C | do | Nov. 10, 1863 |
| Lynch, Thomas | do | Sep. 20, 1864 |
| Levi, M. B | do | Sep. 20, 1864 |
| Larkins, Martin | do | Sep. 20, 1864 |
| Lacy, Francis | do | Sep. 20, 1864 |
| Lawler, John | do | Sep. 20, 1864 |
| Lands, John | do | Sep. 20, 1864 |
| Lauden, Jm | do | Sep. 20, 1864 |
| Ligheser, F | do | Sep. 20, 1864 |
| Ling, J | do | Sep. 20, 1864 |
| Ludden, William | do | Sep. 20, 1864 |
| Lameck, H | do | Sep. 20, 1864 |
| Loran, Thomas | do | Sep. 20, 1864 |
| Laurence, J | Milwaukee | Nov. 15, 1864 |
| Loyd, William | do | Nov. 15, 1864 |
| Lilly, William | do | Nov. 15, 1864 |
| Lundar, M | do | Nov. 15, 1864 |
| Leach, William | do | Nov. 15, 1864 |
| Laney, John | do | Nov. 15, 1864 |
| Linnen, J | do | Jan. 11, 1865 |
| Lewis, John | do | Nov. 10, 1863 |
| Lincoln, Willard | do | Nov. 10, 1863 |
| Lela, Samuel | do | Nov. 10, 1863 |
| Lovering, George | do | Nov. 10, 1863 |
| Lawton, Thomas | do | Sep. 21, 1864 |
| Lynch, Peter | do | Sep. 21, 1864 |
| Linny, Joseph | do | Sep. 21, 1864 |
| Laury, John, W | do | Sep. 21, 1864 |
| Linka, John | do | Nov. 10, 1863 |
| Larson, Andrew | do | Nov. 10, 1863 |
| Lempke, Ludwig | do | Nov. 10, 1863 |
| Laugin, Thomas | do | Nov. 10, 1863 |
| Lueve, John | do | Sep. 27, 1864 |
| Luepke, Fritz | do | Sep. 27, 1864 |
| Lescher, John | do | Sep. 27, 1864 |

| *Name.* | *Residence.* | *Date.* |
|---|---|---|
| Loessel, John | Milwaukee | Sep. 27, 1864 |
| Laire, J. A. | do | Nov. 10, 1863 |
| Laion, John | do | Nov. 10, 1863 |
| Leveland, Edward | do | Nov. 11, 1863 |
| Larkham, Fritz | do | Nov. 11, 1863 |
| Larry, Fred | do | Nov. 11, 1863 |
| Lough, Jacob | do | Nov. 11, 1863 |
| Lerst, Joseph | do | Jan. 19, 1865 |
| Leonard, Hall | do | Jan. 19, 1865 |
| Louden, John | do | Sep. 21, 1864 |
| Lax, Charles | do | Sep. 21, 1864 |
| Lam, Michael | do | Sep. 21, 1864 |
| Loveland, Zachmas | do | Nov. 25, 1864 |
| Loepert, Ernst | do | Nov. 25, 1864 |
| Luder, Daniel | do | Nov. 25, 1864 |
| Le Febre, Abram | do | Nov. 25, 1864 |
| Lienhardt, Theodore | do | Nov. 11, 1863 |
| Leidendorf, Carl | do | Nov. 11, 1863 |
| Laudgraf, ——— | do | Nov. 11, 1863 |
| Lauer, Peter | do | Nov. 11, 1863 |
| Leudhofer, John | do | Sep. 21, 1864 |
| Larone, Purre Alesis | do | Sep. 21, 1864 |
| Lorey, Gottfried | do | Sep. 21, 1864 |
| Lint, Gustav | do | Sep. 21, 1864 |
| Laich, Johann | do | Sep. 21, 1864 |
| Larbegs, Andreas | do | Sep 21, 1864 |
| Lehman, Johann | do | Nov. 25, 1864 |
| Lefevre, Abraham | do | Nov. 25, 1864 |
| Leipert, Godfrey | do | Nov. 30, 1864 |
| Laverenz, August | do | Jan. 26, 1865 |
| Liesener, Charles | do | Jan. 26, 1865 |
| Luneberg, Johann | do | Sep. 22, 1864 |
| Le Brun, John | do | Sep. 22, 1864 |
| Lempke, Gottleib | do | Sep. 22, 1864 |
| Lass, Frederick | do | Dec. 7, 1864 |
| Lubke, Willhelm | do | Dec. 7, 1864 |
| Laugherty, Richard | Granville | Nov. 11, 1863 |
| Littlefield, Moses | Wheatfield | Sep. 24, 1864 |
| Lais, Herman | do | Dec. 14, 1864 |
| Lane, M. | do | Dec. 14, 1864 |
| Lauchlin, James | East Troy | Dec. 2, 1864 |
| Leuz, Ludwig | Summit | Nov. 12, 1863 |
| Leuz, August | do | Nov. 30, 1864 |
| Laman, Edgar | Pewaukee | Nov. 12, 1863 |
| Linch, Daniel | do | Sep. 22, 1864 |
| Lippert, Frank | do | Dec. 2, 1864 |
| Lee, W W. | Waukesha | Sep. 23, 1864 |
| Lahee, William | Vernon | Sep. 24, 1864 |
| Laufler, Henry | do | Sep. 24, 1864 |
| Letke, Charles | do | Sep. 24, 1864 |
| Lanehart, Stopp | Menomonee | Dec. 1, 1864 |
| Leinhart, Blanc | do | Dec. 1, 1864 |
| Lichtgeble, Christian | do | Nov. 25, 1864 |
| Lamb, John | Brookfield | Sep. 23, 1864 |
| Lynch, Daniel | Muskego | Sep. 24, 1864 |
| La Feber, Abram | Harmony | Nov. 12, 1863 |
| Lucas, Nicholas | Berry | Oct. 22, 1864 |
| Lahey, Thomas | Mazomanie | Nov. 13, 1863 |
| Lambert, Nicholas | Roxbury | Nov. 13, 1863 |

| *Name.* | *Residence.* | *Date.* |
| --- | --- | --- |
| Leek, Christian | York | Nov. 13, 1863 |
| Lindel, John | Farmington | Sep. 20, 1864 |
| Lendorf, Leonard | do | Oct. 28, 1864 |
| Ludwick, Charles | do | Oct. 28, 1864 |
| Lary, James | Watertown | Oct. 22, 1864 |
| Laflin, Luke | Lewiston | Sept. 21, 1864 |
| Laughlin, Thomas | Concord | Sep. 20, 1864 |
| Lovell, Edward | Watertown | Nov. 15, 1863 |
| Lynch, Timothy | Ridgeway | Sep. 28, 1864 |
| Lewis, William | do | Sept. 28, 1864 |
| Larson, William | do | Oct. 28, 1864 |
| Lee, Hugh | do | Oct. 28, 1864 |
| Lee, Leonard | do | Oct. 28, 1864 |
| Lott, Isaac | Clyde | Nov. 19, 1863 |
| La Bounty, William | Dodgeville | Sep. 28, 1864 |
| Larson, John | do | Sep. 28, 1864 |
| Letcher, William H | do | Oct. 28, 1864 |
| Larson, Lars | do | Oct. 28, 1864 |
| La Bounty, Louis | do | Oct. 28, 1864 |
| Lander, Matthew | do | Oct. 28, 1864 |
| Letan, Andrew | Highland | Sep. 28, 1864 |
| Lewison, Ans | do | Sep. 28, 1864 |
| Lee, Robert | do | Oct. 28, 1864 |
| Lee, George | do | Oct. 28, 1864 |
| Lamb, Winfield S | do | Oct. 28, 1864 |
| Laverly, William | Waldwick | Oct. 4, 1864 |
| Longham, Edward | New Diggings | Sep. 29, 1864 |
| Leary, Timothy | do | Sep. 29, 1864 |
| Lynch, Michael | do | Sep. 29, 1864 |
| Linzy, Henry | Clarno | Nov. 17, 1863 |
| Lowery, Franklin | Jefferson | Sep. 27, 1864 |
| Lawrence, Jacob | Sylvan | Sep. 26, 1864 |
| Lawrence, Thomas | Spring Grove | Oct. 5, 1864 |
| Lenehan, Dennis | Seneca | Sep. 30, 1864 |
| Lynch, John | do | Sep. 30, 1864 |
| Loby, Edward | Eastman | Sep. 30, 1864 |
| Lewison, Lewis | do | Nov. 19, 1863 |
| Langridge, George | Scott | Sep. 30, 1864 |
| Lame, Robert | Monroe Co | Nov. 17, 1863 |
| Laven, I | do | Nov. 17, 1863 |
| Lenihen, Thomas | Tomah | Nov. 10, 1864 |
| Loschwiski, Andrew | Trempealeau Co | Nov. 18, 1863 |
| Lanning, Edward | Juneau Co | Nov. 17, 1863 |
| Lenahan, John | Kildare | Sep. 19, 1864 |
| Lenahan, Daniel | do | Sep. 19, 1864 |
| Lenahan, M | do | Oct. 31, 1864 |
| Leffingwell, James | Plymouth | Sep. 19, 1864 |
| Lyon, Myron F | do | Sep. 19, 1864 |
| Leyson, Townes | Vernon Co | Nov. 18, 1863 |
| Lalan, William | Bergen | Sep. 21, 1864 |
| Lord, Charles | Wood Co | Nov. 18, 1863 |
| Longhton, Bazil | Centralia | Nov 15, 1863 |
| Lesert, Linn | do | Nov. 15, 1863 |
| La Claire, Lewis | Campbell | Sep. 19, 1864 |
| Lelâukin, John | Washington | Sep. 19, 1864 |
| Lamphear, Ezra | Linwood | Sep. 28, 1864 |
| Leonard, Patrick | Sharon | Sep. 22, 1864 |
| Lane, Marquis D | Lanark | Sept. 22, 1864 |

| *Name.* | *Residence.* | *Date.* |
|---|---|---|
| Laran, Thomas | Lanark | Nov. 15, 1864 |
| Larson, Helle | Eau Galle | Sep. 23, 1864 |
| Lemrand, Prudent | Somerset | Oct 5, 1864 |
| Leberto, Paul | do | Oct. 5, 1864 |
| Lavalle, Thomas | Erin Prairie | Sep. 23, 1864 |
| Loomis, Abijah | Gilmanton | Sep. 26, 1864 |
| Langney, Palsey | New Haven | Sep. 26, 1864 |
| Lyman, Oshen G | Springville | Sep. 26, 1864 |
| Lyman, Henry C | do | Nov. 14, 1864 |
| Lightfall, John | Monroe | Sep. 26, 1864 |
| Litchfield, Thomas | Easton | Nov 14, 1864 |
| Linden, Christ | Eau Galle | Sep. 27, 1864 |
| Lanahan, Thomas | do | Nov. 2, 1864 |
| Langdell, Nyles | Spring Brook | Nov. 2, 1864 |
| La Chappell, Paul | Chippewa Falls | Sep. 27, 1864 |
| Lewezell, E | do | Nov. 2, 1864 |
| Larson, Andrew | Martell | Nov. 3, 1864 |
| Loveless, Joseph jr | St. Croix Falls | Nov. 15, 1864 |
| Leitch, Alexander | Pepin | Nov 16, 1864 |
| Lecapitaine, J B | Lincoln | Nov. 20, 1863 |
| Looze, Perie | Red River | Dec 29, 1864 |
| Lefevre, Chas | do | Dec. 29, 1864 |
| Linair, Arvis | Casco | Dec 29, 1864 |
| Larkin, Thomas | do | Dec. 29, 1864 |
| Lanis, Joseph | do | Dec. 29, 1864 |
| Levanes, Joseph | Franklin | Dec. 29, 1864 |
| Luniage, Joseph | Lincoln | Dec 29, 1864 |
| Luck, William | Cooperstown | Nov. 21, 1863 |
| La Bell, David | Manitowoc Rapids | Nov. 21, 1863 |
| Levely, Horace | do | Dec. 29, 1864 |
| Lynk, George | Liberty | Nov. 21, 1863 |
| Lanzen, Stephen | Meeme | Nov. 21, 1863 |
| Lour, Peter | do | Nov. 21, 1863 |
| Loskoski, Nicholas | do | Dec. 29, 1864 |
| Lehnekamp, Fred | Two Creeks | Dec. 29, 1864 |
| Leach, John | Gibson | Dec. 29, 1864 |
| Lokojicik, Francis | do | Dec. 29, 1864 |
| Lienivan, Mathias | Maple Grove | Dec. 29, 1864 |
| Luchow, Frederick | Newton | Dec. 29, 1864 |
| Lang, Charles | Oshkosh city | Nov. 23, 1864 |
| Lipke, Charles | do | Nov. 23, 1864 |
| Lee, Thomas | Nepeuskin | Nov. 23, 1864 |
| Lisby, Jacob | Wolf River | Nov. 5, 1864 |
| Livermore, L | Berlin city | Nov. 24, 1863 |
| Lantis, George | Brooklyn | Nov. 24, 1863 |
| Lee, John | Kingston | Nov. 24, 1863 |
| Lynch, Michael | Seneca | Nov. 5, 1864 |
| Larrimain, Hugh | Marquette Co | Nov. 21, 1863 |
| Leedler, William | Mecan | Nov. 1, 1864 |
| Leedki, Emil | do | Dec. 31, 1864 |
| Lilly, Norman | Royalton | Nov. 25, 1863 |
| Lieb, Charles F | Caledonia | Nov. 5, 1864 |
| Larson, Gregor | St. Lawrence | Nov. 5, 1864 |
| Larson, Lane | do | Nov. 5, 1864 |
| Larson, Lars | do | Dec. 31, 1864 |
| Lorenson, Aslack | Iola | Dec. 31, 1864 |
| Lansurch, Ole O | do | Dec. 31, 1864 |
| Larson, Ole | do | Nov. 5, 1864 |
| Lerman, John | Grand Chute | Nov. 27, 1863 |

| *Name.* | *Residence.* | *Date.* |
|---|---|---|
| Lanze, Joseph | Grand Chute | Dec. 28, 1864 |
| Lewis, Edward | | Nov. 27, 1863 |
| Lallendorf, Christian | Hortonia | Dec. 28, 1864 |
| Lapland, Nelson | Green Bay | Nov. 27, 1863 |
| Lemminse, Francois | do | Dec. 28, 1864 |
| Linne, Edward | Fort Howard | Nov. 27, 1863 |
| Lau, Alexander | Marinette | Nov. 28, 1863 |
| Lawrence, Mortimore | Pensaukee | Nov. 28, 1863 |
| Londe, Alfred | do | Nov. 28, 1863 |
| Livermore, Randall G | do | Nov. 28, 1863 |
| Leaner, Joseph | Peshtigo | Nov. 28, 1863 |
| Lanwauder, Joseph | Stiles | Nov. 28, 1863 |
| Lapens, Frank | do | Nov. 28, 1863 |
| Lnsha, Elisha | Little Suamico | Dec. 29, 1864 |
| Lapsey, John | Bloomfield | Nov. 2, 1864 |
| Louden, Franklin | do | Nov. 2, 1864 |
| Loch, B. Z | do | Dec. 31, 1864 |
| Lally, Philip | Aurora | Nov. 2, 1864 |
| Larson, Christian | do | Dec. 31, 1864 |
| Lloanoeck, John | Warren | Nov. 2, 1864 |
| Lane, Lawrence A | Springwater | Nov. 2, 1864 |
| Lewis, Shubel | Deerfield | Nov. 2, 1864 |
| Leddick, Philip | do | Nov. 2, 1864 |
| Lock, William | Oasis | Nov. 2, 1864 |
| Lord, Hiram | do | Nov. 2, 1864 |
| Lane, Jacob | do | Nov. 2, 1864 |
| Lane, Oliver | do | Nov. 2, 1864 |
| Lake, E. W | Plainfield | Nov. 2, 1864 |
| Lamkin, Wales | do | Dec. 31, 1864 |
| Loftes, Thomas | Rantoul | Dec. 28, 1864 |
| Lutnei, Engleworth | Brothertown | Dec. 28, 1864 |
| Lecog, Ch | Brussells | Dec. 29, 1864 |
| Laduren, Louis | do | Dec. 29, 1864 |

## M

| | | |
|---|---|---|
| Miky, Thomas | Farmington | Jan. 27, 1865 |
| Miller, Jacob | do | Jan. 27, 1865 |
| Miller, August | do | Jan. 27, 1865 |
| Mauz, Nicholas | Belgium | Dec. 1, 1864 |
| Morse, Michael | do | Nov. 21, 1863 |
| Morson, Michael | do | Nov. 21, 1863 |
| Martz, Peter | do | |
| Michaels, John | do | Oct. 13, 1864 |
| Mockley, Gerhard | do | Oct. 13, 1864 |
| Masenes, Nicholas | do | Oct. 13, 1864 |
| May, Nicholas | do | Oct. 13, 1864 |
| May, John | do | Oct. 13, 1864 |
| Mors, Getter | do | Oct. 13, 1864 |
| Muller, John | do | Oct. 13, 1864 |
| Mart, Nicholas | do | Dec. 1, 1864 |
| Michels, Henry | do | Dec. 1, 1864 |
| Molinger, Peter | do | Dec. 1, 1864 |
| Muller, John | Fredonia | Dec. 1, 1864 |
| Martin, Peter | do | Dec. 1, 1864 |
| Marris, Illard | Cedarburg | Nov. 23, 1863 |
| Myers, Bart G | Grafton | Oct. 13, 1864 |
| Meeder, Benjamin | do | Oct. 13, 1864 |
| Mathews, Mathew | do | Oct. 13, 1864 |
| Misser, John | do | Oct. 13, 1864 |

| *Name.* | *Residence.* | *Date.* |
|---|---|---|
| Mahar, John | Grafton | Oct. 13, 1864 |
| Male, Carl | do | Dec. 1, 1864 |
| Morehouse, S | Barton | Oct. 12, 1864 |
| Martines, Gerhard | do | Dec. 1, 1864 |
| Muller, Peter jr | do | Dec. 1, 1864 |
| Martin, Jacob | Polk | Oct. 12, 1864 |
| Mann, John Christopher | do | Oct. 12, 1864 |
| Michel, John | do | Dec. 8, 1864 |
| Mertz, John | do | Dec. 8, 1864 |
| Malony, Michael | Richfield | Oct. 12, 1864 |
| Malone, John | do | Dec. 1, 1864 |
| Molzet, John | do | Dec. 1, 1864 |
| Mahem, Andrew | do | Dec. 1, 1864 |
| Maner, William | do | Jan. 27, 1865 |
| Mahen, John | do | Jan. 27, 1865 |
| Messer, Andrew | do | Jan. 27, 1865 |
| Motts, Godfrey Jr | do | Jan. 27, 1865 |
| Manis, Edwin M | do | Jan. 27, 1865 |
| Marigle, Peter | do | Jan. 27, 1865 |
| Morgenroth, Carl | Farmington | Oct. 18, 1864 |
| Miller, George | do | Oct. 18, 1864 |
| Mahoney, John | do | Oct. 18, 1864 |
| Murphy, Daniel | do | Dec. 1, 1864 |
| Moths, Heinrich | do | Dec. 1, 1864 |
| Mulraney, James | do | Dec. 1, 1864 |
| Mulan, Thomas | do | Dec. 1, 1864 |
| Marhman, Frederick | do | Dec. 1, 1864 |
| Midweed, Angust | Lima | Dec. 2, 1864 |
| Margtete, S. C | do | Dec. 2, 1864 |
| Marek, John | do | Jan. 27, 1865 |
| Maas, Ludwig | Abbott | Oct. 18, 1864 |
| Miller, Herman | do | Oct. 18, 1864 |
| Mehloes, Frederick | do | Oct. 18, 1865 |
| Mead, J. A | do | Oct. 18, 1864 |
| Murphy, Thomas | do | Dec. 2, 1864 |
| Murphy, Patrick | do | Dec. 2, 1864 |
| Moll, William | do | Jan. 27, 1865 |
| Miller, William | Plymouth | Dec. 6, 1864 |
| Maguire, Michael | Grafton | Dec. 1, 1864 |
| Malony, Dennis | do | Dec. 1, 1864 |
| Moro, Godlip | do | Jan. 27, 1865 |
| Miller, David | do | Jan. 27, 1865 |
| Muller, Mike | Mequon | Nov. 23, 1863 |
| Maul, Well | do | Nov. 23, 1863 |
| Michel, John | Port Washington | Nov. 23, 1863 |
| Mack, Nicholas | do | Nov. 23, 1863 |
| Miller, Louis | do | Nov. 23, 1863 |
| Montag, Bernard | Saukville | Nov. 23, 1863 |
| Miller, Nicholas | do | Oct. 14, 1864 |
| Munes, John | do | Oct. 14, 1864 |
| Montag, Christian | do | Oct. 14, 1864 |
| Miller, William | Sheboygan | Nov. 23, 1864 |
| Manger, Phil | do | Oct. 25, 1864 |
| Manning, James | do | Dec. 2, 1864 |
| Mue, Ernest | do | Dec. 2, 1864 |
| Muller, William | do | Dec. 2, 1864 |
| Meyer, Joseph | do | Oct. 18, 1864 |
| Moller, George | do | Oct. 18, 1864 |
| Maegs, Richard | do | Dec. 2, 1864 |

| Name. | Residence. | Date. |
|---|---|---|
| Miller, Theodore | Moselle | Nov. 24, 1863 |
| Maser, Lukas | do | Dec. 2, 1864 |
| Murphy, James | Lima | Oct. 21, 1864 |
| Moses, R | do | Oct. 21, 1864 |
| Margaret, Adam | do | Dec. 2, 1864 |
| Manly, Riley | Fond du Lac | Nov. 19, 1863 |
| Murry, Gilford | do | Nov. 19, 1863 |
| Martin, Orlando | Eden | Nov. 19, 1863 |
| Mabel, Henry | Byron | Nov. 19, 1863 |
| Myer, William | Alto | Nov. 19, 1863 |
| Moor, James M | Ripon | Nov. 19, 1863 |
| Millard Robert | do | Nov. 19, 1863 |
| Morgan, William | Eldorado | Oct. 5, 1864 |
| Meiers, Charles | do | Oct. 5, 1864 |
| Moran, John | do | Oct. 5, 1864 |
| Murtha, Patrick | do | Oct. 5, 1864 |
| Morrison, James | do | Dec. 1, 1864 |
| Masters, Ephram | Fox Lake | Nov. 19, 1863 |
| Muand, Patrick | Beaver Dam | Nov. 20, 1863 |
| Morey, Winzel | Emmett | Oct. 11, 1864 |
| Mauty, Diedrick | do | Oct. 11, 1864 |
| Morisy, Dennis | do | Oct. 11, 1864 |
| Morrey, John | do | Oct. 11, 1864 |
| Mastersen, John | do | Oct. 11, 1864 |
| Morgan, David | do | Oct. 11, 1864 |
| Manning, John, jr | Clyman | Nov. 20, 1863 |
| Muher, Patt | do | Oct. 6, 1864 |
| Mahoney, Jarreti | do | Oct. 6, 1864 |
| Mariaty, Michael, jr | do | Oct. 6, 1864 |
| March, Winchel | do | Oct. 6, 1864 |
| Merrill, Alexander | Oak Grove | Nov. 20, 1863 |
| Madison, Albert | Chester | Nov. 20, 1863 |
| Mudling, William | Watertown | Oct. 6, 1864 |
| Mohr, William | do | Oct. 6, 1864 |
| Mattes, Henry | do | Jan. 27, 1865 |
| Mads, Martin | do | Jan. 27, 1865 |
| Moon, David, jr | Leroy | Oct. 4, 1864 |
| Minnich, Wm. H | do | Oct. 4, 1864 |
| Miscinger, Joseph | do | Dec. 1, 1864 |
| Morton, Dexter | Lomira | Nov. 20, 1863 |
| Malony, Edwin | do | Oct. 6, 1864 |
| Mayers, Charles | do | Oct. 6, 1864 |
| Murphy, John W | do | Jan. 27, 1864 |
| Moldenhauer, Charles | Theresa | Nov. 20, 1863 |
| Merg, Henry | Herman | Nov. 24, 1863 |
| Mueller, George | do | Oct. 18, 1864 |
| Mueller, Peter | do | Oct. 18, 1864 |
| Martin, Adolph | do | Oct. 18, 1864 |
| Meyre, Henry, jr | do | Oct. 18, 1864 |
| Mueller, Bemhard | do | Oct. 18, 1864 |
| Murphy, John | Hubbard | Nov. 21, 1863 |
| Mead, David | Hartford | Nov. 21, 1863 |
| Munson, Olace | Erin | Oct. 12, 1864 |
| Murphy, Thomas | do | Dec. 1, 1864 |
| Markham, Milton | Kewaskum | Nov. 21, 1863 |
| Miller, William | Barton | Nov. 21, 1863 |
| Murray, James | do | Nov. 21, 1863 |
| McDonald, Barney | Fond du Lac | Nov. 19, 1863 |
| McAuly, Byron W | Waupun Village | Nov. 19, 1863 |

| *Name* | *Residence.* | *Date.* |
|---|---|---|
| McLaughlin, James | Eldorado | Nov. 19, 1863 |
| McKinney, John | do | Oct. 5, 1864 |
| McCauley, George H | Metomen | Nov. 19, 1863 |
| McCauly, L | Elba | Nov. 19, 1863 |
| McGronty, Patrick | Beaver Dam | Nov. 20, 1863 |
| NcNulty, Michael | Clyman | Oct. 6, 1864 |
| McGregor, Thomas | Watertown | Jan. 27, 1865 |
| McCan, Oliver | Leroy | Nov. 20, 1863 |
| McCoy, John | Lomira | 1863 |
| McCoy, Pearce | do | Oct. 6, 1864 |
| McCoy, Peter | do | Oct. 6, 1864 |
| McRoberts, Edward | Trenton | Nov. 20, 1863 |
| McCarty, John, jr. | Erin | Nov. 21, 1863 |
| McCarty, Patrick | do | Oct. 12, 1864 |
| McCarty, Geo. W | Barton | Oct. 12, 1864 |
| McQuake, William | Polk | Oct. 12, 1864 |
| McQuaker, James | do | Oct. 12, 1864 |
| McKinney, James | Richfield | Oct. 12, 1864 |
| McMannus, Edward | do | Oct. 12, 1864 |
| McGarrett, Barney | do | Jan. 27, 1865 |
| McAllister, James | Fredonia | Dec. 1, 1864 |
| Mc Cuen, James | Grafton | Oct. 13, 1864 |
| McCuen, John, jr | do | Dec. 1, 1864 |
| McCausland, Charles | Shehoygan | Dec. 2, 1864 |
| McGaroey, Joseph | Sheboygan Falls | Oct. 25, 1864 |
| McElroy, Charles | Abbott | Oct. 18, 1864 |
| McElroy, John | do | Dec. 2, 1864 |
| McDaniel, Michael | Scott | Oct. 21, 1864 |
| Meyer, Michael | Waukesha | Sep. 23, 1864 |
| Michle, John | Vernon | Sep 24, 1864 |
| Martin, Hiram | Menomenee | Nov. 12, 1863 |
| Milbarter, Michael | do | Nov. 12, 1863 |
| Martin, Thomas | do | Nov. 12, 1863 |
| Morgan, William | do | Nov. 12, 1863 |
| Mitchel (or Martin) Mil | do | Sep. 24, 1864 |
| Madden, Michael | do | Sep. 24, 1864 |
| Milmore, M. E | do | Sep. 24, 1864 |
| Murphy, Edward | do | Dec. 1, 1864 |
| Mills, John G | do | Dec 1, 1864 |
| Metzger, Leonardt | do | Nov. 25, 1864 |
| Meyer, George | Brookfield | Sep. 23, 1864 |
| Murphy, Michael | New Berlin | Nov. 12, 1863 |
| Moore, Patrick | do | Nov 12, 1863 |
| Martin, Christian | do | Nov. 12, 1863 |
| Malahoney, John | Milwaukee | Nov. 19, 1863 |
| Merchant, Henry | do | Nov. 9, 1863 |
| Mirchnahan, Tim | do | Nov. 9, 1863 |
| Mirrigan, Timothy | do | Nov. 9, 1863 |
| Melline, Geo | do | Nov. 9, 1863 |
| Mather, Martin | do | Nov. 9, 1863 |
| Mathews, ——— | do | Sep. 19, 1864 |
| Mannahan, Jacob | do | Sep. 19, 1864 |
| Morgan, Jas | do | Sep 19, 1864 |
| Montel, Timothy | do | Sep. 19, 1864 |
| Morris, Wm | do | Sep. 19, 1864 |
| Map, John | do | Nov. 14, 1864 |
| Mason, Nenison | do | Nov. 14, 1864 |
| Meroughs, Fred | do | Nov. 14, 1864 |
| Munson, Andrus | do | Nov. 14, 1864 |

| *Name* | *Residence.* | *Date* |
|---|---|---|
| Martin, Jas. | Milwaukee | Dec. 22, 1864 |
| Max, Phelix | do | Dec. 22, 1864 |
| Mullaty, Wm | do | Dec. 22, 1864 |
| Mason, Theo | do | Dec 22, 1864 |
| Meyer, H. H. | do | Nov. 9, 1863 |
| Morgan, Jas. | do | Nov. 9, 1863 |
| Morava, Joseph | do | Nov. 9, 1863 |
| Muller, Julius | do | Nov. 9, 1863 |
| Milldown, C. R. | do | Nov. 9, 1863 |
| Mattes, John | do | Nov. 19, 1863 |
| Miller, Ernest | do | Sep. 20, 1864 |
| Maier, John | do | Sep. 20, 1864 |
| Meyer, Fred | do | Sep. 20, 1864 |
| Mausle, John | do | Nov. 14, 1864 |
| Mally, J. | do | Nov. 10, 1863 |
| Mulholland, Andrew | do | Nov. 10, 1863 |
| Murphy, Pat. | do | Nov. 10, 1863 |
| Mulhein, J. | do | Nov 10, 1863 |
| Morton, A. H. | do | Nov. 10, 1863 |
| Mingea, J. | do | Nov 10, 1863 |
| Madden, John | do | Nov. 10, 1863 |
| Morrin, Pat. | do | Nov. 10, 1863 |
| Miller, Andrew E. | do | Nov. 10, 1863 |
| Mannin, C. | do | Nov. 10, 1863 |
| Munan, E. | do | Nov. 10, 1863 |
| Meloy, John | do | Nov. 10, 1863 |
| Madpan, Thomas | do | Nov 10, 1863 |
| Morgan, Stephen | do | Nov. 10, 1863 |
| Murphy, James | do | Nov. 10, 1863 |
| Melony, Patrick | do | Nov. 10, 1863 |
| Madder, M. | do | Nov. 10, 1863 |
| Myrath, M. | do | Nov. 10, 1863 |
| Maheny, Jerry | do | Sep 20, 1864 |
| Maran, J. W. | do | Sep. 20, 1864 |
| Messenger, M. C. | do | Sep. 20, 1864 |
| Murray, James | do | Sep. 20, 1864 |
| Martin, Thomas | do | Sep. 20, 1864 |
| Meyer, Leonard | do | Sep. 20, 1864 |
| Mooney, John | do | Sep. 20, 1864 |
| Murphy, E. | do | Sep. 20, 1864 |
| Murphy, H. | do | Sep. 20, 1864 |
| Molton, Amos | do | Sep. 20, 1864 |
| Murther, Edward | do | Sep. 20, 1864 |
| Murphy, Thomas | do | Sep. 20, 1864 |
| Mack, Peter | do | Nov. 15, 1864 |
| Maher, D. | do | Nov 15, 1864 |
| Molling, John | do | Nov. 15, 1864 |
| Malony, James | do | Nov. 15, 1864 |
| Maginnis, J. | do | Nov. 15, 1864 |
| Milligan, J. | do | Nov. 15, 1864 |
| Meper, Ed. | do | Nov. 15, 1864 |
| Mayhew, M. M. | do | Nov. 15, 1864 |
| Manerer, Christ | do | Nov. 15, 1864 |
| Megonniger, J. M. | do | Nov 15, 1864 |
| Mayer, John | do | Nov. 15, 1864 |
| Murphy, Patrick | do | Nov. 15, 1864 |
| Making, Michael | do | Nov. 15, 1864 |
| Murphy, James | do | Nov. 15, 1864 |
| Mason, James. | do | Nov. 15, 1864 |

| *Name.* | *Residence.* | *Date.* |
|---|---|---|
| Myer, M | Milwaukee | Nov. 15, 1864 |
| Murphy, John | do | Nov. 15, 1864 |
| Murray, Nicholas | do | Nov. 15, 1864 |
| Miller, Charles | do | Nov. 15, 1864 |
| Milonce, John | do | Nov. 15, 1864 |
| Mally, C. | do | Nov. 15, 1864 |
| Myrath, Hugh | do | Nov. 15, 1864 |
| Morgan, Henry | do | Nov. 16, 1864 |
| Maske, August | do | Nov. 16, 1864 |
| Mahan, Frederick | do | Nov. 16, 1864 |
| Michel, Pat | do | Nov. 16, 1864 |
| Millard, Samuel N. | do | Nov. 10, 1863 |
| Millard, Jesse | do | Nov. 10, 1863 |
| Miller, Joseph | do | |
| Mayer, Hugo | do | |
| Martin, Oliver | do | |
| Miser, Gotlieb | do | Nov. 10, 1863 |
| Maiser, Peter | do | Nov. 10, 1863 |
| Mullen, Thomas | do | Nov. 10, 1863 |
| Mockriezer, William | do | Nov. 10, 1863 |
| Mullen, Patrick | do | Sep. 21, 1864 |
| Mansing, August | do | Sep. 21, 1864 |
| Munce, John | do | Sep. 21, 1864 |
| Miehoff, Charles | do | Sep. 21, 1864 |
| Money, Walfram | do | Sep. 21, 1864 |
| Miller, Adam | do | Sep. 21, 1864 |
| Mopman, August | do | Sep. 21, 1864 |
| Morske, Lawrence | do | Sep. 21, 1864 |
| Marker, Lary | do | Sep. 21, 1864 |
| Magher, Michael | do | Sep. 21, 1864 |
| Muchter, or Wuchter, Andrew | do | Sep. 21, 1864 |
| Markwick, Joseph | do | Sep. 21, 1864 |
| Messy, J. | do | Nov. 25, 1864 |
| Murphy, John | do | Nov. 25, 1864 |
| Myer, Christian | do | Nov. 25, 1864 |
| Murphy, Pat | do | Jan. 11, 1865 |
| Murphy, John | do | Jan. 11, 1865 |
| Murray, Patrick | do | Jan. 11, 1865 |
| Martin, John | do | Nov. 10, 1863 |
| Moody, ——— | do | Nov. 10, 1863 |
| Macan, Pat | do | Nov. 10, 1863 |
| Murry, William | do | Nov. 10, 1863 |
| Manning, W. C. | do | Nov. 10, 1863 |
| Miga, *Miza* Conrad | do | Nov. 10, 1863 |
| Mannix, Thomas | do | Sep. 21, 1864 |
| Monroe, James | do | Sep. 21, 1864 |
| Mellag, John | do | Sep. 21, 1864 |
| Mahar, John | do | Sep. 21, 1864 |
| Merrill, Julius | do | Sep. 21, 1864 |
| Morgan, James | do | Nov. 10, 1863 |
| Manning, Luke | do | Nov. 10, 1863 |
| Messing, Peter | do | Nov. 10, 1863 |
| Mathias, George | do | Nov. 10, 1863 |
| Muller, Ustamus | do | Nov. 10, 1863 |
| Muller, William | do | Nov. 10, 1863 |
| Mick, Joseph | do | Nov. 10, 1863 |
| Mung, Michael | do | Nov. 10, 1863 |
| Marremer, John | do | Nov. 10, 1863 |
| Matskia, Charles | do | Nov. 10, 1863 |

| *Name.* | *Residence.* | *Date* |
|---|---|---|
| Morgan, John | Milwaukee | Nov. 10, 1863 |
| Marsch, William | do | Nov. 10, 1863 |
| Mack, Thomas | do | Nov. 15, 1864 |
| Memetz, John | do | Nov. 15, 1864 |
| Mery, Conrad | do | Nov. 15, 1864 |
| Murphy, Edward | do | Jan. 19, 1865 |
| Morgenworth, Ernist | do | Jan. 19, 1865 |
| Moroyce, Charles | do | Jan. 19, 1865 |
| Miller, Charles | do | Jan. 19, 1865 |
| Mitchel, James | do | Nov. 11, 1863 |
| Matzke, A | do | Sep. 21, 1864 |
| Michaels, ——— | do | Sep. 21, 1864 |
| Mollett, Christian | do | Sep. 21, 1864 |
| Meppamock, K. Johann | do | |
| Madler, Heinrich | do | Sep. 21, 1864 |
| Merow, Heinrich | do | Sep. 21, 1864 |
| Michell, Jos ph | do | Sep. 21, 1864 |
| Messinger, John | do | Nov. 25, 1864 |
| Mackey, Andrew | do | Nov. 30, 1864 |
| Miller, Fritz | do | Nov. 30, 1864 |
| Miller, Henry | do | Nov. 30, 1864 |
| Meyer, Johann | do | Jan. 26, 1865 |
| Matheuvers, Nick | do | Jan. 26, 1865 |
| Meyer, George | do | Nov. 11, 1863 |
| Mull, Henry | do | Dec. 7, 1864 |
| Meyer, John | do | Dec. 7, 1864 |
| Mitchel, Jacob | do | Dec. 7, 1864 |
| Mickelray, James | Granville | Sep. 22, 1864 |
| Morl, George | do | Sep. 22, 1864 |
| Miller, John | do | Sep. 22, 1864 |
| Miller, John | Wauwatosa | Nov. 11, 1863 |
| Morrison, James | do | Nov. 11, 1863 |
| Mason, John | do | Nov. 11, 1863 |
| Meitz, James | Greenfield | Nov. 11, 1863 |
| Mages, Wolfgang | do | Sep. 22, 1864 |
| Martin, N. W | Lake | Sep. 22, 1864 |
| Morlit, John | Caledonia | Sep. 23, 1864 |
| Martin, John | do | Sep. 23, 1864 |
| Miller, George D | do | Sep. 23, 1864 |
| Miller, Nicholas | do | Dec. 7, 1864 |
| Michels, Peter | Kenosha | Nov. 12, 1863 |
| Myson, Henry | Wheatland | Dec. 14, 1864 |
| Meres, Jacob | Paris | Sep. 24, 1864 |
| Mellor, Samuel H | Salem | Nov. 12, 1863 |
| Murphy, Michael | Bristol | Nov. 12, 1863 |
| Monroe, Alfred | do | Nov. 12, 1863 |
| Martin, Robert | Richmond | Nov. 12, 1863 |
| Murphy, John | Whitewater | Nov. 12, 1863 |
| Mulharen, Patrick | do | Nov. 12, 1863 |
| Mattocks, Chris | Linn | Nov. 12, 1863 |
| Mist, James | East Troy | Sep. 24, 1864 |
| Motherway, John | do | Dec. 2, 1864 |
| Morey, J. H | do | Dec. 2, 1864 |
| Medberry, George W | do | Dec. 2, 1864 |
| Mullinger, Wm. R | Spring Prairie | Nov. 12, 1863 |
| Melgrave, John | Bloomfield | Nov. 12, 1863 |
| Manny, Michael | Summit | Sep. 22, 1864 |
| Meyers, Julius | Oconomowoc | Sep. 22, 1864 |
| Meyers, Conrad | do | Sep. 22, 1864 |

| *Name.* | *Residence.* | *Date.* |
|---|---|---|
| Mayhew, John | Oconomowoc | Nov. 12, 1863 |
| Martiron, William | Pewaukee | Nov. 12, 1863 |
| Malkins, James | do | Sep. 22, 1864 |
| Molton, John S | do | Sep. 22, 1864 |
| Murphy, James A | Waukesha | Nov. 12, 1863 |
| Meurs, Henry | Lake | Sep. 22, 1864 |
| Marks, Peter | do | Sep. 22, 1864 |
| Munech, Anthony | Oak Creek | Nov. 11, 1863 |
| Minch, John | do | Nov. 11, 1863 |
| Mangan, Edward | do | Sep. 22, 1864 |
| May, Mat | Racine | Nov. 11, 1863 |
| Morgan, E. H | do | Nov. 11, 1863 |
| Mills, John | do | Nov. 11, 1863 |
| Malone, Martin | do | Nov. 11, 1863 |
| Meiv, John | do | Sep. 24, 1864 |
| Mainland, Sinclair | do | Sep. 24, 1864 |
| Miller, John | do | Sep. 24, 1864 |
| March, John | do | Sep. 24, 1864 |
| Meinzer, Gottleib | do | Sep. 24, 1864 |
| Muller, Mat | do | Nov. 11, 1863 |
| Monitson, P. C | do | Sep. 22, 1864 |
| Megehan, Edward | do | Sep. 22, 1864 |
| Mullin, John | do | Sep. 22, 1864 |
| Martin, Peter | do | Sep. 22, 1864 |
| Madsen, Mathias L | do | Jan. 19, 1865 |
| Mashek, V | do | Jan. 19, 1865 |
| Mathew, John | do | Nov. 11, 1863 |
| Mow, Orrin | Dover | Dec. 10, 1864 |
| Miller, Hans | Raymond | Sep. 23, 1864 |
| More, William H | do | Dec. 9, 1864 |
| Mahaffy, Alexander | do | Dec. 9, 1864 |
| Moyle, Robert | do | Dec. 9, 1864 |
| Melville, Moses | Caledonia | Nov. 11, 1863 |
| McPhillips, Henry | do | Nov. 15, 1864 |
| McClive, James | do | Nov. 15, 1864 |
| McGregor, William H | do | Nov. 15, 1864 |
| McKenzie, George | do | Nov. 15, 1864 |
| McCoum, —— | do | Nov. 15, 1864 |
| McCamvay, Michael | do | Nov. 15, 1864 |
| McElegate, B | do | Nov. 15, 1864 |
| McCarley, James | do | Nov. 15, 1864 |
| McCumins, James | do | Nov. 15, 1864 |
| McCurdy, Peter | do | Nov. 15, 1864 |
| McCarty, H | do | Jan. 11, 1865 |
| McBride, Terance | do | Jan. 11, 1865 |
| McHenry, —— | do | Jan. 11, 1865 |
| McCarthy, John | do | Jan. 11, 1865 |
| McGrath, Edward | do | Nov. 10, 1863 |
| McCreany, Thomas | do | Nov. 10, 1863 |
| McCuskor, John | do | Sep. 21, 1864 |
| McGrath, Daniel | do | Sep. 21, 1864 |
| McMannis, John | do | Sep. 21, 1864 |
| McKay, Alexander | do | Sep. 21, 1864 |
| McDenny, Edward | do | Sep. 21, 1864 |
| McCready, William | do | Sep. 21, 1864 |
| McGrath, Thomas | do | Nov. 10, 1863 |
| McCall, Hughst | do | Nov. 10, 1863 |
| McGee, Michael | do | Nov. 10, 1863 |
| McGregor, —— | do | Nov. 10, 1863 |

| *Name.* | *Residence.* | *Date.* |
|---|---|---|
| McCrevey, Henry | Caledonia | Nov. 10, 1863 |
| McGrath, Michael | Milwaukee | Nov. 9, 1863 |
| McCarty, Flurty | do | Nov. 9, 1863 |
| McGorun, Edwin | do | Nov. 9, 1863 |
| McHardy, Peter | do | Sep. 19, 1864 |
| McGee, George | do | Sep. 19, 1864 |
| McLane, Thomas | do | Sep. 19, 1864 |
| McGinnis, John | do | Sep. 19, 1864 |
| McGoven, Edgar | do | Sep. 19, 1864 |
| McGoren, Edwin | do | Sep. 19, 1864 |
| McGrery, James | do | Nov. 14, 1864 |
| McNorton, Duncan | do | Dec. 22, 1864 |
| McDowell, ——— | do | Nov. 9, 1863 |
| McGrath, Michael | do | Nov. 10, 1863 |
| McHealy, ——— | do | Nov. 10, 1863 |
| McLanden, F | do | Nov. 10, 1863 |
| McLaughlin, Pat | do | Nov. 10, 1863 |
| McEran, E. H | do | Nov. 10, 1863 |
| McCrittick, Charles | do | Nov. 10, 1863 |
| McCarty, James | do | Nov. 10, 1863 |
| McKitrick, James | do | Nov. 10, 1863 |
| McDougherty, Luke | do | Nov. 10, 1863 |
| McManus, B | do | Nov. 10, 1863 |
| McMann, John | do | Nov. 10, 1863 |
| McNaughton, Thomas | do | Sep. 20, 1864 |
| McBride, Mathew | do | Sep. 20, 1864 |
| McIntire, Peter | do | Sept. 20, 1864 |
| McKinley, T. J | do | Nov. 15, 1864 |
| McGryn, John | do | Sep. 21, 1864 |
| McCane, Michael | do | Sep. 21, 1864 |
| McShane, John | do | Nov. 30, 1864 |
| McCohnahy, Hugh | do | Nov. 30, 1864 |
| McGulpin, Frederick | do | Sep. 22, 1864 |
| McCarta, Andrew | Greenfield | Nov 11, 1863 |
| McCready, Henry | Lake | Sep. 22, 1864 |
| McKittrich, William | Franklin | Nov. 11, 1863 |
| McDonald, Daniel | Oak Creek | Sep. 22, 1864 |
| McLane, Joel | Racine | Nov. 11, 1863 |
| McQuinn, Patrick | do | Sep. 22, 1864 |
| McLaughlin, J | do | Nov. 11, 1863 |
| McCarty, Timothy | Dover | Sep. 23, 1864 |
| McManus, Charles | do | Sep. 23, 1864 |
| McCarty, Arty | do | Dec. 10, 1864 |
| McCovey, Michael | Rochester | Nov. 11, 1864 |
| McNamara, Martin | Waterford | Nov. 11, 1864 |
| McDonald, ——— | Caledonia | Nov. 11, 1863 |
| McDonald Thomas | Brighton | Nov. 12, 1863 |
| McFee, J. S | do | Nov. 12, 1863 |
| McFee, H B | do | Nov. 12, 1863 |
| McCormick, David | Randall | Sep. 24, 1864 |
| McFadden, Archer | do | Dec. 16, 1864 |
| McMulty, Patrick | Sugar Creek | Nov. 12, 1863 |
| McGraw, Edward | Geneva | Nov. 12, 1863 |
| McClure, William | Ottawa | Nov. 12, 1863 |
| McMahon, John | Oconomowoc | Sep. 22, 1864 |
| McCornnock, Roger | do | Sep. 22, 1864 |
| McMullen, Angus | Vernon | Sep. 24, 1864 |
| McCarty, James | Menomonee | Sep. 24, 1864 |
| McCarty, Dennis | do | Sep. 24, 1864 |

| *Name.* | *Residence* | *Date.* |
|---|---|---|
| McCarty, Philip | Menomonee | Dec. 1, 1864 |
| McBride, John jr | do | Dec. 1, 1864 |
| McGarity, Patrick | Muskego | Sep. 24, 1864 |
| Mack, John | Turtle | Nov. 12, 1863 |
| Morgan, Erick | Clinton | Nov. 12, 1863 |
| Mackey, Ganson B | Center | Nov. 12, 1863 |
| Mannering, William | Janesville | Nov. 12, 1863 |
| Mealy, Hiram O | Lima | Nov. 12, 1863 |
| Mahana, Daniel | Dunn | Nov. 13, 1863 |
| Maloy, Patrick | Fitchburg | Nov. 13, 1863 |
| Moore, Thomas | Blue Mounds | Sep. 19, 1864 |
| Miller, Herman | Sun Prairie | Nov. 13, 1863 |
| Murdaugh, James E | do | Oct. 15, 1864 |
| Murphy, Pat | Westport | Nov. 13, 1863 |
| Myers, Harry | Bristol | Nov. 13, 1863 |
| Masterson, John | Sullivan | |
| Martin, A. S | Lake Mills | |
| Moore, Henry T | West Point | Nov. 16, 1863 |
| Malone, Patrick | Columbus | Nov. 16, 1863 |
| Muldoon, James | Pacific or Portage City | Nov. 16, 1863 |
| Maratz, William | Randolph | Nov. 16, 1863 |
| Marquhart, William | Scott | Nov. 16, 1863 |
| Macking, Michael | Milford | Oct. 22, 1864 |
| Merrin, Thomas | Watertown | Sep. 20, 1864 |
| Mesic, Peter J | do | Oct 15, 1864 |
| Mourn, Thomas | do | Oct. 15, 1864 |
| Marshall, Thomas | Fort Winnebago | Sep. 21, 1864 |
| McCarty, John | Janesville | Nov. 12, 1863 |
| McCoy, Andrew | Madison | Nov. 13, 1863 |
| McNeeley, T | Burke | Nov. 13, 1863 |
| McIntosh, Henry | Arlington | Nov. 16, 1863 |
| McCormick, Michael | Pacific | Sep. 21, 1864 |
| McCae, Edward | Watertown | Sep. 20, 1864 |
| Mack, Timothy | Ithaca, Orion or BuenaVista | Nov. 14, 1863 |
| Manahaney, Dan'l | Ridgeway | Sep. 28, 1864 |
| Murrey, Peter | do | Oct. 28, 1864 |
| Mahoney, Thos | do | Oct. 28, 1864 |
| Mehan, John | Henrietta | Sep. 26, 1864 |
| Murphey, Edward | Rockbridge | Sep. 26, 1864 |
| Murry, Christopher | Clyde | Sep. 27, 1864 |
| Minor, Jacob | Dodgeville | Sep. 28, 1864 |
| Muer, Jacob | do | Sep. 28, 1864 |
| Mitchell, Joseph | do | Oct. 28, 1864 |
| Mann, J. H | do | Oct. 28, 1864 |
| Martin, Sam'l | do | Oct. 28, 1864 |
| Miller, Aaron | do | Nov. 19, 1864 |
| Mitchell, Herman | Highland | Sep. 28, 1864 |
| Mills, Thos | do | Sep. 28, 1864 |
| Marten, Frank | do | Sep. 28, 1864 |
| Manning, Edward | do | Sep. 28, 1864 |
| Metcalf, Geo | do | Oct. 28, 1864 |
| Marming, John | do | Oct. 28, 1864 |
| More, Morty | do | Nov. 19, 1864 |
| Mills, Jas | do | Nov. 19, 1864 |
| Mera, Dan'l | do | Dec. 7, 1864 |
| Madden, John | Moscow | Nov. 14, 1863 |
| Miller, John | Willow Springs | Oct. 4, 1864 |
| Magee, Arthur | WhiteOak Springs or M'tcello | Nov. 16, 1863 |
| Meloy, Jas | Benton | Sep. 29, 1864 |

| *Name* | *Residence.* | *Date.* |
|---|---|---|
| Meloy, John | Benton | Sep. 29, 1864 |
| Monahan, John, sr | do | Sep. 29, 1864 |
| Mulligan, Jas | do | Sep. 29, 1864 |
| Malone, John | do | Sep. 29, 1864 |
| Murphy, Pat | New Diggings | Sep. 29, 1864 |
| Murphy, John | do | Sep. 29, 1864 |
| Martin, Miles | Elk Grove | Nov. 16, 1863 |
| Murphy, Arthur | Clayton | Sept. 30, 1864 |
| Meloin, Thos | Utica | Oct. 29, 1864 |
| Meyers, John | Beetown | Oct. 1, 1864 |
| Maker, J. O | do | Oct. 1, 1864 |
| Morshead, Wm | Potosi | Nov. 19, 1863 |
| Morshead, John | Harrison | Nov. 19, 1863 |
| Metcalf, Hillory | Hazel Green | Nov. 19, 1863 |
| Martin, John Hardy | Prairie du Sac | Nov. 20, 1863 |
| Mally, Peter | Seneca | Sep. 30, 1864 |
| Miller, Sylvester | Eastman | Oct. 29, 1864 |
| Miller, Albert | do | Oct. 29, 1864 |
| Morris, Robert | do | Jan. 6, 1865 |
| Mulligan, Thos | Dellona | Oct. 3, 1864 |
| Murphy, John | do | Oct. 3, 1864 |
| Maxwell, Lewis | Washington | Oct. 3, 1864 |
| Meryner, Mathias | Bear Creek | Oct. 3, 1864 |
| Morawa, Menzel | Blue River | Nov. 19, 1864 |
| Mackham, Edgar | do | Dec. 7, 1864 |
| McDonald, Thos | Ithaca, Orion or BuenaVista | Nov. 14, 1863 |
| McDermott, Thos | Ridgeway | Nov. 14, 1863 |
| McMullin, John | do | Nov. 14, 1863 |
| McDowell, John | Dodgeville | Oct. 28, 1864 |
| McClarky, Patrick | do | Oct. 28, 1864 |
| McGiff, Thos | Highland | Sep. 28, 1864 |
| McFarland, Marshall | do | Sep. 28, 1864 |
| McNair, John | do | Sep. 28, 1864 |
| McGuire, Mathew | do | Nov. 19, 1864 |
| McMullen, Sam'l | do | Nov. 19, 1864 |
| McGuire, Jas., jr | do | Dec. 7, 1865 |
| McWilliams, Rob't | Moscow | Sep. 28, 1864 |
| McCartney, Pat | Kendall or Belmont | Nov. 16, 1863 |
| McGuin, H | do | Oct. 4, 1864 |
| McDermott, John | do | Oct. 4, 1864 |
| McIntee, Jas | do | Nov. 19, 1864 |
| McCoffrey, John | Benton | Nov. 16, 1864 |
| McMahon, Jas | do | Nov. 16, 1864 |
| McCabe, Peter | do | Nov. 16, 1864 |
| McMahon, B | do | Nov. 16, 1864 |
| McGuire, M | do | Nov. 16, 1864 |
| McMann, Jas | do | Nov. 16, 1863 |
| McMannus, John | do | Sep. 29, 1864 |
| McCabe H | do | Sep. 29, 1864 |
| McGaffrey B | do | Sep. 29, 1864 |
| McManus, Jas | do | Sep. 29, 1864 |
| McDonald, John, jr | do | Sep. 29, 1864 |
| McCabe, John | do | Sep. 29, 1864 |
| McGrain, Pat | do | Sep. 29, 1864 |
| McDonnell, Thos | Fayette | Nov. 14, 1863 |
| McDonald, John | New Diggins | Nov. 16, 1863 |
| McManus, Jas | do | Sep. 29, 1864 |
| McKenna, Pat'k | do | Sep. 29, 1864 |
| McGlouchlin, Pat'k | Clayton or Utica | Nov. 18, 1863 |

| *Name.* | *Residence.* | *Date.* |
|---|---|---|
| McMillan, Henry, jr. | Clayton or Utica | Nov. 18, 1863 |
| McCormick, John | Clayton | Sep. 30, 1864 |
| McEvoy, John | Troy or Spring Green | Nov. 20, 1863 |
| McGee, Thos. | Bloom | Sep. 26, 1864 |
| McCarthy, Dennis | Blue River | Oct. 1, 1864 |
| McDonald, Enis | Dellona | Oct. 3, 1864 |
| McLaughlin, M. | do | Oct. 3, 1864 |
| McCarvill, James | Bear Creek | Oct. 3, 1864 |
| McGuire, Jas. | Franklin | Oct. 3, 1864 |
| McKinney, Rich'd | Millville | Oct. 28, 1864 |
| Martin, Sam'l | La Crosse Co. | Nov. 16, 1863 |
| Maise, Sam'l | do | Nov. 16, 1863 |
| Melone, Wm. | Campbell | Sep. 19, 1864 |
| McGuire, Pat | Chippewa Co. | Nov. 20, 1863 |
| Meagher, Wm. | do | Nov. 20, 1863 |
| Massell, Jocko | do | Nov. 20, 1863 |
| McKinley, Mike | do | Nov. 20, 1863 |
| Merin, Emmor | do | Nov. 20, 1863 |
| Margeson, Ole | Bloomer Prairie | Sep. 27, 1864 |
| McDonald | Anson | Sep. 27, 1864 |
| McMellan, Duncan | do | Sep. 27, 1864 |
| Mason, Harvey | do | Sep. 28, 1864 |
| McCenville, Dan | Chippewa Falls | Nov. 2, 1864 |
| Mulligan, Dan | do | Nov. 2, 1864 |
| Mulligan, J. | do | Nov. 2, 1864 |
| Mandalert, Jos. | do | Nov. 2, 1864 |
| Miller, J. W. | Jackson Co. | Nov. 18, 1863 |
| McGregor, Jno. | Adams Co. | Nov. 28, 1863 |
| Miller, Ferdinand | do | Nov. 23, 1863 |
| Manley, Lewis | Richfield | Sep. 26, 1864 |
| Mosher, Jas. H. | New Haven | Sep. 26, 1864 |
| McClemarch, Hugh | Jackson | Sep. 26, 1864 |
| Morris, Jno. | Springville | Sep. 26, 1864 |
| Morris, Thos. | do | Sep. 26, 1864 |
| Miller, Henry | Portage Co. | Nov. 23, 1863 |
| Morris, Winchell | Juneau Co. | Nov. 23, 1863 |
| Matthews, Moses E. | Kildare | Sep. 19, 1864 |
| McEntee, Chas. | do | Sep. 19, 1864 |
| Murphy, Lawrence | do | Oct. 31, 1864 |
| Mackin, John | Seven Mile Creek | Sept. 19, 1864 |
| McGee, Edward I. | do | Sep. 19, 1864 |
| McEvoy, Michael | Plymouth | Sep. 19, 1864 |
| Murphy, Morris | do | Sep. 19, 1864 |
| McEvoy, James | do | Oct. 31, 1864 |
| McEvoy, Patrick | do | Oct. 31, 1864 |
| Matthews, Thomas | Lemonweir | Sep. 19, 1864 |
| Monroe, Samuel | do | Sep. 19, 1864 |
| Meaton, Robert | do | Oct. 31, 1864 |
| Murphy, Jeremiah | Wonewoc | Sep. 19, 1864 |
| Morehead, J. A. | do | Sep. 19, 1864 |
| Mosier, David | do | Oct. 31, 1864 |
| Martin, Thomas | Summit | Sep. 19, 1864 |
| McMurphy, Iva | do | Sep. 19, 1864 |
| Miller, William | do | Sep. 19, 1864 |
| Matthews, Charles | do | Oct. 31, 1864 |
| Milan, Thomas | Clearfield | Sep. 19, 1864 |
| Morris, George | do | Sep. 19, 1864 |
| Michael, Christian | do | Sep. 19, 1864 |
| McDowell, William | Dunn Co. | Nov. 23, 1863 |

| *Name.* | *Residence.* | *Date.* |
|---|---|---|
| Murphy, John | Eau Galle | Sep. 27, 1864 |
| Murray, Thomas | do | Sep. 27, 1864 |
| Moore, William | do | Sep. 27, 1864 |
| Murray, Patrick | do | Sep. 27, 1864 |
| McGilton, William | do | Sept. 27, 1864 |
| Murphy, Patr'k (2d) | do | Sept. 27, 1864 |
| Mulligan, James | do | Sept. 27, 1864 |
| McCarty, Joel | do | Nov. 2, 1864 |
| Myer, Joseph | do | Nov. 2, 1864 |
| Morrisett, Frank | Wood Co. | Nov. 18, 1863 |
| Montgomery, Henry | Dexter | Sep. 22, 1864 |
| McEwen, James | Centralia | Sep. 22, 1864 |
| Martin, D | do | Sep. 22, 1864 |
| McClure, Charles B | Eaton | Sep 20, 1864 |
| Maynard, Elisha | Adrian | Sep. 20, 1864 |
| Morgans, David | do | Nov. 10, 1864 |
| Mahr, Peter | Tomah | Sep. 20, 1864 |
| McCauley, Peter | Oak Dale | Sep. 20, 1864 |
| Murphy, James | Clifton | Sep. 20, 1864 |
| Murphy, Richard | do | Nov. 10, 1864 |
| Manning, Edward | Glendale | Nov. 10, 1864 |
| McDermott, Brian | do | Nov. 10, 1864 |
| Martin, Charles | Ettrick | Sep. 21, 1864 |
| Mahoney, Patrick | do | Sep. 21, 1864 |
| Manson, Andrew | do | Sep. 21, 1864 |
| McCarty, James | do | Sep. 21, 1864 |
| McDonald, David | Bergen | Sep. 21, 1864 |
| Morgan, Eleazer A | Genoa | Sep. 21, 1864 |
| Martin, George | do | Sep. 21, 1864 |
| Mines, Neil | Franklin | Sep. 21, 1864 |
| Munyon, Thomas | do | Sep. 21, 1864 |
| Maxwell, James | do | Sep. 21, 1864 |
| Mines, Michael | do | Nov. 15, 1864 |
| McShane, Barney | do | Nov. 15, 1864 |
| Munyon, Wesley | do | Nov. 15, 1864 |
| McHenry, Joseph | Webster | Nov. 15, 1864 |
| Mallory, Porter | Lincoln | Nov. 14, 1864 |
| Munson, Nels | Monroe | Nov. 14, 1864 |
| Marshall, Josiah | New Haven | Nov. 14, 1864 |
| Morgan, Henry | Linwood | Sep. 22, 1864 |
| Murphy, Patrick | do | Sep. 22, 1864 |
| Martin, Edward | Sharon | Sep. 22, 1864 |
| Martin, Horace | do | Sep. 22, 1864 |
| McInvoe, James | Belmont | Sep. 22, 1864 |
| Moore, Patrick | Hull | Sep. 22, 1864 |
| McNally, John | Emerald | Sep. 23, 1864 |
| Murphy, William | St. Croix | Sep. 23, 1864 |
| McNaton, Alex | Eau Galle | Sep. 23, 1864 |
| McRoberts, David | do | Nov. 3, 1864 |
| McCartney, Michael | Rush River | Sep. 23, 1864 |
| Martin, Michael | Erin Prairie | Sep. 23, 1864 |
| McCartney, John | do | Sep. 23, 1864 |
| Meath, Peter | do | Sep. 23, 1864 |
| Meath, William | do | Sep. 23, 1864 |
| Martin, Patrick | do | Nov. 3, 1864 |
| McNamara, Thomas | do | Nov. 3, 1864 |
| Madison, John | Naples | Sep. 26, 1864 |
| Mathing, Frederick | Albany | Sep. 27, 1864 |
| Mithin, William | Waubeck | Sep. 27, 1864 |

| *Name.* | *Residence.* | *Date.* |
|---|---|---|
| Mundy, J. L. | Waudeck | Nov. 16, 1864 |
| McKernan Felix | Pleasant Valley | Sep. 27, 1864 |
| McKernan, Thomas | do | Sep. 27, 1864 |
| Moon, George | do | Sep. 27, 1864 |
| Moon, Samuel | do | Sep. 27, 1864 |
| Merriman, J. M. | Trimbell | Nov. 3, 1864 |
| Moser, Frank | Union | Nov. 3, 1864 |
| Miles, S. A. | Kewaunee | Nov. 20, 1863 |
| Marthiensen, Peter | Carlton | Nov. 20, 1863 |
| Miller, Joseph | do | Dec. 29, 1864 |
| Manferts, Gabriel | Red River | Dec. 29, 1864 |
| Maset, Jean | do | Dec. 29, 1864 |
| Maceaux, Julian | do | Dec. 29, 1864 |
| Muly, Peter | do | Dec. 29, 1864 |
| Michaels, John | Pierce | Dec. 29, 1864 |
| Montford, Mansel | do | Dec. 29, 1864 |
| Martle, Isadore | Coryville | Dec. 29, 1864 |
| Maher, John | Franklin | Dec. 29, 1864 |
| Mennier, John | Lincoln | Dec. 29, 1864 |
| Mullins, James | Maple Grove | Nov. 21, 1863 |
| Morseck, Martin | do | Dec. 29, 1864 |
| Metz, Ejetus | Cato | Nov 21, 1863 |
| Michelson, Andrew | Two Creeks | Dec. 28, 1864 |
| Martinick, John | Cooperstown | Dec 29, 1864 |
| McCarthy, Timothy | Kossuth | Dec. 29, 1864 |
| McKeough, Michael | do | Dec. 29, 1864 |
| Marsck, John | Newton | Dec. 29, 1864 |
| Maloney, Timothy | Neenah | Nov. 25, 1863 |
| McDowell, Jasper | Oshkosh | Nov. 23, 1863 |
| McCloud, James | do | Nov. 23, 1863 |
| McClure, Amos | do | Nov. 23, 1863 |
| Murphy, Henry | Omro | Nov. 23, 1863 |
| Martin, Frederick | Rushford | Nov. 24, 1863 |
| Marata, John | do | Nov. 24, 1863 |
| McAlister, John | | Nov. 24, 1863 |
| McMahon, Patrick | | Nov. 24, 1863 |
| Matthew, Kelley | Utica | Nov. 24, 1863 |
| Mongan, Timothy | Poygan | Nov. 5, 1864 |
| McAllister, Jno | Berlin city | Nov. 24, 1863 |
| Midhurst, Thos | do | Nov. 24, 1863 |
| Mahoney, Jno | Mackford | Nov. 24, 1863 |
| Miller, Henry | Manchester | Nov. 24, 1863 |
| McQueen, Thomas | Waupaca Co | Nov. 25, 1863 |
| Minton, Henry | do | Nov. 25, 1863 |
| McIntyre, W. B. D | Iola | Nov. 25, 1863 |
| Mattenson, Andreas | do | Nov. 5, 1864 |
| Martin, Horace | do | Dec. 31, 1864 |
| Martin, Nathan | Larabee | Nov. 5, 1864 |
| Matteson, Charles | do | Nov. 5, 1864 |
| Muntcet, Frederick | Bear Creek | Nov. 5, 1864 |
| Martin, Andrew | Lebanon | Nov. 5, 1864 |
| McCarty, Patriek | do | Nov. 5, 1864 |
| Maloy, Michael | do | Nov. 5, 1864 |
| McClellan, Samuel | Caledonia | Nov. 5, 1864 |
| Marsh, Jno | do | Nov. 5, 1864 |
| McHugh, Alexander | do | Dec. 31, 1864 |
| Morris, Hiram | Weyauwega | Nov. 5, 1865 |
| Mumbim, Henry | do | Dec. 31, 1864 |
| McCall, Alexander | do | Dec. 31, 1864 |

| *Name.* | *Residence.* | *Date.* |
|---|---|---|
| Moon, Myron G | St. Lawrence | Nov. 5, 1864 |
| Moses, Lorenzo D | do | Nov. 5, 1864 |
| McInnery, Thomas | do | Nov. 5, 1864 |
| Maas, William | Appleton | Nov. 27, 1863 |
| Miller, B. F | do | Nov. 27, 1863 |
| Mitchel, —— | Center | Nov. 27, 1863 |
| Mather, Martin | do | Nov. 27, 1863 |
| Mathes, Jno | do | Dec. 28, 1864 |
| McDonald, Wm | Outagamie Co | Nov. 27, 1863 |
| McNoett, Ezekiel | Black Creek | Dec. 28, 1864 |
| Miller, Dedric | Freedom | Dec. 28, 1864 |
| Mitchell, James | Grand Chute | Dec. 28, 1864 |
| McMurdo, Jas. jr | Hortonia | Dec. 28, 1864 |
| Mass, Frederick | do | Dec. 28, 1863 |
| Manis, Wm | Green Bay | Nov. 27, 1863 |
| Madigan, Dennis | Holland | Nov. 27, 1863 |
| McCabe, Peter | do | Dec. 28, 1864 |
| McCabe, Patrick | do | Dec. 28, 1864 |
| Manin, Patrick | Lawrence | Nov. 27, 1863 |
| Mamsaid, Leopold | Humboldt | Dec. 28, 1864 |
| Moore, Wm | Wrightstown | Dec. 28, 1864 |
| Moran, Wm | Suamico | Dec. 28, 1864 |
| Montgomery, Jno | Marinette | Nov. 28, 1863 |
| McDonald, Geo | Oconto | Nov. 28, 1863 |
| Mister, Frederick | do | Nov. 28, 1863 |
| Monroe, Jno | do | Nov. 28, 1863 |
| McDonald, D. J | Peshtigo | Nov. 28, 1863 |
| McPhail, Wm | do | Nov. 28, 1863 |
| Mann, Wm | do | Nov. 28, 1864 |
| Mann, Peter | Stiles | Nov. 28, 1864 |
| McQuarin, —— | Little Suamico | Nov. 28, 1864 |
| Moles. Luke | Pensaukee | Dec. 29, 1864 |
| Mathess, Rudolf | Mecan | Nov. 1, 1864 |
| McIntire, James | Buffalo | Nov. 1, 1864 |
| McQuaters, Jno | Springfield | Nov. 1, 1864 |
| Munroe, G. H | Newton | Nov. 1, 1864 |
| Meers, Jas. K | do | Nov. 1, 1863 |
| McGever, Jno | Douglas | Dec. 31, 1864 |
| Murphy, James | do | Dec. 31, 1864 |
| Morris, Thomas W | Aurora | Nov. 2, 1864 |
| Moran, Christy | Warren | Nov. 2, 1864 |
| Minor, Reuben | Richford | Nov. 2, 1864 |
| Monrone, Maxton | do | Nov. 2, 1864 |
| Miller, Jno | do | Nov. 2, 1864 |
| Mullen, Nelson | do | Dec. 31, 1864 |
| Mott, Gideon | do | Dec. 31, 1864 |
| Montgomery, Geo. B | Coloma | Dec. 31, 1864 |
| Maxon, Jas. W | do | Nov. 2, 1864 |
| McFarlin, Wm | do | Nov. 2, 1864 |
| McClaughlin, Clandius | do | Nov. 2, 1864 |
| Mitchell, J. B | Plainfield | Nov. 2, 1864 |
| Menz, A | Poysippi | Dec. 31, 1864 |

## N

| *Name.* | *Residence.* | *Date.* |
|---|---|---|
| Newman, Abel | Springville | Nov. 19, 1863 |
| Niles, Albert | Fox Lake | Nov. 19, 1863 |
| Nairy, John | Elba | Nov. 20, 1863 |
| Nimuon, Frederick | Emmett | Oct. 11, 1864 |

| *Name.* | *Residence.* | *Date.* |
|---|---|---|
| Nemis, Yacum | Leroy | Oct. 4, 1864 |
| Neumeisler, Loui | Herman | Oct. 18, 1864 |
| Nail, William jr | Trenton | Nov. 20, 1863 |
| Nelson, Christopher | Ashippun | Nov. 21, 1863 |
| Nelson, Andrew | Erin | Dec. 1, 1864 |
| Nelson Christopher | do | Dec. 1, 1864 |
| Ney, William | Barton | Oct. 12, 1864 |
| Numins, Peter | Polk | Oct. 12, 1864 |
| Neiderkon, John | Belgium | Oct. 13, 1863 |
| Nepper, John | do | Oct. 13, 1863 |
| Neis, Peter Jerome | do | Oct. 13, 1863 |
| Nappel, Peter | do | Dec. 1, 1864 |
| Niesen, Gerhard | Fredonia | Oct. 14, 1864 |
| Noesen, Peter | do | Dec. 1, 1864 |
| Nenens, Peter | do | Nov. 21, 1863 |
| Nolsy, Charles | Grafton | Oct. 13, 1864 |
| Neuthal, August | do | Jan. 27, 1865 |
| Nelson, Lars | Saukville | Oct. 14, 1864 |
| Nack, Christolf | Sheboygan | Oct. 25, 1864 |
| Nenig, Nick | Moselle | Oct. 18, 1864 |
| Nenig —— | do | Oct. 18, 1864 |
| Norwood, John H | Sheboygan Falls | Oct. 25, 1864 |
| Neasenberger, Chas. F | do | Dec. 2, 1864 |
| Neule, William | Lima | Oct. 24, 1864 |
| Nytes, Antonie | do | Oct. 21, 1864 |
| Nussen, Ferdinand | Abbott | Dec. 2, 1864 |
| Nathanson, —— | Milwaukee | Nov. 9, 1863 |
| Nilsen, Carnee | do | Sep. 19, 1864 |
| Norton, James | do | Sep. 19, 1864 |
| Nicholas, Henry | do | Sep. 19, 1864 |
| Nicholas, Julius | do | Sep. 19, 1864 |
| Neuman, Mathias | do | Nov. 14, 1864 |
| Nardle, George | do | Nov. 14, 1864 |
| Nicholas, Johann | do | Nov. 14, 1864 |
| Naetz, —— | do | Nov. 14, 1864 |
| Neuman, Dedrich | do | Dec. 22, 1864 |
| Nelis, Wenzel | do | Dec. 1, 1864 |
| Nunemacher, Anton | do | Nov. 9, 1863 |
| Nelson, John | do | Sep. 20, 1864 |
| Nichols, Mark | do | Nov. 10, 1863 |
| Norris, Thomas A | do | Nov. 10, 1863 |
| Nodmire, W | do | Nov. 10, 1863 |
| Nieman, Charles | do | Sep. 20, 1864 |
| Norsh, W. W | do | Sep. 20, 1864 |
| Nolan, Peper | do | Nov. 15, 1864 |
| Nighman, G. W | do | Nov. 15, 1864 |
| Ness, Henry | do | Nov. 15, 1864 |
| Nowark, Charles | do | Nov. 15, 1864 |
| Norman, John | do | Nov. 10, 1863 |
| Nolan, John | do | Nov. 10, 1863 |
| Nolan, Larry | do | Nov. 10, 1863 |
| Neary, John | do | Sep. 21, 1864 |
| Nelson, Gudrin | do | Nov. 10, 1863 |
| Newel, John | do | Nov. 10, 1863 |
| Nock, Charles | do | Nov. 10, 1863 |
| Nusse, John | do | Nov. 10, 1863 |
| Nelson, John | do | Nov. 10, 1863 |
| Nore, Frank | do | Nov. 10, 1863 |
| Niles, Thomas | do | Sep. 21, 1864 |

| *Name.* | *Residence.* | *Date.* |
|---|---|---|
| Nelson, James | Milwaukee | Nov. 10, 1863 |
| Nuzcum, Thomas | do | Nov. 10, 1863 |
| Nicheld, John | do | Nov. 10, 1863 |
| Nugen, James Z. | do | Nov. 10, 1863 |
| Nigfall, Noel | do | Sep. 21, 1864 |
| Nouke, Christian | do | Sep. 21, 1864 |
| Nicholas, Fred | do | Nov. 25, 1864 |
| Nessler, —— | do | Sep. 21, 1864 |
| Nansen, Cornelius | do | Sep. 21, 1864 |
| Neberman, Angust | do | Sep. 21, 1864 |
| Niewelock, Henry | do | Nov. 11, 1863 |
| Neissing, Albert | do | Jan. 19, 1865 |
| Neghtschrigin, Antony | Greenfield | Nov. 11, 1863 |
| Nwka, Carl | Franklin | Nov. 11, 1863 |
| Newcomb, John | Oak Creek | Sep. 22, 1864 |
| Nieson, Frank | do | Sep. 22, 1864 |
| Near, Geo | Racine | Sep. 24, 1864 |
| Newman, —— | do | Sep. 22, 1864 |
| Nixon, James H | Mount Pleasant | Sep. 23, 1864 |
| Nelson, Henry | Caledonia | Dec. 7, 1864 |
| Niger, Matt | Randall | Sep. 24, 1864 |
| Nolan, Patrick | do | Sep. 24, 1864 |
| Nixon, Geo. R | Bristol | Nov. 12, 1863 |
| Nelson, Ennis | Summit | Sep. 22, 1864 |
| Neunham, Henry | do | Sep. 22, 1864 |
| Neunham, Howard | do | Nov. 30, 1864 |
| Norton, John | Oconomowoc | Sep. 22, 1864 |
| Nugent, Wm. T. | | |
| Nelson, John J. | Pewaukee | Dec 2, 1864 |
| Newbery, Robert O. | Menomonee | Sep. 24, 1864 |
| Nusbauba, Joseph | do | Sep. 24, 1864 |
| Nelson, Anfin | Deerfield | Nov. 13, 1863 |
| Nehemiah, Henry | Sun Prairie | Nov. 13, 1863 |
| Nutter, Walter | do | Nov. 13, 1863 |
| Notter, Richard | Fountain Prairie | Nov. 16, 1864 |
| Norton, John | Lewiston | Sep. 21, 1864 |
| Naker, Charles | Milford | Sep. 20, 1864 |
| Nieiks, Jonathan | Henrietta | Oct. 28, 1864 |
| Nicholas, John | Dodgeville | Nov. 14, 1864 |
| Nelson, Amund | do | Sep. 28, 1864 |
| Nelson, Gunder | Highland | Oct. 28, 1864 |
| Newmyre, Fred | do | Oct. 28, 1864 |
| Nichols, J. C. | do | Nov. 19, 1864 |
| Nelson, Ole | do | Jan. 6, 1865 |
| Newman, Richard | New Diggings | Sep. 29, 1864 |
| Needham, Martin | Waterloo | Oct. 1, 1864 |
| Noggle, Jacob | Jamestown | Oct. 6, 1864 |
| Nuss, Henry | Prairie du Sac | Nov. 20, 1863 |
| Norton, Edward | Franklin | Oct. 29, 1864 |
| Newton, Polk | do | Nov. 19, 1864 |
| Nelson, Peter | La Crosse city | Nov. 16, 1863 |
| Nason, Joseph | Jackson | Nov. 18, 1863 |
| Newbauer, Valentine | Adams Co | Nov. 19, 1863 |
| Neff, Jacob | Easton | Nov. 26, 1863 |
| Neisbit, Henry | Lincoln | Oct. 31, 1863 |
| North, Thomas L | Springville | Oct. 31, 1863 |
| Noonan, John | Juneau Co | Nov. 17, 1863 |
| Nourse, Harper | do | Nov. 17, 1863 |
| Noonan, Patrick | Summit | Sep. 19, 1864 |

| *Name.* | *Residence.* | *Date* |
|---|---|---|
| Nelson, William A. L | Lyndon | Sep. 19, 1864 |
| Nichols, W. H | Kildare | Oct. 31, 1864 |
| Noble, John | Dunn Co | Nov. 23, 1863 |
| Nesbit, W | Eau Galle | Sep. 27, 1864 |
| Neilan, Michael | do | Sep. 27, 1864 |
| Noram, Hans | Spring Brook | Sep. 27, 1864 |
| Nooman, Nels J | do | Sep. 27, 1864 |
| Nelson, Elias | Vernon Co | Nov. 18, 1863 |
| Neneson, Asner | Coon | Sep. 19, 1864 |
| Nelson, David S | Harmony | Sep. 19, 1864 |
| Norris, James | Webster | Sep. 19, 1864 |
| Nixon, R T | Jefferson | Sep. 19, 1864 |
| Nelson, Niels | Amherst | Sep. 22, 1864 |
| Noloff, Joseph | Sharon | Oct. 31, 1864 |
| Newville, John | Door Co | Nov. 20, 1863 |
| Nequette, Ferdinand | Two Rivers | Nov. 21, 1863 |
| Norton, Wm. W | Manitowoc | Nov. 21, 1863 |
| Nilson, Loren | Liberty | Nov. 21, 1863 |
| Naumer, Nicholas | Gibson | Dec. 29, 1864 |
| Nettekoven, Hubert | Calumet Co | Nov. 21, 1863 |
| Newbert, George | New Holstein | Nov. 23, 1863 |
| Nolen, William | Brothertown | Dec. 28, 1864 |
| Noyse, Charles | Oshkosh | Nov. 23, 1863 |
| Noe, John | Nekimi | Nov. 23, 1863 |
| Noonan, Dennis | Nepeuskin | Nov. 23, 1863 |
| Nohni, George | Marquette Co | Nov. 24, 1863 |
| Nelson, Ole | Scandinavia | Nov. 25, 1863 |
| Nowland, Thomas | Lebanon | Nov. 5, 1864 |
| Neigenfind, August | Caledonia | Nov. 5, 1864 |
| Nelson, Jens Peter | Iola | Nov. 5, 1864 |
| Nelson, Simon | do | Nov. 5, 1864 |
| Neubauer, Michael | Caledonia | Nov. 5, 1864 |
| Nelson, Lars | Iola | Nov. 5, 1864 |
| Nelson, Peter | do | Nov. 5, 1864 |
| Naylor, Jerome H | Freedom | Nov. 27, 1863 |
| Nickle, Thomas C | Outagamie Co. | Nov. 27, 1863 |
| Noble, Arthur | Stiles | Nov. 28, 1863 |
| Nulting, Warren | Aurora | Nov. 2, 1864 |
| Nichols, Charles W | Richford | Nov. 2, 1864 |
| Nicolys, James | Scott | Dec. 28, 1864 |
| Noloen, John | Humboldt | Dec. 28, 1864 |
| Noel, John B | Lincoln | Dec. 29, 1864 |
| Nase, Eugene | do | Dec. 29, 1864 |

## O

| *Name.* | *Residence.* | *Date* |
|---|---|---|
| Orins, Eugener | Eden | Nov. 19, 1863 |
| O'Herne, John O | Fox Lake | Nov. 19, 1863 |
| Osborn, Willis H | Westford | Nov. 20, 1863 |
| Owens, Hugh | Elba | Nov. 20, 1863 |
| O'Brion, George | do | Nov. 20, 1863 |
| O'Neil, John | Shields | Nov. 20, 1863 |
| O'Connell, John | do | Nov. 20, 1863 |
| Otto, Frederick | Watertown | Nov. 20, 1863 |
| Ottman, Jacob | Leroy | Dec. 1, 1864 |
| Otle, Leopold | Lomira | Jan. 27, 1865 |
| Olner, Frederick | Herman | Oct. 18, 1864 |
| O'Bryan, Patrick | Trenton | Nov. 20, 1863 |
| Ogsbury, William | Hubbard | Nov. 21, 1863 |
| O'Connell, Patrick | Hartford | Nov. 21, 1863 |

| *Name.* | *Residence.* | *Date* |
|---|---|---|
| O'Brian, John | Erin | Oct. 12, 1864 |
| O'Heary, Thomas | do | Oct. 12, 1864 |
| O'Connell, Patrick | do | Dec. 1, 1864 |
| O'Connell, Edward | do | Dec. 1, 1864 |
| Oswander, A. | Barton | Dec. 1, 1864 |
| Otto, Henry | Richfield | Jan. 27, 1865 |
| O'Brier, Thomas | Farmington | Oct. 18, 1864 |
| Ohler, Ernst | do | Dec. 1, 1864 |
| Oswald, Nicholas | Belgium | Oct. 13, 1864 |
| O'Kief, John | Fredonia | Dec. 1, 1864 |
| O'Brien, John | Grafton | Oct. 13, 1864 |
| Oushits, Henry | do | Jan. 27, 1865 |
| Owden, Mathias | Saukville | Oct. 14, 1864 |
| Oster, Peter | do | Oct. 14, 1864 |
| Ohel, Michael | Moselle | Oct. 18, 1864 |
| Oliver, Henry | Sheboygan Falls | Nov. 24, 1863 |
| Otis, John | do | Oct 25, 1864 |
| Oglris, Daniel | Lima | Oct. 21, 1864 |
| O'Hara, James | Holland | Dec 2, 1864 |
| O'Connor, Thomas | Milwaukee | Nov. 9, 1863 |
| Olden, S. G. | do | Sep. 19, 1864 |
| Ott, Fred | do | Nov. 14, 1864 |
| O'Connell, Daniel | do | Nov 14, 1864 |
| Osterday, George | do | Nov. 14, 1864 |
| Owens, John D | do | Nov. 9, 1863 |
| Ormsby, William | do | Nov. 9, 1863 |
| O'Marah, Timothy | do | Nov. 10, 1863 |
| O'Neal, David | do | Nov. 10, 1863 |
| O'Stock, Theodore | do | Nov. 10, 1863 |
| O'Brian, Michael | do | Nov. 10, 1863 |
| Onnan, G. | do | Nov 10, 1863 |
| O'Bryne, Mathew | do | Sep. 20, 1864 |
| O'Harren, Patrick | do | Sep. 20, 1864 |
| O'Leary, Joseph | do | Nov 15, 1864 |
| O'Halland, Edward | do | Nov. 15, 1864 |
| O'Hare, John | do | Nov. 15, 1864 |
| O'Heal, Bart | do | Nov. 15, 1864 |
| O'Hare, James | do | Nov. 15, 1864 |
| O'Hare, Patrick | do | Jan. 11, 1865 |
| O'Connell, M | do | Jan. 11, 1865 |
| O'Brien, ——— | do | Nov. 10, 1863 |
| O'Conner, Martin | do | Nov. 10, 1863 |
| Olin, George | do | Sep. 21, 1864 |
| Oswald, Carl | do | Jan. 19, 1865 |
| Ormond Charles | do | Sep. 21, 1864 |
| O'Mealey, George | do | Sep. 21, 1864 |
| O'Brien, Philp | do | Sep. 21, 1864 |
| O'Niel, James | do | Sep. 21, 1864 |
| Olson, Hart | do | Nov. 10, 1863 |
| Oht, Charles | do | Nov. 10, 1863 |
| Oleson, John | do | Nov. 10, 1863 |
| O'Brien, ——— | do | Nov. 10, 1863 |
| Oht, Joseph | do | Nov. 10, 1863 |
| Oesterle, Crowell | do | Nov. 10, 1863 |
| O'Brien, James | do | Sep. 21, 1864 |
| O'Donhue, Byron | do | Nov. 10, 1863 |
| O'Brien, Michael | do | Sep. 21, 1864 |
| Odenbreit, John | do | Sep. 21, 1864 |
| Ormers, Charles | do | Nov. 25, 1864 |

| *Name.* | *Residence.* | *Date.* |
|---|---|---|
| Odenbute, John | Milwaukee | Nov. 26, 1864 |
| O'Haron, James, jr | Granville | Nov. 11, 1863 |
| Oberheite, Henry | do | Sep. 22, 1864 |
| O'Connel, William | Lake | Nov. 11, 1863 |
| O'Herrin, John | Oak Creek, | Nov. 11, 1863 |
| Oleson, Ole | Norway | Nov. 11, 1863 |
| Orth, Charles | Kenosha | Nov. 12, 1863 |
| Omarah, John | Salem | Sep. 24, 1864 |
| Oatman, Joseph | do | Sep. 24, 1864 |
| O'Donnel, Michael | Whitewater | Nov. 12, 1863 |
| Owen, W. W. A | Bloomfield | Nov. 12, 1863 |
| Olwell, Philip | Oconomowoc | Sep. 22, 1864 |
| Owen, James | Genesee | Nov. 12, 1863 |
| Owen, John | do | Nov. 12, 1863 |
| Oleson, Henry | Muskego | Sept. 24, 1864 |
| O Brien, John | Oregon | Nov. 12, 1863 |
| O'Neil, Hugh | Fitchburg | Nov. 13, 1863 |
| O'Brien, John | Middleton | Nov. 13, 1863 |
| Oleson, Christ | Madison | Nov. 13, 1863 |
| Oleson, Heinrich | Deerfield | Nov. 13, 1863 |
| Oret, Martin | York | Nov. 13, 1863 |
| O'Connor, John | Waterloo | |
| O'Donalds, John | Watertown | |
| O'Rourke, John | Columbus | Nov. 16, 1863 |
| O'Neil, Patrick | Dekorrah | Sep. 21, 1864 |
| O'Neal, Timothy | Lewiston | Sep. 21, 1864 |
| O'Neal, Mathew | Ridgeway | Sep. 28, 1864 |
| Olson, Andrew, (1st) | Dodgeville | Sep. 28, 1864 |
| Owens, John | do | Sep. 28, 1864 |
| Olson, Lewis | do | Sep. 28, 1864 |
| Oliver, John | do | Sep. 28, 1864 |
| Olson, Henry | do. | Nov. 19, 1864 |
| Oleson, Errick | Highland | Sep. 28, 1864 |
| Oleson, Harrel | do | Sep. 28, 1864 |
| Oleson, John | do | Sep. 28, 1864 |
| Olson, Nils | Moscow | Sep. 28, 1864 |
| Olson, Peter | do | Sep. 28, 1864 |
| Oldham, Geo | Benton | Nov. 16, 1863 |
| O'Brien, Dennis | do | Nov. 16, 1863 |
| Oldham, Wm | do | Nov. 16, 1863 |
| O'Brien, Dennis | New Diggins | Sep. 29, 1864 |
| Oinderkafter, O. H | New Glarus or Exeter | Nov. 17, 1863 |
| O'Neil, Daniel | Utica | Sep. 30, 1864 |
| O'Kaafa, Timothy | Fennimore | Nov. 19, 1863 |
| O'Neil, Jas | Seneca | Sep. 30, 1864 |
| Oleson, Thos | Blue River | Oct. 1, 1864 |
| Olson, Andrew | La Crosse | Nov. 16, 1863 |
| Oleson, W | Washington | Sep. 19, 1863 |
| Osweiler, Jno | do | Sep. 19, 1863 |
| Ottona, O | Chippewa Co | Nov. 20, 1863 |
| Oleson, Ole | do | Nov. 20, 1863 |
| O'Brien, Dan'l | Chippewa Falls | Sep. 27, 1864 |
| O'Connell, Edw'd | do | Nov. 2, 1864 |
| O'Brien, Jno | St. Croix Co | Nov. 16, 1863 |
| Oleson, Jno | Eau Galle | Sep. 23, 1864 |
| Oleson, Aleek | do | Nov. 3, 1864 |
| Oleson, Peter, (1st) | Rush River | Sep. 23, 1864 |
| Olson, Lewis | Dunn Co | Nov. 23, 1863 |
| O'Leary, Jno | Eau Galle | Sep. 27, 1864 |

| *Name.* | *Residence.* | *Date.* |
|---|---|---|
| Olson, Thoel | Eau Galle | Nov. 2, 1864 |
| O'Brine, Pearce | Seven Mile Creek | Sep. 19, 1864 |
| O'Brine, Thos | do | Sep. 19, 1864 |
| O'Connor, Jas | Plymouth | Sep. 31, 1864 |
| Olavy, Dan'l | Tomah | Sep. 19, 1864 |
| O'Blaizer, Jno | do | Sep. 19, 1864 |
| Oleson, Andrew | Ettrick | Sep. 21, 1864 |
| Oleson, Ole | Bergen | Sep. 21, 1864 |
| Oleson, Ole | do | Nov. 15, 1864 |
| Oenllett, Hubert | Linwood | Sep. 22, 1864 |
| Oboine, James | Pleasant Valley | Sep. 23, 1864 |
| Owens, Jno | Martell | Sep. 23, 1864 |
| Olson, Borre | do | Nov. 3, 1864 |
| Oleson, Christopher | Perry | Nov. 3, 1864 |
| O'Connell, Timothy | New Haven | Nov. 14, 1864 |
| Oleson, Andrew (Osby) | Manitowoc Rapids | Nov. 21, 1863 |
| Obervogeke, Fred'k | Centerville | Nov. 21, 1863 |
| Oleson, Neils | Liberty | Nov. 21, 1863 |
| Oleson, Swan | Gibson | Dec. 29, 1864 |
| Oleson, Henry | Rockland | Dec. 29, 1864 |
| O'Conner, Timothy | Chilton | Nov. 23, 1863 |
| O'Neill, John | do | Dec. 28, 1864 |
| Osher, John | Oshkosh city | Nov. 23, 1863 |
| Olmstead, Geo | Omro | Nov. 23, 1863 |
| Odell, Henry | do | Nov. 24, 1863 |
| Oliver, Benj. N | Poygan | Nov. 5, 1864 |
| Oliver, Wm | do | Nov. 5, 1864 |
| Overans, Thos | Lebanon | Nov. 25, 1863 |
| Olmstead, James J | Matteson | Nov. 25, 1863 |
| Owns, Judson | St. Lawrence | Nov. 5, 1864 |
| Oleson, Ole | do | Dec. 31, 1864 |
| Olesen, Annond | Iola | Dec. 31, 1864 |
| Oleson, John | do | Dec. 31, 1864 |
| Oleson, Alfred | do | Nov. 5, 1864 |
| O'Connell, —— | Caledonia | Dec. 31, 1864 |
| Ovitt, Lanson L | Outagamie Co | Nov. 27, 1863 |
| Otis, Marshall | Dale | Nov. 27, 1863 |
| O'Brien, Timothy | Holland | Nov. 27, 1863 |
| O'Brien, Michael | Ft. Howard | Nov. 27, 1863 |
| O'Brien, Patrick | Morrison | Dec. 28, 1864 |
| Olmstedt, Dan'l | Bellville | Dec. 28, 1864 |
| Oately, Simeon | Suamico | Dec. 28, 1864 |
| O'Connell, Jno | Packwaukee | Nov. 1, 1864 |
| Owens, Evan M | Springwater | Nov. 2, 1864 |
| O'Coine, Newton J | do | Dec. 31, 1864 |
| Oleson, Martin | do | Dec. 31, 1864 |
| Owen, Roswell | Plainfield | Dec. 31, 1864 |
| Ostrom, Jno. C | Aurora | Dec. 31, 1864 |
| Oleson, Olie | Little Suamico | Dec. 31, 1864 |

## P

| | | |
|---|---|---|
| Padden, John | Fond du Lac | Nov. 19, 1863 |
| Pappinau, Adolph | do | Nov. 19, 1863 |
| Powell, John | do | Nov. 19, 1863 |
| Powers, Lester | do | Nov. 19, 1863 |
| Pottle, Benjamin | do | Nov. 19, 1863 |
| Pesh, John | Auburn | Oct. 5, 1864 |
| Powers, William A | Eldorado | |
| Pern, Francis | Lamartine | Nov. 19, 1863 |

| *Name.* | *Residence.* | *Date.* |
|---|---|---|
| Pond, L. P | Alto | Nov. 19, 1863 |
| Patch, Andrew J | do | Nov. 19, 1863 |
| Pierce, Edwin R | Waupun Village | Nov. 19, 1863 |
| Porter, William | Portland | Nov. 20, 1863 |
| Percotz, Frederick, jr | Emmett | Nov. 20, 1863 |
| Paulfrantz, M F | Watertown | Oct. 6, 1864 |
| Passak, Wingel | do | Oct. 6, 1864 |
| Phelps, Ava C | Leroy | Dec. 1, 1864 |
| Parrott, James | do | Jan. 27, 1865 |
| Phillips, Adam | Trenton | Nov. 20, 1863 |
| Past, Henry | do | Nov. 20, 1863 |
| Piper, John | Lebanon | Nov. 21, 1863 |
| Peters, Frank | Wayne | Nov. 21, 1863 |
| Pieters, John | Addison | Nov. 21, 1863 |
| Peper, John | Erin | Dec. 1, 1864 |
| Peterson, Engrebet | do | Dec. 1, 1864 |
| Peter, Franz | Barton | Oct. 12, 1864 |
| Pies, Michael | do | Oct. 12, 1864 |
| Pies, Nich | do | Dec. 1, 1864 |
| Pickard, William | Polk | Nov. 21, 1863 |
| Peterson, Peter | Richfield | Oct. 12, 1864 |
| Porter, Henry | Farmington | Nov. 21, 1863 |
| Putnam, Lafayette | do | Oct. 18, 1864 |
| Pratts, Henry | do | Oct. 18, 1864 |
| Palmer, Joseph | do | Oct. 18, 1864 |
| Perthold, Louis | do | Dec. 1, 1864 |
| Peterman, H | Jackson | Oct. 11, 1864 |
| Prahl, C | do | Oct. 11, 1864 |
| Pastoral, Peter | Belgium | Dec. 1, 1864 |
| Pfeifer, John | do | Nov. 12, 1863 |
| Pohl, Joseph | do | Oct. 13, 1864 |
| Phiel, Frank | do | Oct. 13, 1864 |
| Piever, Peter | do | Oct. 13, 1864 |
| Plier, Nicholas | do | Oct. 13, 1864 |
| Peening, Peter T | do | Oct. 13, 1864 |
| Pierny, Nicholas | do | Oct. 13, 1864 |
| Petz, Henry | do | Oct. 13, 1864 |
| Perong, Peter | do | Dec. 1, 1864 |
| Porly, Nicholas | do | Dec. 1, 1864 |
| Pastoral, Hendrick | do | Dec. 1, 1864 |
| Paulen, Theodore | do | Dec. 1, 1864 |
| Paulus, John | do | Dec. 1, 1864 |
| Paule, Tioder | Fredonia | Dec. 1, 1864 |
| Puerling, Andrew | Grafton | Nov. 23, 1863 |
| Powell, Charles B | Saukville | Nov. 23, 1863 |
| Peterson, Ant | Sheboygan | Oct. 25, 1864 |
| Peterson, John Jacob | do | Dec. 2, 1864 |
| Pautz, Fr | do | Oct. 25, 1864 |
| Pflong, Gottleib | do | Oct. 25, 1864 |
| Pott, Aug | do | Dec. 2, 1864 |
| Pash, Frederick | do | Dec. 2, 1864 |
| Pruden, John | do | Dec. 2, 1864 |
| Pfan, Gottlob | do | Dec. 2, 1864 |
| Perselin, Frederick | Moselle | Oct. 18, 1864 |
| Porkhart, Niclaus | do | Jan. 27, 1865 |
| Patterson, James | Sheboygan Falls | Nov. 24, 1863 |
| Poderman, William | do | Nov. 24, 1863 |
| Pringe, William | do | Dec. 2, 1864 |
| Peterson, Bartolff | do | Dec. 2, 1864 |

| *Name.* | *Residence.* | *Date.* |
|---|---|---|
| Pierce, George | Lima | Oct. 24, 1864 |
| Peopper, John | do | Oct. 24, 1864 |
| Phelan, J. E | do | Oct. 24, 1864 |
| Prinsen, W. G | Holland | Oct. 21, 1864 |
| Pierce, Martin | do | Oct. 21, 1864 |
| Pierce, Robert | Abbott | Oct. 18, 1864 |
| Pfeifer, Carl | do | Oct. 18, 1864 |
| Pratt, Henry | Milwaukee | Nov. 9, 1863 |
| Power, Julius | do | Nov. 9, 1863 |
| Parker, Martin | do | Nov. 9, 1863 |
| Pork, John | do | Nov. 9, 1863 |
| Peterson, Peter | do | Sep. 19, 1864 |
| Pisket, Michael | do | Sep. 19, 1864 |
| Plankinhom, Chas | do | Nov. 14, 1864 |
| Pryor, Peter | do | Nov. 14, 1864 |
| Paris, John | do | Nov. 9, 1863 |
| Pritzlaff, E. S | do | Nov. 9, 1863 |
| Prichard, O | do | Nov. 9, 1863 |
| Parker, J. B | do | Sep. 20, 1864 |
| Peilony, Aug | do | Sep. 20, 1864 |
| Philan, Thomas | do | Nov. 10, 1863 |
| Potts, Wm | do | Nov. 10, 1863 |
| Pueill, J | do | Nov. 10, 1863 |
| Parsons, L | do | Sep. 20, 1864 |
| Poake, James | do | Sep. 20, 1864 |
| Powers, S. L | do | Sep. 20, 1864 |
| Prescott, Charles | do | Sep. 20, 1864 |
| Piper, Charles | do | Sep. 20, 1864 |
| Putow, Christopher | do | Sep. 20, 1864 |
| Powers, J | do | Jan. 11, 1865 |
| Phealon, J | do | Jan. 11, 1865 |
| Phillips, S. E | do | Jan. 11, 1865 |
| Phillips, S. W | do | Jan. 11, 1865 |
| Palmer, E | do | Jan. 11, 1865 |
| Powers, Michael | do | Jan. 11, 1865 |
| Pattenden, Fred | do | Jan. 11, 1865 |
| Powers, Henry | do | Jan. 11, 1865 |
| Pans, William | do | Sep. 21, 1864 |
| Plesser, John | do | Nov. 10, 1863 |
| Popper, Charles | do | Nov. 10, 1863 |
| Paul, George | do | Nov. 10, 1863 |
| Phalon, Lewis | do | Nov. 10, 1863 |
| Park, Hiram | do | Nov. 10, 1863 |
| Patterson, Joseph | do | Sep. 21, 1864 |
| Pothiman, John | do | Sep. 21, 1864 |
| Papcock, David | do | Sep. 21, 1864 |
| Poppert, George | do | Nov. 15, 1864 |
| Pretz, Philip | do | |
| Parkinson, Robert | do | |
| Patchkowsky, T. W | do | Nov. 16, 1864 |
| Pless, Nathan | do | Nov. 10, 1863 |
| Pierce, Richard | do | Nov. 10, 1863 |
| Pfiels, Henry | do | Sep. 21, 1864 |
| Piefel, Peter | do | Sep. 21, 1864 |
| Prazer, Andrew | do | Nov. 25, 1864 |
| Peck, John | do | Nov. 25, 1864 |
| Paul, Christian | do | Nov. 25, 1864 |
| Pheeps, Delancy | do | Nov. 11, 1863 |
| Potrat, Charley | do | Sep. 21, 1864 |

| *Name.* | *Residence.* | *Date.* |
|---|---|---|
| Pieer, Charley | Milwaukee | Sep. 21, 1864 |
| Polord, Frederick | do | Sep. 21, 1864 |
| Peul, John | do | Sep. 21, 1864 |
| Pittelkow, William | do | Sep. 21, 1864 |
| Pauli, Peter | do | Nov. 16, 1863 |
| Pudit, August | do | Jan. 19, 1865 |
| Phale, Anton | do | Jan. 19, 1865 |
| Pesch, —— | do | Sep. 21, 1864 |
| Prager, Johann | do | Nov. 25, 1864 |
| Peck, Henry M | do | Nov. 30, 1864 |
| Peters, Johann | do | Sep. 22, 1864 |
| Prohl, John | do | Dec. 7, 1864 |
| Palmer, —— | Granville | Sept. 22, 1864 |
| Phillips, Wm | Racine | Sep. 24, 1864 |
| Phillips, Louis H | do | Sep. 24, 1864 |
| Pitts, Anthony | do | Sep. 22, 1864 |
| Parker, William | do | Nov. 11, 1863 |
| Pferdesteller, Fredrick | do | Sep. 22, 1864 |
| Pulling, Frank | Mount Pleasant | Nov. 11, 1863 |
| Plummer, Geo. F | do | Nov. 11, 1863 |
| Patterson, David | Raymond | Dec. 9, 1864 |
| Perkins, Fred B | do | Dec. 9, 1864 |
| Palmer, Thomas | do | Dec. 9, 1864 |
| Peterson, Hans | do | Dec. 9, 1864 |
| Palmerton, Homer | Wheatland | Dec. 14, 1864 |
| Pierce, Carlton C | Paris | Sep. 24, 1864 |
| Pomeroy, Luther | Randall | Sep. 24, 1864 |
| Pearson, John | do | Dec. 16, 1864 |
| Philips, Walter | Bristol | Sep. 24, 1864 |
| Pheld, James | Delavan | Nov. 12, 1863 |
| Phelps, Arthur | Walworth | Nov. 12, 1863 |
| Petzor, Wilson | Geneva | Nov. 12, 1863 |
| Piercell, Lawrence | Lynn | Nov. 12, 1863 |
| Pier, Michael | East Troy | Dec. 24, 1864 |
| Price, Adelmer | Bloomfield | Nov. 12, 1863 |
| Pratt, Wm | Summit | Sep. 22, 1864 |
| Peur, Frederick | Waukesha | Sep. 23, 1864 |
| Pierce, J. E | do | Sep. 23, 1864 |
| Phillips, John | do | Sep. 23, 1864 |
| Pierce, Hiram M | Vernon | Sep. 24, 1864 |
| Pickett, Seymour S | Menomonee | Sep. 24, 1864 |
| Phillips, Frank | do | Dec. 1, 1864 |
| Poth, Jacob | do | Nov. 25, 1864 |
| Pfanschmidt, Andreas | do | Nov. 25, 1864 |
| Polson, John | Brookfield | Sep. 23, 1864 |
| Phillips, Leander | New Berlin | Nov. 12, 1863 |
| Peffer, George F | Muskego | Nov. 30, 1864 |
| Post, John | do | Nov. 30, 1864 |
| Peterson, Martin C | Delafield | Sep. 22, 1864 |
| Parks, R D | Avon | Nov. 12, 1863 |
| Persow, Ferdinand | Bradford | Nov. 12, 1863 |
| Patton, O. D | Magnolia | Nov. 12, 1863 |
| Patwin, Richard | Oregon | Nov. 12, 1863 |
| Perry, George | Sun Prairie | Sep. 19, 1864 |
| Pwar, Henry | Berry | Nov. 13, 1863 |
| Parr, Martin | do | Sep. 19, 1864 |
| Pratt, Patrick | York | Nov. 13, 1863 |
| Pickett, Edward | do | Nov. 13, 1863 |
| Probert, James | Sullivan | Nov. 13, 1863 |

| *Name.* | *Residence.* | *Date.* |
|---|---|---|
| Perkins, T. C | Lake Mills | Nov. 13, 1863 |
| Packhass, J | Farmington | Sep. 20, 1864 |
| Peek, Justin | Portage City | Sep. 21, 1864 |
| Peterson, Andrew | Perry | Feb. 27, 1865 |
| Pouche, Wm | Milford | Oct. 20, 1864 |
| Paul, Thomas | Ridgeway | Nov. 19, 1864 |
| Philips, David | Willow | Sep. 26, 1864 |
| Phillips, Leonard | Clyde | Sep. 27, 1864 |
| Pearcy, John | do | Sep. 27, 1864 |
| Parry, Thomas | Dodgeville | Sep. 28, 1864 |
| Pollard, Samuel | do | Oct. 28, 1864 |
| Peterson, Amilo | do | Oct. 28, 1864 |
| Palkinghorn, Richard | do | Oct. 28, 1864 |
| Parsons, Henry | do | Oct. 28, 1864 |
| Polkinghorn, Edwin | do | Nov. 19, 1864 |
| Patterson, Thomas | Highland | Nov. 14, 1863 |
| Pugh, David | do | Oct. 28, 1864 |
| Pugh, Wm | do | Oct. 28, 1864 |
| Peterson, Eli | do | Oct. 28, 1864 |
| Patterson, Robert | do | Oct. 28; 1864 |
| Pierce, Thomas | Benton | Sep. 29, 1864 |
| Powers, John | do | Sep. 29, 1864 |
| Page, Wm | New Diggings | Sep. 29, 1864 |
| Price, Richard | Albany | Nov. 17, 1863 |
| Peterson, Peter | Clayton | Sep. 30, 1864 |
| Peterson, Peter | Utica | Sep. 30, 1864 |
| Prise, David | Freeman or Lynxville | Nov. 18, 1863 |
| Parks, Robert | Beetown | Oct. 1, 1864 |
| Pester, John | Prairie du Sac | Nov. 20, 1863 |
| Patterson, John | Little Grant | Oct. 6, 1864 |
| Palmer, Henry | Paris | Oct. 1, 1864 |
| Prouty, Barnaba | Bear Creek | Oct. 3, 1864 |
| Prouty, Joshua | do | Oct. 29, 1864 |
| Palmer, I. E | La Crosse city | Nov. 13, 1863 |
| Pearsoo, Jeremiah | Campbell | Nov. 18, 1863 |
| Poppel, Henry | Chippewa Co | Nov. 20, 1863 |
| Phillips, Charles | do | Nov. 20, 1863 |
| Pollock, John | do | Nov. 20, 1863 |
| Patneant, Tophuld | La Fayette | Sep. 27, 1864 |
| Prew, Joseph | do | Nov. 2, 1864 |
| Pratt, Jonathan | Jackson Co | Nov. 18, 1863 |
| Porter, William | Juneau Co | Nov. 17, 1863 |
| Powers, Patrick | Seven Mile Creek | Sep. 19, 1864 |
| Porter, Frederick | Lemonweir | Sep. 19, 1864 |
| Platt, John | Summit | Sep. 19, 1864 |
| Poler, Orvill C | Lyndon | Sep. 19, 1864 |
| Paley, Martin | Germantown | Sept. 19, 1864 |
| Persons, Wallace | Kildare | Oct. 31, 1864 |
| Putford, Woodward | Plymouth | Oct. 31, 1864 |
| Parker, Thomas | Eau Claire Co | Nov. 20, 1863 |
| Peters, Cris | Vernon Co | Nov. 18, 1863 |
| Parl, Frank | do | Nov 18, 1863 |
| Pedretta, Lorenzo | do | Nov. 18, 1863 |
| Powell, S. S | Harmony | Sep. 20, 1864 |
| Petit, Henry | Clinton | Sep. 20, 1864 |
| Page, David | Nelson | Nov. 18, 1863 |
| Peterson, Johannes | Portland | Sep. 20, 1864 |
| Phillips, John | do | Sep. 20, 1864 |
| Parasol, Charles | Linwood | Sep. 22, 1864 |

| *Name.* | *Residence.* | *Date.* |
|---|---|---|
| Potter, James | Pine Grove | Sep. 22, 1864 |
| Pierce, George W | do | Sep. 22, 1864 |
| Prell, Gahart | Sharon | Oct. 31, 1864 |
| Phillips, John | Stockton | Sep. 22, 1864 |
| Phillips, Darius | Amherst | Sep. 22, 1864 |
| Polley, Andrew | Belmont | Nov. 15, 1864 |
| Peterson, Christian | Martell | Sep. 23, 1864 |
| Phillips, James | do | Sep. 23, 1864 |
| Peterson, John | do | Nov. 3, 1864 |
| Plumb, Augustus | Eau Galle | Sep. 23, 1864 |
| Pidd, Darius E | do | Sep. 23, 1864 |
| Perrant, Anthony | Somerset | Oct. 5, 1864 |
| Prevard, Sveir | do | Oct. 5, 1864 |
| Perrant, Lewis | do | Oct. 5, 1864 |
| Peralt, Zephyr | do | Oct. 5, 1864 |
| Pross, Thomas | Erin Prairie | Nov. 3, 1864 |
| Peck, Jason | Lincoln | Sep. 26, 1864 |
| Potter, John W | Big Flats | Sep. 26, 1864 |
| Pierce, Avery L | Richfield | Sept. 26, 1864 |
| Palms, Jesse | New Haven | Sep. 26, 1864 |
| Palmer, Jacob | do | Sep. 26, 1864 |
| Palms, Henry B | do | Nov. 15, 1864 |
| Poorfine, Charles | Jackson | Sep. 26, 1864 |
| Powers, Byron H. | Easton | Sep. 26, 1864 |
| Phillips, J. H | Adams | Sep. 26, 1864 |
| Poble, Dane | Monroe | Sep. 26, 1864 |
| Page, Rodney | Waubeck | Sep. 27, 1864 |
| Prescott M | do | Sep. 27, 1864 |
| Peters, Charles | Pepin | Nov. 16, 1864 |
| Parkinson, William | do | Nov. 16, 1864 |
| Post, John | Eau Galle | Sep. 27, 1864 |
| Patterson, John | do | Sep. 27, 1864 |
| Palmer, Eugene | do | Nov. 2, 1864 |
| Page, Henry | Spring Brook | Nov. 2, 1864 |
| Proutz, Albert | Berlin | Nov. 14, 1864 |
| Pool, William | New Holstein | Nov. 23, 1863 |
| Potter, Sheldon | Woodville | Dec. 28, 1864 |
| Peters, Peter | do | Dec. 28, 1864 |
| Phillips, Samuel | Stockbridge | Dec. 28, 1864 |
| Peterson, George | do | Dec. 28, 1864 |
| Proper, Henry | Brothertown | Dec. 28, 1864 |
| Peans, Lewis | Oshkosh city | Nov. 23, 1863 |
| Phelps, Cleveland P | Omro | Nov. 23, 1863 |
| Potter, Albert | Rushford | Nov. 23, 1863 |
| Peterson, A. C | Berlin City | Nov. 24, 1863 |
| Phoenix, Philo | Brooklyn | Nov. 24, 1863 |
| Pond, Simon | Marquette Co | Nov. 24, 1863 |
| Peltre, Carl | Shields | Nov. 1, 1864 |
| Pond, William | Springfield | Nov. 1, 1864 |
| Potter, Joseph | Marion | Nov. 25, 1863 |
| Porter, Clinton | Richford | Nov. 2, 1864 |
| Pope, John L | do | Dec. 31, 1864 |
| Potter, Asil J. | do | Dec. 31, 1864 |
| Phineas, Jaquith | Deerfield | Nov. 2, 1864 |
| Peevey, John R | Oasis | Nov. 2, 1864 |
| Peevey, William | do | Dec. 31, 1864 |
| Pierce, George | Plainfield | Nov. 2, 1864 |
| Packard, C. W | Mukwa | Nov. 25, 1863 |
| Peterson, Egbert | Weyauwega | Nov. 25, 1863 |

| *Name* | *Residence.* | *Date.* |
|---|---|---|
| Patterson, J. G | Weyauwega | Nov. 5, 1863 |
| Pound, Samuel | do | Nov. 5, 1863 |
| Pound, J. S | do | Nov. 5, 1863 |
| Patney, F. B | Lind | Nov. 25, 1863 |
| Packard, S. C | Bear Creek | Nov. 5, 1864 |
| Phillips, F. N | do | Nov. 5, 1864 |
| Prokenon, John | Lebanon | Nov. 5, 1864 |
| Prebnow, Frederick | Caledonia | Nov. 5, 1864 |
| Parks, Phineas H | St. Lawrence | Nov. 5, 1864 |
| Paulson, Ole | Iola | Nov. 5, 1864 |
| Pederson, Gregor | do | Nov. 5, 1864 |
| Paulsen, Samuel | do | Dec. 31, 1864 |
| Petty, Christian | Wolf River | Nov. 5, 1864 |
| Phillips, Charles | Kaukama | Nov. 27, 1863 |
| Pickwin, Michael | Appleton | Nov. 27, 1863 |
| Palmer, F. B | do | Nov. 27, 1863 |
| Prest, William | do | Nov. 27, 1863 |
| Peeble, Morris | | Nov. 27, 1863 |
| Preboonow, Augustus | | Nov. 27, 1863 |
| Purath, Frederick | Center | Dec. 28, 1863 |
| Papp, Herman | do | Dec. 28, 1863 |
| Petram, August | do | Dec. 28, 1863 |
| Plieger, August | Greenville | Dec. 28, 1863 |
| Perry, William A | Marinette | Nov. 28, 1863 |
| Pettit, John | Stiles | Nov. 28. 1863 |
| Phillips, George | Little Suamico | Dec. 29, 1864 |
| Polzin, Gottlieb | Gibson | Dec. 29, 1864 |
| Phillips, Matthias | Meeme | Dec. 29, 1864 |
| Petigean, Simon | Casco | Dec. 29, 1864 |
| Pawleck, Vincene | do | Dec. 29, 1864 |
| Pauli, Frank | Kewaunee | Dec. 29, 1864 |
| Paris, John | Lincoln | Dec. 29, 1864 |
| Pierre, Alex | Brussells | Dec. 29, 1864 |
| Piette, L | do | Dec. 29, 1864 |
| Piette, Joseph | do | Dec. 29, 1864 |
| Piette, Charles | do | Dec. 29, 1864 |

## Q

| *Name* | *Residence.* | *Date.* |
|---|---|---|
| Quintin, John | Clyman | Oct. 6, 1864 |
| Quinn, Michael | Trenton | Nov. 20, 1863 |
| Quassins, Christop | Sheboygan Falls | Dec. 2, 1864 |
| Quindt, Fred | Milwaukee | Sep. 20, 1864 |
| Quirk, Peter | do | Nov. 10, 1863 |
| Quinter, James | do | Sep. 20, 1864 |
| Quirk, J | do | Sep. 20, 1864 |
| Quirk, P. H | do | Jan. 11, 1865 |
| Quigley, Edward | do | Nov. 25, 1864 |
| Quinn, James | do | Nov. 25, 1864 |
| Quinn, Barthelet | do | Nov. 25, 1864 |
| Quig, John | Racine | Nov. 11, 1863 |
| Quirk. John | Dover | Dec. 10, 1864 |
| Quakenbush, Monroe T. | Rochester | Sep. 24, 1864 |
| Quirk, John | Waukesha | Sep. 23, 1864 |
| Quinn, James | Centre | Nov. 12, 1863 |
| Quinn, Michael | Watertown | Dec. 19, 1864 |
| Queest, Joseph | Platteville | Nov. 19, 1863 |
| Queenane, John | Seven Mile Creek | Oct. 31, 1864 |
| Quinn, Peter | Rudolph | Nov. 15, 1864 |
| Quimby, George | Waupaca Co | Nov. 25, 1863 |

| *Name.* | *Residence.* | *Date.* |
|---|---|---|
| Quimbey, Martin | Suamico | Dec. 28, 1864 |
| Quinn, William | Richford | Dec. 31, 1864 |

## R

| | | |
|---|---|---|
| Ragan, Thomas O | Grafton | Dec. 1, 1864 |
| Runert, Frederick | do | Dec. 1, 1864 |
| Rodica, Christian | do | Jan. 27, 1864 |
| Russell, George | Sheboygan | Nov. 23, 1863 |
| Reinhwein, Simon | do | Oct. 25, 1864 |
| Resenoetter, William | do | Oct. 25, 1854 |
| Reirdon, Charles | do | Dec. 2, 1864 |
| Raufuss, ——— | do | Oct. 18, 1864 |
| Russel, Alanson | do | Jan. 27, 1865 |
| Rassebamr, Christopher | Sheboygan Falls | Nov. 24, 1863 |
| Retinger, Seaman | do | Oct. 25, 1864 |
| Raer, Frederick | do | Dec. 2, 1864 |
| Restman, John | do | Dec. 2, 1864 |
| Rahn, Antha | Lima | Oct. 24, 1864 |
| Redman, Adam | do | Oct. 21, 1864 |
| Ruelink, William | do | Dec. 2, 1864 |
| Ruelink, H. J | do | Dec. 2, 1864 |
| Reddink, John | do | Jan. 27, 1865 |
| Rook, J. S | do | Jan. 27, 1865 |
| Reink, Carl | Abbott | Nov. 24, 1863 |
| Reed, Philip | do | Oct. 18, 1864 |
| Ritschdorf, ——— | do | Oct. 18, 1864 |
| Riley, James | do | Oct. 18, 1864 |
| Riddle, Daniel | Scott | Oct. 21, 1864 |
| Row, George | do | Dec. 2, 1864 |
| Rath, George | do | Dec. 2, 1864 |
| Robinson, Ira | Hubbard | Nov. 21, 1863 |
| Roll, Ferdinand | Hustisford | Nov. 21, 1863 |
| Rad, William | Wayne | Nov. 21, 1863 |
| Ryan, Thomas | Erin | Oct. 12, 1864 |
| Ring, James | do | Dec. 1, 1864 |
| Rumpel, Michael | Barton | Nov. 21, 1863 |
| Reinhardt, Michael | do | Oct. 12, 1864 |
| Roecker, Diedrick | do | Dec. 1, 1864 |
| Roshong, Frank | West Bend | Nov. 21, 1863 |
| Rice, Wahore | Polk | Oct. 12, 1864 |
| Reiss, Philip | do | Oct. 12, 1864 |
| Ruhl, Christian | do | Oct. 12, 1864 |
| Rykowskey, Andreas | do | Oct. 12, 1864 |
| Rulles, Jacob | do | Oct. 12, 1864 |
| Roesch, Reinhardt | do | Oct. 12, 1864 |
| Rost, Gustave | do | Oct. 12, 1864 |
| Rosenhemer, Max | do | Dec. 8, 1864 |
| Rai, Martin | Richfield | Nov. 21, 1863 |
| Rowell, F. H | do | Oct. 12, 1864 |
| Rummins, William | do | Oct. 12, 1864 |
| Rissing, John | do | Jan. 27, 1865 |
| Radwigher, Arnst | do | Jan. 27, 1865 |
| Ruchel, Henry | Jackson | Nov. 21, 1863 |
| Ringans, Jacob | do | Oct. 11, 1864 |
| Riebe, William | do | Oct. 11, 1864 |
| Rohn, James | Germantown | Nov. 21, 1863 |
| Reif, Nicholas | Belgium | Nov. 21, 1863 |
| Rupert, Cornelius | do | Nov. 21, 1863 |
| Rinchen, Michael | do | Oct. 13, 1864 |

| *Name.* | *Residence.* | *Date.* |
|---|---|---|
| Renick, Peter John | Belgium | Oct. 13, 1864 |
| Roller, Peter | do | Oct. 13, 1864 |
| Rober, Henry | do | Oct. 13, 1864 |
| Rueling, Nicholas | do | Oct. 13, 1864 |
| Reif, Michael | do | Oct. 13, 1864 |
| Rappert, William | do | Oct. 13, 1864 |
| Rannen, John | do | Oct. 13, 1864 |
| Ruffing, William | do | Oct. 13, 1864 |
| Reiter, Michael | do | Oct. 13, 1864 |
| Risch, Nicholas | do | Dec. 1, 1864 |
| Retzer, George | Fredonia | Oct. 14, 1864 |
| Reilly, Michael | do | Oct. 14, 1864 |
| Ragan, William | do | Oct. 14, 1864 |
| Regner, Lorenz | do | Oct. 14, 1864 |
| Rodsticker, Philip | do | Dec. 1, 1864 |
| Rilly, Michael | do | Dec. 1, 1864 |
| Roder, John | do | Dec. 1, 1864 |
| Rocell, Zaver | do | Dec. 1, 1864 |
| Ratford, George | do | Dec. 1, 1864 |
| Roseler, August | Grafton | Oct. 13, 1864 |
| Reily, James | Byron | Nov. 19, 1863 |
| Rehder, Nicholas | Auburn | Oct. 5, 1864 |
| Ranch, Thomas | Taycheedah | Oct. 5, 1864 |
| Roidink, Henry J | Alto | Oct. 5, 1864 |
| Race, Virgil | do | Oct. 5, 1864 |
| Root, Jeremiah | Ripon | Oct. 5, 1864 |
| Reed, Richard | Rosendale | Oct. 5, 1864 |
| Ritz, Anton | Metomen | Oct. 5, 1864 |
| Rogers, Hiram | Lowell | Nov. 20, 1863 |
| Rhames, Thomas | Beaver Dam | Nov. 20, 1863 |
| Ruense, Samuel | Emmett | Nov. 20, 1863 |
| Roth, Charles | do | Oct. 11, 1864 |
| Reed, Sanford | Watertown | Nov. 20, 1863 |
| Reibet, Julius | do | Oct. 6, 1864 |
| Rades, Otto | do | Oct. 6, 1864 |
| Ramp, John | do | Oct. 6, 1864 |
| Rohn, Henry | do | Dec. 1, 1864 |
| Ryan, John | do | Jan. 27, 1865 |
| Reynolds, Charles | Leroy | Nov. 20, 1863 |
| Runnels, James | do | Dec. 1, 1864 |
| Roden, Carl | Lomira | Dec. 1, 1864 |
| Radhey, William | Theresa | Nov. 20, 1863 |
| Rierson, Thomas J | Hermon | Nov. 20, 1863 |
| Roehboun, John H | do | Oct. 18, 1864 |
| Ran, Michael | do | Oct. 18, 1864 |
| Rehberg, Daniel | do | Oct. 18, 1864 |
| Roeber, Gustave | do | Dec. 2, 1864 |
| Reynolds, Ebon | Trenton | Nov. 20, 1863 |
| Rane, John | Milwaukee | Nov. 9, 1863 |
| Rhule, Bernard | do | Nov. 9, 1863 |
| Richey, John | do | Nov. 9, 1863 |
| Rusha, ——— | do | Nov. 9, 1863 |
| Ryan, Thomas | do | Nov. 9, 1863 |
| Ralf, Christ | do | Nov. 9, 1863 |
| Reisch Carl | do | Sep. 19, 1864 |
| Reannier, Peter | do | Sep. 19, 1864 |
| Ritsche, William | do | Sep. 19, 1864 |
| Racsch, Joseph H | do | Sep. 19, 1864 |
| Reek, John | do | Sep. 19, 1864 |

| *Name.* | *Residence.* | *Date.* |
|---|---|---|
| Rickert, Christian | Milwaukee | Nov. 14, 1864 |
| Raeser, James | do | Nov. 14, 1864 |
| Resser, Samuel | do | Nov. 14, 1864 |
| Rowe, F | do | Nov. 14, 1864 |
| Renhard, John | do | Dec. 22, 1864 |
| Ramsey, Chas | do | Nov. 9, 1863 |
| Rosherscheidt, J | do | Nov. 9, 1863 |
| Rath, Conrad | do | Nov. 9, 1863 |
| Rolloff, Charles | do | Sep. 20, 1864 |
| Raback, J | do | Nov. 14, 1864 |
| Rothe, Frank | do | Nov. 14, 1864 |
| Raster, John | do | Nov. 10, 1863 |
| Ryan, Pat | do | Nov. 10, 1863 |
| Rickly ——— | do | Nov. 10, 1863 |
| Rogers, Michael | do | Nov. 10, 1863 |
| Rapp, David | do | Nov. 10, 1864 |
| Roberts, Roland | do | Jan. 11, 1865 |
| Rice, F. P | do | Jan. 11, 1865 |
| Rae, E. B | do | Jan. 11, 1865 |
| Reed, George | do | Jan. 11, 1865 |
| Roughan, James | do | Nov. 10, 1864 |
| Riley, William | do | Nov. 10, 1864 |
| Rown, James | do | Nov. 10, 1864 |
| Rodman, George | do | Nov. 10, 1864 |
| Riley, Edward | do | Sep. 21, 1864 |
| Rodgen, Edgar | do | Sep. 21, 1864 |
| Riemer, 2d ——— | do | Sep. 21, 1864 |
| Roderer, Joseph G | do | Sep. 21, 1864 |
| Raenck, Herman | do | Nov. 10, 1863 |
| Rungstein, Christ | do | Nov. 10, 1863 |
| Richard, Arther | do | Sep. 21, 1864 |
| Rosenholf, Peter | do | Sep. 21, 1864 |
| Rochl, Joachim | do | Sep. 21, 1864 |
| Rueckof, Henry | do | Nov. 15, 1863 |
| Rempton, August | do | Nov. 10, 1863 |
| Remer, John | do | Nov. 11, 1863 |
| Redeske, Henry | do | Sep. 21, 1864 |
| Renkel John | do | Sep. 21, 1864 |
| Rlein, William | do | Nov. 25, 1864 |
| Raasa, William | do | Nov. 25, 1864 |
| Remming, Frederick | do | Nov. 11, 1863 |
| Rotz, Jacob | do | Sep. 21, 1864 |
| Rhineholt, Fred | do | Nov. 10, 1863 |
| Rogers, Patrick | do | Nov. 10, 1863 |
| Rice, Ratrick | do | Sep. 20, 1864 |
| Rafers, John | do | Sep. 20, 1864 |
| Rogers, William | do | Sep. 20, 1864 |
| Robinson, William | do | Sep. 20, 1864 |
| Rogers, Edward | do | Sep. 20, 1864 |
| Riens, James | do | Sep. 20, 1864 |
| Regly, J | do | Sep. 20, 1864 |
| Rastell, James | do | Sep. 20, 1864 |
| Reagan, J | do | Sep. 20, 1864 |
| Robinson, M | do | Sep. 20, 1864 |
| Ryan, Michael | do | Sep. 20, 1864 |
| Rabis, John | do | Sep. 20, 1864 |
| Ryan, Thomas | do | Sep. 20, 1864 |
| Reed, M | do | Sep. 20, 1864 |
| Rastick, Theodore | do | Sep. 20, 1864 |

| *Name* | *Residence* | *Date* |
| --- | --- | --- |
| Ryan, John | Milwaukee | Sep. 20, 1864 |
| Rees, C | do | Sep. 20, 1864 |
| Roysineke, P | do | Nov. 15, 1864 |
| Ready, Thomas | do | Nov. 15, 1864 |
| Ryan, Sam | do | Nov. 15, 1864 |
| Reily, James | do | Nov. 15, 1864 |
| Regnal, James | do | Nov. 15, 1864 |
| Reily, J | do | Nov. 15, 1864 |
| Robfer, John | do | Nov. 15, 1864 |
| Raymond, Peter | do | Jan. 19, 1865 |
| Reichardt, Jacob | do | Sep. 21, 1864 |
| Roderler, Johann | do | Sep. 21, 1864 |
| Roth, Johann | do | Sep. 21, 1864 |
| Romberg, J. F | do | Sep. 21, 1864 |
| Riemensahler, George | do | Sep. 21, 1864 |
| Reiman, Heinrich | do | Sep. 21, 1864 |
| Rausch, David | do | Sep. 21, 1864 |
| Ritschman, Heinerich | do | Sep. 21, 1864 |
| Ransen, G. S | do | Sept. 21, 1864 |
| Rickert, Herman P | do | Sept. 21, 1864 |
| Roth, Wilhelm | do | Nov. 25, 1864 |
| Rust, Frederick | do | Nov. 25, 1864 |
| Rath, Johann | do | Nov. 25, 1864 |
| Rusch, Wilhelm | do | Nov. 25, 1864 |
| Ramaker, John W | do | Nov. 25, 1864 |
| Ronsinthal, John | do | Nov. 11, 1863 |
| Razel, Andreas | Granville | Nov. 11, 1863 |
| Ryan, Daniel | Greenfield | Sep. 21, 1864 |
| Riley, John | do | Sep. 21, 1864 |
| Reichenbach, John | Lake | Sep. 22, 1864 |
| Ruhle, Charles | do | Sep. 22, 1864 |
| Rusdorf, Joseph | do | Dec. 13, 1864 |
| Ready, Jerry | Franklin | Nov. 11, 1863 |
| Ray, John | | |
| Radish, William | Oak Creek | Sep. 22, 1864 |
| Richardson, Solomon | Racine | Sep. 24, 1864 |
| Relham, Joseph | do | Sep. 24, 1864 |
| Roney, James | do | Nov. 11, 1863 |
| Roberts, William | do | Sep. 22, 1864 |
| Rada, Christian | Pewaukee | Nov. 12, 1863 |
| Rhodes, Nicholas | do | Sep. 22, 1864 |
| Reagen, Richasd | do | Sep. 22, 1864 |
| Regan, Michael | do | Sep. 22, 1864 |
| Rosebrooks, S. E | do | Dec. 2, 1864 |
| Roberts, George | do | Dec. 2, 1864 |
| Riford, Ephraim | do | Dec. 2, 1864 |
| Rhong, Jacob | Menomonee | Sep. 24, 1864 |
| Richard, Henry | do | Sep. 24, 1864 |
| Read, Philip | do | Sep. 24, 1864 |
| Roetts, Peter | do | Sep. 24, 1864 |
| Roetts, Consten | do | Dec. 1, 1864 |
| Repeats, Henry | do | |
| Rabel, Julius | do | |
| Rapin, John C | do | Nov. 25, 1864 |
| Ramlen, Charles | Brookfield | Sep. 23, 1864 |
| Ramstack, George | do | Sep. 23, 1864 |
| Rodahan, John | do | Sep. 23, 1864 |
| Rickert, Joseph | Muskego | Sep. 24, 1864 |

| *Name.* | *Residence.* | *Date.* |
|---|---|---|
| Reed, John | Muskego | Nov. 30, 1864 |
| Ricks, George | Racine | Jan. 19, 1865 |
| Ritting, Jake | do | Nov. 11, 1863 |
| Rigney, Thomas | do | Sep. 22, 1864 |
| Rontlas, Henry | Mount Pleasant | Nov. 11, 1863 |
| Rutka, Jacob | Rochester | Sep. 24, 1864 |
| Robinson, Joshua | Raymond | Nov. 11, 1863 |
| Ransmusen, Hans | do | Sep. 23, 1864 |
| Road, Frederick | Caledonia | Sep. 22, 1864 |
| Ray, Samuel, H | do | Sep. 22, 1864 |
| Rosewal, Franz | do | Dec. 7, 1864 |
| Ryan, Thomas | Paris | Sep. 24, 1864 |
| Reeves, Winfield S | Salem | Sep. 24, 1864 |
| Riggs, John | do | Sep. 24, 1864 |
| Robbins, Charles B | do | Sep. 24, 1864 |
| Ritter, Jacob | do | Sep. 24, 1864 |
| Root, Austin | Randall | Sep. 24, 1864 |
| Robertson, John | do | Dec. 16, 1864 |
| Rowe, William P | Bristol | Sep. 24, 1864 |
| Rogers, John | Richmond | Nov. 12, 1863 |
| Regan, John | La Grange | Nov. 12, 1863 |
| Riggs, James | La Fayette | Nov. 12, 1863 |
| Russell, E. B | East Troy | Dec. 24, 1864 |
| Robinson, James | Boomfield | Nov. 12, 1863 |
| Rust, Alvin | do | Nov. 12, 1863 |
| Robinson, William | Summit | Nov. 30, 1864 |
| Rider, Niliet | Oconomowoc | Sep. 22, 1864 |
| Rollins, Hugh R | Genesee | Nov. 12, 1864 |
| Ranons, Spencer | Beloit | Nov. 12, 1863 |
| Ricker, Pardon | Janesville | Nov. 12, 1863 |
| Rercter, Adolph | Blooming Grove | Nov. 13, 1863 |
| Ripp, Herman | Berry | Feb. 27, 1865 |
| Runge, August | do | Feb. 27, 1865 |
| Ryan, Philip | Mazomanie | Nov. 13, 1863 |
| Rickerman, Nicholas | Sullivan | Nov. 13, 1863 |
| Ritter, Fraye | do | Nov. 13, 1863 |
| Riesner, George | Farmington | Nov. 13, 1863 |
| Ripley, George | Portage city | Sep. 21, 1864 |
| Rose, Daniel | Springvale | Nov. 16, 1863 |
| Riordon, Morris | Lewiston | Sept. 21, 1864 |
| Rolison, Smith | Newport | Nov. 13, 1863 |
| Rye, Ole C | Perry | Sep. 19, 1864 |
| Riley, William | Watertown | Sep. 20, 1864 |
| Rustin Samuel | do | Oct. 15, 1864 |
| Roughten Oeba | Marcellon | Sep. 21, 1864 |
| Riley, Patrick | Ridgeway | Nov. 14, 1863 |
| Ryan, Edward | do | Sep. 28, 1864 |
| Roberts, Sam'l | do | Sep. 28, 1864 |
| Rule, Rich'd | do | Sep. 28, 1864 |
| Riley, Michael | do | Oct. 28, 1864 |
| Reed, Nicholas | do | Nov. 19, 1864 |
| Rowe, R. H. D | Dodgeville | Sep. 28, 1864 |
| Richards, Wm | do | Sep. 28, 1864 |
| Rhinerson, Bennett | do | Oct. 28, 1864 |
| Rundell, Robt | do | Oct. 28, 1864 |
| Roach, Richd | do | Oct. 28, 1864 |
| Richards, Jas | do | Nov. 19, 1864 |
| Reiley, John | Waldwick | Oct. 4, 1864 |
| Rogan, Michael | Moscow | Sep. 28, 1864 |

| *Name* | *Residence* | *Date.* |
|---|---|---|
| Roberts, Matthew | White Oak Springs | Nov. 16, 1863 |
| Reisbeck, Robt | Benton | Nov. 16, 1863 |
| Richardson, John | do | Sep. 29, 1864 |
| Ross, Robt | do | Sep. 29, 1864 |
| Rule, John | do | Sep. 29, 1864 |
| Rogus, Jas | Shullsburg | Nov. 16, 1863 |
| Red, Jas | Beetown | Oct. 1, 1864 |
| Rand, H. C | do | Oct. 1, 1864 |
| Rodda, Edward | Hazel Green | Nov. 19, 1863 |
| Rice, W. A | Excelsior | Nov. 20, 1863 |
| Russ, John | Prairie du Sac | Nov. 20, 1863 |
| Ronshcoup, Jonothan | Bloom | Sep. 26, 1864 |
| Rogus, David | do | Sep. 26, 1864 |
| Ryan, Joseph | Eastman | Oct. 29, 1864 |
| Rathburn, Wm | Lavalle | Oct. 29, 1864 |
| Ryan, Daniel | Marshall | Nov. 19, 1864 |
| Reuchlian, Pat'k | Franklin | Nov. 19, 1864 |
| Ross, Jno | Chippewa Co | Nov. 20, 1863 |
| Raff, Anthony | Jackson | Nov. 18, 1863 |
| Reiser, Andreas | Buffalo Co | Nov. 18, 1863 |
| Ressell, Conrad | Belvidere | Sep. 26, 1864 |
| Rick, Chas | Eagle Mills | Sep. 26, 1864 |
| Riley, James | Kildare | Sep. 19, 1864 |
| Riley, Michael | do | Oct. 31, 1864 |
| Riley, Pat | do | Oct. 31, 1864 |
| Robbins, Jno | Plymouth | Sep. 19, 1864 |
| Robinson, Jno | Lemonweir | Oct. 31, 1864 |
| Root, Chauncey | do | Oct. 31, 1864 |
| Richards, Thos | Adrian | Sep. 20, 1864 |
| Reel, Prospere | Tomah | Sep. 20, 1864 |
| Robinson, Jno | do | Sep. 20, 1864 |
| Rieber, Bonnepart | do | Sep. 20, 1864 |
| Rieber, Sebastian | Oak Dale | Sep. 20, 1864 |
| Robson, Jno | Franklin | Sep. 21, 1864 |
| Richardson, Lewis | do | Sep. 21, 1864 |
| Rich, Edwin, F | Pine Grove | Sep. 22, 1864 |
| Roe, Jarons | Stockton | Sep. 22, 1864 |
| Ridding, Wm | Hull | Sep. 22, 1864 |
| Ramo, Geo | Amherst | Sep. 22, 1864 |
| Remier, Jno | Berlin | Sep. 22, 1864 |
| Roach, Edw'd | Erin Prairie | Sep. 23, 1864 |
| Riley, Patrick | do | Nov. 3, 1864 |
| Raradon, Con | Oak Dale | Nov. 3, 1864 |
| Raymond, Anthony | Lincoln | Sep. 26, 1864 |
| Reed, Orson | do | Sep. 26, 1864 |
| Ross, Edwin R | do | Nov. 14, 1864 |
| Rice, Dwight B | New Haven | Sep. 26, 1864 |
| Risk, Thos | Easton | Sep. 26, 1864 |
| Renmington, Dan'l | do | Nov. 14, 1864 |
| Rowley, Geo. W | Jackson | Nov. 14, 1864 |
| Ripley, Judson S | Springvale | Sep. 26, 1864 |
| Ridgeway, Mahlon | Pepin | Sep. 27, 1864 |
| Richland, N | Waubeek | Sep. 27, 1864 |
| Richie, C. C | do | Sep. 27, 1864 |
| Rombark, Mark | Eau Galle | Sep. 27, 1864 |
| Rivert, Louis | do | Nov. 2, 1864 |
| Reede, W. H | Spring Brook | Sep. 27, 1864 |
| Reede, Robert | do | Sep. 27, 1864 |
| Rowly, Warren | Door Co | Nov. 20, 1863 |

| *Name.* | *Residence.* | *Date* |
|---|---|---|
| Riley, Patrick | Brussells | Dec. 29, 1864 |
| Rock, Fred'k | Gibson | Nov. 21, 1863 |
| Rubitze, Matthias | do | Dec. 29, 1864 |
| Rick, John | do | Dec. 29, 1864 |
| Ready, John | Franklin | Nov. 21, 1863 |
| Robinson, Albert, L | Cato | Nov. 21, 1863 |
| Rumelfaenger, Martin | Meeme | Nov. 21, 1863 |
| Reed, Thos | Cooperstown | Dec. 29, 1864 |
| Ruell, Portas | Manitowoc Rapids | Dec. 29, 1864 |
| Rheinhard, Fred'k | Newton | Dec. 29, 1864 |
| Ruchoft, Henrick | do | Dec. 29, 1864 |
| Renn, John | Menasha | Nov. 23, 1863 |
| Reynolds, Jas. H | Oshkosh city, 1st ward | Nov. 23, 1863 |
| Rooks, Andrew | Nepeuskin | Nov. 23, 1863 |
| Ryan, Patrick | Rushford | Nov. 24, 1863 |
| Richards, Solon, jr | do | Nov. 24, 1863 |
| Reechel, Christopher | Mecan | Nov. 1, 1864 |
| Radethke, Michael | do | Nov. 1, 1864 |
| Reinke, Chas | do | Dec. 31, 1864 |
| Rasler, August | Shields | Nov. 1, 1864 |
| Russell, James | Moundville | Dec. 31, 1864 |
| Rande, James | do | Dec. 31, 1864 |
| Ropersteine, Michael | Newton | Dec. 31, 1864 |
| Rest, Chas | Waushara Co | Nov. 25, 1863 |
| Ringling, Fred'k | Poysippi | Nov. 2, 1864 |
| Ringling, Fred'k | do | Dec. 31, 1864 |
| Roberts, Robt G | Springwater | Nov. 2, 1864 |
| Rozel, Wm. A | Plainfield | Nov. 2, 1864 |
| Rathermiel, Franklin | do | Nov. 2, 1864 |
| Reed, John H | Plainfield | Nov. 25, 1863 |
| Rowley, Andrew | Richford | Dec. 31, 1864 |
| Richmond, Welcom W | Coloma | Dec. 31, 1864 |
| Rogers, Crandall | Oasis | Dec. 31, 1864 |
| Rice, Henry | Waupaca Co | Nov. 25, 1863 |
| Richdassle, Jno. K | Lebanon | Nov. 25, 1863 |
| Rughan, Edw'd | do | Nov. 5, 1864 |
| Roughan, Edw'd | do | Nov. 5, 1864 |
| Richdassle, Lawrence | do | Nov. 25, 1863 |
| Richdassle, Paul | do | Dec. 31, 1864 |
| Rendman, Martin | do | Nov. 25, 1863 |
| Redfield, C. E | Waupaca | Nov. 25, 1863 |
| Rice, Thos | Bear Creek | Nov. 5, 1864 |
| Rice, Bartley | do | Nov. 5, 1864 |
| Rich, O. A | Royalton | Nov. 5, 1864 |
| Richie, Sam'l | do | Nov. 5, 1864 |
| Russell, Lewis A | St. Lawrence | Nov. 5, 1864 |
| Rogers, H | do | Dec. 31, 1864 |
| Ratcliff, James | do | Dec. 31, 1864 |
| Rierson, Ole | Iola | Dec 31, 1864 |
| Rolfson, Runert A | do | Dec. 31, 1864 |
| Russ, Jas. C | do | Nov. 5, 1864 |
| Rombirg, Henry | Caledonia | Dec. 31, 1864 |
| Reifland, H. G | do | Dec. 31, 1864 |
| Randall, M. M | Appleton | Nov 27, 1863 |
| Ryer, Joseph | do | Nov. 27, 1863 |
| Rohrback, Fred | Center | Nov 27, 1863 |
| Room, Jno. Carl | do | Nov. 27, 1863 |
| Rogers, James | do | Nov. 27, 1863 |
| Rogers, Jno | do | Dec. 28, 1864 |

| *Name.* | *Residence.* | *Date.* |
|---|---|---|
| Rhinehart, Jno | Hortonia | Dec. 28, 1864 |
| Reedy, Martin | Morrison | Nov. 27, 1863 |
| Raunotte, Jaque J | Bellville | Nov. 27, 1863 |
| Rahr, Augustus | do | Dec. 28, 1864 |
| Renward, Francoine | Green Bay | Dec. 28, 1864 |
| Reed, Jno | Washington | Dec. 28, 1864 |
| Radamach, Wm | Marinette | Nov. 28, 1863 |
| Redmond, P | Pensuakee | Nov. 28, 1863 |
| Richaboo, Adam | Stiles | Nov. 28, 1863 |
| Rabe, Henry | do | Dec. 29, 1864 |
| Rexnell, Theodore | Little Suamico | Dec. 29, 1864 |
| Redman, Leroy | do | Dec. 29, 1864 |
| Ryan, Thos | do | Dec. 29, 1864 |
| Ryan, Patrick | do | Nov. 28, 1863 |
| Rolf, Wm | Woodville | Dec. 28, 1864 |
| Rummaph, Martin | Harrison | Dec. 28, 1864 |
| Robinson, Joel | Stockbridge | Dec. 28, 1864 |
| Rembold, F | do | Dec. 28, 1864 |
| Rogler, John | Brothertown | Dec. 28, 1864 |
| Ruscan, Francis | Casco | Dec. 29, 1864 |
| Retler, Wm | Carlton | Dec. 29, 1864 |

## S

| Name | Residence | Date |
|---|---|---|
| Schumner, Casper | Belgium | Dec. 1, 1864 |
| Steffer, Antone | do | Dec. 1, 1864 |
| Schuller, Lawrence | do | Dec. 1, 1864 |
| Steinmeitzer, Nicholas | do | Dec. 1, 1864 |
| Schumner, Lambert | do | Dec. 1, 1864 |
| Sehumining, Henry | do | Dec. 1, 1864 |
| Striff, John | Fredonia | Oct. 14, 1864 |
| Shoeger, Luthmid | do | Oct. 14, 1864 |
| Sanman, John | do | Oct. 14, 1864 |
| Sheno, Jacob | do | Oct. 14, 1864 |
| Schueler, John | do | Dec. 1, 1864 |
| Sauerepry, Daniel | do | Dec. 1, 1864 |
| Short, Felix | do | Dec. 1, 1864 |
| Steffens, Nicholas | do | Dec. 1, 1864 |
| Shforog, John P | do | Dec. 1, 1864 |
| State, George | Grafton | Oct. 13, 1864 |
| Smith, John | do | Oct. 13, 1864 |
| Shellhon, ——— | do | Oct. 13, 1864 |
| Shafer, John D | do | Dec. 1, 1864 |
| Sulfow, Godlip | do | Dec. 1, 1864 |
| Smoka, George | do | Dec. 1, 1864 |
| Strange, Peter | do | Jan. 27, 1865 |
| Seil, Anthony | Port Washington | Nov. 23, 1863 |
| Schengen, Michael | do | Nov. 28, 1863 |
| Schneider, Nicholas | Farmington | Dec. 1, 1864 |
| Shaunor, William | Jackson | Nov. 21, 1863 |
| Strelow, Henry | do | Oct. 11, 1864 |
| Schustler, Jacob | Germantown | Nov. 21, 1863 |
| Schorsch, Nicholas | Belgium | Nov. 21, 1863 |
| Schorsh, Michael | do | Nov. 21, 1863 |
| Steess, Nicholas J | do | Oct. 13, 1864 |
| Schmidt, Peter | do | Oct. 13, 1864 |
| Stief, Peter | do | Oct. 13, 1864 |
| Schmidt, Peter | do | Oct. 13, 1864 |
| Schmidt, Nicholas | do | Oct. 13, 1864 |
| Scheller, John | do | Oct. 13, 1864 |

| *Name.* | *Residence.* | *Date.* |
|---|---|---|
| Scholler, John | Belgium | Oct. 13, 1864 |
| Stief, Jacob | do | Oct. 13, 1864 |
| Scholl, Joseph | do | Oct. 13, 1864 |
| Schreiner, Jacob | do | Oct. 13, 1864 |
| Steinback, Nicholas | do | Oct. 13, 1864 |
| Steimnetch, Nick jr | do | Oct. 13, 1864 |
| Schmid, Valarius | do | Oct. 13, 1864 |
| Schreiner, Hubert | do | Oct. 13, 1864 |
| Schorsch, John | do | Oct. 13, 1864 |
| Steinback, Nicholas | do | Oct. 13, 1864 |
| Scharmen, Nicholas | do | Oct. 13, 1864 |
| Strans, Nicholas jr | do | Oct. 13, 1864 |
| Schitz, Michael | do | Oct 13, 1864 |
| Sanem, John | do | Oct. 13, 1864 |
| Schubwaber Math | do | Dec. 1, 1864 |
| Schuly, William | do | Dec. 1, 1864 |
| Schmitz, Sebastian | do | Dec. 1, 1864 |
| Schaack, John | do | Dec. 1, 1864 |
| Schanen, Nicholas | do | Dec. 1, 1864 |
| Stack, Wm | Polk | Dec. 8, 1864 |
| Schuck, David | do | Dec. 8, 1864 |
| Stoft, John | do | Dec. 8, 1864 |
| Schmidt, Philip | do | Dec. 8, 1864 |
| Shaffer, Apolorases | Richfield | Nov. 21, 1864 |
| Susony, Joseph | do | Oct. 12, 1864 |
| Schneider, Nathan | do | Oct. 12, 1864 |
| Shannon, John | do | Oct. 12, 1864 |
| Shanner, James | do | Oct. 12, 1864 |
| Suson, John | do | Oct. 12, 1864 |
| Sufron, Heinrich | do | Dec. 1, 1864 |
| Schmitt, John | do | Dec. 1, 1864 |
| Schmitz, John | do | Dec. 1, 1864 |
| Schuster, John | do | Jan. 27, 1865 |
| Sieffer, Richard | do | Jan. 27, 1865 |
| Sullivan, John | do | Jan. 27, 1865 |
| Stow, Wm | do | Oct. 18, 1864 |
| Shenn, John | do | Oct 18, 1864 |
| Schmidt, Peter | do | Oct. 18, 1864 |
| Schuster, Mortez | do | Oct. 18, 1864 |
| Smitz, John | do | Oct. 18, 1864 |
| Seedeman, Carl | do | Oct. 18, 1864 |
| Seagel, George | do | Oct. 18, 1864 |
| Strong, Jacob | do | Oct. 18, 1864 |
| Swin, Peter | Farmington | Dec. 1, 1864 |
| Shoemaker, Joseph | do | Dec. 1, 1864 |
| Smith, Mathias | do | Dec. 1, 1864 |
| Schnier, Chas | do | Dec. 1, 1864 |
| Stopfer, Joseph | Saukville | Oct. 14, 1864 |
| Sunish, Peter | do | Oct. 14, 1864 |
| Sumach, John | do | Oct. 14, 1864 |
| Schleich, Peter | do | Oct 14, 1864 |
| Stein, John | Sheboygan | Nov. 23, 1863 |
| Schubel, Gottfried | do | Nov. 24, 1863 |
| Schwartz, Frank | do | Oct. 25, 1864 |
| Sindel, Andreas | do | Oct. 25, 1864 |
| Spiettel, August | do | Oct. 25, 1864 |
| Stecging, Fr | do | Oct. 25, 1864 |
| Schilling, Mathias | do | Oct. 25, 1864 |
| Sindel, Ambeas | do | Dec. 2, 1864 |

| *Name.* | *Residence.* | *Date.* |
|---|---|---|
| Schwanekampf, Henry | Sheboygan | Oct. 18, 1864 |
| Sommer, Carl | do | Oct. 18, 1864 |
| Sticker, Jokin | do | Oct. 18, 1864 |
| Schwarzbeck, Anton | do | Dec. 2, 1864 |
| Schmidt, Adolph | do | Oct. 18, 1864 |
| Schubert, Joseph | do | Oct. 18, 1864 |
| Schrader, Fred | do | Oct. 18, 1864 |
| Schumble, Joseph | do | Oct. 18, 1864 |
| Schmidt, George | do | Oct. 18, 1864 |
| Stresser, Herman | do | Oct. 18, 1864 |
| Sieber, Nicholas | do | Oct. 18, 1864 |
| Schutz, Sigmond | do | Oct. 18, 1864 |
| Schuller, Peter | Moselle | Oct. 18, 1864 |
| Schubez, Martin | Sheboygan Falls | Nov. 24, 1864 |
| Stemiel, Eugene | Plymouth | Dec. 6, 1864 |
| Schumburg, Conrad | Sheboygan Falls | Oct. 25, 1864 |
| Sweeting, Thomas J | do | Oct. 25, 1864 |
| Smith, Frederick | do | Dec. 2, 1864 |
| Sargeant, Wm. | do | Dec. 2, 1864 |
| Storm, Gasper | do | Dec. 2, 1864 |
| Shoemaker, John | do | Dec. 2, 1864 |
| Suratovey, William | do | Dec. 2, 1864 |
| Squires, G. C | Lima | Oct. 24, 1864 |
| Stammers, John | do | Oct. 24, 1864 |
| Smith, Hiram | do | Oct. 24, 1864 |
| Schooner, Fritz | do | Dec. 2, 1864 |
| Samson, John | do | Jan. 27, 1865 |
| Scheher, P | Holland | Oct. 21, 1864 |
| Schons, Nichola | do | Oct. 21, 1864 |
| Schwezerhart, Mathy | do | Dec. 2, 1864 |
| Shaver, John jr | do | Dec. 2, 1864 |
| Scholte, H. J | do | Jan. 27, 1865 |
| Schwantz, Nicholas | Abbott | Oct. 18, 1864 |
| Stanley, Merit | do | Oct. 18, 1864 |
| Scerilin, Patrick | do | Oct. 18, 1864 |
| Scheovmart, August | do | Jan. 27, 1865 |
| Stiller, Jacob | Scott | Oct. 21, 1864 |
| Seifert, Herman | do | Oct. 21, 1864 |
| Stanley, Julius | do | Dec. 2, 1864 |
| Suhrke, John | Plymouth | Oct. 21, 1864 |
| Savage, John | Herman | Nov. 20, 1863 |
| Steinheal, George | do | Nov. 20, 1863 |
| Schreiber, Gotheib | do | Dec. 2, 1864 |
| Schultz, Martin | do | Dec. 2, 1864 |
| Schumer, Peter | Trenton | Nov. 20, 1863 |
| Stanton, Geo | do | Nov. 20, 1863 |
| Smith, Monroe | Rubicon | Nov. 21, 1863 |
| Sawger, Alexander. | Wayne | Nov. 21, 1863 |
| Shiners, William | Hartford | Nov. 21, 1863 |
| Sullivan, James | Erin | Nov. 21, 1863 |
| Sewhm, John | do | Nov. 21, 1863 |
| Scollard, James jr | do | Oct. 12, 1864 |
| Sullivan, David | do | Dec. 1, 1864 |
| Scollard, William | do | Dec. 1, 1864 |
| Siebenstien, Phil | Barton | Dec. 1, 1864 |
| Slazer, John A | do | Dec. 1, 1864 |
| Seipp, Wm | do | Dec. 1, 1864 |
| Staff, Geo. G | West Bend | Nov. 21, 1863 |
| Schmidt, John (4th) | Polk | Nov. 21, 1863 |

| *Name.* | *Residence.* | *Date* |
|---|---|---|
| Seele, Norman | Polk | Nov. 21, 1863 |
| Stegenmyer, Geo | do | Oct. 12, 1864 |
| Streder, Anton | do | Oct. 12, 1864 |
| Strietz, Adam | do | Oct. 12, 1864 |
| Schmeiss, Peter | do | Oct. 12, 1864 |
| Schuss, Johann | do | Oct. 12, 1864 |
| Staab, John | do | Oct. 12, 1864 |
| Sheber, Franz | Emmett | Oct. 11, 1864 |
| Seefeld, Frederick | do | Oct. 11, 1864 |
| Stoffel, John | do | Oct. 11, 1864 |
| Schuttre, August H | do | Oct. 11, 1864 |
| Shrader, Charles | Burnett | Nov. 20, 1863 |
| Sisson, Henry | Chester | Nov. 20, 1863 |
| Schreiber, Christian | Watertown | Oct. 6, 1864 |
| Sack, Carl | do | Oct. 6, 1864 |
| Schmidt, Albert | do | Oct. 6, 1864 |
| Shmutzter, Fred | do | Oct. 6, 1864 |
| Shultz, Henry | do | Oct. 6, 1864 |
| Sputman, Robert | do | Dec. 1, 1864 |
| Seckander, G | do | Dec. 1, 1864 |
| Sattig, Henry | do | Dec. 1, 1864 |
| Schmidt, John | do | Dec. 1, 1864 |
| Schenk, John | do | Dec. 1, 1864 |
| Snider, Jacob H | Leroy | Nov. 20, 1863 |
| Shermerhorn, ——— | do | Nov. 20, 1863 |
| Smith, Charles | do | Oct. 4, 1864 |
| Sprague, Oscar F | do | Oct. 4, 1864 |
| Seigle, Joseph | do | Dec. 1, 1864 |
| Sidler, Christopher | Lomira | Nov. 20, 1863 |
| Schultz, Frederick | do | Nov. 20, 1863 |
| Sumner, James | do | Nov. 20, 1863 |
| Shultze, Julius | do | Oct. 6, 1864 |
| Schisco, Louis | do | Oct. 6, 1864 |
| Seefelt, Theodore | do | Oct. 6, 1864 |
| Scherr, Casper | do | Jan. 27, 1865 |
| Seskie, Anson | do | Jan. 27, 1865 |
| Schmidt, Eberhard | do | Jan. 27, 1865 |
| Scheiler, Carl | do | Jan. 27, 1865 |
| Sylvester, Seaman | Fond du Lac | Nov. 19, 1863 |
| Smith, Henry | do | Nov. 19, 1863 |
| Secor, John | do | Nov. 19, 1863 |
| Seacord, John | do | Nov. 19, 1863 |
| Strayckmons, Filician | do | Nov. 19, 1863 |
| Stevens, R. G | do | Nov. 19, 1863 |
| Strannell, Nicholas | do | Nov. 19, 1863 |
| Sanders, John | Osceola | Nov. 19, 1863 |
| Shay, Thomas | Oakfield | Nov. 19, 1863 |
| Seuft, Frederick | Ashford | Nov. 19, 1863 |
| Sie, John | Calumet | Nov. 19, 1863 |
| Smith, Ira H | Lamartine | Nov. 19, 1863 |
| Shaw, Ame | do | Nov. 19, 1863 |
| Shultz, Joel J | Alto | Nov. 19, 1863 |
| Stepte, Nathan | Ripon | Nov. 19, 1863 |
| Spriggle, William | do | Nov. 19, 1863 |
| Smith, John | Eldorado | Oct. 5, 1864 |
| Shermon, Theron | do | Oct. 5, 1864 |
| Shweper, John | do | Dec. 1, 1864 |
| Smith, William | do | Dec. 1, 1864 |
| Sherman, Duton | do | Dec. 1, 1864 |

| *Name.* | *Residence.* | *Date.* |
|---|---|---|
| Sheverim, Laurich | Eldorado | Dec. 1, 1864 |
| Sulivan, Eugene | Fox Lake | Nov. 19, 1863 |
| Seward, Edward | Calamus | Nov. 20, 1863 |
| Schustes, Adam | Shields | Nov. 20, 1863 |
| Stacy, Wm | Emmett | Nov. 20, 1863 |
| Shanahan, Thomas | Milwaukee | Sep. 21, 1864 |
| Shanahan, James | do | Sep. 21, 1864 |
| Streeper, James D | do | Sep. 21, 1864 |
| Stickling, William | do | Sep. 21, 1864 |
| Strou, George | do | Sep. 21, 1864 |
| Sehr, ——— | do | Sep. 21, 1864 |
| Sully, Patrick | do | Sep. 21, 1864 |
| Seymour, James L. | do | Sep. 21, 1864 |
| Smith, B. | do | Nov. 10, 1863 |
| Shrimer, Franz | do | Nov. 10, 1863 |
| Schennaker, G | do | Nov. 10, 1863 |
| Schrieber, Charles | do | Nov. 10, 1863 |
| Sleusby, Dennis | do | Nov. 10, 1863 |
| Schermey, Vincent | do | Nov. 10, 1863 |
| Seriedke, John | do | Nov. 10, 1863 |
| Steinke, Joseph | do | Nov. 10, 1863 |
| Stock, T. T | do | Nov. 10, 1863 |
| Schrieber, Ernst | do | Nov. 10, 1863 |
| Sullbrandt, Henry | do | Nov. 10, 1863 |
| Scofield, John | do | Nov. 10, 1863 |
| Schaly, William | do | Nov. 10, 1863 |
| Stroebel, George | do | Nov. 10, 1863 |
| Schmidt, Christopher | do | Nov. 10, 1863 |
| Schmidt, Henry | do | Nov. 10, 1863 |
| Shuler, Domenick | do | Sep. 21, 1864 |
| Stevenson, Charles | do | Sep. 21, 1864 |
| Seeman, Anton | do | Sep. 21, 1864 |
| Schwaller, John | do | Sep. 21, 1864 |
| Schroefer, Charles | do | Sep. 21, 1864 |
| Smith, Frederick | do | Nov. 11, 1863 |
| Sander, Gustav | do | Nov. 11, 1863 |
| Seeger, Jacob | do | Nov. 11, 1863 |
| Sherman, August | do | Nov. 11, 1863 |
| Smith, Charles | do | Sep. 21, 1864 |
| Schmidt, Rothelf | do | Sep. 21, 1864 |
| Sauss, John | do | Sep. 21, 1864 |
| Shue, William | do | Nov. 25, 1864 |
| Stein, Nicholas | do | Nov. 25, 1864 |
| Smith, Jacob | do | Nov. 25, 1864 |
| Sittser, John | do | Nov. 25, 1864 |
| Schiess, Louis | do | Nov. 25, 1864 |
| Schaeder, George | do | Nov. 25, 1864 |
| Stein, Nichodemus | do | Nov. 25, 1864 |
| Strautmire, Jaeck | do | Nov. 25, 1864 |
| Schlein, Heinrich | do | Nov. 11, 1863 |
| Schimmer, Joseph | do | Nov. 11, 1863 |
| Schmidt, Bernhard | do | Nov. 11, 1863 |
| Schwermann, Johann | do | Nov. 11, 1863 |
| Schmidt, Christopher | do | Nov. 11, 1863 |
| Stiehl, Johann | do | Nov. 11, 1863 |
| Schutner, Frederick | do | Sep. 21, 1864 |
| Scherr, Frank | do | Sep. 21, 1864 |
| Stuewahs, ——— | do | Sep. 21, 1864 |
| Sepsen, Johann | do | Sep. 21, 1864 |

| *Name.* | *Residence.* | *Date.* |
|---|---|---|
| Sprinke, Gerd William | Milwaukee | Sep. 21, 1864 |
| Schneider, Paul | do | Sep. 21, 1864 |
| Sebold, Heinrich | do | Sep. 21, 1864 |
| Sturk, Frederick | do | Sep. 21, 1864 |
| Schaefer, Anton | do | Sep. 21, 1864 |
| Schermerhorn, John | do | Sep. 21, 1864 |
| Schwautus, Fred | do | Sep. 21, 1864 |
| Stroebe, Charles | do | Nov. 15, 1864 |
| Schoen, Jacob | do | Nov. 15, 1864 |
| Stauf, Hans | do | Nov. 16, 1864 |
| Strack, William | do | Nov. 16, 1864 |
| Smith, John D | do | Nov. 16, 1864 |
| Shumacher, John | do | Nov. 16, 1864 |
| Schmidt, Charles | do | Nov. 16, 1864 |
| Schmeissner, John | do | Nov. 16, 1864 |
| Smith, David | do | Nov. 16, 1864 |
| Schuster, Freder'k Schroeder | do | Nov. 16, 1864 |
| Sindorf, Mathias | do | Nov. 16, 1864 |
| Soipel, Jacob | do | Nov. 16, 1864 |
| Salmon, Casper | do | Nov. 16, 1864 |
| Shaver, Charles | do | Nov. 10, 1863 |
| Soldgis, Edward | do | Nov. 10, 1863 |
| Smith, Patrick | do | Nov. 10, 1863 |
| Schmeling, Fred. Wm | do | Nov. 10, 1863 |
| Selben, Ernest | do | Sep. 21, 1864 |
| Stodolkd, ——— | do | Sep. 21, 1864 |
| Sander, Henry | do | Sep. 21, 1864 |
| Scumockys, Charles | do | Sep. 21, 1864 |
| Steig, Carl | do | Sep. 21, 1864 |
| Shafer, Herman | do | Sep. 21, 1864 |
| Stanley, Henry A | do | Sep. 21, 1864 |
| Sacarason, Gabriel | do | Sep. 21, 1864 |
| Saus, Charles | do | Sep. 21, 1864 |
| Sergers, Heinrich | do | Sep. 21, 1864 |
| Schoen, ——— | do | Sep. 21, 1864 |
| Schrodd, Johann | do | Sep. 21, 1864 |
| Schulbert, Paulus | do | Sep. 21, 1864 |
| Schul, Peter | do | Sep. 21, 1864 |
| Stoll, Carl | do | Sep. 21, 1864 |
| Schebeck, Johann | do | Sep. 21, 1864 |
| Stelling, Johann | do | Sep. 21, 1864 |
| Stoll, Heinrich | do | Sep. 21, 1864 |
| Schmidt, Jacob | do | Sep. 21, 1864 |
| Schroeder, Albert | do | Sep. 21, 1864 |
| Schlaegel, Xavier | do | Sept. 21, 1864 |
| Schultz, Gottlied Aug | do | Nov. 25, 1864 |
| Shue, Philip | do | Nov. 25, 1864 |
| Steiner, John | do | Nov. 25, 1864 |
| Schuler, Charles | do | Nov. 25, 1864 |
| Schauss, Nicholas | do | Nov. 25, 1864 |
| Stark, Wilhelm | do | Nov. 25, 1864 |
| Stull, Henry | do | Nov. 25, 1864 |
| Semmer, Frederick | do | Nov. 25, 1864 |
| Sanders, Gerhard | do | Nov. 30, 1864 |
| Schinke, Gottleib | do | Jan. 26, 1865 |
| Swiens, G. H | do | Jan. 26, 1865 |
| Schultz, Heinrich | do | Jan. 26, 1865 |
| Schmidt, Carl | do | Jan. 26, 1865 |
| Schwartz, Carl | do | Jan. 26, 1865 |

| *Name.* | *Residence.* | *Date.* |
|---|---|---|
| Stark, Matthias | Milwaukee | Jan. 26, 1865 |
| Schalock, Gottleib | do | Jan. 26, 1865 |
| Sullivan, F. | do | Sep. 20, 1864 |
| Shaw, George | do | Sep. 20, 1864 |
| Sullivan, Charles | do | Sep. 20, 1864 |
| Smith, B. | do | Sep. 20, 1864 |
| Simmonds, D. | do | Sep. 20, 1864 |
| Samuel, James | do | Nov. 15, 1864 |
| Sullivan, Louran | do | Nov. 15, 1864 |
| Sweeney, Ed | do | Nov. 15, 1864 |
| Shumaker, T. | do | Nov. 15, 1864 |
| Spellan, William | do | Nov. 15, 1864 |
| Shanley, John | do | Nov. 15, 1864 |
| Shepler, B S | do | Nov. 15, 1864 |
| Sullivan, Dennis | do | Nov. 15, 1864 |
| Stone, E | do | Nov. 15, 1864 |
| Slettr, Charles | do | Nov. 15, 1864 |
| Smith, C. S. | do | Jan. 11, 1865 |
| Shea, Patrick | do | Jan. 11, 1865 |
| Spell, George | do | Jan. 11, 1865 |
| Sinnopp, John | do | Jan. 11, 1865 |
| Slingsby, P. | do | Jan. 11, 1865 |
| Smith, Michael | do | Nov. 10, 1863 |
| Sisson, Wm. B. | do | Nov. 10, 1863 |
| Storks, James | do | Nov. 10, 1863 |
| Souther, Frederick | do | Nov. 10, 1863 |
| Shannon, Joseph | do | Nov. 10, 1863 |
| Smith, Thomas | do | Sep. 21, 1864 |
| Schroener, Adam | do | Sep. 21, 1864 |
| Semr, ——— | do | Sep. 21, 1864 |
| Smith, Thomas | do | Sep. 21, 1864 |
| Schiffner, George | do | Jan. 19, 1865 |
| Syinky, August | do | Jan. 19, 1865 |
| Shased, Charley | do | Jan. 19, 1865 |
| Steinhart, Fred | do | Jan. 19, 1865 |
| Schroeter, Wm | do | Sep. 20, 1864 |
| Schnick, Wm. | do | Nov. 14, 1864 |
| Strapburger, Wm. | do | Nov. 14, 1864 |
| Schehman, George | do | Nov. 14, 1864 |
| Schmidt, Jacob | do | Nov. 14, 1864 |
| Schrey, Adolph | do | Nov. 14, 1864 |
| Schirkes, A. | do | Nov. 14, 1864 |
| Sullivan, Ed | do | Nov. 10, 1863 |
| Sours, N. | do | Nov. 10, 1863 |
| Sullivan, Pat | do | Nov. 10, 1863 |
| Smith, J. M | do | Nov. 10, 1863 |
| Sure, A | do | Nov. 10, 1863 |
| Staff, J. | do | Nov. 10, 1863 |
| Steel, William | do | Nov. 10, 1863 |
| Savin, J. | do | Nov. 10, 1863 |
| Shawley, M. | do | Nov. 10, 1863 |
| Stone, Charles | do | Nov. 10, 1863 |
| Savin, N. | do | Nov. 10, 1863 |
| Sedin, Edward | do | Nov. 10, 1863 |
| Stapleton, Frank | do | Nov. 10, 1863 |
| Smith, Bryan | do | Nov. 10, 1863 |
| Spice, John | do | Sep. 20, 1864 |
| Sheehan, R. | do | Sep. 20, 1864 |
| Short, M. | do | Sep. 20, 1864 |

| *Name.* | *Residence.* | *Date.* |
|---|---|---|
| Sterns, M. | Milwaukee | Sep. 20, 1864 |
| Shuri, Michael | do | Sep. 20, 1864 |
| Solan, Michael | do | Sep. 20, 1864 |
| Son, Heiches | do | Nov. 9, 1863 |
| Short, George | do | Nov. 9, 1863 |
| Stehan, Charles | do | Nov. 9, 1863 |
| Shaw, Daniel | do | Nov. 9, 1863 |
| Schmidt, George | do | Nov. 9, 1863 |
| Schultz, Daniel | do | Nov. 9, 1863 |
| Schuck, Gottlieb | do | Nov. 9, 1863 |
| Seremar, Paul | do | Nov. 9, 1863 |
| Scott, Wm. B. | do | Nov. 9, 1863 |
| Schmitz, Morritz | do | Nov. 9, 1863 |
| Short, John | do | Nov. 9, 1863 |
| Sill, Wm. | do | Sep. 19, 1864 |
| Stephenson, J. A. | do | Sep. 19, 1864 |
| Stitler, Louis | do | Sept. 19, 1864 |
| Schwimmer, Paul | do | Sep. 19, 1864 |
| Schwitzer, E. | do | Sep. 19, 1864 |
| Smith, Fritz | do | Sep. 19, 1864 |
| Stirns, Henry | do | Sep. 19, 1864 |
| Seckaldach, August | do | Sep. 19, 1864 |
| Sagle, George | do | Nov. 14, 1864 |
| Schmidt, John, Sr. | do | Nov. 14, 1864 |
| Schrader, John | do | Nov. 14, 1864 |
| Senderz, William | do | Nov. 14, 1864 |
| Sullivan, Timothy | do | Nov. 14, 1864 |
| Strauss, Fred | do | Nov. 14, 1864 |
| Stein, Louis | do | Nov. 14, 1864 |
| Stein, Henry | do | Nov. 14, 1864 |
| Schmidt, John, jr. | do | Nov. 14, 1864 |
| Schmidt, Martin | do | Nov. 14, 1864 |
| Schenck, Gottlieb | do | Nov. 14, 1864 |
| Seerge, Jas. | do | Nov. 14, 1864 |
| Shever, Wm. | do | Nov. 14, 1864 |
| Seller, Leonard | do | Nov. 14, 1864 |
| Schofield, J. H. | do | Nov. 14, 1864 |
| Schuck, John | do | Dec. 22, 1864 |
| Schmidt, Fred | do | Dec. 22, 1864 |
| Saltzer, John | do | Dec. 22, 1864 |
| Sharpstein, J. K. | do | Dec. 22, 1864 |
| Schmidt, Ernest | do | Nov. 9, 1863 |
| Struder, John | do | Nov. 9, 1863 |
| Schieke, John | do | Nov. 9, 1863 |
| Schrym, Crokles | do | Nov. 9, 1863 |
| Seebich, John | do | Nov. 9, 1863 |
| Schlund, Johann | do | Nov. 9, 1863 |
| Schein, C. | do | Nov. 9, 1863 |
| Sery, Wm. | do | Nov. 9, 1863 |
| Screiber, Theo | do | Nov. 9, 1863 |
| Schruer, Adam | do | Nov. 9, 1863 |
| Schenck, John | do | Nov. 9, 1863 |
| Steiser, O. | do | Sep. 20, 1864 |
| Schmidt, Adam, jr. | do | Sep. 20, 1864 |
| Schlensker, Henry | do | Sep. 20, 1864 |
| Sren, Jacob | do | Sep. 20, 1864 |
| Scholker, Christian | do | Sep. 20, 1864 |
| Seebenhuner, Louis | do | Sep. 22, 1864 |
| Sorgenprie, Joachim | do | Sep. 22, 1864 |

| *Name.* | *Residence.* | *Date.* |
|---|---|---|
| Schult, Edward | Milwaukee | Dec. 7, 1864 |
| Schearier, Jas. E | do | Dec. 7, 1864 |
| Simmon, Heinrich | do | Dec. 7, 1864 |
| Serth, Joseph | Granville | Nov. 11, 1863 |
| Stork, Henry | do | Sep. 22, 1864 |
| Schurrlets, Ernest | do | Sep. 22, 1864 |
| Schuster, Anthony | do | Sep. 22, 1864 |
| Schnider, Anton | Wauwatosa | Nov. 11, 1863 |
| Sonner, Charles | do | Nov. 11, 1863 |
| Sonnen, Charles | do | Nov. 11, 1863 |
| Schultz, Albert | do | Nov. 11, 1863 |
| Stark, Nicholas | Greenfield | Nov. 11, 1863 |
| Smith, Joseph | do | Sep. 22, 1864 |
| Slater, Henry | do | Sep. 22, 1864 |
| Smith, Daniel | do | Sep. 22, 1864 |
| Stult, Samuel | do | Sep. 22, 1864 |
| Slemmer, Frederick | do | Sep. 21, 1864 |
| Stedler, Henry | do | Sep. 21, 1864 |
| Scot, John | do | Sep. 21, 1864 |
| Sanford, Michael | Lake | Nov. 11, 1863 |
| Stiffens, Antony | do | Nov. 11, 1863 |
| Steiner, John | do | Nov. 11, 1863 |
| Schimpgin, John | do | Sep. 22, 1864 |
| Schroeder, John | do | Sep. 22, 1864 |
| Schudar, Gottleib | do | Sep. 22, 1864 |
| Sies, Joseph | do | Sep. 22, 1864 |
| Stowe, Soloman, A. | Randall | Dec. 16, 1864 |
| Stout, Peter | Bristol | Nov. 12, 1864 |
| Stumard, Edward S | do | Sep. 24, 1864 |
| Soloman, George | Delavan | Nov. 12, 1863 |
| Shaw, George D. | Sharon | Nov. 12, 1863 |
| Stafford, John | Whitewater | Nov. 12, 1863 |
| Sharin, John | do | Nov. 12, 1863 |
| Smith, William | Linn | Nov. 12, 1863 |
| Shindler, Richard | East Troy | Sep. 24, 1864 |
| Shinder, John | do | Dec. 2, 1864 |
| Sharp, John | do | Dec. 2, 1864 |
| Street, James | do | Dec. 2, 1864 |
| Sherman, Chas. H | do | Dec. 2, 1864 |
| Snider, Wendel | Hudson | Nov. 12, 1863 |
| Sunnumers, Fred'k | Bloomfield | Nov. 12, 1863 |
| Smith, Theodore | do | Nov. 12, 1863 |
| Spence, James | Ottawa | Nov. 12, 1863 |
| Smith, John | Summit | Nov. 12, 1863 |
| Sibling, Michael | do | Sep. 22, 1864 |
| Spaulding, Thomas | do | Sep. 22, 1864 |
| Shellhom, John | do | Sep. 22, 1864 |
| Stickles, Edward | do | Sep. 22, 1864 |
| Stevens, Philip | do | Nov. 30, 1864 |
| Stohlman, Wm | do | Nov. 30, 1864 |
| Sauter, Thaddeus | Oconomowoc | Nov. 12, 1863 |
| Sanderson, Jacob | do | Sep. 22, 1864 |
| Smith, August | do | Sep. 22, 1864 |
| Shuch, Jacob | Merton | Nov. 12, 1864 |
| Shaffer, Jacob | Pewaukee | Nov. 12, 1864 |
| Sherlds, Thomas | do | Sep. 22, 1864 |
| Stowell, Trueman | do | Dec. 2, 1864 |
| Sears, Burton | do | Dec. 2, 1864 |
| Stillwell, Wm. D | Vernon | Nov. 12, 1863 |

| Name. | Residence. | Date. |
|---|---|---|
| Stuart, Archibald | Vernon... | Sep. 24, 1864 |
| Scarland, Gustave | do | Sep. 24, 1864 |
| Stuart, Thomas | do | Sep. 24, 1864 |
| Shelling, Henry | Menomonee | Sep. 24, 1864 |
| Schmidt. John | do | Sep. 24, 1864 |
| Shontrer, Jonas | do | Sep. 24, 1864 |
| Sauler, John | do | Dec. 1, 1864 |
| Sohn, Frederick | do | Dec. 1, 1864 |
| Sauler, Andrew | do | Dec. 1, 1864 |
| Stillwagen, Conrad | do | Dec 1, 1864 |
| Schow, Carl | do | Nov. 25, 1864 |
| Schwanbeck, Fred | do | Nov. 25, 1864 |
| Spahl, Carl | do | Nov. 25, 1864 |
| Stark, William | Brookfield | Nov. 12, 1863 |
| Stanton, Le Roy | do | Sep. 23, 1864 |
| Sterling, Walter | New Berlin | Nov. 12, 1863 |
| Stroung, Ansel | do | Nov. 12, 1863 |
| Smith, F. A | do | Nov. 12, 1863 |
| Steel, M. R | do | Nov. 12, 1863 |
| Stuart, S. D | Muskego | Sep. 24, 1864 |
| Sullivan, John | do | Sep. 24, 1864 |
| Shean, Patrick | do | Sep. 24, 1864 |
| Sullivan, Timothy | do | Nov. 30, 1864 |
| Shuky, Christopher | do | Dec. 1, 1864 |
| Shauly, William | Delafield | Sep. 22, 1864 |
| Sharer, Thomas | Mount Pleasant | Sep. 23, 1864 |
| Seiver, Adam | Dover | Sept. 23, 1864 |
| Schmidt, Frank | Burlington | Nov. 11, 1863 |
| Smith, John | Rochester | Sep. 24, 1864 |
| Southworth, Seth | do | Sep. 24, 1864 |
| Smith, Henry | Raymond | Nov. 11, 1863 |
| Sumerton, James | do | Dec. 9, 1864 |
| Spencer, Alfred | Caledonia | Sep. 22, 1864 |
| Shultz, Christian | do | Sep. 22, 1864 |
| Schneider, Conrad | do | Sep. 22, 1864 |
| Spaang, William | do | Sep. 22, 1864 |
| Shiding, Gustaves | do | Sep. 22, 1864 |
| Shindell, Jacab J | do | Dec. 7, 1864 |
| Schrawder, William | do | Dec. 7, 1864 |
| Stebbins, Alexander | do | Dec. 7, 1864 |
| Staples, Charles | do | Dec. 7, 1864 |
| Smitz, Franz | Kenosha | Nov. 12, 1863 |
| Snow, Charles | Somers | Nov. 12, 1863 |
| Sullivan, Daniel | Brighton | Nov. 12, 1863 |
| Searles, Thomas | do | Nov. 12, 1863 |
| Smith, C. O | Wheatland | Sep. 24, 1864 |
| Spitzman, Herman | do | Sep. 24, 1864 |
| Smithcamp, John | do | Sep. 24, 1864 |
| Schrader, Ludwic | Salem | Sep. 24, 1864 |
| Schiller, George | do | Sep. 24, 1864 |
| Schownaren, Ludvic | do | Sep. 24, 1864 |
| Schutle, Conrad | Lake | Dec. 13, 1864 |
| Siering, Anthony | do | Dec. 13, 1864 |
| Schuttle, Henry | do | Dec. 13, 1864 |
| Steel, George | do | Dec. 13, 1864 |
| Stefer, Henry | Franklin | Nov. 11, 1863 |
| Stitzman, John | do | Nov. 11, 1863 |
| Scanlen, Luke | Oak Creek | Nov. 11, 1863 |
| Seymer, Christian | do | Nov. 11, 1863 |

| *Name* | *Residence* | *Date* |
|---|---|---|
| Sullivan, Owen | Oak Creek | Nov. 11, 1863 |
| Sutter, Fudel | do | Sep. 22, 1864 |
| Stuffel, John | do | Sep. 22, 1864 |
| Skintzelus, F. T | Racine | Nov. 11, 1863 |
| Simpson, S | do | Nov. 11, 1863 |
| Stofhel, C | do | Nov. 11, 1863 |
| Shepherd, August | do | Nov. 11, 1863 |
| Simmer, Peter | do | Sept. 24, 1864 |
| Swift, Edward | do | Sep. 24, 1864 |
| Stoleway, Michael | do | Sep. 24, 1864 |
| Smith, Charles | do | Sep. 24, 1864 |
| Sullivan, James | do | Sep. 22, 1864 |
| Sullivan, William | do | Sep. 22, 1864 |
| Saunders, Joe | do | Jan. 19, 1865 |
| Shuba, Ignatz | do | Jan. 19, 1865 |
| Sullivan, Daniel | do | Jan. 19, 1865 |
| Smith, Frederick | do | Sep. 22, 1864 |
| Starkey, Henry | do | Sep. 22, 1864 |
| Stiechen, Nicholas | Mount Pleasant | Nov. 11, 1863 |
| Smith, Mortimer | Bradford | Nov. 12, 1863 |
| Spring, John | Prairie | Nov. 12, 1863 |
| Salmon, John | Oregon | Nov. 12, 1863 |
| Sanderson, Andrew | Dunkirk | Nov. 12, 1863 |
| Sjurson, Nel | Pleasant Springs | Nov. 13, 1863 |
| Stewart, James | Madison | Nov. 13, 1863 |
| Shanesey, John | do | Nov. 13, 1863 |
| Saugsbery, James | do | Nov. 13, 1863 |
| Sthurg, Fred | Blooming Grove | Nov. 12, 1863 |
| Soules, Charles A | Cottage Grove | Nov. 13, 1863 |
| Swain, R. V | Sun Prairie | Nov. 18, 1864 |
| Smith, Joseph | do | Dec. 1, 1864 |
| Sutton, Luther | do | Dec. 1, 1864 |
| Stillwell, R | Bristol | Dec. 1, 1864 |
| Shultz, August | Hebron | |
| Stivers, Jeremiah | Sullivan | |
| Sears, Gowel C | do | |
| Sumerville, Wm | Farmington | |
| Shrider, Charles | do | |
| Swamshcuster, John | do | Sep. 20, 1864 |
| Shereder, Charles | do | Sep. 20, 1864 |
| Shoemaker, Charles | do | Sep. 20, 1864 |
| Seteaman, William | Watertown | Nov. 13, 1863 |
| Steans, Christian | do | Sep. 20, 1864 |
| Sirdow, Ferdinand | do | Sep. 20, 1864 |
| Sloan, Thomas | do | Oct. 22, 1864 |
| Schmitt, Charles | Lewiston | Sep. 21, 1864 |
| Srehan, John D | do | Oct. 22, 1864 |
| Stevens, Livingston | Watertown | Oct. 15, 1864 |
| Smith, Isaac | do | Oct. 15, 1864 |
| Spragin, John | do | Oct. 15, 1864 |
| Stube, John | do | Nov. 15, 1864 |
| Sullivan, Mathew | do | Dec. 19, 1864 |
| Shady, Michael | Fort Winnebago | Sep. 21, 1864 |
| Samson, Richard | Ridgeway | Sep. 28, 1864 |
| Smith, John | do | Sep. 28, 1864 |
| Stanton, Thomas | do | Nov. 19, 1864 |
| Smith, James | Henrietta | Sep. 26, 1864 |
| Sutton, Walter | Willow | Sep. 26, 1864 |
| Seffers, Herman | Clyde | Sep. 27, 1864 |

| *Name* | *Residence.* | *Date* |
|---|---|---|
| Smith, Ebenezer B | Clyde | Sep. 27, 1864 |
| Shelton, Patrick | do | Sep. 27, 1864 |
| Shelton, John | do | Sep. 27, 1864 |
| Shnider, Wm | Dodgeville | Sep. 28, 1864 |
| Stephens, Stephen | do | Sep. 28, 1864 |
| Steffis, Matthew | do | Sep. 28, 1864 |
| Shields, Thomas | do | Sep. 28, 1864 |
| Sillars, Jas | do | Sep. 28, 1864 |
| Scaurick, Wm | do | Sep. 28, 1864 |
| Shoenimon, Barnard | do | Sep. 28, 1864 |
| Sillers, Wm | do | Oct. 28, 1864 |
| Sterling, B. D | Highland | Nov. 14, 1863 |
| Spencer, George | do | Sep. 28, 1864 |
| Smith, Wm | do | Sep. 28, 1864 |
| Sander, Henry | do | Oct. 28, 1864 |
| Smeltser, Nicholas | do | Nov. 19, 1864 |
| Shaw, Wm | Benton | Sep. 29, 1864 |
| Slavin, John | Shullsburg | Nov. 16, 1864 |
| Sanneman, Aug | do | Nov. 16, 1864 |
| Sullivan, Dennis | New Diggings | Nov. 16, 1864 |
| Scott, Thomas | do | Nov. 16, 1864 |
| Shea, John P | do | Nov. 16, 1864 |
| Sullivan, Jerry F | do | Sep. 29, 1864 |
| Slee, Edward | do | Sep. 29, 1864 |
| Sullivan, Michael | do | Sep. 29, 1864 |
| Sullivan, Daniel | do | Sep. 29, 1864 |
| Stenssy, Peter | New Glarus or Exeter | Nov. 17, 1863 |
| Stevens, John A | Albany | Nov. 17, 1863 |
| Sheyva, Hysa | Jefferson | Nov. 17, 1863 |
| Skinner, John | do | Sep. 27, 1864 |
| Seaman, M. F | do | Sep. 27, 1864 |
| Smith, Wm. H | Clayton | Sep. 30, 1864 |
| Sherwood, A M | Utica | Oct. 29, 1864 |
| Stackable, Andrew | Waterloo | Oct. 1, 1864 |
| Sabins, Chas | Clifton | Nov. 19, 1863 |
| Schulte, Albert | Harrison | Oct. 29, 1864 |
| Shay, John | Platteville | Nov. 19, 1863 |
| Sanders, Harvey | Fairfield | Nov. 20, 1863 |
| Schlenk, Geo | Prairie du Sac | Nov. 20, 1863 |
| Slayback, Wm | Bloom | Sep. 26, 1864 |
| Silby, Wm | do | Sep. 26, 1864 |
| Snell, John | Seneca | Sep 30, 1864 |
| Shaw, Wm | do | Sep. 30, 1864 |
| Shaw, Fred | do | Oct. 29, 1864 |
| Slater, John | Washington | Oct. 3, 1864 |
| Shanmaker, Anthony | do | Oct. 3, 1864 |
| Smith, Pat | Bear Creek | Oct. 3, 1864 |
| Smith, Peter | do | Oct. 3, 1864 |
| Schneider, Gregory | Monroe Co | Nov. 17, 1864 |
| Squires, Homer | Jefferson | Sep. 19, 1864 |
| Smith, Jacob | Eaton | Sep. 19, 1864 |
| Sullivan, Dan'l | Tomah | Sep. 19, 1864 |
| Sullivan, Jno | do | Nov. 10, 1864 |
| Stow, Benj | Clifton | Sep. 20, 1864 |
| Schumaker, Jno | do | Sep. 20, 1864 |
| Seikel, Herman | do | Nov. 10, 1864 |
| Sturdevant, Leonard | Portland | Sep. 20, 1864 |
| Shelmer, H | Chippewa Co | Nov. 20, 1863 |
| Senoy, Joseph | do | Nov. 20, 1863 |

| *Name.* | *Residence.* | *Date.* |
|---|---|---|
| Sullivan, Jim | Chippewa Falls | Nov. 2. 1864 |
| Shellburne, Wm | do | Nov. 2, 1864 |
| Shellenburg, Geo | Anson | Nov. 2, 1864 |
| Satterlee, Wm | Jackson Co | Nov. 18, 1863 |
| Steppy, Geo. K | Adams Co | Nov. 19, 1863 |
| Sheppard, Orrin | Lincoln | Nov. 14, 1864 |
| Sleppy, Jno | Richfield | Nov. 14, 1864 |
| Severson, Lewis | Monroe | Nov. 14, 1864 |
| Smith, Renald A | New Haven | Nov. 14, 1864 |
| Smith, Lewis | Jackson | Nov. 14, 1864 |
| Smith, Geo W | Springville | Nov. 14, 1864 |
| Shorey, Geo | Quincy | Nov. 14, 1864 |
| Swan, Jno | Portage Co | Nov. 23, 1863 |
| Shornweiller, Nicholas | do | Nov. 23, 1863 |
| Singleton, Jno | do | Nov. 23, 1863 |
| Sparks Wm | Linwood | Oct. 31, 1864 |
| Sayles, Zachariah | Stockton | Oct. 31, 1864 |
| Shoefellow, Nicholas | Sharon | Oct. 31, 1864 |
| Sullivan, Jerry | Hull | Oct. 31, 1864 |
| Stickles, Jacob | Juneau Co | Nov. 17, 1863 |
| Smith, Chas. A | Plymouth | Oct. 31, 1864 |
| Stevens, David | do | Oct. 31, 1864 |
| Scott, Thos | Kildare | Sep. 19, 1864 |
| Sullivan, Jno | do | Sep. 19, 1864 |
| Sullivan, Jno | do | Oct. 31, 1864 |
| Sohnow, T | do | Oct. 31, 1864 |
| Scanlan, Michael | Seven Mile Creek | Sep. 19, 1864 |
| Scully, Patrick | do | Oct. 31, 1864 |
| Scanlain, Jno | do | Oct. 31, 1864 |
| Savage, Joseph | Lemonweir | Sep. 19, 1864 |
| Smith, Patrick | do | Oct. 31, 1864 |
| Smith, Luther | do | Oct. 31, 1864 |
| Smith, Jno | Summit | Sep. 19, 1864 |
| Stirling, Francis | do | Sep. 19, 1864 |
| Smith, Calvin | Germantown | Sep. 20, 1864 |
| Smith, Wm | St. Croix Co | Nov. 23, 1863 |
| Stevens, Thomas | do | Nov. 23, 1863 |
| Shampain, T. B | Somerset | Oct. 5, 1864 |
| Seaver, Jno | Dunn Co | Nov. 23, 1863 |
| Stevens, Henry | do | Nov. 23, 1863 |
| Sherman, Jos | Eau Galle | Sep. 27, 1864 |
| Shay, Dan'l | do | Sept. 27, 1864 |
| Sullivan, J | do | Sep. 27, 1864 |
| Shannon, Edward | do | Sep. 27, 1864 |
| Smith, Sylvester | do | Nov. 2, 1864 |
| Smith, James | do | Nov. 2, 1864 |
| Stoddard, James | Buffalo Co | Nov. 18, 1863 |
| Shanks, M. G | Waubeck | Nov. 20, 1863 |
| Scott, H. A | Wood Co | Nov. 18, 1863 |
| Stedwell, Geo | Campbell | Sep. 19, 1864 |
| Swenson, Halvor | Martell | Nov. 3, 1864 |
| Saline ——— | Berlin | Nov. 14, 1864 |
| Smith, Augustus | do | Nov. 14, 1864 |
| Shackleton, Isaac | Durand | Sep. 27, 1864 |
| Swift, Robert | do | Sep. 27, 1864 |
| Sharp, Abram | Bergen | Nov. 15, 1864 |
| Silburg, Sebastian | Webster | Nov. 15, 1864 |
| Sathan, Neils M | Sterling | Nov. 15, 1864 |

| *Name.* | *Residence.* | *Date.* |
|---|---|---|
| Stevens, H. J | Door Co | Nov. 20, 1863 |
| Sieball, Wenzel | Cooperstown | Nov. 21, 1863 |
| Schley, Julius | do | Dec. 29, 1864 |
| Sumner, Jno | Gibson | Nov 21, 1863 |
| Saudhoffer, Paul | Maple Grove | Nov. 21, 1863 |
| Sinder, Andrew | Franklin | Nov. 21, 1863 |
| Spoo, Joseph | Two Rivers | Nov. 21, 1863 |
| Schwalby, Chas | Eaton | Nov. 24, 1863 |
| Sprowd, Herman | do | Nov. 24, 1863 |
| Sweet, Jonathan | do | Nov. 24, 1863 |
| Stracka, Anton | Kossuth | Dec. 29, 1864 |
| Strange, Joseph | Mishicott | Dec. 29, 1864 |
| Shila, ——— | Two Creeks | Dec. 29, 1864 |
| Schweegert, Jno | Manitowoc Rapids | Dec. 29, 1864 |
| Seiger, Wilhelm | do | Dec. 29, 1864 |
| Schroeder, Christian | do | Dec. 29, 1864 |
| Shinnick, Joseph | do | Dec. 29, 1864 |
| Schmudt, Stephen | Meeme | Dec. 29, 1864 |
| Stein, Adam | do | Dec. 29, 1864 |
| Schneider, Jacob | do | Dec. 29, 1864 |
| Stock, Simon | Newton | Dec. 29, 1864 |
| Schultz, Johann | do | Dec. 29, 1864 |
| Scherer, Mathias | do | Dec. 29, 1864 |
| Stoeder, Micholas | do | Dec. 29, 1864 |
| Saych, Phillip | do | Dec. 29, 1864 |
| Stinge, Wilhelm | do | Dec. 29, 1864 |
| Schase, Ludwig | do | Dec. 29, 1864 |
| Snme, Berthold | Centerville | Nov. 21, 1863 |
| Schumaker, Peter | Stockbridge | Nov. 21, 1863 |
| Stephenson, Stephens | Oshkosh | Nov. 23, 1863 |
| Scholtz, Jno | do | Nov. 23, 1863 |
| Store, Wm. A | do | Nov. 23, 1863 |
| Staples, Chas | do | Nov. 23. 1863 |
| Schmidt, Lambert | Algoma | Nov. 23, 1863 |
| Smith, Jno | Nekimi | Nov. 23, 1863 |
| Smith, Geo. C | do | Nov. 23, 1863 |
| Statson, Burns | Omro | Nov. 23, 1863 |
| Stevens, Henry | do | Nov. 23, 1863 |
| Schmidt, Jno | | Nov. 24, 1863 |
| Scharz, Carl | | Nov. 28, 1863 |
| Shuffett, Lewis | Poygan | Nov. 5, 1864 |
| Shuffett, Robert | do | Nov. 5, 1864 |
| Simmons, Stephen | Berlin city | Nov. 24, 1863 |
| Salt, Jno | Brooklyn | Nov. 24, 1863 |
| Savage, Jno | Dayton | Nov. 24, 1863 |
| Saunders, Geo. W | Marquette Co | Nov. 24, 1863 |
| Stillman, Franklin | do | Nov. 24, 1863 |
| Stiles, Albert D | do | Nov. 24, 1863 |
| Stunzell, Gottfreid | Mecan | Nov. 1, 1864 |
| Schwanke, Chas | do | Dec. 31, 1864 |
| Stibb, Chas | do | Dec. 31, 1864 |
| Sanboine, Joseph | Buffalo | Nov. 1, 1864 |
| Shea, Patrick | do | Nov. 1, 1864 |
| Shower, August | Crystal Lake | Nov. 1, 1864 |
| Stunk, Hiram | Shields | Nov. 1, 1864 |
| Stiles, Wayne A | Springfield | Nov. 1, 1864 |
| Stubbins, Geo | Moundville | Dec. 31, 1864 |
| Singleton, Jno | Douglas | Dec. 31, 1864 |
| Shaurtleff, Jason | Newton | Dec. 31, 1864 |

| *Name* | *Residence.* | *Date.* |
|---|---|---|
| Snyder, Peter | Waushara Co | Nov. 24, 1863 |
| Sweat, Benj. C | Wautoma | Nov. 25, 1863 |
| Spawn, Jno | Plainfield | Nov. 25, 1863 |
| Stone, Ranceler | do | Nov. 2, 1864 |
| Smith, Norman | do | Nov. 2, 1864 |
| Smith, Benzilla | do | Nov. 2, 1864 |
| Stillwell, Wm | do | Nov. 2, 1864 |
| Steven, S. Horton | do | Nov. 2, 1864 |
| Sparon, G. S. | do | Dec. 21, 1864 |
| Steward, Jno | Poysippi | Nov. 2, 1864 |
| Stewart, Jno | Springwater | Nov. 2, 1864 |
| Stillman, G. R | Coloma | Nov. 2, 1864 |
| Stowell, Benj | do | Nov. 2, 1864 |
| Staples, Roscoe | Oasis. | Nov. 2, 1864 |
| Skellons, Hugh | do | Nov. 2, 1864 |
| Sleight, Peter | do | Nov. 2, 1864 |
| Shead, Chas | Aurora | Dec. 31, 1864 |
| Segworth, Alvis | Waupaca Co | Nov. 25, 1864 |
| Stevens, Jno | do | Nov. 25, 1863 |
| Sloan, Hugh | Lebanon | Nov. 25, 1863 |
| Sullivan, Jerry | do | Nov. 25, 1864 |
| Starks, Chas. A | Weyauwega | Nov. 25, 1863 |
| Sutherland, Geo. W | do | Nov. 5, 1863 |
| Smith, Henry | Royalton | Nov. 5, 1864 |
| Snits, Geo | do | Nov. 25, 1864 |
| Salverson, Hans | | Nov. 25, 1863 |
| Shaw, Jno. W | Lind | Nov. 25, 1863 |
| Smith, Gilderoy | Larabee | Nov. 5, 1864 |
| Swenmingson, Torger | St. Lawrence | Nov. 5, 1864 |
| Shamtan, William | do | Nov. 5, 1864 |
| Stuart, Winfield | do | Dec. 31, 1864 |
| Staples, Peter K | Iola | Dec. 31, 1864 |
| Shepherd, Thomas L | Osborne | Dec. 28, 1864 |
| Sharp, G | do | Dec. 28, 1864 |
| Swinkles, Thomas | Freedom | Nov. 27, 1863 |
| Sheriff, Robert | do | Dec. 28, 1864 |
| Sanderfoot, Sanborn | do | Dec. 28, 1864 |
| Schwader, George | do | Dec. 28, 1864 |
| Stillman, David B. | do | Dec. 28, 1864 |
| Snyder, Thomas S | Kaukama | Nov. 27, 1863 |
| Smart, Peter | Appleton | Nov. 27, 1863 |
| Smith, James H | do | Nov. 27, 1863 |
| Smith, James | do | Nov. 27, 1863 |
| Schultz, Waltz. K | Center | Nov. 27, 1863 |
| Schreiter, Wenzel | do | Dec. 28, 1863 |
| Schelly, Volney | do | Dec. 28, 1863 |
| Schultz, Frederick | Hortonia | Dec. 28, 1863 |
| Sanborn, Horatio B | do | Dec. 28, 1863 |
| Strinsky, Anthony | do | Dec. 28, 1863 |
| Schultz, Gustav | Maple Creek | Dec. 28, 1863 |
| Schultz, Ludwig | do | Dec. 28, 1863 |
| Seamour, Herman | do | Dec. 28, 1863 |
| Seiler, John | | Nov. 27, 1863 |
| Sweany, Patrick | Humboldt | Nov. 27, 1863 |
| Shauer, Theodore | do | Dec. 28, 1864 |
| Splingair, Charles | do | Dec. 28, 1864 |
| Sweany, Patrick | Glenmore | Dec. 28, 1864 |
| Schroeder, Christian | do | Nov. 27, 1863 |
| Shehan, John | Holland | Nov. 27, 1863 |

| *Name.* | *Residence.* | *Date.* |
|---|---|---|
| Seymour, Charles | Green Bay city | Nov. 27, 1863 |
| Scheller, Adam | Scott | Dec. 28, 1864 |
| Snyder, Henry | Morrison | Dec. 28, 1864 |
| Sanders, Thomas E | Marinette | Nov. 28, 1863 |
| Sanders, Nathan | do | Nov. 28, 1863 |
| Sanders, Thomas E | do | Nov. 28, 1863 |
| Smith, Frank | do | Nov. 28, 1863 |
| Sheffer, Henry | Oconto | Nov. 28, 1863 |
| Saute, Theodore | do | Nov. 28, 1863 |
| Surally, John | do | Nov. 28, 1863 |
| Sullivan, Jerry | Peshtigo | Nov. 28, 1863 |
| Seely, William | Stiles | Dec. 29, 1864 |
| Sharlon, Joseph | do | Dec. 29, 1864 |
| Senal, Joseph | do | Nov. 28, 1863 |
| Seivers, Garrett | do | Nov. 28. 1863 |
| Salmon, Thomas | Harrison | Dec. 28, 1864 |
| Schwallbach, Franz | do | Dec. 28, 1864 |
| Schmalz, Nicholaus | do | Dec. 28, 1864 |
| Sears, John | Stockbridge | Dec. 28, 1864 |
| Sentner, Joseph | Brothertown | Dec. 28, 1864 |
| Spellecy, Patrick | Montpelier | Dec. 29, 1864 |
| Sleporn, Joseph | Franklin | Dec. 29, 1864 |
| Schonmack, William | do | Dec. 29, 1864 |
| Sager, John | Carlton | Dec. 29, 1864 |
| Seibert, Charles | do | Dec. 29, 1864 |
| Samproux, ——— | Lincoln. | Dec. 29, 1864 |

## T

| *Name.* | *Residence.* | *Date.* |
|---|---|---|
| Thill, Nicholas | Fredonia | Oct. 14, 1864 |
| Thiess, John | do | Oct. 14, 1864 |
| Theiss, Peter | do | Oct. 14, 1864 |
| Teusher, Anthony | do | Oct. 14, 1864 |
| Thigs, John | do | Oct. 14, 1864 |
| Thags, Henry C | do | Dec. 1, 1864 |
| Trumer, Jacob | Grafton | Oct. 13, 1864 |
| Thelu, John | Saukville | Oct. 14, 1864 |
| Tuember, Louis | Sheboygan | Oct. 24, 1864 |
| Taucer, August | do | Oct. 18, 1864 |
| Teshneeyer, Fred | Sheboygan Falls | Oct. 25, 1864 |
| Tupper, Rufus | Lima | Jan. 27, 1865 |
| Tupper, Arnel | do | Jan. 27, 1865 |
| Thull, Michael | Holland | Oct. 21, 1864 |
| Thuell, M. | do | Oct. 21, 1864 |
| Tife, J | do | Oct. 21, 1864 |
| Terguson, M | do | Dec. 2, 1864 |
| Thieme, Carl | Abbott | Oct. 18, 1864 |
| Thorp, S. V. | Plymouth | Oct. 21, 1864 |
| Thorpe, Albert | Fond du Lac | Nov. 19, 1863 |
| Thomas, John | Eldorado | Oct. 5, 1864 |
| Tuck, John C | Fox Lake | Nov. 19, 1863 |
| Tyson, William H | Shields | Nov. 20, 1863 |
| Treanas, Christopher | do | Nov. 20, 1863 |
| Teliry, Charles O | do | Nov. 20, 1863 |
| Toben, William | Emmett | Oct. 11, 1864 |
| Tobin, James | do | Oct. 11, 1864 |
| Tolever, William W | Oak Grove | Nov. 20, 1863 |
| Tilman, Godfrey | Watertown | Dec. 1, 1864 |
| Tement, James H | Leroy | Nov. 20, 1863 |
| Thiel, Martin | Lomira | Jan. 27, 1865 |

| *Name.* | *Residence.* | *Date.* |
|---|---|---|
| Taylor, John | Trenton | Jan. 27, 1865 |
| Tollefson, T. | Erin | Oct. 12, 1864 |
| Toland, John H. | do | Dec. 1, 1864 |
| Taylor, Frank | Barton | Dec. 1, 1864 |
| Tschudy, John | Richfield | Jan. 27, 1865 |
| Traffer, Julius | do | Jan. 27, 1865 |
| Thorp, James | Farmington | Oct. 18, 1864 |
| Tickler, John | do | Jan. 27, 1865 |
| Tircher, D | Jackson | Oct. 11, 1864 |
| Thill, Nicholas | Belgium | Dec. 1, 1864 |
| Thery, Nicholas | do | Oct. 13, 1864 |
| Thiel, Jacob | do | Oct. 13, 1864 |
| Thill, John Baptist | do | Dec. 1, 1864 |
| Ternes, John | do | Dec. 1, 1864 |
| Terry, G. A. | Milwaukee | Nov. 9, 1863 |
| Tirs, Jacob | do | Nov. 9, 1863 |
| Thrinipper, Louis | do | Sep. 19, 1864 |
| Taney, James | do | Nov. 14, 1864 |
| Tiego, Ed | do | Nov. 9, 1863 |
| Teigo, William | do | Sept. 20, 1864 |
| Tannakus, Ignatz | do | Sep. 20, 1864 |
| Teschel, Ernest | do | Sep. 20, 1864 |
| Threadel, Adam | do | Sep. 20, 1864 |
| Tomson, Peter | do | Sep. 20, 1864 |
| Truetel, S | do | Nov. 14, 1864 |
| Treutel, Henrich | do | Nov. 14, 1864 |
| Thomas, John | do | Nov. 14, 1864 |
| Tager, John | do | Nov. 10, 1864 |
| Tulay, John | do | Nov. 10, 1864 |
| Tiger, Nicholas | do | Nov. 10, 1864 |
| Taylor, Francis | do | Sep. 20, 1864 |
| Tamsley, Wesley | do | Sep. 20, 1864 |
| Turrann, John | do | Sep. 20, 1864 |
| Tompkins, John | do | Sept. 20, 1864 |
| Thompson, John | do | Sep. 20, 1864 |
| Tarrel, J. W | do | Nov. 15, 1864 |
| Tully, Mark | do | Nov. 15, 1864 |
| Touhay, James | do | Nov. 15, 1864 |
| Thompson, James | do | Nov. 15, 1864 |
| Trippin, James | do | Nov. 10, 1863 |
| Travis, John | do | Sep. 26, 1864 |
| Thorson, Thomas | do | Nov. 10, 1863 |
| Thonson, Andrew | do | Nov. 10, 1863 |
| Treinor, Charles | do | Nov. 10, 1863 |
| Treadwell, George | do | Nov. 10, 1863 |
| Towod, Charles | do | Sep. 21, 1864 |
| Terry, Abraham | do | Sept. 21, 1864 |
| Tenis, Henry | do | Sep. 21, 1864 |
| Thoman, Joseph | do | Nov. 16, 1863 |
| Tress, Fred | do | Nov. 16, 1863 |
| Teil, Anton | do | Sep. 21, 1864 |
| Tries, Gotfried | do | Sep. 21, 1864 |
| Thom, Jacob | do | Sep. 21, 1864 |
| Tezan, Frederick | do | Sep. 21, 1864 |
| Tapalsky, Charles | do | Nov. 25, 1864 |
| Treible, Aberhart | do | Nov. 25, 1864 |
| Tohn, Jacob | do | Nov. 25, 1864 |
| Triechner, Fritz | do | Nov. 11, 1863 |
| Tarch, William | do | Sep. 21, 1864 |

| Name. | Residence. | Date. |
|---|---|---|
| Trim, John | Milwaukee | Sep. 21, 1864 |
| Thries, John | do | Sep. 21, 1864 |
| Ties, Johann | do | Sep. 21, 1864 |
| Theins, Hans | do | Sep. 21, 1864 |
| Trapp, John Jacob | do | Nov. 25, 1864 |
| Trentelaar, Jozias | do | Nov. 25, 1864 |
| Toerg, —— | do | Nov. 25, 1864 |
| Tieg, Ferdinand | do | Jan. 26, 1865 |
| Tenant, Philip | do | Jan. 26, 1865 |
| Tesch, Charles | do | Jan. 26, 1865 |
| Teetsloff, William | do | Jan. 19, 1865 |
| Tuers, Benedict | do | Jan. 19, 1865 |
| Trease, Daniel | Delafield | Nov. 12, 1863 |
| Taylor, John | Pewaukee | Dec. 2, 1864 |
| Thomas, Charles E. | Menomenee | Sep. 24, 1864 |
| Tetter, Charles | do | Nov. 25, 1864 |
| Trautmann, Casper | do | Nov. 25, 1864 |
| Tenny, Thomas | Brookfield | Sep. 23, 1864 |
| Torbinson, Halver | Muskego | Sep. 24, 1864 |
| Tews, John | Milwaukee | Sep. 22, 1864 |
| Tager, Carl | Granville | Nov. 11, 1863 |
| Teaching, Henry | Greenfield | Sep. 21, 1864 |
| Tucker, Robert S. | Lake | Dec. 13, 1864 |
| Traumer, Charles | Oak Creek | Sep. 22, 1864 |
| Tooming, Richard | Racine | Nov. 11, 1863 |
| Tyrrell, Harry | do | Sep. 24, 1864 |
| Taylor, Lafayette | do | Nov. 11, 1863 |
| Tyler, James | Mount Pleasant | Sep. 23, 1864 |
| Tye, Joseph | Dover | Sep. 23, 1864 |
| Thayer, William | do | Sep. 23, 1864 |
| Traves, Michael | Rochester | Sep. 24, 1864 |
| Thorpe, William | Caledonia | Sep. 22, 1864 |
| Taukin, Anton | Wheatland | Dec. 14, 1864 |
| Terry, William | Paris | Sep. 24, 1864 |
| Tom, John | do | Sep. 24, 1864 |
| Toner, Charles | do | Sep. 24, 1864 |
| Turnbelly, —— | Salem | Sep. 24, 1864 |
| Threshman, Adam | do | Sep. 24, 1864 |
| Thomas, Frank | Sharon | Nov. 12, 1863 |
| Taylor, Jeff (col'd) | do | Nov. 12, 1863 |
| Teanell, John | East Troy | Nov. 12, 1863 |
| Tonny, Richard | do | Sep. 24, 1864 |
| Tomrow, John | do | Dec. 2, 1864 |
| Tiler, Jacob | Bloomfield | Nov. 12, 1863 |
| Thomas, Isaac | Summit | Sep. 22, 1864 |
| Thorn, August | Oconomowoc | Sep. 22, 1864 |
| Travis, William | do | Sep. 22, 1864 |
| Tierman, Peter | Magnolia | Nov. 12, 1863 |
| Thayer, James | Johnson | Nov. 12, 1863 |
| Ten Eyck, Andrew | Fulton | Nov. 12, 1863 |
| Tronson, Erick | Blue Mounds | Oct. 22, 1864 |
| Tolefson, Ole | do | Oct. 22, 1864 |
| Turgleson, John | Vermont | Nov. 13, 1863 |
| Towle, Henry | Sun Prairie | Nov. 15, 1864 |
| Ters, William | Jefferson | |
| Tyrany, Patrick | do | |
| Thomas, George | Farmington | Sep. 20, 1864 |
| Thom, August | Ixonia | Nov. 13, 1863 |
| Thieler, Niclaus | Lewiston | Sep. 21, 1864 |

| *Name.* | *Residence.* | *Date.* |
|---|---|---|
| Thompson, Tovor | | Dec. 13, 1864 |
| Thompson, Jim | Springdale | Sep. 19, 1864 |
| Tarnell, William | Ridgeway | Nov. 14, 1863 |
| Tophy, Michael | do | Sep. 28, 1864 |
| Tullifson, Summon | do | Sep. 28, 1864 |
| Turison, Taldef | do | Oct. 28, 1864 |
| Trarees, Henry | Henrietta | Sep. 26, 1864 |
| Thomas, Henry | Dodgeville | Sep. 28, 1864 |
| Thomas, Wm | do | Sep. 28, 1864 |
| Torgumson, Andrew | do | Sep. 28, 1864 |
| Torkelson, John | Highland | Sep. 28, 1864 |
| Trelour, Joseph | do | Sep. 28, 1864 |
| Telters, Bernard | do | Sep. 28, 1864 |
| Torkleson, Torke | do | Oct. 28, 1864 |
| Taleen, John | Waldwick | Nov. 14, 1863 |
| Teagul, Thos | do | Oct. 4, 1864 |
| Timmoos, James | do | Oct. 4, 1864 |
| Tellefson, Ole | Moscow | Nov. 14, 1863 |
| Tamblin, William | Willow Springs | Nov. 16, 1863 |
| Thompson, J. E | Benton | Nov. 16, 1863 |
| Thomas, Thos | do | Sep. 29, 1864 |
| Tunry Michael | do | Sep. 29, 1864 |
| Toppins, James | do | Sep. 29, 1864 |
| Thomas, John | do | Sep. 29, 1864 |
| Trainer, Thos | do | Sep. 29, 1864 |
| Thompson, Job | New Diggins | Nov. 16, 1863 |
| Temby, Samuel | Clayton or Utica | Nov. 18, 1863 |
| Tulley, Michael | Utica | Sep. 30, 1864 |
| Tusck, 'Joseph | Prairie du Chien | Nov. 18, 1863 |
| Taylor, Saloman | do | Nov. 18, 1863 |
| Thiossel, Robert | Cassv'le, B'twn or Waterloo | Nov. 19, 1863 |
| Turneal, Thomas | Hazel Green | Nov. 19, 1863 |
| Thompson, Richardson | Adams Co | Nov. 23, 1863 |
| Tuperfal, Frederick | do | Nov. 23, 1863 |
| Teaffach, Frederick | do | Nov. 23, 1863 |
| Tenney, William | Monroe | Sep. 26, 1864 |
| Tooney, John | Juneau Co | Nov. 17, 1863 |
| Teffany, John | Kildare | Sep. 19, 1864 |
| Trumbell, Andrew | do | Oct. 31, 1864 |
| Trainor, Dan | do | Oct. 31, 1864 |
| Troup, Nelson | do | Oct. 31, 1864 |
| Thompson, Victor | Lemonweir | Sep. 19, 1864 |
| Thompson, Hiram | Marion | Sep. 19, 1864 |
| Trumble, Michael | Lyndon | Sep. 19, 1864 |
| Taylor, John | do | Sep. 19, 1864 |
| Truell, William | do | Sep. 19, 1864 |
| Thatcher, Johnson | Plymouth | Oct. 31, 1864 |
| Tufto, Christian | Pierce Co | Nov. 23, 1863 |
| Tuscan, James | Trimbell | Sep. 22, 1864 |
| Taylor, J. H | do | Sep. 22, 1864 |
| Thompson, Eri | Jefferson | Sep. 19, 1864 |
| Thomas, William | Ettrick | Sep. 21, 1864 |
| Theel, August | Hamburg | Sep. 21, 1864 |
| Tuhler, August | do | Sep. 21, 1864 |
| Taylor, James J | Franklin | Sep. 21, 1864 |
| Taylor, William | Forest | Sep. 21, 1864 |
| Tanner, G. W | Harmony | Sep. 21, 1864 |
| Taylor, William | Rodolph | Sep. 21, 1864 |
| Thompson, Ole | Amherst | Sep. 22, 1864 |

| Name. | Residence. | Date. |
|---|---|---|
| Turner, Albert | Amherst | Sept. 22, 1864 |
| Turner, John | Belmont | Sep. 22, 1864 |
| Taylor, Charles | do | Sep. 22, 1864 |
| Timlan, Anthony | Lanark | Sep. 22, 1864 |
| Tubbs, Grey | do | Nov. 15, 1864 |
| Tubbs, Hosea | Linwood | Oct. 31, 1864 |
| Thompson, Wm. H | Eau Galle | Sep. 27, 1864 |
| Thompson, Hiram C | do | Sep. 27, 1864 |
| Taylor, Chas | do | Nov. 2, 1864 |
| Thompson, Andrew | Chippewa Falls | Sep. 27, 1864 |
| Turney, John | do | Sep. 27, 1864 |
| Tacks, Hugo | Somerset | Sep. 27, 1864 |
| Torgerson, Ole | Eau Galle | Nov. 3, 1864 |
| Tolvson, L | Rush River | Nov. 3, 1864 |
| Tudes, Wilhelm | Berlin | Nov. 14, 1864 |
| Terry, C. D | Waubeek | Nov. 15, 1864 |
| Timerlin, Edward | Nelson | Nov. 16, 1864 |
| Taoha, Wenzel | Cooperstown | Nov. 21, 1863 |
| Thompson, Even | Liberty | Nov. 21, 1863 |
| Thomas, Theodore | Two Creeks | Dec. 28, 1864 |
| Trasson, Jacob | Mishicott | Dec. 28, 1864 |
| Thurston, Isack | Gibson | Dec. 28, 1864 |
| Thomas, Owen N | Neenah | Nov. 23, 1863 |
| Tuttle, Howard | Oshkosh | Nov. 23, 1863 |
| Taylor, George N | do | Nov. 23, 1863 |
| Twecken, Michael | Black Wolf | Nov. 23, 1863 |
| Townsend, John H | Nepeuskin | Nov. 23, 1863 |
| Taylor, Truman | Omro | Nov. 23, 1863 |
| Tucker, Alfred L | Berlin city | Nov. 24, 1863 |
| Thompson, Geo. W | Brooklyn | Nov. 24, 1863 |
| Truesdell, V. J | Wautoma | Nov. 25, 1863 |
| Thomas, David | Springwater | Nov. 2, 1864 |
| Topham, Chas | Coloma | Nov. 2, 1864 |
| Tibbitts, John | Plainfield | Nov. 2, 1864 |
| Timm, Daniel | Bloomfield | Dec. 31, 1864 |
| Thomas, J | Aurora | Dec. 31, 1864 |
| Thomas, John | do | Dec. 31, 1864 |
| Tubbs, Wm | Richford | Dec. 31, 1864 |
| Thurston, Joseph | Oasis | Dec. 31, 1864 |
| Taylor, J. A | Waupaca Co | Nov. 25, 1864 |
| Tealks, Louis | Bear Creek | Nov. 25, 1864 |
| Theulon, Amos | St. Lawrence | Nov. 25, 1864 |
| Tanner, Wm | do | Dec. 31, 1864 |
| Thompson, Luevin | Iola | Nov. 25, 1864 |
| Tubas, Halver K | do | Nov. 25, 1864 |
| Tubas, Ole K | do | Nov. 25, 1864 |
| Tubas, Kettle K. | Iola | Nov. 5, 1864 |
| Tullfesen, Bjoven | do | Nov. 25, 1863 |
| True, Nelson | Outagamie Co | Nov. 27, 1863 |
| Turney, Jno. S | do | Nov. 27, 1863 |
| True, Joseph E | Hortonia | Dec. 28, 1864 |
| Thede, Joachum | Humboldt | Nov. 27, 1863 |
| Tivito, Jean Baptist | Fort Howard | Nov. 27, 1863 |
| Tuyls, Anton | Preble | Dec. 28, 1864 |
| Tals, Philip | Bellville | Dec. 28, 1864 |
| Taylor, Jno. T | Peshtigo | Nov. 28, 1863 |
| Taggart, Christopher | Crystal Lake | Nov. 1, 1864 |
| Tremel, Joseph | Rantoul | Dec. 28, 1864 |
| Tillman, Frank | Woodville | Dec. 28, 1864 |

| *Name.* | *Residence.* | *Date.* |
|---|---|---|
| Thomas, Henry | Harrison | Dec. 28, 1864 |
| Tewer, Franz | Stockbridge | Dec. 28, 1864 |
| Thiry, Constant | Red River | Dec. 29, 1864 |
| Tracy, Martin | Franklin | Dec. 29, 1864 |
| Tyrell, Aherd | Clay Banks | Dec. 29, 1864 |

## U

| *Name.* | *Residence.* | *Date.* |
|---|---|---|
| Utrem, Peter | Leroy | Jan. 27, 1865 |
| Uthrer, Herman | Barton | Oct. 12, 1864 |
| Utteg, William | Jackson | Oct. 11, 1864 |
| Underwood, Elijah | Scott | Nov. 24, 1863 |
| Urich, Jacob | Milwaukee | Sep. 20, 1864 |
| Ukrow, —— | do | Nov. 10, 1863 |
| Umpherson, Wm. | Greenfield | Sep. 21, 1864 |
| Ulrich, Adam | Menomonee | Nov. 12, 1863 |
| Urich, Anton | do | Sep. 24, 1864 |
| Uchelach, John | do | Dec. 1, 1864 |
| Ulealt, Ferdinant | Watertown | Oct. 22, 1864 |
| Uldrick, Fred | Pacific or Portage City | Nov. 16, 1863 |
| Ullman, Joseph | Outagamie Co | Nov. 27, 1863 |
| Underwood, Ira | Lebanon | Nov. 5, 1864 |

## V

| *Name.* | *Residence.* | *Date.* |
|---|---|---|
| Vogt, Edward | Forest | Nov. 19, 1863 |
| Varnum, Isaac | Clyman | Oct. 6, 1864 |
| Voget, Ludwig | Watertown | Oct. 6, 1864 |
| Vaugne, Godey | Leroy | Dec. 1, 1864 |
| Voalacum, Peter | Lomira | Dec. 1, 1864 |
| Vokt, Paul | West Bend | Nov. 21, 1863 |
| Voss, Hubbard | Richfield | Dec. 1, 1864 |
| Vanderbough, John | Grafton | Jan. 27, 1865 |
| Vineda, Louis | Lima | Oct. 21, 1864 |
| Vandeler, Wilkilm | do | Oct. 21, 1864 |
| Veuenson, Gerhardt | do | Jan. 27, 1865 |
| Verrlins, C | Holland | Oct. 21, 1864 |
| Valett, J. B | Milwaukee | Sep. 19, 1864 |
| Verait, Joseph | do | Dec. 22, 1864 |
| Vliet, —— | do | Dec. 22, 1864 |
| Vochting, Christian | do | Nov. 9, 1863 |
| Volkman, Wm | do | Sep. 20, 1864 |
| Vincent, Sam'l | do | Sep. 20, 1864 |
| Voight, Wm | do | Nov. 14, 1864 |
| Vamicke, Ernest | do | Nov. 15, 1864 |
| Vurbryke, Parklow | do | Nov. 15, 1864 |
| Vandercook, D | do | Jan. 11, 1865 |
| Velwod, Ludwig | do | Nov. 10, 1863 |
| Valentine, Adam | do | Nov. 10, 1863 |
| Voight, Charles | do | Sep. 21, 1864 |
| Van Kerk, David | do | Nov. 16, 1864 |
| Valkenstein, Christian | do | Nov. 11, 1863 |
| Venhall, William | do | Nov. 30, 1864 |
| Volbrecht, Martin | do | Jan. 26, 1865 |
| Vliet, Joseph | do | Nov. 11, 1863 |
| Vogel, John | do | Sep. 22, 1864 |
| Voss, Ludwig | do | Dec. 7, 1864 |
| Vernon, Louis | Greenfield | Sep. 21, 1864 |
| Verboort, William | Lake | Sep. 22, 1864 |
| Van Dusen, Horace | Racine | Sep. 22, 1864 |

| *Name.* | *Residence.* | *Date.* |
|---|---|---|
| Van Valkenburg, Andrew | Racine | Sep. 22, 1864 |
| Vandiglo, Henry | Yorkville | Nov. 11, 1863 |
| Vogeling, Franz | Waterford | Nov. 11, 1863 |
| Vilman, Henry | Salem | Sep. 24, 1864 |
| Voight, Heinrich | Menomonee | Nov. 25, 1864 |
| Volbrecht, —— | Brookfield | Sep. 23, 1864 |
| Veronger, Martin | do | Sep. 23, 1864 |
| Volkner, Frederiek | Watertown | |
| Van Buren, Martin | Dodgeville | Oct. 28, 1864 |
| Van Lesky, Frank | Prairie du Chien | Nov. 18, 1863 |
| Vance, Wm | Beetown | Oct. 1, 1864 |
| Vanalstine, Charles | Ridgeway | Sep. 20, 1864 |
| Van Seckle, Francis | Tomah | Nov 10, 1864 |
| VanWagner, Felix K | Franklin | Sep. 21, 1864 |
| Van Count, Jno | Hull | Sep. 22, 1864 |
| Verafskaski, Jacob | Sharon | Oct. 31, 1864 |
| Vileet, David | Eau Galle | Sep. 27, 1864 |
| Vileet, John | do | Sep. 27, 1864 |
| Villue, Joseph | Somerset | Oct. 5, 1864 |
| Vaughan, Jno. H | New Haven | Nov. 14, 1864 |
| Van Hover, Umbau | Jackson | Nov. 14, 1864 |
| Vernett Isaac | Door Co | Nov. 20, 1863 |
| Vordekee, Savre | Casco | Nov. 20, 1863 |
| Vantanhanten, Franz | do | Nov. 20, 1863 |
| Vannol Jaque | Red River | Dec. 29, 1864 |
| Vandervel, Ferdinand | do | Dec. 29, 1864 |
| Vancaster, J | Pierce | Dec. 29, 1864 |
| Verana, Wenzel | Carlton | Nov. 20, 1863 |
| Vamer, Ezra | Two Rivers | Nov. 21, 1863 |
| Vader, Calvin | Manitowoc | Nov. 21, 1863 |
| Voboset, Mathias | Rockland | Nov. 21, 1863 |
| Vee, Sam'l | Manasha | Nov. 23, 1863 |
| Valentine, Julius G | do | Nov 23, 1863 |
| Vaughan, O. D | Waupaca | Nov. 25, 1863 |
| Vanvochis, C. H | Weyauwega | Nov. 5, 1864 |
| Veiker, Chas | do | Nov. 5, 1864 |
| Vellun, Ole Paulsen | Iola | Dec. 31, 1864 |
| Vander, Siders Jno | Freedom | Nov. 27, 1863 |
| Van Driel, Anthony | Kaukama | Nov. 27, 1863 |
| Van Oven, Arie | Grand Chute | Nov. 27, 1863 |
| Van Beek, Martin | Green Bay | Nov. 27, 1863 |
| Vander Barg, Francis | Humboldt | Nov. 27, 1863 |
| Van Ess, Peter | do | Dec. 28, 1864 |
| Vanderburg, Mehlans | Holland | Nov. 27, 1863 |
| Varkile, Jno | do | Nov 27, 1863 |
| Vanding, James | Green Bay city | Nov. 27, 1863 |
| Vancaster, Joseph | Green Bay | Dec. 28, 1864 |
| Verbois, Peter | Scott | Dec. 28, 1864 |
| Vanlannene, Jno | do | Dec. 28, 1864 |
| Valentin, Chas | Eaton | Dec. 28, 1864 |
| Venderavend —— | Bellville | Dec. 28, 1864 |
| Valoisi, Gilbert | Stiles | Nov. 28, 1863 |
| Vandolph, Lewis | Little Suamico | Dec. 29, 1864 |
| Vandervest, Joseph | do | Dec. 29, 1864 |
| Vreeland, Enock | Packwaukee | Dec. 29, 1864 |

## W

| | | |
|---|---|---|
| Weber, Peter | Polk | Dec. 8, 1864 |
| Wildner, Valentine | do | Dec. 8, 1864 |

| *Name.* | *Residence.* | *Date.* |
|---|---|---|
| Weenert, Mathias | Polk | Dec. 8, 1864 |
| With, Leonhart | Richfield | Oct. 12, 1864 |
| Weber, Anton | do | Oct. 12, 1864 |
| Wolf, Peter | do | Dec. 1, 1864 |
| Webber, Henry | do | Jan. 27, 1865 |
| Wilger, John | Farmington | Nov. 21, 1863 |
| Walter, Otto | do | Oct. 18, 1864 |
| Wercotts, Timothy | do | Oct. 18, 1864 |
| Waber, Julius | do | Oct. 18, 1864 |
| Weinrich, Fred'k | do | Oct. 18, 1864 |
| Willis, David | do | Dec. 1, 1864 |
| Wercott, Dennis | do | Dec. 1, 1864 |
| Wescott, Gramtis | do | Jan. 27, 1865 |
| Winters, August | Jackson | Oct. 11, 1864 |
| Wechroiler, Jacob | do | Oct. 11, 1864 |
| Wolett, Edward | do | Oct. 11, 1864 |
| Wolf, George | Germantown | Nov. 21, 1863 |
| Wetter, Nicholas | Belgium | Nov. 21, 1863 |
| Wesler, Peter | do | Nov. 21, 1863 |
| Weycher, Michael | do | Oct. 13, 1864 |
| Watry, John | do | Oct. 13, 1864 |
| Waltz, John | do | Dec. 1, 1864 |
| Weyker, Nicholas | do | Dec. 1, 1864 |
| Witt, Frederick | do | Oct. 13, 1864 |
| Westor, Melchior | do | Oct. 13, 1864 |
| Weyker, Baptist | do | Oct. 13, 1864 |
| Welter, Nicholas | do | Oct. 13, 1864 |
| Wester, Henry | do | Oct. 13, 1864 |
| Wiltchen, Baptist | do | Oct. 13, 1864 |
| Wallenstein, John | do | Oct. 13, 1864 |
| Wagner, Peter | do | Oct. 13, 1864 |
| Weyker, John | do | Oct. 13, 1864 |
| Weller, Theodore | do | Dec. 1, 1864 |
| Weiland, John | do | Dec. 1, 1864 |
| Wagner, John | do | Dec. 1, 1864 |
| Weiland, John M | do | Dec. 1, 1864 |
| Willard, Frank | do | Dec. 1, 1864 |
| Wisler, Justor | do | Dec. 1, 1864 |
| Weimond, John | Fredonia | Oct. 14, 1864 |
| Wagner, Antius | do | Oct. 14, 1864 |
| Wonderly, Bernard | do | Oct. 14, 1864 |
| Wagner, Englebret | do | Oct. 14, 1864 |
| Welsh, Lawrence | do | Oct. 14, 1864 |
| Wagner, Ben | Grafton | Oct. 13, 1864 |
| Windels, Gerhard | Mequon | Nov. 23, 1863 |
| Wagner, Theodore | do | Nov. 23, 1863 |
| Wagoner, Joseph | Port Washington | Nov. 23, 1863 |
| Weck, William | Saukville | Oct. 14, 1864 |
| Wadsworth, Hiram | do | Oct. 14, 1864 |
| Wauke, Conrad | Sheboygan | Nov. 23, 1863 |
| Wein, Hr | do | Dec. 2, 1864 |
| Weisbrocker, Fred'k | do | Oct. 18, 1864 |
| Wiffin, George | Sheboygan Falls | Nov. 24, 1863 |
| Wilson, Samuel O | do | Oct. 25, 1864 |
| Wassendorff, Louis | do | |
| Wiescelenk, Charles | do | Dec. 2, 1864 |
| Winthe, Fritz | do | Dec. 2, 1864 |
| Whiffind, A. C | do | Dec. 2, 1864 |
| Weyner, William | do | Jan. 27, 1864 |

| *Name.* | *Residence.* | *Date.* |
|---|---|---|
| Whipple, Charles | Lima | Oct. 24, 1864 |
| Wichser, Joseph | do | Dec. 2, 1864 |
| White, James | Abbott | Dec. 2, 1864 |
| Wolf, Andrew | do | Dec. 2, 1864 |
| Walsh, Patrick | do | Dec. 2, 1864 |
| Whitford, Sam'l W | Plymouth | Oct. 21, 1864 |
| Wortz, John | do | Oct. 21, 1864 |
| Warn, Patrick | do | Oct. 21, 1864 |
| Wheeler, Alonzo | Fond du Lac | Nov. 19, 1863 |
| Washburn, Edwin L | do | Nov. 19, 1863 |
| Wringer, Philip | Eden | Nov. 19, 1863 |
| Winters, John | do | Nov. 19, 1863 |
| Wilke, Godfrey | Oakfield | Nov. 19, 1863 |
| Winter, John | Ashford | Nov. 19, 1863 |
| Wauder, Joseph | Auburn | Oct. 5, 1864 |
| Wieurip, Henry | Calumet | Oct. 5, 1864 |
| Wright, William A | Lamartine | Oct. 5, 1864 |
| Whiteman, George | Alto | Oct. 5, 1864 |
| Wentworth, Henry | do | Oct. 5, 1864 |
| Webb, Charles | Waupun Village | Oct. 5, 1864 |
| Welch, John | Eldorado | Oct. 5, 1864 |
| Wiggins, William H | do | Dec. 1, 1864 |
| Weston, James, H | Metomen | Dec. 1, 1864 |
| Wright, Lambert | Fox Lake | Dec. 1, 1864 |
| Williams, Robert T | Calamus | Nov. 20, 1863 |
| White, Andrew | Elba | Nov. 20, 1863 |
| Wallace, Thomas | Shields | Nov. 20, 1863 |
| Warner, James | do | Nov. 20, 1863 |
| Wanmaker, Nelson | Beaver Dam | Nov. 20, 1863 |
| Waterhouse, David | Clyman | Nov. 2, 1863 |
| Woyciehoroske, Julius | do | Oct. 6, 1864 |
| Weiss, Robert | Watertown | Nov. 20, 1863 |
| Wessel, Peter | do | Oct. 6, 1864 |
| Wilber, Henry | do | Oct. 6, 1864 |
| Werlandorf, Fred | do | Oct. 6, 1864 |
| Webber, William | Watertown | Oct. 6, 1864 |
| Wilt, John | Leroy | Oct. 4, 1864 |
| Wilt, Sebastian | do | Oct. 4, 1864 |
| Waugh, James M | do | Oct. 4, 1864 |
| Walner, Peter | do | Dec. 1, 1864 |
| Weiglan, Andrew | do | Jan. 27, 1865 |
| Wheeler, Alfred | Lomira | Nov. 20, 1863 |
| Walsh, Andrew | do | Oct. 6, 1864 |
| Webber, Philip | do | Dec. 1, 1864 |
| Weins, Louis | Herman | Oct. 18, 1864 |
| Wagener, Fritz | do | Oct. 18, 1864 |
| Wartophol, Wm | Wayne | Nov. 21, 1863 |
| Whellen, John | Erin | Oct. 12, 1864 |
| Werner, Mathew | do | Dec. 1, 1864 |
| Weir, Francis | do | Dec. 1, 1864 |
| Wendall, James | Barton | Oct. 12, 1864 |
| Wendall, Jacob | do | Oct. 12, 1864 |
| Wagenknecht, Lorenzo | do | Oct. 12, 1864 |
| Wolfrum, Henry | West Bend | Nov. 21, 1863 |
| Walebenstein, Louis | Polk | Nov. 21, 1863 |
| Waleabenstein, Frederick | do | Nov. 21, 1863 |
| Wagner, Peter | do | Oct. 12, 1864 |
| Weger, Peter | do | Oct. 12, 1864 |
| Werle, Jacob | do | Oct. 12, 1864 |

| *Name.* | *Residence.* | *Date.* |
|---|---|---|
| Wagner, Nicholas | Polk | Oct. 12, 1864 |
| Wallace, J. T | Milwaukee | Nov. 9, 1863 |
| Weise, Jacob | do | Nov. 9, 1863 |
| White, ——— | do | Nov. 9, 1863 |
| Wilsmann, Henry | do | Nov. 9, 1863 |
| Weising, Carl | do | Nov. 9, 1863 |
| Wither, E. C | do | Sept. 19, 1864 |
| Wimmler, Theodore | do | Nov. 14, 1864 |
| Weiss, Anth | do | Nov. 14, 1864 |
| Wilson, T. M | do | Nov. 14, 1864 |
| Weiurschem, John | do | Nov. 14, 1863 |
| Wallace, J. W | do | Nov. 14, 1863 |
| Winckel, Fred | do | Nov. 14, 1863 |
| Watkins, V | do | Dec. 22, 1864 |
| Wilson, John G | do | Dec. 22, 1864 |
| Weichman, John | do | Dec. 22, 1864 |
| Williams, Chas | do | Dec. 22, 1864 |
| Wergen, Wm | do | Nov. 9, 1863 |
| Wilson, John | do | Nov. 9, 1863 |
| Wallich, Fern'd | do | Nov. 9, 1863 |
| Wallert, James | do | Nov. 9, 1863 |
| Weiss, Edwin | do | Nov. 9, 1863 |
| Wanderer, Leonard | do | Nov. 9, 1863 |
| Weingartuer, Neil | do | Nov. 9, 1863 |
| Wagner, Chas | do | Sep. 20, 1864 |
| Waltz, Robert | do | Sep. 20, 1864 |
| Wanderer, Heinrich | do | Sep. 20, 1864 |
| Wreds, Wm | do | Sep. 20, 1864 |
| Wilson, B. B | do | Nov. 10, 1863 |
| Winsell, Lue | do | Nov. 10, 1863 |
| Wigfall, Rob't. W | do | Nov. 11, 1863 |
| White, H. C | do | Sep. 21, 1864 |
| Wiasa, Frederick | do | Sep. 21, 1864 |
| Wael, Chas | do | Sep. 21, 1864 |
| Wright, Wm | do | Sep. 21, 1864 |
| Wright, Geo. W | do | Sep. 21, 1864 |
| Ward, Frank | do | Sep. 21, 1864 |
| Wright, Geo. W | do | Sep. 21, 1864 |
| Weasburg, Geo | do | Sep. 21, 1864 |
| Welduman, Nicholas | do | Nov. 25, 1864 |
| Wench, Godfred | do | Nov. 25, 1864 |
| Winzonter, John | do | Nov. 25, 1864 |
| Wise, Jacob | do | Nov. 25, 1864 |
| Wilford, Ruton | do | Nov. 25, 1864 |
| Weitzmann, Gerhart | do | Nov. 25, 1864 |
| Williams, Harry | do | Nov. 25, 1864 |
| Wasnock, Frank | do | Nov. 25, 1864 |
| Walter, Wm | do | Nov. 11, 1863 |
| Weshek, Weit | do | Nov. 11, 1863 |
| Wendel, Carl | do | Nov. 11, 1863 |
| Winkler, Christian | do | Nov. 11, 1863 |
| Wahbit, Heinrich | do | Sep. 21, 1864 |
| Walleze, Michael | do | Sep. 21, 1864 |
| Wilke, Heinrich | do | Sep. 21, 1864 |
| Werle, Frank | do | Sep. 21, 1864 |
| Wild, Ludwig | do | Sep. 21, 1864 |
| Williams, Wm | do | Jan. 11, 1865 |
| Welch, Thos | do | Jan. 11, 1865 |
| Walsh, Geo | do | Jan. 11, 1865 |

| *Name.* | *Residence.* | *Date.* |
|---|---|---|
| Whalin, Thos | Milwaukee | Jan. 11, 1865 |
| Whaley, Edmond | do | Jan. 11, 1865 |
| Warucke, Johann | do | Jan. 11, 1865 |
| Withen, G | do | Jan. 11, 1865 |
| Whaling, James | do | Nov. 10, 1863 |
| Williams, Ed | do | Nov. 10, 1863 |
| Wesley, Geo | do | Nov. 10, 1863 |
| Wenelker, Wm | do | Nov. 10, 1863 |
| William, Michael | do | Sep. 21, 1864 |
| William, Adam | do | Sep. 21, 1864 |
| Wright, Patrick | do | Sep. 21, 1864 |
| Walsh, Mathew | do | Sep. 21, 1864 |
| Wuhlke, Peter | do | Nov. 10, 1863 |
| Waterman, Carl | do | Nov. 10, 1863 |
| Weir, Henry | do | Nov. 10, 1863 |
| Winkle, Jacob | do | Nov. 10, 1863 |
| Winners, Wm | do | Sep. 21, 1864 |
| Westphal, John | do | Sep. 21, 1864 |
| Wambold, Abram | do | Sep. 21, 1864 |
| Welk, John | do | Sep. 21, 1864 |
| Winkler, ——— | do | Sep. 21, 1864 |
| Wentzlof, Chas | do | Sep. 21, 1864 |
| Wellzin, Martin | do | Nov. 15, 1864 |
| Werner, Fritz | do | Nov. 16, 1864 |
| Wade, Joseph | do | Nov. 16, 1864 |
| Weid, Frederick | do | Nov. 10, 1863 |
| Waben, Frederick | do | Sep. 20, 1864 |
| Woods, W. H | do | Nov. 10, 1863 |
| Wauke, A | do | Nov. 10, 1863 |
| Walsh, Thomas | do | Nov. 10, 1863 |
| Webler, E | do | Nov. 10, 1863 |
| Whigdel, I | do | Nov. 10, 1863 |
| Witherill, I. Milton | do | Nov. 10, 1863 |
| Walsh, William | do | Nov. 10, 1863 |
| Whaling, Thomas | do | Nov. 10, 1863 |
| Welch, Patrick | do | Sep. 20, 1864 |
| Wiener, Gerhard | do | Sep. 20, 1864 |
| Waln, Thomas | do | Sep. 20, 1864 |
| Withorell, Peter | do | Sep. 20, 1864 |
| Willough, George | do | Sep. 20, 1864 |
| Wall, Michael | do | Sep. 20, 1864 |
| Willoughoby, H. C | do | Sep. 20, 1864 |
| Wiltshire, Stephen | do | Sep. 20, 1864 |
| Woods, William | do | Sep. 20, 1864 |
| Workman, James | do | Sep. 20, 1864 |
| Wilkins, A. W | do | Sep. 20, 1864 |
| Wood, Thomas | do | Nov. 15, 1864 |
| Williams, William | do | Nov. 15, 1864 |
| Winters, Joseph | do | Nov. 15, 1864 |
| Wheeler, J. A | do | Nov. 15, 1864 |
| Walsh, Peter | do | Nov. 15, 1864 |
| Wallis, G. D | do | Nov. 15, 1864 |
| Wearer, Tom | do | |
| Wright, John | do | Jan. 19, 1865 |
| Wikolashego, Johann | do | Jan. 19, 1865 |
| Wickmann, Henry | do | Jan. 19, 1865 |
| Wenden, John | do | Jan. 19, 1865 |
| Wemdering, John | do | Sep. 21, 1864 |
| Weiland, Nicholas | do | Sep. 21, 1864 |

| *Name.* | *Residence.* | *Date.* |
|---|---|---|
| Wiede, Wilhelm | Milwaukee | Nov. 25, 1864 |
| Wolf, George | do | Nov. 25, 1864 |
| Wusen, Johann | do | Nov. 25, 1864 |
| Wundering, —— | do | Nov. 25, 1864 |
| Ward, Simon | do | Nov. 25, 1864 |
| Weber, Mathew | do | Nov. 25, 1864 |
| Wackle, Carl | do | Nov. 25, 1864 |
| Wichardt, Heinrich | do | Nov. 25, 1864 |
| Wes-enburg, Fred'k | do | Nov. 25, 1864 |
| Wendt, Joachim | do | Nov. 25, 1864 |
| Walter, William | do | Nov. 30, 1864 |
| Wieder, Edmond | do | Jan. 26, 1865 |
| Wehren, Joseph | do | Jan. 26, 1865 |
| William, Halle | do | Jan. 26, 1865 |
| Wecke, Fred | do | Nov. 11, 1863 |
| Wasserberger, Henry | do | Dec. 7, 1864 |
| Westphall, Carl | do | Dec. 7, 1864 |
| Wezlie, John | Granville | Nov. 11, 1863 |
| Wieland, Nicholas | do | Nov. 11, 1863 |
| Washburn, William | Greenfield | Sep. 22, 1864 |
| Wood, Stephen | do | |
| Wallace, Alex. C. | do | Sep. 21, 1864 |
| Wagen, Charles | Lake | Nov. 11, 1863 |
| Wertz, Michael | do | Sep. 22, 1864 |
| Wellard, George L. | do | Sep. 22, 1864 |
| Wenterer, Anthony | do | Dec. 13, 1864 |
| Willman, George | Brookfield | Sep. 23, 1864 |
| Webber, John | New Berlin | Nov. 12, 1863 |
| Wallace, John | do | Nov. 12, 1863 |
| Wintzfield, Fred'k | Muskego | Sep. 24, 1864 |
| Waltz (or Walter), Henry | do | Sep. 24, 1864 |
| Wild, Joseph | do | Dec. 1, 1864 |
| Williams, Robert | Delafield | Sep. 22, 1864 |
| Wrightman, Chas. F. | do | Sep. 22, 1864 |
| Woodhouse, John | Bristol | Sep. 24, 1864 |
| Wales, John | East Troy | Sep. 24, 1864 |
| Welch, John | Bloomfield | Nov. 12, 1864 |
| Weir, Patrick | Elk Horn | Nov. 12, 1864 |
| Wiseman, Henry | Summit | Sep. 22, 1864 |
| Whitney, John | Oconomowoc | Nov. 12, 1863 |
| Weltner, Jacob | do | Dec. 5, 1864 |
| Waller, Gunder | do | Dec 5, 1864 |
| Wautey, William | Mukwanego | Nov. 12, 1863 |
| Walfren, Ludwig | Pewaukee | Sep. 22, 1864 |
| Weise, John | Waukesha | Sep. 23, 1864 |
| Wells, Henry | do | Sep. 23, 1864 |
| Wolfe, Adam | do | Sep. 23, 1864 |
| Williams, Evan J. | do | Sep. 23, 1864 |
| Welch, Soloman Z. | Vernon | Sep. 24, 1864 |
| Welch, William | Menomonee | Nov. 12, 1863 |
| Winter, Matthias | do | Sep. 23, 1864 |
| Will, Joseph | do | Sep. 23, 1864 |
| Walter, John | do | Sep. 23, 1864 |
| Werhesh, Herbert | do | Sep. 23, 1864 |
| Wietz, Matthias | do | Dec. 1, 1864 |
| Willie, Theodore | do | Dec. 1, 1864 |
| Wagli, Benedict | do | Nov. 25, 1864 |
| Wusen, Joseph | do | Nov. 25, 1864 |
| Witt, Matthias | do | Dec. 1, 1864 |

| *Name.* | *Residence.* | *Date.* |
|---|---|---|
| Willewer, Conrad | Brookfield | Sep. 23, 1864 |
| Wisenhelm, John, Jr | do | Sep. 23, 1864 |
| Webber, J | Oak Creek, | Sep. 22, 1864 |
| Wallust, Benjamin | do | Sep. 22, 1864 |
| Walfender, John | Racine | Sep. 24, 1864 |
| Winsch, Frederick | do | Sep. 24, 1864 |
| Wright, Christian | do | Sep. 22, 1864 |
| Welsh, Edward | do | Sep. 22, 1864 |
| Wallen, Dominecus | do | Sep. 22, 1864 |
| White, Marshall | do | Sep. 22, 1864 |
| Wirth, Andrew | do | Jan. 19, 1865 |
| Wardell, Thomas | Mount Pleasant | Nov. 11, 1863 |
| Welsh, Edmond | do | Sep. 23, 1864 |
| Williams, John E. | do | Sep. 23, 1864 |
| Worsley, Thomas | Dover | Dec. 10, 1864 |
| Weirich, Fred | Burlington | Nov. 11, 1863 |
| Weimas, Clemence | Rochester | Sep. 24, 1864 |
| Winars, Joseph | do | Sep. 24, 1864 |
| Wille, Mathias | Raymond | Sep. 23, 1864 |
| Walker, Anson E | do | Sep. 23, 1864 |
| White, Peter | Caledonia | Nov. 11, 1863 |
| Winkle, Louis | do | Dec. 7, 1864 |
| Wilson, J. L | Kenosha | Nov. 12, 1863 |
| Wright, N. D | do | Nov. 12, 1863 |
| Williams, Louis J | Paris | Sep. 24, 1864 |
| Woolf, John | Salem | Nov. 12, 1863 |
| White, Patrick | do | Sept. 24, 1864 |
| Welsh, Henry | Randall | Sep. 24, 1864 |
| Wesnet, John | do | Sep. 24, 1864 |
| Wieson, William | do | Sep. 24, 1864 |
| Wing, John D. | do | Dec. 16, 1864 |
| Winchell, William | Bradford | Nov. 12, 1863 |
| Wilson, John | Johnson | Nov. 12, 1863 |
| Wheeler, Jefferson | Lima | Nov. 12, 1863 |
| Weaver, J. A | Milton | Nov. 12, 1863 |
| Whitney, John | Oregon | Nov. 12, 1863 |
| Walsh, Nicholas | Middleton | Nov. 13, 1863 |
| Williams, William | Madison | Nov. 13, 1863 |
| Wheeler, James | Sun Prairie | Sep. 19, 1864 |
| Walker, John | do | Sep. 19, 1864 |
| Warner, Franklin | do | Oct. 15, 1864 |
| Werthawser, John | Mazomanie | Nov. 13, 1863 |
| Whipple, Melton | Bristol | Nov. 13, 1863 |
| Whitman, George | Farmington | Sep. 20, 1864 |
| Waters, William | do | Sep. 20, 1864 |
| Warner, John | Watertown | Nov. 13, 1863 |
| Weyner, Henry | do | Nov. 13, 1863 |
| Winspear, Horatio | Arlington | Nov. 16, 1863 |
| Williams, Alfred A | Dekorrah | Sep. 21, 1864 |
| Walter, James H | Pacific | Nov. 16, 1863 |
| Whipple, Irwin | Randolph | Nov. 16, 1863 |
| Wilch, Michael | Lewiston | Oct. 2, 1864 |
| Wildrick, Patrick | Newport | Nov. 13, 1863 |
| Woods, Thomas | Milford | Sep. 20, 1864 |
| Williams, John | Ridgeway | Nov. 14, 1863 |
| Weirs, Peter | do | Sep. 28, 1864 |
| Wheeler, Ira | do | Sep. 28, 1864 |
| Wescoat, Peter | do | Sep. 28, 1864 |
| Weirs, John | do | Sep. 28, 1864 |

| *Name.* | *Residence.* | *Date.* |
|---|---|---|
| Williams, John | Ridgeway | Sep. 28, 1864 |
| Williams, John T | do | Sep. 28, 1864 |
| Weirs, Nicholas | do | Sep. 28, 1864 |
| Williams, Samuel | Dodgeville | Nov. 14, 1864 |
| Williams, John | do | Nov. 14, 1864 |
| Wall, William | do | Oct. 28, 1864 |
| Williams, Morgan | do | Oct. 28, 1864 |
| Williams, Evan | do | Nov. 19, 1863 |
| Williams, Morgan J | do | Nov. 19, 1863 |
| Wittman, Jacob | Highland | Sep. 18, 1864 |
| Woodward, Thomas | do | Sep. 18, 1864 |
| Wasley, James | do | Sep. 18, 1864 |
| Wells, John R | do | Dec. 7, 1864 |
| Woods, Patrick | Willow Springs | Nov. 16, 1863 |
| Webster, Elijah | Wayne or Gratiot | Nov. 16, 1863 |
| Walker, Thomas | Benton | Nov. 16, 1864 |
| Welsh, Michael | do | Sep. 29, 1864 |
| Worth, John | Elk Grove | Nov. 16, 1863 |
| Wheeler, Jefferson | Albany | Nov. 17, 1863 |
| Wilhelm, Amos | Sylvester | Nov. 17, 1863 |
| Welch, H | do | Nov. 17, 1863 |
| Wheelock, Jas | Utica | Sep. 30, 1864 |
| Winsor, Eugene | Cassv'le, Beet'n or Waterloo | Nov. 19, 1863 |
| Waters, Juba | Beetown | Oct. 29, 1864 |
| Wright, G. W | Waterloo | Oct. 1, 1864 |
| Wunderlin, Wm | Harrison | Oct. 1, 1864 |
| Wilson, L. C | Jamestown | Oct. 6, 1864 |
| Wait, Lorenzo | Sylvan | Sep. 26, 1864 |
| Woodman, Samuel | Dayton | Sep. 26, 1864 |
| Weeks, James | Millville | Oct. 1, 1864 |
| Williams, David | Ellenboro | Oct. 1, 1864 |
| Wilson, Geo | Lavalle | Oct. 3, 1864 |
| Whitas, Joseph M | Franklin | Oct. 3, 1864 |
| Willey, Edwin | Paris | Oct. 29, 1864 |
| Welch, Wm | Franklin | Oct. 29, 1864 |
| Winslow, E | La Crosse city | Nov. 16, 1863 |
| Williams, Geo., (col'd) | do | Nov. 16, 1863 |
| Waller, Thos | Monroe Co | Nov. 17, 1863 |
| Williams, Jas | Jefferson | Sep. 19, 1864 |
| Wait, W | Chippewa Co | Nov. 20, 1863 |
| Winter, J | Chippewa Falls | Sep. 27, 1864 |
| Whaler, Mike | do | Nov. 2, 1864 |
| Wolfe, Peter | Adams Co | Nov. 23, 1863 |
| Weker, Lewis | do | Nov. 23, 1863 |
| Watson, Jno | Lincoln | Sep. 26, 1864 |
| Wilson, Ziba | Richfield | Sep. 26, 1864 |
| Winsin, Eleazin | Leola | Sep. 26, 1864 |
| Weld, Wm. D | do | Nov. 14, 1864 |
| Williamson, Albert | Easton | Nov. 14, 1864 |
| Whitter, Geo | do | Nov. 14, 1864 |
| Worden, Wm | Linwood | Nov. 23, 1863 |
| Warren, Aaron G | do | Nov. 23, 1863 |
| Welch, Wm | do | Sep. 22, 1864 |
| Wilson, Robt | Amherst | Sep. 22, 1864 |
| Welty, Geo | do | Sep. 22, 1864 |
| White, Jeremiah | Belmont | Sep. 22, 1864 |
| White, Jonas B | do | Nov. 15, 1864 |
| Wolcott, Jno | Juneau Co | Nov. 17, 1863 |

| *Name.* | *Residence.* | *Date.* |
|---|---|---|
| Wilcox, H. | Kildare | Sep. 19, 1864 |
| Wright, Wm. | do | Sep. 19, 1864 |
| Webster, Jno. C. | do | Sep. 19, 1864 |
| Weber, Leopold | do | Sep. 31, 1864 |
| Wood, Martin C. | Plymouth | Sep. 19, 1864 |
| Ward, Wm. | Lemonweir | Sep. 19, 1864 |
| Williams, Jno | do | Sep. 31, 1864 |
| Walker, Jacob | Marion | Sep. 19, 1864 |
| Walker, Franklin | do | Sep. 19, 1864 |
| Wiggins, Jesse, P. | do | Sep. 19, 1864 |
| Walker, G. W. | Lyndon | Sep. 20, 1863 |
| Williams, Geo. | Oak Dale | Sep. 20, 1863 |
| Wright, Geo. | Sheldon | Sep. 20, 1864 |
| Walch, Patrick | Seven Mile Creek | Sep. 31, 1864 |
| Walsh, James | do | Sept. 31, 1864 |
| Walton, Geo. | St. Croix Co | Sept. 23, 1864 |
| Welch, Wm. | do | Nov. 20, 1863 |
| Walsh, Thos. | Erin Prairie | Nov. 3, 1864 |
| Walters, Jas. | Rush River | Nov. 3, 1864 |
| White, C. M. | Dunn Co | Nov. 23, 1863 |
| Ward, Henry | Eau Galle | Nov. 2, 1864 |
| Wright, Henry | do | Nov. 2, 1864 |
| Wiland, Jno | do | Nov. 2, 1864 |
| Wetmore, Jas | Spring Brook | Nov. 2, 1864 |
| Williams, Beasly | Bergen | Sep. 21, 1864 |
| Wearing, Henry B. | Kickapoo | Sep. 21, 1864 |
| Wier, Augustus | Franklin | Sep. 21, 1864 |
| Welsh, Michael | Greenwood | Sep. 21, 1864 |
| White, Moses | Harmony | Sep. 21, 1864 |
| White, Jesse | do | Sep. 21, 1864 |
| White, Albert | Union | Sep. 21, 1864 |
| Wagoner, Jacob | Starks | Sep. 21, 1864 |
| Wiggins, Jno. | Dexter | Sep. 22, 1864 |
| Warner, Austin | Centralia | Sep. 22, 1864 |
| Winter, Jacob | Rudolph | Nov. 15, 1864 |
| Wagner, Theo | Berlin | Sep. 22, 1864 |
| Woodbridge, Cyrus | Manchester | Sep. 23, 1864 |
| Wilkinson, R. | Perry | Sep. 23, 1864 |
| White, Newton | Trimbell | Sep. 23, 1864 |
| Wheeler, Peter H. | do | Nov. 3, 1864 |
| Warner, Hans | Martell | Nov. 3, 1864 |
| Walworth, Peter | Nelson | Sep. 26, 1864 |
| Williams, Oreson | Durand | Sep. 27, 1864 |
| Ward, Lyman T. | Waubeek | Sep. 27, 1864 |
| Weis, Nicholas | do | Nov. 16, 1864 |
| Winters, J. | do | Nov. 16, 1864 |
| Welch, Jno. | Eau Galle | Sep. 27, 1864 |
| Webber, Bernhard | do | Sep. 27, 1864 |
| Waterson, Jas. B | do | Sep. 27, 1864 |
| White, Patrick | do | Sep. 27, 1864 |
| Wocedalek, Joseph | Kewaunee | Nov. 20, 1863 |
| Watson, Chas. | Carlton | Nov. 20, 1863 |
| Wiscock, Joseph | Franklin | Dec. 31, 1864 |
| Wagones, John | Eaton | Nov. 24, 1863 |
| Williamson, Wm. | Two Creeks | Sep. 28, 1864 |
| Winters. Therin | Gibson | Sep. 28, 1864 |
| Winters, Nathan | do | Sep. 28, 1864 |
| Wilson, Chas. | do | Sep. 28, 1864 |
| Wittencamp, Wm. | Manitowoc Rapids | Sep. 28, 1864 |

| *Name.* | *Residence.* | *Date.* |
|---|---|---|
| Waterbach, Anton | Meeme | Sep. 28, 1864 |
| Wagner, Peter | do | Sep. 28, 1864 |
| White, Mitchell | Neenah | Nov. 23, 1863 |
| Warner, Orange | Oshkosh | Nov. 23, 1863 |
| Wentworth, Henry | Rushford | Nov. 24, 1863 |
| Wilbur, Alorn | Utica | Nov. 24, 1863 |
| Wussow, Chas | do | Nov. 1, 1864 |
| Walker, Wills | Poygan | Dec. 31, 1864 |
| Wadsworth, H. J | Berlin City | Nov. 24, 1863 |
| Wilson, Isaac | Waushara Co | Nov. 25, 1863 |
| Wilson, Salmon | do | Nov. 25, 1863 |
| Whiting, Jacob | do | Nov. 25, 1863 |
| Wood, A. H | Plainfield | Nov. 25, 1863 |
| Wiggins, Benj | do | Nov. 2, 1864 |
| Walker, H. | do | Nov. 2, 1864 |
| Wilson, Fredk | Bloomfield | Nov. 2, 1864 |
| Wells, Harvey | Aurora | Nov. 2, 1864 |
| Williams, Rich'd | do | Dec. 31, 1864 |
| Williams, Ebenezer | Springvale | Nov. 2, 1864 |
| Williams, Jno. R | do | Nov. 2, 1864 |
| Wilson, Andrew | do | Nov. 2, 1864 |
| Wilson, James | do | Nov. 2, 1864 |
| Wright, Ransom K | Deerfield | Nov. 2, 1864 |
| Wright, Orin L | do | Dec. 31, 1864 |
| Wright, Orin | Oasis | Nov. 2, 1864 |
| Wood, Alfred | do | Nov. 2, 1864 |
| Wood, Alfred | do | Dec. 31, 1864 |
| Wordin, Henry | Poysippi | Dec. 31, 1864 |
| Wordin, Henry K | do | Dec. 31, 1864 |
| Wetherby, Luke | Richford | Dec. 31, 1864 |
| Wilcox, Rufus | Mukwa | Nov. 25, 1863 |
| Warriner, Horace | Waupaca | Nov. 25, 1863 |
| Woolsey, Richard | do | Nov. 25, 1863 |
| White, N. L | Lind | Nov. 25, 1863 |
| Wait, Thomas | Farmington | Nov. 25, 1863 |
| Warren, Harrison | Iola | Nov. 25, 1863 |
| Wipf, Conrad | do | Dec. 31, 1864 |
| Wipf, Jacob | do | Dec. 31, 1864 |
| Will, C. G. | Bear Creek | Nov. 5, 1864 |
| Welsh, Patrick | Union | Nov. 5, 1864 |
| Wundlandt, August | Caledonia | Nov. 5, 1864 |
| Wood, Melvin | Weyauwega | Nov. 5, 1864 |
| Wilson, Charles | do | Nov. 5, 1864 |
| Williams, F. J | do | Nov. 5, 1864 |
| Waterhouse, Henry | do | Nov. 5, 1864 |
| Whiteman, Byron | Royalton | Nov. 5, 1864 |
| White, John M. | Matteson | Nov. 5, 1864 |
| Wallengfang, Adam | Suamico | Nov. 5, 1864 |
| Webb, A. M | do | Nov. 5, 1864 |
| Williams, Adam | St. Lawrence | Dec. 31, 1864 |
| Westfall, August | Greenville | Nov. 27, 1863 |
| Weisenburg, Wm | do | Nov. 27, 1863 |
| Williams, W. C | do | Nov. 27, 1863 |
| Welcine, Wm | do | Nov. 27, 1863 |
| Weisenberg, Fred'k | do | Dec. 28, 1864 |
| Wood, James | Hortonia | Nov. 27, 1863 |
| Williamson, Antoine | Freedom | Nov. 5, 1864 |
| Waters, John | Center | Dec. 28, 1864 |
| Weis, Wolfgang | do | Dec. 28, 1864 |

| Name. | Residence. | Date. |
|---|---|---|
| Wieland, Jacob | Center | Dec. 28, 1864 |
| Ward, Howard | Wrightstown | Nov. 27, 1863 |
| Wristle, Conrad | Marinette | Nov. 28, 1863 |
| Wilkey, Charles | do | Nov. 28, 1863 |
| Welch, Michael | Oconto | Nov. 28, 1863 |
| Welch, John | Peshtigo | Nov. 28, 1863 |
| Wilson, Ed | do | Nov. 28, 1863 |
| White, Capt. John F. | do | Nov. 28, 1863 |
| Williams, James | Stiles | Nov. 28, 1863 |
| Whitney, Franklin L. | Pensaukee | Dec. 29, 1864 |
| Wilson, Harry W. | do | Dec. 29, 1864 |
| Winshnoe, August | Neshkora | Nov. 1, 1864 |
| Waretok, Joseph | Mecan | Nov. 1, 1864 |
| Woffle, Conrad | Newton | Nov. 1, 1864 |
| Wishner, August | do | Dec. 31, 1864 |
| Welke, Robert | Shields | Dec. 31, 1864 |
| Welke, Gustoph | do | Dec. 31, 1864 |
| Weltig, G. | Harrison | Dec. 28, 1864 |
| Wallis, James | do | Dec. 28, 1864 |
| Williams, Renice | do | Dec. 28, 1864 |
| Whalen, Daniel | Stockbridge | Dec. 28, 1864 |
| Warrent, Thomas | Brothertown | Dec. 28, 1864 |

## Y

| Name. | Residence. | Date. |
|---|---|---|
| Yager, Frederick | Watertown | Oct. 6, 1864 |
| Young, Francis J. | Leroy | Oct. 4, 1864 |
| Yuzor, Julius | Theresa | Nov. 20, 1863 |
| Young, Edwin | Richfield | Jan. 27, 1865 |
| Yhagle, Anton | Farmington | Jan. 27, 1865 |
| Yoelk, Henry | Jackson | Oct 11, 1864 |
| Youngerz, Nicholas | Belgium | Dec. 1, 1864 |
| Yunker, Lawrence | Saukville | Oct. 14, 1864 |
| Young, William C. | Scott | Nov. 24, 1863 |
| Young, John | Milwaukee | Nov. 9, 1863 |
| Young, Wm. | do | Nov. 9, 1863 |
| Young, James. | do | Sept. 19, 1864 |
| Young, Lorin | do | Nov. 11, 1863 |
| Yung, Ferdinando | Greenfield | Sep. 22, 1864 |
| York, William | Dover | Sep. 23, 1864 |
| Yickerman, Frank | Menomonee | Sep. 24, 1864 |
| Yorker, Nicholas | do | Sep. 24, 1864 |
| Youngblood, Amos | do | Sep. 24, 1864 |
| Youngblood, John | do | Sep. 24, 1864 |
| Yaney, John R. | Highland | Sep. 28, 1864 |
| Yates, George | Lanark | Sep. 22, 1864 |
| Young, Wm. C. | Hull | Sep. 22, 1864 |
| Yocum, Walter F. | Springville | Sep. 26, 1864 |
| Yenger, Andrew | Calumet Co. | Nov. 21, 1863 |
| Young, John | Weyauwega | Dec. 31, 1864 |

## Z

| Name. | Residence. | Date. |
|---|---|---|
| Zong, Alois | Alto | Nov. 19, 1863 |
| Zimmerman, Wm. | Beaver Dam | Nov. 20, 1863 |
| Zulsdorff, Carl | Burnett | Nov. 20, 1863 |
| Zerbert, Ferdinand | Watertown | Oct. 6, 1864 |
| Zimmerman, John | Lomira | Oct. 6, 1864 |
| Zimmer, Simon | Herman | Oct. 18, 1864 |
| Zena, August | Jackson | Oct. 11, 1864 |

STATE OF WISCONSIN } ss.
OFFICE OF THE SECRETARY OF STATE, }

I, Thomas S. Allen, Secretary of State of the State of Wisconsin, do hereby certify, that the foregoing is a full and complete list of non-reporting drafted men and deserters after reporting, under the various military drafts in the State of Wisconsin, together with their places of residence and the dates of their desertion, as appears from the certified list procured from the War Department of the United States, pursuant to the provisions of section 1, of chapter 67, of the General Laws of 1867.

IN WITNESS WHEREOF, I have hereunto set my hand and affixed the Great Seal of the State of Wisconsin, at the capitol in Madison, this 9th day of July, A. D., 1867.

[L. S.]

THOS. S. ALLEN,
Secretary of State.

www.ingramcontent.com/pod-product-compliance
Lightning Source LLC
LaVergne TN
LVHW011207110826
845150LV00006B/1347

* 9 7 8 1 4 2 5 5 1 7 8 7 8 *